Reformers and war

Reformers and war

American progressive publicists and the First World War

JOHN A. THOMPSON

Lecturer in History, University of Cambridge,
and Fellow of St. Catharine's College, Cambridge

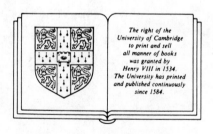

The right of the
University of Cambridge
to print and sell
all manner of books
was granted by
Henry VIII in 1534.
The University has printed
and published continuously
since 1584.

CAMBRIDGE UNIVERSITY PRESS

Cambridge
New York   New Rochelle
Melbourne   Sydney

Published by the Press Syndicate of the University of Cambridge
The Pitt Building, Trumpington Street, Cambridge CB2 1RP
32 East 57th Street, New York, NY 10022, USA
10 Stamford Road, Oakleigh, Melbourne 3166, Australia

First published 1987

Printed in the United States of America

Library of Congress Cataloging-in-Publication Data
Thompson, John A.
Reformers and war.
1. World War, 1914–1918 – Public opinion, American.
2. Press – United States – History – 20th century.
3. United States – Politics and government – 1901–1953.
4. United States – Foreign relations – 20th century.
5. Reformers – United States – History – 20th century.
6. Public opinion – United States.   I. Title.
D632.T46   1987   973.91   86-26329
ISBN 0 521 25289 X

British Library Cataloging-in-Publication data applied for.

Contents

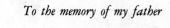

To the memory of my father

Preface

This book has been in the making more years than I care to recall and it would probably never have been finished at all but for the assistance and encouragement I have received from others. First and foremost, I wish to thank for their generosity and patience those friends and fellow historians who have read the entire manuscript in draft, and from whose critical judgment (and stylistic decisiveness) it has greatly benefited: John Burrow, Peter Clarke, Stefan Collini, David Lieberman, David Reynolds, and Quentin Skinner. Distinguished as this company is, its members have not labored in the particular field of history with which this book is concerned. For that, among other reasons, the reading and suggestions of Robert H. Wiebe had a special value. At an earlier stage, the comments of Michael O'Brien and Roy Rosenzweig were most helpful. The doctoral dissertation from which the book developed was written under the shrewd supervision of William R. Brock and took shape under the guidance of William E. Leuchtenburg and Lawrence W. Levine. To Charles B. Forcey, I am indebted not only for valuable advice but also for permitting me to consult his notes on Walter Weyl's diary, a source to which I had no direct access. Indebted as I am for all this assistance, the final product is, of course, my responsibility alone.

A scholar living outside the United States is even more dependent than his American counterparts on financial assistance for research. In this respect, I have been extremely fortunate. Indeed, both as a Harkness Fellow and a Fellow of the Woodrow Wilson International Center for Scholars, I enjoyed support that went far beyond the financial, as well as a rich variety of American experiences. I have also gained a great deal of stimulation and encouragement over the years from my colleagues in the History Department of University College, London, the Cambridge History Faculty, and St. Catharine's College.

Finally, I wish to acknowledge three vital contributions. Patricia Williams, a spur throughout, encouraged me to seek a publisher's contract at a time when my faith in the project was flagging. My mother typed the manuscript with a care and attention to detail that saved me from several misstatements. Above all, my wife, Dorothy J. Thompson, has helped at every stage in innumerable ways and with a selflessness especially remarkable in one writing her own book at the same time. Indeed, I doubt that the book would have been finished without this help, but this is the least of my debts to her.

Acknowledgments

Portions of this work appeared in different form in "American Progressive Publicists and the First World War, 1914–1917," *Journal of American History,* 58 (Sept. 1971), pp. 364–83; and in the pamphlet *Progressivism* (Durham, England: British Association for American Studies, 1979); and appear here with permission.

Location of manuscript collections

Bibliographical details for published sources may be found in the notes. The manuscript collections cited are located as follows:

Newton D. Baker Papers. Manuscript Division, Library of Congress
Ray Stannard Baker Papers. Manuscript Division, Library of Congress
Albert J. Beveridge Papers. Manuscript Division, Library of Congress
Randolph Bourne Papers. Butler Library, Columbia University
George Creel Papers. Manuscript Division, Library of Congress
Felix Frankfurter Papers. Manuscript Division, Library of Congress
Franklin H. Giddings Papers. Butler Library, Columbia University
Hamilton Holt Papers. Rollins College Library, Winter Park, Florida
E. M. House Papers. Sterling Memorial Library, Yale University
Paul U. Kellogg Papers. Social Welfare History Archives, University of
    Minnesota Library
Walter Lippmann Papers. Sterling Memorial Library, Yale University
George F. Peabody Papers. Manuscript Division, Library of Congress
Amos Pinchot Papers. Manuscript Division, Library of Congress
Gifford Pinchot Papers. Manuscript Division, Library of Congress
Louis F. Post Papers. Manuscript Division, Library of Congress
Chester Rowell Papers. Bancroft Library, University of California,
    Berkeley
Charles Edward Russell Papers. Manuscript Division, Library of Congress
John Spargo Papers. Bailey/Howe Library, University of Vermont,
    Burlington
Lincoln Steffens Papers. Butler Library, Columbia University
J. G. Phelps Stokes Papers. Butler Library, Columbia University
Oswald Garrison Villard Papers. Houghton Library, Harvard University
William English Walling Papers. State Historical Society of Wisconsin,
    Madison, Wisconsin
William Allen White Papers. Manuscript Division, Library of Congress
Woodrow Wilson Papers. Manuscript Divison, Library of Congress

xi

CHAPTER I

Introduction

The confrontation of the American reform tradition with the world conflicts in which the United States has been involved is a major theme in modern American history. With regard to the First World War, two questions have attracted particular attention. The first is the part played by the war in the decline of the progressive movement. The second is whether a commitment to domestic reform produced a particular approach to foreign affairs, and if so what the nature of this approach may have been. This latter issue has generated a lively historiographical debate.[1] On the former, however, there has been general agreement that the war weakened the forces of reform in America. This has been conceded even by those who wish to stress the extent to which the progressive impulse persisted through the war and into the 1920s.[2]

There has been less agreement, however, about the nature of the connection between war and the decline of progressivism. The suggestion is sometimes made that war always puts an end to reform.[3] This generalization does not bear scrutiny. Even within the history of the United States, Radical Republicanism reached its apogee shortly after the Civil War, while the Progressive Era itself followed the Spanish-American War. From a wider perspective, there are many more examples of a tendency for war to promote reform or revolution. Unsuccessful war certainly endangers regimes, as the First World War demonstrated in Russia, Austria-Hungary, Germany, and Turkey. Even when unaccompanied by defeat, the experience of war can help to stimulate a desire for radical change, as it did in Britain in 1945.

---

[1] See the introductory remarks in Chapter 5.

[2] Arthur S. Link, "What Happened to the Progressive Movement in the 1920s?" *American Historical Review*, 64 (July 1959), pp. 833–51 at pp. 837–44; Allen F. Davis, "Welfare, Reform and World War I," *American Quarterly*, 19 (Fall 1967), pp. 516–33 at pp. 532–3; Clarke A. Chambers, *Seedtime of Reform: American Social Service and Social Action, 1918–1933* (Minneapolis, 1963), pp. ix–xi, 89.

[3] For example, Richard Hofstadter, *The Age of Reform: From Bryan to F.D.R.* (New York, 1955), pp. 270–1.

If, then, American progressivism was damaged by the First World War, the reason must be sought in some aspect of this particular case. A number of such aspects have been pointed to by historians. One possibility is that the pre-war reform movement depended upon assumptions about human progress that were discredited by the occurrence of such an appalling conflict. Another is that progressivism was fatally weakened by the divisions created among its supporters by the new issues of foreign policy, above all the question of American intervention. Still another is that domestic reform suffered from the postwar public reaction against American involvement just because the Wilson Administration had justified this so largely in terms of "the Progressive values and the Progressive language."[4] Each of these explanations possesses at least some truth, yet no one of them is adequate in itself. The first implies a more radical discontinuity in the whole tradition of American reform thought than most historians have observed. The second does not explain why differences of view on foreign policy questions – which, however important, were transitory – had a more fatal effect upon the progressive movement than the deep divisions that had always existed within it over such enduring domestic issues as the trusts or prohibition. The third applies only to the period after the war, by which time the strength of progressive sentiment had clearly been much reduced. The relative significance of these and other connections between the war and progressivism can be assessed only by studying the subject as a whole.

It might seem that all these questions rest upon an outdated assumption – that there was in early twentieth-century America a "progressive movement." In 1970 Peter G. Filene produced "an obituary for 'the progressive movement'" on the grounds that in respect of each of the essential characteristics of a movement – goals, values, members, and supporters – progressivism displayed "a puzzling and irreducible incoherence."[5] Such a conclusion was a logical response to the very different interpretations of the nature of progressivism advanced by historians in the previous twenty years. George Mowry and Richard Hofstadter had portrayed it as a movement led by middle-class Americans, usually of a "Yankee-Protestant" background, who were seeking to reestablish tradi-

---

[4] Ibid., p. 276.
[5] "An Obituary for 'The Progressive Movement,'" *American Quarterly*, 22 (Spring 1970), pp. 20–34 at p. 31.

tional moral and civic values that seemed to them threatened by the growth of large corporations, labor unions, and machine politics. Since such men were generally self-employed professionals or independent businessmen, the movement represented, in Hofstadter's words, "the complaint of the unorganized against the consequences of organisation."[6] By contrast, Samuel P. Hays and Robert H. Wiebe stressed the role of organized interest groups, including business lobbies, in promoting reform. These historians attributed progressivism to the rise of what Wiebe called "a new middle class" committed to the "bureaucratic" values of efficiency, expertise, and rationality.[7] Some writers have seen such values as inspiring those in the emerging "profession" of social work,[8] but most who have studied the notable contribution to reform movements of settlement house residents and social gospel ministers have continued to attribute their motivation to democratic idealism and humanitarian concern.[9] Whereas all these interpretations focused on middle-class Americans, J. Joseph Huthmacher and John D. Buenker have argued that the political representatives of the urban, immigrant lower class in the industrial states of the Northeast and Middle West provided indispensable support for many political and economic reforms.[10] To New Left historians, however, the nature of the changes that actually occurred was effectively determined by the big business interests that dominated the economy; the ideology of progressivism represented a "corporate liber-

[6] Hofstadter, *Age of Reform*, p. 214. See also George E. Mowry, *The California Progressives* (Berkeley and Los Angeles, 1951), and *The Era of Theodore Roosevelt and the Birth of Modern America, 1900–1912* (New York, 1958).

[7] Samuel P. Hays, *The Response to Industrialism, 1885–1914* (Chicago, 1957), chap. 3; "The Politics of Reform in Municipal Government in the Progressive Era," *Pacific Northwest Quarterly*, 55 (Oct. 1964), pp. 157–69; "Political Parties and the Community–Society Continuum, 1865–1929," in *The American Party Systems*, ed. William N. Chambers and Walter Deal Burnham (New York, 1967), pp. 152–81; and "The New Organizational Society," in *Building the Organizational Society: Essays on Associational Activities in Modern America*, ed. Jerry Israel (New York, 1972), pp. 1–15; Robert H. Wiebe, *Businessmen and Reform: A Study of the Progressive Movement* (Cambridge, 1962); *The Search for Order, 1877–1920* (New York, 1967), chaps. 5–8.

[8] John F. McClymer, *War and Welfare: Social Engineering in America, 1890–1925* (Westport, Conn., 1980). In an earlier and more comprehensive study of the professionalization of social work, Roy Lubove had seen it as a process distinct from, and antithetical to, involvement with social reform. See Lubove, *The Professional Altruist: The Emergence of Social Work as a Career, 1880–1930* (Cambridge, Mass., 1965), especially pp. 220–1.

[9] For example, Allen F. Davis, *Spearheads for Reform: The Social Settlements and the Progressive Movement, 1890–1914* (London, 1967); Clarke A. Chambers, *Paul U. Kellogg and the Survey: Voices for Social Welfare and Social Justice* (Minneapolis, 1971).

[10] J. Joseph Huthmacher, "Urban Liberalism and the Age of Reform," *Mississippi Valley Historical Review*, 49 (Sept. 1962), pp. 231–41; John D. Buenker, *Urban Liberalism and Progressive Reform* (New York, 1973).

alism" that succeeded in legitimatizing, while gently socializing, the new capitalist order. [11]

Although several of these interpretations reflected a particular angle of politial vision or special preoccupations of the time in which they were conceived, they nearly all rested upon a sufficiently solid basis of evidence to suggest that they captured at least some of the historical realities. This has naturally led some historians to stress the diversity of progressivism and to seek to analyze the movement's various components and their interrelationships. Works that have applied this approach – notably those of Otis Graham – have brought further illumination to the complex interplay of different interests and impulses, but they have served only to underline what Buenker has called "the vast divergence of forces demanding change in the era." [12] It has become impossible to sustain the old notion of a single progressive movement, which set the agenda of politics in early twentieth-century America and largely determined the course of events.

Those seeking a new "synthesis" for the period have moved naturally toward a higher level of generality, attempting to delineate patterns of development that would encompass the variety of impulses and particular political purposes at work. Long ago Hays suggested the rubric "response to industrialism," and more recently Buenker has recommended "viewing the era as the work of shifting coalitions." [13] More elaborate and sophisticated have been the various versions of what Louis Galambos has called "the organizational synthesis." [14] These stress the fundamental implications for all aspects of American life of the decline of local communities and informal groups and their replacement by the structured organizations and formal procedures of a great society. The period of transition is seen as marked by what Wiebe called a "search for order," which underlay the various and often conflicting demands for reform.

[11] Gabriel Kolko, *The Triumph of Conservatism: A Reinterpretation of American History, 1900–1916* (New York, 1963); James Weinstein, *The Corporate Ideal in the Liberal State, 1900–1918* (Boston, 1968).

[12] John D. Buenker, "The Progressive Era: The Search for a Synthesis," *Mid-America*, 51 (July 1969), p. 179; Otis L. Graham, Jr., *The Great Campaigns: Reform and War in America, 1900–1928* (Englewood Cliffs, N.J., 1971), and *An Encore for Reform: The Old Progressives and the New Deal* (New York, 1967).

[13] John D. Buenker, "Essay," in *Progressivism*, ed. John D. Buenker, John C. Burnham, and Robert M. Crunden (Cambridge, Mass., 1977), p. 31; Hays, *Response to Industrialism*, pp. 188–92.

[14] Louis Galambos, "The Emerging Organizational Synthesis in Modern American History," *Business History Review*, 44 (Autumn 1970), pp. 279–90; Wiebe, *Search for Order*; Hays, "The New Organizational Society."

Despite its value in suggesting connections and parallels between developments in different fields, this approach does not succeed in indicating what, if anything, was distinctive about the Progressive Era. The broad, social, institutional, and attitudinal changes upon which it focused attention are those generally associated with "modernization," a process that has surely been a continuous one since at least the nineteenth century.[15] Although Galambos, like Wiebe, suggested that the years around the turn of the century (which predate slightly the conventional Progressive Era) were "a crucial period in organizational terms," he also stressed that the new forces "became more, and not less, important during the 1920's, the New Deal, and World War II."[16] Ideologically as well as chronologically, the interpretation is too broad to provide the necessary definition. As Galambos, Wiebe, and Hays all emphasize (with varying degrees of enthusiasm), the changes they are concerned with include some that have never previously been considered liberal or "progressive."[17]

For similar reasons, the Progressive Era cannot be satisfactorily characterized by such broad notions as "response to industrialism" or "shifting coalitions." The emergence of the latter, like the growth of interest groups, should surely be seen, as Daniel T. Rodgers has suggested, as part of a long-term process: "the rise of modern, weak-party, issue-focused politics."[18] Indeed, none of the diverse forces that historians have identified as contributing to the pressure for reform in the early twentieth century was confined to that period. This applies as much to the attempt to uphold traditional American values in the face of the challenges presented by urbanization and immigration as it does to the promotion of the virtues of organization, efficiency, and technical expertise. Neither the critics of "political capitalism" nor the devotees of urban liberalism would wish to end their stories in 1920.

Yet there seems little doubt that there was something distinctive about the Progressive Era. Historians of various points of view have seen the early twentieth century as marked by a particular "mood," "temper," or

---

[15] For explicit evocation of the model of modernization, see Robert H. Wiebe, "The Progressive Years, 1900–1917," in *The Reinterpretation of American History and Culture*, ed. William H. Cartwright and Richard L. Watson (Washington, D.C., 1973), p. 425.

[16] Galambos, "The Emerging Organizational Synthesis," pp. 288, 284; Wiebe, *Search for Order*, p. 127.

[17] On this point, see David M. Kennedy, "Overview: The Progressive Era," *Historian*, 36 (May 1975), p. 464.

[18] Daniel T. Rodgers, "In Search of Progressivism," *Reviews in American History*, 10 (Dec. 1982), p. 117. See also Richard L. McCormick, "The Party Period and Public Policy: An Exploratory Hypothesis," *Journal of American History*, 66 (Sept. 1979), pp. 279–98.

"ethos" – one sympathetic to calls for reform. [19] This was also the perception of many at the time, not least some ambitious and alert politicians. "I have been carefully studying the present popular unrest and interviewing numbers of people about it," Senator Albert J. Beveridge of Indiana reported to his closest political confidant in the spring of 1906. "I am coming to the conclusion that it is not a passing whim, but a great and natural movement such as occurs in this country, as our early history shows, once about every forty years. It is not like the granger episode or like the Debs episode. The former of these affected only the farmers; the latter only the 'workingmen.' The present unrest, however, is quite as vigorous among the intellectuals, college men, university people, etc., as it is among the common people."[20] In Minnesota, the Democratic Governor, John A. Johnson, adopted a progressive stance. "When a political leader of Johnson's style and temperament became a reformer, it could only mean that the reform spirit had captured public opinion," Carl H. Chrislock has concluded. "At the same time, spokesmen for all groups within Minnesota adapted progressive rhetoric to the promotion of their particular interests. Precisely what politics deserved to be called progressive became a moot question, but nearly everyone claimed the label."[21]

This mood seems to have crystallized around 1905–6, when, as Richard L. McCormick has pointed out, a number of corruption scandals were uncovered across the nation.[22] In the next few years, the language of successful political leaders like Theodore Roosevelt and Woodrow Wilson emphasized the need for reform if traditional American ideals were to be preserved in the novel circumstances created by economic and social change. The climate of opinion was evidently very different from that of the 1890s, when the platform of the Populist Party, and even that of William Jennings Bryan in 1896, had seemed threateningly revolutionary to most middle-class Americans, including many who later became progressives.

One of the earliest signs of the new temper had been the muckraking articles that started to appear in popular magazines around 1903, and the

---

[19] See, for example, Hofstadter, *Age of Reform*, p. 280; Wiebe, *Search for Order*, p. 157; James C. Burnham and John D. Buenker in *Progressivism*, ed. Buenker et al., pp. 5, 124.

[20] Beveridge to John C. Shaffer, 27 Mar. 1906, quoted in John Braeman, *Albert J. Beveridge: American Nationalist* (Chicago, 1971), pp. 99–100.

[21] Carl H. Chrislock, *The Progressive Era in Minnesota, 1899–1918* (St. Paul, Minn., 1971), p. 22.

[22] "The Discovery That Business Corrupts Politics: A Reappraisal of the Origins of Progressivism," *American Historical Review*, 86 (Apr. 1981), pp. 247–74.

appetite of the reading public for reform literature of various kinds remained a striking characteristic of the Progressive Era. The muckraking vogue itself, which lasted several years, produced many books as well as hosts of articles. Studies were made of the nature and character of urban poverty, and those by the socialist authors Robert Hunter and John Spargo achieved notable sales. In time, the exposure of social ills, economic exploitation, and political corruption was supplemented by the celebration of reform achievements and the mapping of further advances. Some writers, including Herbert Croly, Walter Weyl, and Walter Lippmann, came to offer somewhat more theoretical analyses of the problems America faced, and of the solutions required.

The central importance to progressivism of these writings and of those who produced them has always been recognized by historians. In one of the earliest scholarly accounts of the period, Harold U. Faulkner concluded that "in encouraging the movement for reform no influence was greater than that of the popular magazines."[23] A generation later, Richard Hofstadter considered it "hardly an exaggeration to say that the Progressive mind was characteristically a journalistic mind, and that its characteristic contribution was that of the socially responsible reporter-reformer."[24] These observations remain valid even if it now seems that the distinguishing feature of the Progressive Era was a climate of opinion sympathetic to calls for reform, which generated among diverse groups and individuals a somewhat ill-founded feeling that they were participants in a broadly based and generally united "progressive movement." Wiebe has stressed the role of the muckrakers and of later reform literature, together with "some wishful thinking," in generating the "growing sense of interrelatedness" that created the picture of "an entire nation in the process of a grand metamorphosis."[25]

The perspective of its leading publicists, then, provides a good vantage point from which to reassess the character and fate of progressivism. Since such writers have to deal more directly and extensively with ideas than do inarticulate voters, or even politicians, it is also an appropriate point from which to consider how the First World War, in its various aspects and phases, affected the thinking of American reformers.

---

23 Harold U. Faulkner, *The Quest for Social Justice, 1898–1914* (New York, 1931), p. 112.
24 *Age of Reform*, p. 185.
25 *Search for Order*, pp. 198–9.

My interest in the evolution of ideas in response to public events has led me to concentrate on selected writers and editors. A general survey of the liberal press in these years would not serve this purpose so well. For to cite some as holding certain opinions at one time and others as expressing different points of view at another would not, of course, reveal the elements of continuity and change in the ideas of either. The size of the group is limited by practical considerations, not only of research but also of presentation. (As it is, I am very conscious that the thinking of some at least of the people considered here is treated inadequately, even cursorily.) I have tried, however, to include a sufficiently large number of writers and editors to give a fair indication of the range and diversity of progressive opinion.

It is in this way that I hope this book may add another dimension to the existing historical literature. Several of the men considered here have been studied individually, in biographies, scholarly articles, or dissertations. In addition, some excellent studies have focused on particular journals – especially the *New Republic* – or on particular issues, such as international peace.[26] To these works, as will be evident, I am greatly indebted. By placing such stories in a somewhat wider context, however, one can map the more general currents of opinion among progressive commentators – and thereby highlight distinctively individual reponses.

This study is concerned almost exclusively, then, with a group of about twenty individuals. These include the editors of several weekly magazines that were associated with the cause of reform in 1914 – namely, the *New Republic, Harper's Weekly,* the *Independent,* the *Public,* and the *Survey* – as well as a number of the best-known progressive publicists and journalists. They have been chosen because of their national prominence, but with some regard for diversity. A prerequisite was a clear commitment to some form of progressivism in the pre-war years.[27] Although the principle of selection is to this extent clear, the choice of particular individuals is too arbitrary for any great significance to be attached to the comparative

[26] In particular, Charles B. Forcey, *The Crossroads of Liberalism: Croly, Weyl, Lippmann and the Progressive Era, 1900–25* (New York, 1961); and C. Roland Marchand, *The American Peace Movement and Social Reform, 1898–1918* (Princeton, N.J., 1972).

[27] This criterion led to the exclusion of, for example, Albert Shaw and Oswald Garrison Villard. By this time, Shaw had come to adopt a fairly complacent view of the status quo, while Villard, who owned the *Nation* as well as the *New York Evening Post,* was a firm defender of the laissez-faire doctrines that these papers had upheld since the days of E. L. Godkin. Like his dedication to black civil rights, Villard's commitment to pacifism, which was to lead him to a more radical political outlook during the war, was, of course, quite consistent with this Manchester version of liberalism.

numbers adopting different points of view. The general balance of opinion among them is often indicated, but I do not wish to imply that this is necessarily representative of any wider segment of the population. Thus there seemed no compelling reason to treat each of these writers at equal length, and I have not hesitated to devote more attention to those whose views seemed more interesting or significant, or were simply more fully expressed.

A few words are in order on the form in which the material is presented, particularly the extensive use of direct quotation. I have no illusion that this does much to reduce the extent to which the reader has to trust the historian to give a fair account of the view he or she is reporting. Indeed, short quotations, which those that follow mostly are, may well carry a greater risk of distortion than paraphrase or exegesis. A phrase or a sentence torn from its context can easily give a misleading impression even of the particular document in which it appears, let alone of the general character of its author's writings. Nevertheless, there are some countervailing considerations. In the first place, direct quotation (provided it is accurate) always has some minimal value as evidence − these very words were written on some specific occasion by a particular individual. More important, perhaps, some of the tone and flavor, as well as the substance, of the original can be directly conveyed. Not least, such quotations may enliven the reading. For, however much (or little) else these men had in common, they had all made their names through writing.

CHAPTER 2

Progressive publicists

In the early twentieth century, progressive publicists seemed to play an important role in politics. A number of them were national figures, their support sought by candidates for office and widely advertised when obtained. Political organizations such as the National Progressive Republican League of 1911 and the Woodrow Wilson Independent League of 1916 included men who had made their reputation primarily through writing.[1] This situation owed much to muckraking, which had left many politicians with a healthy respect for the influence of certain well-known journalists. After the elections of 1905, Lincoln Steffens received telegrams from successful reform candidates in Ohio and Missouri thanking him for "your essential and great part in our victory."[2] "Can you give me a hearing?" the recently defeated presidential candidate had beseeched him a year earlier. "I am anxious to have a few minutes talk with you on a matter in which I am very much interested."[3] "They 'swung the world by the tail,'" recalled one liberal editor, admiringly, of the muckrakers.[4]

It was not all the writers of muckraking articles who acquired, or even sought, such status and influence. The phenomenon was, from óne point of view, simply a journalistic vogue and in its heyday several capable reporters produced material of this type with the same facility and skill, but no more special commitment than they brought to earlier and later

---

[1] Of the publicists considered here, Ray Stannard Baker, Frederic C. Howe (who was the secretary), Amos Pinchot, and William Allen White were among the charter members of the National Progressive Republican League in January 1911. Norman Hapgood and Lincoln Steffens became members of the auxiliary "Progressive Federation of Publicists and Editors" formed "to work for the nomination and election of a Progressive president." See George Mowry, *Theodore Roosevelt and the Progressive Movement* (Madison, Wisc., 1946), pp. 172–3. In 1916, as vice-chairman, Norman Hapgood virtually ran the Woodrow Wilson Independent League, and Ray Stannard Baker, among others, served on its national committee.

[2] Edward W. Bemis to Lincoln Steffens, 9 Nov. 1905, Steffens Papers, reel 1. Also Justin Kaplan, *Lincoln Steffens: A Biography* (New York, 1974), p. 143.

[3] Alton B. Parker to Steffens, 20 Dec. 1904, Steffens Papers, reel 4.

[4] Paul U. Kellogg, "Annual Report," *Survey*, 37 (11 Nov. 1916), pp. 7–8.

stories of very different character.[5] For some of its most famous practi-
tioners, however, muckraking was more than a routine assignment or
passing fashion. Representatives of that new breed of journalists who had
been to college and sometimes also to graduate school, they tended to take
themselves and their work seriously.[6] Even if they had not before held
strong political views, the authority they acquired as muckrakers led them
to see themselves thereafter as social critics, moral guides, or, simply,
reformers. In this role, they joined other writers and editors, who by
different routes and in various ways sought to express, shape, and inspire
the demand for reform in the Progressive Era. Before analyzing the main
patterns of their thinking in the pre-war years, and the ways they responded to the several challenges presented by the events of 1914 to
1920, we need to introduce these men and briefly sketch their individual
careers and characters.

Freelances

Among the muckrakers who retained an identification with reform were
three of the most famous – Lincoln Steffens, Ray Stannard Baker, and
Charles Edward Russell. The three were very different personalities.
Steffens, the only son of a successful hardware merchant, whose house is
now the governor's residence in Sacramento, California, was an urbane,
confident man who had made his way in the world by cultivating personal
relationships. As a postgraduate student in Germany, where he explored
in a somewhat dilettante manner the naturalistic basis of ethics under the
influence of Wilhelm Wundt, he formed a friendship with a certain
Johann Krudewolf who, on his early death in 1894, left Steffens his entire
estate of about twelve thousand dollars.[7] Upon his return to America,
Steffens began his career as a reporter on E. L. Godkin's *New York Evening
Post*. As one of his biographers has written, with his "genteel bearing and

---

[5] Such men as Samuel Hopkins Adams, C. P. Connolly, Burton J. Hendrick, Will Irwin, and
George Kibbe Turner. Irwin, for instance, won much praise during the First World War for his
reports from European battlefronts, which were published in book form as *Men, Women and War*
(New York, 1915), *The Latin at War* (New York, 1917), and *A Report at Armageddon* (New York,
1918). Hendrick turned increasingly to history as the vein of muckraking ran out. See Graham,
Encore for Reform, p. 161.

[6] See Hofstadter, *Age of Reform*, pp. 190–1.

[7] Harry H. Stein, "Lincoln Steffens: An Intellectual Portrait" (Ph.D. dissertation, University of
Minnesota, 1965), pp. 35–6; Irving G. Cheslaw, "An Intellectual Biography of Lincoln Steffens"
(Ph.D. dissertation, Columbia University, 1952), pp. 26–7.

demeanour, good education, Mugwump sympathies," he was "the *Post's* idea of a gentleman."[8] It was as the *Post's* police reporter that he became friendly with that other gentleman, the Commissioner of Police, Theodore Roosevelt, following the Lexow Committee revelations of 1895. In 1897, Steffens and some other university graduates, including Norman Hapgood, took over the venerable *New York Commercial Advertiser*, which they turned into a journal combining the advocacy of high-minded reform with self-consciously literary sketches of city life. It was from here that Steffens joined *McClure's* magazine in June 1901, supposedly as managing editor. However, he lacked the patience for office work and was soon on the road, gathering the stories of municipal corruption that were to inaugurate muckraking. A small man, whose elegant dressing bordered on dandyism – in Harold S. Wilson's phrase, "the bantam sophisticate with the pince-nez who asked his political informants what the hell was *really* going on in municipal politics"[9] – he retained through a lifetime of changing political opinions a fascination with the character and crucial role of strong leaders or "bosses."

If Steffens never quite lost some of the lighthearted irresponsibility of the "boy on horseback" he was fondly to recall in his *Autobiography*, life had always been a more serious business for Ray Stannard Baker. As the eldest of six sons, he had a high degree of responsibility thrust upon him even before the death of his mother, a minister's daughter, when he was thirteen. His father, who proudly traced his family back to Massachusetts in the 1630s, had attained the rank of major in the Union Army before settling as a land agent at St. Croix Falls in northwestern Wisconsin. The "characteristically American" frontier environment of his upbringing was to inspire the rural idylls Baker later published under the pseudonym of "David Grayson," but as a young man he resisted pressure from his father to return to the land office following his graduation from Michigan Agricultural College in order to pursue a journalistic career in Chicago.[10] On the staff of the *Chicago Record* in the 1890s, following Coxey's Army, the Pullman strike, and the movement for municipal reform, Baker was educated in the realities of urban, industrial society. He learned the skills of his trade so well that after joining *McClure's* in 1897 he became one of

[8] Stein, "Lincoln Steffens," p. 19.
[9] Harold S. Wilson, *"McClure's Magazine" and the Muckrakers* (Princeton, N.J., 1970), p. 96.
[10] Notebook 15, 8 Jan. 1918, pp. 12–16, R. S. Baker Papers; John E. Semonche, *Ray Stannard Baker: A Quest for Democracy in Modern America, 1870–1918* (Chapel Hill, N.C., 1969), pp. 182, 58–61.

the outstanding reporters of his generation. In the same year, in what he was to call "the most fruitful discovery in literary method I ever made," he began the practice of keeping notebooks or journals where he wrote "spontaneously exactly what I saw, heard, thought, felt at the moment when the impression was sharpest."[11] Naturally, much of what he recorded was ephemeral or inconsistent, but these fascinating and valuable historical documents also reveal the tension between a deep-seated puritanism and an imaginative sympathy with different types of people that shaped this earnest, introspective man's often ambivalent responses to his experience as he investigated labor unionism, the railroads, race relations, and other aspects of early twentieth-century America.

The most prominent and prolific of the muckrakers not associated with *McClure's* was Charles Edward Russell. Fifty in 1910, he was ten years older than Baker and six years older than Steffens, but in some ways the age gap seems greater. In part this was because, unlike many progressive publicists (including both Steffens and Baker), Russell was not a recent convert from mugwumpish conservatism but a reform veteran from the campaigns of Henry George and the Populists. The son of a staunchly Republican newspaper editor in Davenport, Iowa, Russell had been educated at a small Congregational college in Vermont. Although most of his career had been spent in newspaper journalism, where he had risen by the 1890s to be city editor of the New York *World* and managing editor of the New York *American,* he had artistic and literary tastes and aspirations. His publications include not only numerous political tracts but studies of poets and composers and some volumes of rather uninspired verse. These, like much about Russell, have an old-fashioned, Victorian style. His overwritten prose abounds in archaisms, hyperbole, and unqualified moral judgments. But if a certain provincial unsophistication seems to have survived his metropolitan experience and considerable foreign travel, so, too, did the straightforward sincerity that helped to make him a popular figure in the Socialist Party, which he joined in 1908. Following several heroic election campaigns (at his own expense) in New York State, he was generally recognized to be the leading contender for the Socialist presidential nomination in 1916 after Eugene Debs had indicated he did not wish to run again.

When, as a result of his views on the war, Russell ceased to be acceptable as a candidate, the position fell to another journalist (Allen L. Ben-

[11] *American Chronicle: The Autobiography of Ray Stannard Baker* (New York, 1945), pp. 66–7.

son), which fact may be seen as further testimony to the particularly prominent role of writers in a party that lacked both officeholders and politicians not exclusively identified with some particular locality or community. Perhaps the most notable of the many publicists in the pre-war Socialist Party were John Spargo and William English Walling, each of whom wrote works that are often included in the muckraking movement,[12] though both – in very different fashion, as befitted two very different, indeed antagonistic, personalities – were primarily concerned with the exposition and development of Socialist doctrine. Spargo was born and brought up in Cornwall, England, where he left school before he was twelve years old to follow his father into the trade of stonecutting. He soon became active in trade union affairs and labor politics. When at the age of twenty-five he found himself destitute in New York City following the untimely death of his stepfather, it was to the Socialist community that he naturally turned for assistance. Although he was found temporary jobs with the publishers, Funk and Wagnalls, and (notwithstanding his lack of legal qualifications) in Morris Hillquit's law firm,[13] Spargo experienced real hardship in his early years in America, during which time both his first wife and a baby son died of lung infections.[14] None of this lessened the energy with which he campaigned and wrote on behalf of socialism, and after the success of his first book, *The Bitter Cry of the Children* (1906), he was able to work full time for the cause. Despite a slightly touchy and belligerent manner, Spargo, who in his teens had been a lecturer for the Band of Hope and a Methodist lay preacher, seems to have been an effective and popular speaker, and in 1904 he was elected to the National Committee of the Socialist Party. His several books on socialism included one of the earliest biographies of Karl Marx to be published in any language. Characteristically, this presented Marx's doctrines in rather denatured form, for Spargo was strongly committed to a nonrevolutionary, revisionist variant of socialism.[15]

Whereas Spargo was a right-wing Socialist of proletarian origins and foreign birth, Walling was a left-wing Socialist from an impeccable, established American background – indeed, his maternal grandfather,

[12] John Spargo, *The Bitter Cry of the Children* (New York, 1906); William English Walling, "The Race War in the North," *Independent,* 65 (3 Sept. 1908), 529–34.

[13] "The Reminiscences of John Spargo," (Oral History Research Office, Columbia University, 1957), pp. 119, 122–4.

[14] Gerald Friedberg, "Marxism in the United States: John Spargo and the Socialist Party of America" (Ph.D. dissertation, Harvard University, 1964), pp. 70–82, 98.

[15] Ibid., pp. 4, 40, 82, 147, xi.

William Hayden English, had been governor of Illinois and in 1880 Democratic vice-presidential candidate. Walling himself had been educated in private schools in both Louisville, Kentucky, where he was born, and in Edinburgh, Scotland, where his father, a prosperous physician, was for a time American consul. Although, like other so-called millionaire Socialists, Walling was not quite so wealthy as the term implied, he did possess sufficient independent means to allow him to devote himself to writing and political work after leaving the University of Chicago in 1900 at the age of twenty-three. In 1903, he joined Jane Addams and others in founding the National Women's Trade Union League, and between 1905 and 1907 he traveled a good deal in Russia where Tolstoy and Lenin were among those he met in the course of studying the revolutionary movement. [16] But his most notable achievement was inspiring the creation of the National Association for the Advancement of Colored People (NAACP) in 1908–9. [17] Walling had become a socialist some time before he joined the party in 1910 and he has been described as "one of the few serious theoretical minds American socialism has produced." [18] Certainly his writings are more scholarly and sophisticated than Spargo's, but they are also idiosyncratic and less clearly consistent. Yet if Walling's judgments were often unpredictable, they were generally emphatic, and he had already demonstrated that the passion which fired his unquestionable idealism could easily be diverted into intraparty polemics. [19]

Others somewhat on the fringes of muckraking, while never becoming Socialists, also firmly committed themselves to the cause of reform. One such was William Allen White, who joined with Baker, Steffens, and others in the *McClure's* group in the cooperative of writers and editors that took over the *American Magazine* in 1906. White was born in 1868 in Emporia, Kansas, the small town he was to make famous, and was the only surviving child of a doctor and storekeeper who was one of the leading Democrats in the state. But his father died when he was fourteen and it was the influence of his mother, devout Congregationalist and

---

[16] William English Walling, *Russia's Message: The True World Import of the Revolution* (New York, 1908), pp. 432–5, 369–70.

[17] Anna Strunsky Walling, ed., *William English Walling: A Symposium* (New York, 1938), pp. 75–81.

[18] By Irving Howe in "To *The Masses* – With Love and Envy," in *Echoes of Revolt: The Masses, 1911–1917*, ed. William L. O'Neill (Chicago, 1966), p. 5.

[19] For example, in a bitter dispute over the issue of collaboration with the American Federation of Labor in 1909–10, which not only originated Walling's feud with Spargo but led A. M. Simons to feel that a personal friendship had been betrayed. See Friedberg, "Marxism in the United States," pp. 103–12.

Republican, lover of English literature, ardent supporter of woman suffrage and prohibition, that was the more profound. White had worked as a journalist even before he left the University of Kansas and, after a few years on the *Kansas City Star,* he borrowed three thousand dollars in 1895 to buy the *Emporia Gazette,* which then had only five hundred subscribers. It was his anti-Populist editorial in that journal a year later, widely distributed as a campaign document by the Republicans, that suddenly gave him a national reputation and led to a friendship with Theodore Roosevelt that greatly influenced the next phase of his career. He was serving as a conduit of political information from the Middle West to Roosevelt and was heavily involved in state Republican politics long before Roosevelt's bolt of 1912 so he was well placed to take the lead in organizing the Bull Moose campaign in Kansas – "Boss White" some then called him.[20] By this time he was combining the roles of political activist, nationally known publicist, and author of slightly sentimental short stories and novels, while retaining his distinctive base as editor of a small-town Midwestern newspaper. His very individual style of writing, peppered with vivid, humorous, and extravagant images, seemed, like his mixture of good nature, shrewdness, and unreticent moralism, to epitomize his region. Yet he was also a more sensitive and self-aware man than his somewhat solid appearance and extrovert manner might at first lead one to assume.

For ambitious young journalists without White's calm confidence, charm, and talent, the East was likely to be both more beguiling and less easy to conquer. This was certainly the experience of George Creel who had been deprived of any sort of college education, along with much else, by his upbringing in the genteel poverty of a Missouri home where his father, reared before the Civil War to be a Southern gentleman, had turned to "diligent drinking" as an escape from his failure as a farmer.[21] Creel's first expedition to New York, as a young man of twenty-one, had ended with his selling jokes to the yellow press during the Spanish-American War, which, while it earned him a decent living, did not measure up to his idea of a literary career. It was after his return to the Middle West to be first the producer of a "journal of opinion" in Kansas City and later a crusading editor in Denver – where he had a brief and eventful period of office as police commissioner in a reform administration

---

[20] John DeWitt McKee, *William Allen White: Maverick on Main Street* (Westport, Conn., 1975), p. 117.

[21] George Creel, *Rebel at Large: Recollections of Fifty Crowded Years* (New York, 1947), p. 10.

– that he succeeded in making a name for himself. In these years, Creel energetically built up his contacts with others in the insurgent movement, and he relied on better-known muckrakers such as Steffens and Russell to open doors for him in the East[22] – a quest made more urgent after his marriage to the actress, Blanche Bates, brought him back to live in New York. Creel's drive and fighting spirit were unquestionable; less so the balance and moderation of his judgments. "To Creel there are only two classes of men," Mark Sullivan once wrote. "There are skunks, and the greatest man that ever lived. The greatest man that ever lived is plural, and includes everyone who is on Creel's side in whatever public issue he happens at the moment to be concerned with."[23]

When Creel was publicizing and organizing for the reform movement in Denver, Chester Rowell had for some time been engaged in similar activities in California, yet two men could hardly have been more different in background and temperament. Rowell was as firmly born into the Republican Party as Creel was into the Democratic, for his father, Jonathan Rowell, was a lawyer from Bloomington, Illinois, who served as a Republican congressman from 1883 to 1891. For part of this period, Chester Rowell, the eldest of five children, attended the University of Michigan, where John Dewey was among his instructors. A scholarly and serious young man, Rowell was another who went to Germany for postgraduate work – in philology and philosophy at the Universities of Halle and Berlin – although his money ran out before he was able to complete a degree. Upon his return to America he spent a few rather unsatisfying years in college teaching before in 1898 at the age of thirty he was installed by his uncle, Dr. Chester Rowell, a prominent doctor in Fresno, California, as editor of the town's major newspaper, the *Republican*.[24] By 1912, when he inherited the ownership of the paper from his uncle, Rowell had more than quadrupled its circulation, and had also played a major role in the insurgent movement that had led to the nomination and election of Hiram Johnson as governor of California in 1910. Although he boasted in 1913 that the *Fresno Republican* was "one of the three small-town newspapers in the United States which has a national reputation,"[25] Rowell himself never became as widely known as William

[22] *Ibid.*, pp. 50, 94; Creel to Steffens, [Oct. 1910], Steffens Papers, reel 1.

[23] "Creel – Censor," *Collier's Weekly*, 60 (10 Nov. 1917), p. 13.

[24] Miles Chapman Everett, "Chester Harvey Rowell: Pragmatic Humanist and California Progressive" (Ph.D. dissertation, University of California, Berkeley, 1966), pp. 60–6, 94–122.

[25] *Ibid.*, pp. 285–7.

Allen White, but his importance within Californian politics earned him, too, a place on the National Committee of the Progressive Party in 1912.

Not all progressive publicists were professional journalists, although in the case of one of the most prolific of them, Frederic C. Howe, this was not as a result of choice. Howe, the only son of a small businessman in Meadville, Pennsylvania, where he spent five unhappy years at the local sectarian college, took a Ph.D. at Johns Hopkins specifically to prepare himself to "become an editorial writer on a city newspaper." But although he had worked his way through college largely by selling articles to newspapers and magazines, his attempt to break into New York journalism was unsuccessful and he turned, unenthusiastically, to law. His teachers at Johns Hopkins, notably Albert Shaw, James Bryce, and Woodrow Wilson, had supplemented his inherited, pietistic Republicanism with a commitment to high-minded, mugwumpish reform. It was as an upright young Republican that he was elected in 1901 as a city councilman in Cleveland, where he was a partner in the law firm of James and Harry Garfield, the president's sons. But the charismatic personality of Tom L. Johnson – who was for Howe "one of the greatest statesmen America has produced" – converted him to the Single Tax philosophy and he became one of the Democratic mayor's lieutenants on the council and later in the Ohio state senate and as a member of the Cleveland Tax Commission. Inspired by Johnson's vision and remembering Shaw's teaching, in these years he "studied cities as one might study art" and published a number of books which earned him a national reputation as an authority on municipal reform. He had planned a series of ten volumes "on the general subject of democracy," and it was in order to acquire more leisure for his writing that he moved in 1910 to New York City where he and his wife, a former Unitarian minister, lived on the fringes of Greenwich Village in its halcyon days.[26] A founder of the National Progressive Republican League, he switched his support to Woodrow Wilson when Robert M. La Follette was forced out of the race, and in August 1914 Wilson appointed this honest, sensitive, and humane man to be commissioner of immigration at the Port of New York.

Like Howe, Amos Pinchot had been trained as a lawyer, and was a founding member of the National Progressive Republican League who

---

[26] This account is based upon Howe's autobiography, *The Confessions of a Reformer* (New York, 1925). Quotations on pp. 20, 145, 114, 235.

eventually became a Wilson supporter. Uniquely among these men, Pinchot was really wealthy – just after the war his post-tax income from property and bonds was more than 60,000 dollars a year.[27] His paternal grandfather, a captain in Napoleon's army, had emigrated to Pennsylvania after he was expelled from France by the Bourbons for taking part in an unsuccessful plot to rescue the deposed emperor from St. Helena. Cyril Desiré Constantin Pinchot prospered in America, but his son greatly augmented the family fortune by marrying the beautiful daughter of Amos Eno, a successful real estate dealer and builder in New York City. Born in Paris, while his parents were traveling, Amos Pinchot was educated at exclusive private schools and at Yale, where he was a typical undergraduate, more interested in sport and social life than academic work. Soon after graduation, he enlisted as a private in the brief Spanish-American War before completing his law studies. He never practiced law on a regular basis, instead devoting himself to managing the family estates and enjoying the life of New York society. His political involvement dated only from 1909–10, when he acted for his famous elder brother Gifford in the Pinchot–Ballinger case. An article in *McClure's* in September 1910, comparing the progressive insurgency with the antislavery origins of the Republican Party, marked his debut as a publicist – its success, Gifford proudly wrote their mother, "has given Amos an important position at one stroke."[28] Amos naturally followed Gifford into the Bull Moose Progressive Party in 1912 – and, indeed, ran for Congress in a solidly Democratic district in New York City – but he began to establish an independent position for himself by taking the lead in attacking George Perkins's role in the Progressive Party and by an increasing identification with labor and radical causes. He was one of the most important patrons of the *Masses* and he spoke at meetings in almost every major strike between 1912 and 1916, though he was not, apparently, an impressive orator. His *penchant* for detailed statistical analysis was better suited to written presentation, where, lightened by somewhat contemptuous images, it made him an effective and forthright advocate.

---

[27] Sumner Gerard to Amos Pinchot, 19 Feb. 1912, 11 Aug. 1922, Amos Pinchot Papers, boxes 39, 43.

[28] Gifford to Mrs. James Pinchot, Sept. 1910, cited in Amos Pinchot, *A History of the Progressive Party, 1912–1916*, ed. Helene Maxwell Hooker (New York, 1958), p. 20. I am much indebted for the information in this paragraph to Professor Hooker's "Biographical Introduction," pp. 8–68.

The weeklies and their editors

Long before the outbreak of the First World War, most of the more famous muckraking periodicals had either abandoned the genre or expired. However, in the immediate pre-war years, two weekly magazines with a long history, the *Independent* and *Harper's Weekly*, had a decidedly progressive editorial slant. For most of its history the *Independent* was primarily a religious publication, having been founded, as its name implied, by a group of Congregationalists in 1848. Vehemently antislavery from the beginning, it had been edited during the 1860s by Henry Ward Beecher and Theodore Tilton until the famous scandal ended their collaboration. In 1858, Henry C. Bowen, a tough, austere New York merchant, acquired control of the magazine and it remained in his family after his death. Bowen's grandson, Hamilton Holt, became managing editor in 1897 at the age of twenty-five. Holt, the son of a scholarly Brooklyn lawyer of old New England stock, had already been working on the journal part-time for three years while pursuing graduate studies in sociology and economics at Columbia University following a disappointing academic career at Yale. In collaboration with the chief editor, William Hayes Ward, Holt transformed the *Independent* from a religious weekly into a secular magazine covering all matters of general interest. It deliberately eschewed the more sensational varieties of muckraking, but both Spargo's "The Bitter Cry of the Children" and Walling's "The Race War in the North" were first published in its pages. Holt himself had been connected to several social settlements and, according to his biographer, persuaded his Southern bride to move into a cooperative dwelling at 3 Fifth Avenue "in order to live near a slum district."[29] He was a progressive on most domestic issues, although from 1903 his major enthusiasm was world federation. In 1900, a distinguished if rather idiosyncratic note was introduced into a number of the editorials when Holt recruited Franklin H. Giddings as a regular contributor. Giddings, a professor of sociology at Columbia, where his courses had much impressed Holt, derived from a firmly Darwinian view of social evolution a belief in such values as efficiency, organization, and disiplined liberty, which, together with some other prejudices, he propounded with passion and style. In 1912, Holt borrowed forty thousand dollars to purchase the *Independent*

---

[29] Warren F. Kuehl, *Hamilton Holt: Journalist, Internationalist, Educator* (Gainesville, Fla., 1960), p. 46.

from his uncle, and, as editor-in-chief, he presided during the next two years over a remarkable increase in circulation from 20,000 to 125,000.

This success contrasted with the position of *Harper's Weekly,* which in these years had proved commercially unable to meet the challenge of the newer magazines. Despite its famous attacks on the Tweed Ring in the days of George William Curtis and Thomas Nast, under the editorship of Colonel George Harvey the paper had taken no part in muckraking and had opposed most progressive reforms. By April, 1913, after twelve consecutive years of losses and with circulation down to 70,000, Harpers was happy to sell the *Weekly* for a hundred thousand dollars to a group headed by Charles R. Crane, who wished to secure more journalistic support for the incoming Wilson administration. To Wilson's pleasure, Crane installed in the editorial chair Norman Hapgood, who had gained a reputation as an enterprising and crusading editor at *Collier's Weekly.*[30] Hapgood was born in Alton, Illinois, where his father was a prosperous manufacturer of farm equipment, whose firm moralism had been in no way diminished by his lapse from his Unitarian faith. The eldest of three brothers, Norman Hapgood had graduated from Harvard with artistic tastes and literary ambitions. After an unenthusiastic encounter with law, at Harvard Law School and then briefly in practice in Chicago, he gravitated to journalism. Like Steffens, he was one of those who moved from the *New York Evening Post* to the *Commercial Advertiser,* where he became a sharp and influential theater critic. It was only after his move to *Collier's Weekly* in 1902 that Hapgood, a busy, active little man, became seriously interested in politics and broadened his mugwump outlook into a commitment to progressivism. The Pinchot–Ballinger controversy, in which *Collier's* played a key role, brought him, as it did Amos Pinchot, into close association with the persuasive Louis Brandeis, and Hapgood's wholehearted endorsement of Woodrow Wilson in 1912 doubtless owed much to this influence. As editor of *Harper's Weekly,* Hapgood was unsuccessful in his attempt to secure a contribution from Wilson himself,[31] but he did publish articles by Brandeis that later became *Other People's Money* as well as some muckraking pieces by Creel in which any paucity of documentation was compensated for by an abundance of rhetorical denunciation.[32]

---

[30] Woodrow Wilson to Charles R. Crane, 26 May 1913, Woodrow Wilson Papers, ser. 4, case file 510.

[31] Norman Hapgood to Woodrow Wilson, 20 May 1913. Woodrow Wilson Papers, ser. 4, case file 510.

[32] See, for instance, "Harvesting the Harvest Hands," "Where Is the Vice Fight?" "Poisoners of

However, the hoped-for rise in circulation did not materialize and the paper continued to incur heavy losses until, in April 1916, Crane simply gave the title, together with the obligation to meet paid subscriptions, to Holt, who merged it with the *Independent*.[33]

According to one account, the inadequacies of *Harper's Weekly* under Hapgood were responsible for the birth of the *New Republic* since they prompted Willard and Dorothy Straight to promise Herbert Croly the financial support necessary to produce a rival weekly.[34] It is true that for such strong partisans of the Bull Moose as Croly and the Straights the deficiencies of Hapgood's magazine would have been much aggravated by its unwavering loyalty to Wilson. Nevertheless, it is hard to believe that this was more than an incidental reason, at least for Croly, who was to confess that "the opportunity of starting it [the *New Republic*] fulfilled an ambition which I cherished for over twenty years."[35] For most of that period, Croly, whose only regular employment had been six years as an editor of the *Architectural Record,* was too obscure a figure to have had much real hope of achieving his ambition. It was the publication in 1909 of *The Promise of American Life* that transformed the career of this shy, serious man. Hailed by Theodore Roosevelt – surely the last ex-president to be a regular book reviewer – as "the most powerful and illuminating study of our national conditions which has appeared for many years,"[36] the book was widely assumed to have inspired Roosevelt's "New Nationalism." Croly's impressive intellectual independence and integrity, which were to give the *New Republic* a character even its opponents respected,[37] may well have been an inheritance from his remarkable parents. His father, to whose memory *The Promise* was dedicated, was an immigrant from Ireland who had worked his way up through night schools to top editorial posts on the New York *World* and *Daily Graphic*. It was through the world of journalism that he had met his wife, an

Public Opinion," "The Feudal Towns of Texas," and the series on various brands of quack medicines, *Harper's Weekly,* 59 (26 Sept., 10 Oct., 7, 14 Nov. 1914), and 60 (23 Jan., January– May 1915).

33 See Kuehl, *Hamilton Holt,* p. 33. For the biographical information on Norman Hapgood, I am chiefly indebted to Michael D. Marcaccio, *The Hapgoods: Three Earnest Brothers* (Charlottesville, Va., 1977).

34 Charles Forcey, *The Crossroads of Liberalism: Croly, Weyl, Lippmann and the Progressive Era, 1900– 1925* (New York, 1961), pp. 173–4.

35 Croly to O. G. Villard, 6 Oct. 1915, Villard Papers, folder 758.

36 Cited in Forcey, *Crossroads of Liberalism,* p. 139.

37 See *Commonweal,* 12 (28 May 1930), pp. 92–3.

English clergyman's daughter, who, under the pen name Jenny June, eventually became editor of some of the best-known women's magazines in the country. The Crolys were devotees of Comtean Positivism, and on his birth in 1869 Herbert Croly was baptized in accordance with the ritual of "the religion of humanity." The influence of this secular mysticism remained with him, though in the early years of the *New Republic* in particular, it was less apparent than his debt to his philosophy professors at Harvard – George Santayana and, especially, William James.

When in one of its early issues the *New Republic* criticized Roosevelt for an intemperate speech on Mexico, the honeymoon was abruptly terminated and it was not long before the infuriated Roosevelt dismissed the journal as "a negligible sheet, run by two anaemic Gentiles and two uncircumcized Jews."[38] This last was a reference to Walter Weyl and Walter Lippmann, who shared with Croly the chief responsibility for the journal's editorial policy. Both came from comfortable, metropolitan, German-Jewish backgrounds, although in other respects their upbringing differed in ways that left a lasting imprint on their personalities. From the age of seven, when his father died, Walter Weyl grew up in a large household in Philadelphia consisting of a grandmother, three uncles, his mother, and five brothers and sisters. While his ability was recognized and encouraged, he was teased for his absent-mindedness, and he retained as an adult a warmth and sense of humor that enabled him to get on easily with all classes of people. Described by Lippmann as "by far the best trained economist in the progressive movement,"[39] Weyl took a Ph.D. at the University of Pennsylvania's Wharton School of Commerce and Finance under Professor Simon Nelson Patten, who influenced his thinking considerably. Weyl's dissertation, published as *The Traffic of Railways*, illustrated his skill in handling statistics, but upon its completion in 1897, he deliberately rejected an academic career. Instead, he chose to study social and economic conditions as a freelance, with an interest both theoretical and engaged. He conducted some investigations for the U.S. Bureau of Labor in France and Puerto Rico, assisted John Mitchell of the United Mine Workers in the arbitration proceedings following the 1902 coal strike, and lived for some years in University Settlement, New York. Although he later wrote a number of magazine articles, mostly on immi-

---

[38] Quoted by Eric F. Goldman, *Rendezvous with Destiny: A History of Modern American Reform* (New York, 1952), pp. 251–2.

[39] [Howard Brubaker ed.], *Walter Weyl: An Appreciation* (privately printed, 1922), p. 87.

gration, he only attained widespread recognition with the publication in 1912 of *The New Democracy,* which sold close to 10,000 copies. In the same year, he served on the Progressive Party's National Committee, with responsibility for publicity among the foreign-language press. A vivacious but sensitive man, whose oscillation between self-discipline and self-indulgence was epitomized by the number of times he gave up smoking (with elaborate statistical computations of the degree of his success), Weyl aroused much affection, as is evident from the memorial volume privately printed after his death from cancer in 1919 at the age of forty-six.

Most seem to have found Walter Lippmann less lovable, though few could withhold admiration for his intellectual and literary ability. As a founding editor of the *New Republic,* Lippmann was only at the beginning of one of the most famous careers in the history of American journalism, but already, at the age of twenty-five, he had behind him a remarkable record of achievement and experience. The only child of elderly parents, Lippmann spent his childhood on the Upper East Side of New York City in what his biographer had described as "a gilded Jewish ghetto";[40] he himself carried to an extreme the assimilationist tendencies of the affluent German-American Jewish community at the turn of the century. Nevertheless, at Harvard, where he had a brilliant academic career, he doubtless encountered antisemitic prejudice and this may have helped to fire his undergraduate commitment to socialism.[41] He joined the party after leaving Harvard in 1910, and in early 1912 spent a few months as an aide to the Socialist mayor of Schenectady. However, the experience was a disillusioning one, and Croly later reported that Lippmann "had pretty well ceased to be a socialist by the time we started the New Republic."[42] In any case, the greatest influence on Lippmann at this time was Graham Wallas, with whom he had developed a relationsip of mutual admiration since their encounter at Harvard, and Lippmann's major ambition was probably to make a significant contribution to political science. He viewed the two slender volumes he had already published, *A Preface to Politics* (1913) and *Drift and Mastery* (1914), as "terribly inadequate," but they had given him the "reputation" he considered "the only way of meeting the people you've got to know in order to understand the world."[43] Journalism, to which he had been introduced in 1910 as an assistant to Lincoln Steffens, was a

[40] Ronald Steel, *Walter Lippmann and the American Century* (London, 1980), p. 9.
[41] Ibid., pp. 28–30.
[42] Croly to Felix Frankfurter [1921], Frankfurter Papers, box 50, file 000926.
[43] Lippmann diary, 5 July 1914, p. 5, Lippmann Papers.

further means to this end, and Lippmann, through his industry and discrimination as an editor as well as his own pellucid prose, made a large contribution to the success of the early *New Republic*.

The speed with which the *New Republic* established itself as probably the country's leading intellectual weekly was a tribute to the quality of much of the writing, not only in the editorial sections for which Croly, Weyl, and Lippmann were primarily responsible, but in its feature articles and literary comment. To these sections of the magazine, Randolph S. Bourne, attached in a regular but ill-defined role, made notable contributions. A twenty-eight-year old cripple, whose book *Youth and Life*, published in 1913, had in some way established him as a spokesman for his generation, Bourne specialized in cultural criticism in its broadest sense. He was a devotee and exponent of the philosophical and educational ideas of John Dewey, but such hero worship was but the reverse side of an iconoclastic disposition, just as his self-conscious cultural nationalism was balanced by a profound susceptibility to European, particularly French, civilization.

For all its breadth of interests and the famous names who wrote for it, the *New Republic*'s readership did not until 1916 exceed that of a much narrower, thinner, and more cheaply produced weekly published in Chicago. This was the *Public*, which might more appropriately be compared with sectarian magazines since it was the journal of the Single Tax movement. It had been founded in 1898 by Louis F. Post who, after a varied career, chiefly in journalism, had been Henry George's chief lieutenant and had edited previous Single Tax papers. The *Public* proved much more successful than these, not only on account of the subsidies it received from the Joseph Fels Fund after 1911 but also because it had achieved a steadily growing circulation, which by 1914 exceeded 16,000.[44] This may have reflected the wisdom of Post's attempt to supplement the advocacy of George's panacea with support of a broader reform program, but it was certainly the case that, for better or worse, the paper remained reasonably faithful to the undertaking made in its first issue to be a periodical "in which the news reports are not distorted by editorial bias, nor discolored with impertinent opinions, but are simple, direct, compact, lucid, and veracious; a paper which aims to be right rather than sensational; which is not padded; which clearly relates to their appropriate places in general

[44] Dominic Candelero, "The Public of Louis F. Post and Progressivism," *Mid-America*, 56, no. 2 (Apr. 1974), pp. 109–23.

history those events that have historical value; and which in its editorial policy unflinchingly puts public questions to the supreme test of obvious moral principles, and stands by the result."[45] In 1913, Wilson, at the urging of William Jennings Bryan, appointed the sixty-three-year-old Post to be assistant secretary of labor, and the editorship of the *Public* was assumed by Samuel Danziger, from 1916 jointly with Stoughton Cooley.

If the importance of that segment of the reform constituency represented by the *Public* is still not often sufficiently appreciated, the same can no longer be said of the contribution of social workers to pre–World War I progressivism. The shifting emphasis from individual philanthropy to social reform – in the austere language of the professionals, from "correction" to "prevention" – was reflected in the evolution of the leading journal in the field. Founded in 1897 under the bald title, *Charities,* it was published by the New York Charity Organization Society to provide practical information to persons engaged in health and welfare work of all kinds. Its first editor was the society's thirty-one-year-old secretary, Edward T. Devine, who had been a teacher and the principal of a seminary in Iowa before graduate study at the Universities of Pennsylvania and Halle "earned him the title of 'Doctor' by which his associates always knew him." The amalgamation of *Charities* with the *Charities Review* in 1901 and, more significantly, with Graham Taylor's Chicago-based *Commons* in 1905 broadened its coverage in a topical as well as a geographical sense. From 1907 the journal received substantial financial support from the Russell Sage Foundation, and a complete reorganization in 1912 rendered it independent of the Charity Organization Society. At this point, Devine, who had many other commitments, handed over the editorship to the assistant editor, Paul U. Kellogg.[46]

Kellogg, aged thirty-three in 1912, was from Kalamazoo, Michigan, where his father was an unsuccessful businessman who had been unable to afford to send either of his sons to college. After a short period on the *Kalamazoo Daily Telegraph,* Paul Kellogg had moved east in 1901, and a year later this sober and sincere young man had attracted the attention of Devine at a summer school on philanthropic work. By 1912, Kellogg had proved his administrative as well as editorial ability by organizing the famous Pittsburgh Survey. This pioneering piece of social research not only inspired the journal's new name in 1909 but provided a model for the combination of detailed investigation of social facts with unequivocal

[45] Quoted in Post, "Living a Long Life Over Again," p. 263 (renumbered), TS, Post Papers.
[46] Clarke A. Chambers, *Paul U. Kellogg and the Survey: Voices for Social Welfare and Social Justice* (Minneapolis, 1971), pp. 7–11, 24–7, 40–5.

advocacy of social action. Kellogg saw the magazine's role as in part that of filling the void left by the decline of muckraking, and in 1920 Ray Stannard Baker legitimated the succession by warmly praising the *Survey*'s "clear and honest reporting of actual conditions that will inform or convince public opinion."[47] Although the *Survey* explicitly disclaimed any interest in becoming a journal of opinion and contained little direct editorial comment, many of the signed articles, including those by the associate editors – Devine, Jane Addams, and Graham Taylor – served the same function, and Kellogg was, according to his biographer, "not unaware of the competition of the *Masses* and, after 1914, of the *New Republic,* whose mandate and potential readership overlapped with the *Survey*'s."[48]

Whatever their diversities, these writers and editors for the most part conformed to the picture of the typical progressive, as drawn by Mowry, Hofstadter, and others, in at least two respects. In the first place, the majority "came from old American stock with British origins consistently indicated"[49] – and, unless Southerners, had been inclined to view the Republican party as their natural home. Secondly, they were nearly all of "the generation that came of age in the eighteen nineties."[50] Excluding Lippmann and Bourne at one end and Post (who was clearly of an older generation) and Russell at the other, the ages of these men in 1914 ranged from thirty-five to forty-eight, with many in their early and mid-forties. Of course, these facts, as has often been pointed out with regard to the generalizations of Mowry and Hofstadter, may not have much specific connection with a commitment to reform but may simply reflect general characteristics of those prominent in this sphere of American life at this time.

While it is true that viewed as a group they overwhelmingly represented a middle-class, Anglo-Saxon Protestant America, the backgrounds from which most of them came were, as we have seen, of two main types. On the one hand, some, particularly among the editors of national journals, were from well-to-do families, usually on the East Coast. Educated at Harvard or Yale and often enjoying from an early age the habit of transatlantic travel, such men naturally tended to be more in touch with contemporary European ideas and developments than most Americans. It

---

[47] *Survey,* 44 (26 June 1920), p. 426.
[48] Chambers, *Kellogg,* p. 50.
[49] Mowry, *Era of Theodore Roosevelt,* p. 86.
[50] *Age of Reform,* p. 166.

is interesting, though not perhaps of any great significance, that several of those from socially privileged backgrounds – Amos Pinchot, Lippmann, even Croly – were descended from non-English immigrants. On the other hand, the majority of those who had made their careers as professional reporters were from small or medium-size towns, often in the Middle West. As a rule they were from families that were near the apex of the local social pyramid and, with the exception of Creel and Kellogg, they had all attended college, though often one of slight academic pretensions. Not only were they more exclusively of Anglo-Saxon, Protestant background than those from the eastern, upper middle class, but they were all nurtured in the pieties of that pervasive, small-town, middle-class culture which extended from New England to California in the later nineteenth century. Their careers generally took them to the big cities in the 1890s – and this, indeed, often had a major influence on their outlook – but they retained a more vivid sense than some of their metropolitan colleagues that the new realities of urbanization, industrialization, and immigration still constituted only part of American life. Encountering "Dr. Walter Weyl" in January 1918, Ray Stannard Baker "tried to make him feel the America I know best – the small town America, the farm-dwellers' America, the great middle west America – which is the most characteristic American life we have: with its roots deepest in our traditions, such as they are, and stock longest native to our soil."[51]

At least as significant as such differences in background, some might argue, were the differences in intellectual sophistication and independence. The works of Croly, Lippmann, and to a lesser extent Weyl, would have a place in any history of twentieth-century American political thought; not so the homely commonplaces of William Allen White or the assertive rhetoric of Creel and Russell. Considering this group as a whole, however, we are confronted in this respect not with a sharp distinction between two categories but with a spectrum in which such people as Dr. Howe, Walling (widely read in modern European thought), Steffens, and Rowell – who had once been charged by John Dewey "to take T. H. Green's Protegomena to Ethics and show wherein it is logically deficient, and supply the lack!"[52] – would help to bridge the gap. Moreover, all these men were engaged in a broadly similar kind of writing. Even in their most ambitious treatises, Croly, Weyl, and Lippmann were addressing the general educated public rather than an academic audience, and this was certainly no less true of their work for the *New Republic*. The term

[51] Notebook 15, 8 Jan. 1918, pp. 12–16, R. S. Baker Papers.
[52] Rowell to Cora Rowell, 30 Apr. 1891, cited in Everett, "Chester Harvey Rowell," pp. 61–62.

often used at the time to describe this kind of writer was "publicist," defined by Francis Hackett in his memoir of Weyl as one "who gives to political and social thinking the form in which it can be assimilated by educated people."[53] The word generally implied advocacy as well as popularization, as Martin Schutze made clear in his essay in the same volume. "He was a born publicist," Schutze wrote of Weyl. "The driving force in his work was the desire, sustained by an extraordinary ability, to collect and classify the most readily ascertainable factors in life and to transform general conclusions and theories into concrete motives for specific political action."[54] These descriptions do not seem so different from the role White ascribed to himself and his fellow progressive agitators in 1916 – "to present intelligently and in their most attractive form the advanced ideas of the world's soundest thinkers . . . looking forward to the acceptance of these ideas."[55]

On the importance of this activity, there was general agreement among these men. "The real preparation for a creative statesmanship lies deeper than parties and legislatures. It is the work of publicists and educators, scientists, preachers and artists," wrote Lippmann in *A Preface to Politics*.[56] Among these various communicators, journalists seemed to many to have come to occupy a preeminent position. "The American magazines have to a large extent fallen heir to the power exerted formerly by pulpit [and] lyceum . . . in the molding of public opinion," concluded Hamilton Holt in 1914.[57] Croly upbraided Felix Frankfurter for preferring to keep his post at Harvard rather than join the *New Republic* full time. "I am profoundly convinced that we have entered upon a revolutionary period during which the colleges and universities will count for comparatively little. The real call is for a kind of thinking which is half faith and half human insight, and which has an immediate cash value in terms of human activity."[58] In a characteristically less solemn vein, White sent an editor "my September contribution to Government by Magazine."[59]

This exalted view of the social importance of their work naturally gave

53 [Brubaker, ed.], *Walter Weyl*, p. 103.
54 Ibid., p. 59.
55 *New York World*, 11 June 1916, quoted in Pinchot's *History*, ed. Hooker, p. 38.
56 *A Preface to Politics* (New York, 1913), p. 229.
57 "The Editor as Schoolmaster," *Independent* 79 (3 Aug. 1914), p. 169.
58 Croly to Frankfurter, [4 Sept. 1914], file 000920, box 50, Felix Frankfurter Papers. Frankfurter, of course, did come to have close links with the *New Republic*, wrote often for it, and was in frequent contact with the editors, particularly Lippmann. By precept as well as example, Croly had stressed the importance of the critic, not least the social critic, in *The Promise of American Life* (New York, 1909). See especially pp. 26, 175, 439–40, 443–4, 450–2.
59 White to John S. Phillips, 25 May 1908, quoted in McKee, *William Allen White*, p. 78.

many of these publicists a strong sense of purpose and of responsibility. "It seems almost as though I had a mission to perform," Baker wrote to his father in the early days of his fame.[60] Years later, recognizing in his diary that "much of what I asserted in writings some years ago in all sober owlishness, with dogmatic certainty, as a guide to life I either do not now believe or perceive in wholly different perspective," he nevertheless admonished himself that "if the more studious and thoughtful men do not act strongly upon their opinions but yield weakly to doubt, *they are not fulfilling their responsibilities.*"[61] Randolph Bourne, who felt as strongly as any muckraker that "social progress" was "the first, right, and permanent interest for every thinking and true-hearted man or woman," argued that "the young radical today is not asked to be a martyr, but he is asked to be a thinker, an intellectual leader."[62] "Radical journalism," he concluded, "seems to be the most direct means of bringing one's ideal to the people, to be a real fighter on the firing line."[63]

"I am sorry that you think that the dissemination of ideas in print is n.g.," Amos Pinchot wrote to a fellow Progressive. "Somehow or other I have a sneaking suspicion that it is one of the ways to get things done."[64] However, Pinchot, like most of these publicists, also sought "to get things done" in other ways. Many, as we have seen, participated in politics directly, particularly at the time of the Progressive Party campaign of 1912. One of the attractions of this course for some seems to have been the opportunity to become close to leading political figures, as Croly, Lippmann, and Weyl were for a time to Theodore Roosevelt, and Hapgood and, to a lesser extent, Howe were to Wilson. Beyond this, a number of these men were active in some of the plethora of leagues and associations that were created in these years to work for this or that reform. The list of organizations (several, one suspects, having little more than a paper existence) in which Frederic Howe, for example, held office included the National Voters' League, the Committee on Industrial Relations, the League for Municipal Ownership and Operation in New York City, the Association for an Equitable Federal Income Tax, and the Committee for Federal Ownership of Railroads.

[60] Baker to J. S. Baker, 21 Oct. 1903, quoted in David M. Chalmers, "Ray Stannard Baker's Search for Reform," *Journal of the History of Ideas*, 19 (June 1958), p. 424.

[61] Notebook 10, 17, 21 May 1916, pp. 79, 84, R. S. Baker Papers.

[62] *Youth and Life* (London, 1913), p. 352; "The Price of Radicalism," *New Republic*, 6 (11 Mar. 1916), p. 161.

[63] *Youth and Life*, pp. 298–9. See also Russell's "Confessions of a Muckraker," in *Lawless Wealth: The Origin of Some Great American Fortunes* (New York, 1908), pp. 287–8.

[64] Amos Pinchot to George Henry Payne, 27 Nov. 1914, Amos Pinchot Papers, box 18.

Such organizations, like political activity, provided one of the means by which these progressive publicists were brought into contact with each other. Thus, for example, Russell, Steffens, and Holt were among those involved along with Walling in the founding of the NAACP. Professional activity itself, of course, generated other links. The original muckrakers acquired a sense of comradeship and, as we have seen, Steffens, Baker, and White were among those who became business partners on the *American Magazine.* Indeed, this whole group was connected by a complex network of personal relationships. Thus Weyl and Walling had become friends in the early years of the century when they both resided at University Settlement in New York.[65] The Ballinger case created a lasting link between Hapgood and Amos Pinchot, and the Bull Moose campaign one between White and Rowell (which was to have a dramatic climax in the 1920s when the latter saved the former from drowning in the Californian surf).[66] The closest of Howe's several friendships with fellow reformers was probably that with Steffens, who wrote to Mrs. Howe in 1919 that "I think he and I see things more alike than any other two human beings that I know of."[67] These personal, professional, and political ties were supplemented for some by certain social gatherings in New York City in these years. One was Mabel Dodge's famous salon, attended at times by Steffens, Walling, Amos Pinchot, and Lippmann. Another was the so-called X Club, a loosely structured association of radically inclined writers whose membership included Walling, Weyl, Steffens, Amos Pinchot, Lippmann, Baker, Holt, and Giddings.[68]

It would be misleading to present this group of men as entirely a band of brothers. Rivalries and animosities naturally existed among them. Relations between Spargo and Walling were bad, Steffens did not endear himself to all who met him, and a *New Republic* editorial in 1915 gave rise to a feud between Creel and Lippmann. Nevertheless, they did have a common view of their social role as publicists, and this was reinforced by

---

[65] Several of these men, in fact, had been involved in some way with the settlement movement. In addition to Walling and Weyl, Howe and Kellogg had resided for a time in settlement houses, Holt and Lippmann had worked in them, Spargo had founded Prospect House in Yonkers, and Pinchot had been a trustee of the University Settlement itself.

[66] Walter Johnson, *William Allen White's America* (New York, 1947), pp. 392–4.

[67] Steffens to Marie Howe, 16 Apr. 1919; Ella Winter and Granville Hicks, eds., *The Letters of Lincoln Steffens* (New York, 1938), vol. 1, p. 466. Howe was also friendly with Amos Pinchot and Creel. See Howe, *Confessions*, pp. 248, 288–9.

[68] On the X Club, see Walling, ed., *Walling: A Symposium*, p. 96; Stein, "Lincoln Steffens," pp. 96, 148; Weyl to Amos Pinchot, 14 Jan. 1915, and Harold Howland and Edwin E. Slosson to Amos Pinchot, 16 Oct. 1919, Amos Pinchot papers, boxes 19, 38; Weyl circular, 31 Jan. 1918, Lippmann Papers, box 34, folder 1272.

the network of informal friendships and more formal associations. The sense of comradeship rested ultimately, of course, upon the feeling that they were on the same side in the political battles of the time. It was this feeling to which Kellogg appealed when he asked Steffens (whom he hardly knew) to review Judge Ben Lindsey's book free for the *Survey:* "It is a measley job to ask a professional writer to contribute something for nothing; but at the same time it is all part of the campaign."[69]

[69] Kellogg to Steffens, 14 May 1910, Steffens Papers, reel 3.

CHAPTER 3

The pre-war progressive consensus

Progressivism: boundaries and varieties

The assumption in Kellogg's letter to Steffens that the two were allies in the same "campaign" was general among progressive publicists. It highlights a fact about political debate in the early twentieth century that has been somewhat obscured by two, rather contrary, features of much recent historiography. The first is the emphasis on the diversity of the pressures for reform in this period. Most modern studies of progressive thought analyze, sometimes with great insight and subtlety, the important differences in social values and political philosophy between various types of "progressive."[1] The second, which is usually connected with the search for the distinctive character of the Progressive Era, stresses the concerns that were shared by nearly all Americans in these years as they attempted, in various and often conflicting ways, to adjust to and mould the changes that were occurring in American life.[2] Both these approaches undoubtedly illuminate aspects of the intellectual history of the period for, as is generally the case, some values and views were more or less common to the whole society while others were largely confined to particular groups or even a few individuals. However, those goals which gave these publicists the feeling of working in a common cause, yet one that faced resistance and opposition, lay somewhere in the middle of this scale. They were those that divided progressives (in this sense of the term) from conservatives.

To perceive this common ground we must focus upon political debate and the issues that were central to it. Historians interested in more

---

[1] See, particularly, Graham, *Encore for Reform* and *The Great Campaigns*. Also Daniel Levine, *Varieties of Reform Thought* (Madison, Wisc., 1964); Filene, "An Obituary for the Progressive Movement"; William L. O'Neill, *The Progressive Years: America Comes of Age* (New York, 1975), pp. x–xi, 92.

[2] Hays, *Response to Industrialism*, pp. 188–91; Jean B. Quandt, *From the Small Town to the Great Community: The Social Thought of Progressive Intellectuals* (New Brunswick, N.J., 1970); Richard M. Abrams, *The Burdens of Progress, 1900–1929* (Glenview, Ill., 1978), pp. 53–4.

general cultural and moral attitudes have been impressed by the difference between old-style progressives and the "new radicals" whose "innocent rebellion" in the years immediately preceding the First World War was directed as much against puritanically inclined reform as any other aspect of the Genteel Tradition.[3] Our group of publicists includes examples of both types, as well as some, like Howe and Steffens, who by their own account moved from one position to the other. There is no doubt that in aesthetic sensibility and moral attitudes there was a gulf between such men as Russell, Baker, White, and Rowell on the one hand and young iconoclasts like Bourne and Lippmann on the other. These differences had direct implications for certain public questions – such as divorce law and prohibition – though by no means all even of the most firmly moralistic were in favor of the latter.[4] They also, as we shall see, affected the style in which other issues, both of domestic and of foreign policy, were approached and discussed, but they generally seem to have had less influence in determining the positions adopted. Certainly, few of the divisions of opinion within this group on such questions followed this line of cleavage.

This is not to deny that on economic and political matters, too, there were significant differences in outlook or that one can draw certain broad lines of division between them. One of the clearest is that between those who were members of the Socialist Party – Spargo, Walling, Russell, and for a time Lippmann – and the remainder. This distinction, however, was less fundamental than is assumed by those who see "socialism" as constituting a clear alternative to "liberal reform." For, at least since the days of Edward Bellamy and Henry Demarest Lloyd, certain strands of American reformist thought had not been far removed from some versions of socialism.[5] In the early twentieth century, the less sectarian type of socialism enjoyed an institutional existence rare in the American context, not only in the Socialist Party itself but in such organizations as the Intercollegiate Socialist Society. Spargo was a leading member of the right wing of the Socialist Party, which concentrated on a limited program of immediate reforms rather than on Marxist doctrine – especially those

[3] Christopher Lasch, *The New Radicalism in America, 1889–1963: The Intellectual as a Social Type* (London, 1966); Henry F. May, *The End of American Innocence* (London, 1960). See also William L. O'Neill, *Divorce in the Progressive Era* (New Haven, Conn., 1967).

[4] For example, Baker and Creel. See Baker, Notebook 13, Apr. 1917, p. 130, R. S. Baker Papers; Creel, *Rebel at Large*.

[5] See Daniel Aaron, *Men of Good Hope: A Story of American Progressives* (New York, 1951), pp. 93–169; Sidney Fine, *Laissez Faire and the General-Welfare State: A Study of Conflict in American Thought, 1865–1901* (Ann Arbor, Mich., 1956), chap. 9.

aspects of it, such as the inevitability of the class struggle, least attractive to middle-class progressives. Russell was no doctrinaire. He later confessed that, at the time he joined the party in 1908, "I . . . could not have told Karl Marx from Frederick Engels if I had met them walking arm in arm up the street. Few persons can be conceived to have known less about Scientific Socialism, but the party represented a protest and the biggest protest then in sight."[6]

This sort of approach had much appeal to some of his fellow muckrakers, among whom Russell's conversion prompted Steffens to ask, "Is that not what we should all be doing?"[7] Though Steffens did not join the party, Eugene Debs wrote to him that "if you are not a Socialist, I do not know one."[8] The article that prompted this letter had been praised by Howe for the way it presented "socialism as a philosophy of affection for humanity rather than a cold and formal philosophy of history and society."[9] This approach appealed also to Baker who, though repelled by the "materialism" of Marxism, envisaged voting in 1912 for the Socialists, whom he described as "a tremendous force for good." "I like to think I am a Socialist," he wrote a year later.[10] Nor did the editors of progressive journals see socialism simply as a threat. Hamilton Holt supported Morris Hillquit for Congress in 1906 and frequently expressed sympathy with moderate socialism.[11] Of the *New Republic* group, Bourne, like Lippmann, had been attracted to socialism as an undergraduate, and Weyl, though never a member of the party, had many socialist friends and an intimate knowledge of the movement both in America and Europe.[12] Although Croly clearly dissented from "some doctrines frequently associated with socialism," he insisted that he was "not concerned with dodging the odium of the word."[13] White expressed indifference as to "whether or not we shall sow for the socialists to reap," and even Amos Pinchot, who often made it plain that his antimonopoly standpoint was theoretically antithetical to socialism, not only

6 Charles E. Russell, *Bare Hands and Stone Walls: Some Recollections of a Side-Line Reformer* (New York, 1933), p. 193.
7 To Ida Tarbell, cited in Tarbell, *All in the Day's Work* (New York, 1939), p. 298.
8 Debs to Steffens, 21 Sept. 1908, Steffens Papers, reel 1.
9 Howe to Steffens, 7 Oct. 1908, Steffens Papers, reel 2.
10 Baker to Norman F. Woodlock, 2 July 1912, n.d. [July 1912], 8 Sept. 1913, R. S. Baker Papers, ser. 2, box 94. See also David M. Chalmers, "Ray Stannard Baker's Search for Reform," *Journal of the History of Ideas*, 19 (June 1958), p. 424; Robert C. Bannister, *Ray Stannard Baker: The Mind and Thought of a Progressive* (New York, 1966), pp. 132–7.
11 Kuehl, *Hamilton Holt*, pp. 56–8.
12 Forcey, *Crossroads of Liberalism*, p. 77.
13 Croly, *Promise of American Life*, p. 209.

raised money for the *Masses* and received invitations to speak to the Inter-collegiate Socialist Society but at one time thought he might end up as a socialist.[14] Naturally, someone who considered himself a left-wing socialist, as Walling did in the years before the war, saw a rather clearer distinction between progressivism and true socialism, but, interestingly, Walling reserved his greatest hostility for the heresy of state socialism and stressed that the reforms promoted by "the Republicanism of La Follette" and "the Democracy of Tom Johnson" represented a genuine advance.[15]

If it was true, as perceptive observers both then and since have recognized, that "radical Progressives and conservative Socialists . . . could almost meet on common ground,"[16] it could well be argued that the difference between them was less intellectually significant than the division among non-socialist progressives over the proper role of the state in economic and social life. The central issue which divided the schools of thought that have become known by the campaign slogans of 1912 as the New Freedom and the New Nationalism had to do with the extent to which the ideal of a free market economy remained both feasible and desirable. The debate centered on the question of the trusts, but the argument over whether these were artifical creations maintained through essentially unfair competitive methods by those with privileged access to credit and legal protection, or the natural result of the opportunities and requirements produced by technological advance, generally reflected different attitudes both to the ideal of economic individualism and to the prospect of an enlarged state. As Ellis Hawley and others have shown, this division within American liberalism, which focused upon but was not confined to the problem of monopoly, was to remain important into the 1930s and beyond.[17]

The publicists of interest here included firm upholders of both positions. It was as proponents of the New Nationalism that Croly, Weyl, and Lippmann had come together, and they each on occasion lambasted anti-

[14] Amos Pinchot to J. A. H. Hopkins, 24 Oct. 1917. See also AP to George F. Porter, 20 Jan. 1914; to Helen Phelps Stokes, 29 Jan. 1915, Amos Pinchot Papers, boxes 31, 16, 19.

[15] *Progressivism – and After* (New York, 1914); Walling to George M. Shibley, 9 Mar. 1910, Walling Papers.

[16] Benjamin Parke De Witt, *The Progressive Movement: A Non-Partisan, Comprehensive, Discussion of Current Tendencies in American Politics* (New York, 1915), p. 98. See also Hofstadter, *Age of Reform*, p. 240n.; Wiebe, *Search for Order*, p. 207; Graham, *Encore for Reform*, pp. 129–30.

[17] Ellis W. Hawley, *The New Deal and the Problem of Monopoly: A Study in Economic Ambivalence* (Princeton, N.J., 1966).

trust legislation and the idealization of competition from which it derived its justification.[18] On the other side, both Hapgood and Amos Pinchot had been much influenced by Louis Brandeis, the leading theoretician of the New Freedom. Amos Pinchot, whose distrust of George Perkins's role in the Progressive Party fueled his suspicion that New Nationalist doctrine was essentially a rationalization of the interests of big business, became a particularly vehement exponent of the view that monopoly was always an enemy of efficiency as well as the cause of economic inequality and social injustice. The faith in a purified competitive system that underlay this position brought Pinchot quite close to the philosophy of Henry George and he contributed a number of articles to the Single Tax journal, the *Public*. Howe and Steffens, too, were associated with the Single Tax movement, which also appealed at one time to Creel.[19]

This contrast between the Single Tax ideal of a minimalist state and the nationalist collectivism espoused by Croly and Weyl appears stark, yet the division created by this issue was not as clear or as deep as might be expected. In the first place, apart perhaps from some of the editors of the *Public*, none of these writers held consistently to a theoretically pure and unqualified position. In *The Promise of American Life*, Croly attributed "a decisive part" in "the rapid growth of big producing establishments" to "the rebates granted to them by the railroads," and in discussing "natural monopolies" he insisted on the need "to secure for the whole community those elements in value which are made by the community."[20] Lippmann's attempt to locate "the funds of progress" in "unearned wealth" also owed something to Henry George.[21] On the other side, Steffens's commitment to the Single Tax movement was a reflection of his loyalty to Tom Johnson rather than of the nature of his own, eclectic, thinking.[22] Howe, too, though some of his writings were fairly faithful expositions of the doctrine,[23] also advocated social welfare measures that would substantially enhance the role of government.[24] Even the more doctrinally in-

---

[18] Croly, *Promise of American Life*, pp. 274, 359; Weyl, *The New Democracy* (New York, 1912), pp. 75–6, 93–4; Lippmann, *Drift and Mastery* (New York, 1914), pp. 77–88.

[19] Creel to Steffens, [Oct. 1910], Lincoln Steffens Papers, reel 1.

[20] *Promise of American Life*, pp. 109–10, 380–1.

[21] *Drift and Mastery*, pp. 68–76.

[22] Kaplan, *Lincoln Steffens*, pp. 173–4.

[23] See, especially, *Privilege and Democracy in America* (New York, 1910); and Howe to E. M. House, 19 Dec. 1913, E. M. House Papers.

[24] See, for example, "Unemployment: A Problem and a Program," *Century*, 89 (Apr. 1915), pp. 843–8.

clined Amos Pinchot was, as we have seen, very conscious of what he had in common with socialists, and criticized them for their narrow-minded unreadiness to cooperate.[25] Indeed, when Pinchot became engaged in a controversy with the editors of the *New Republic,* it was he who advocated government ownership (admittedly of a "natural monopoly," the railroads), and Lippmann in his reply who emphasized the dangers of an authoritarian bureaucracy.[26]

So muddied were the waters that some progressives do not appear to have seen an issue at all. "Between the New Nationalism and the New Freedom," White concluded, "was that fantastic imaginary gulf that always has existed between tweedle-dum and tweedle-dee."[27] Several regretted the effect of the contest between Roosevelt and Wilson in 1912 in creating what they saw as an unnecessary and damaging division in the ranks of reform. "The presidential campaign, unhappily, split our movement wide-open," wrote Creel of the situation in Colorado.[28] Norman Hapgood, who himself supported both candidates in their respective primaries, recalled that "when the break of 1912 occurred I had many more friends in the Roosevelt than in the Wilson camp."[29] Immediately after the election he urged Wilson to seek the support of Bull Moose Progressives rather than conservative Democrats.[30] In choosing sides in 1912, most of these publicists seem to have been more influenced by traditional party loyalties or their reactions to the personalities of the two candidates than by the ideological differences between the New Freedom and the New Nationalism – both Baker and Amos Pinchot, for example, ended up in the wrong camp in terms of their views on the trust issue.[31] Moreover, when these distracting influences were not present, even the most ideologically sensitive of these publicists evidently still felt that what they had in common was more important than what divided them. The *Public* urged reformers of all kinds to unite in the 1914 elections, while in 1916 Brandeis had no more fervent and energetic supporters in the bitter fight that followed his nomination to the Supreme Court than the *New Republic* and Herbert Croly.[32]

---

[25] To Edmund C. Stucke, 4 Dec. 1914, Amos Pinchot Papers, box 18.
[26] *New Republic,* 3 (29 May 1915), pp. 95–8.
[27] William Allen White, *Woodrow Wilson: The Man, His Times and His Task* (Boston 1924), p. 264.
[28] *Rebel at Large,* p. 101.
[29] Marcaccio, *The Hapgoods,* pp. 108–11; Hapgood, *The Changing Years* (New York, 1930), p. 213.
[30] Hapgood to Woodrow Wilson, 18 Dec. 1912, Woodrow Wilson Papers, ser. 2, box 68.
[31] For Baker's position on trusts, see Bannister, *Baker,* p. 145.
[32] *Public,* 17 (25 Sept. 1914), p. 919; *New Republic,* 6 (5 Feb. 1916), pp. 4–6; Croly to R. S.

What progressivism meant

Thus, though there were indeed significant differences among these publicists not only in their cultural and moral sensibilities but in their economic views, such divisions were not sufficient to undermine the feeling
that they were allies in a common cause. When we turn to examine the
basis of this assumption – that they shared an outlook upon central
political issues from which many of their contemporaries dissented – we
need to begin by recognizing the evolving character of progressivism,
noted at the time by perceptive observers such as Croly and manifested in
the changing views of several of these publicists during the course of the
Progressive Era. The "awakening" of the mid-1900s, in which muckraking played a prominent role, had been chiefly concerned with the discovery of scandal, graft, and corruption and directed to the rigorous enforcement of the law and the purification of public life. To Croly's eyes, "its
dominant characteristic was that of resentment against individuals."[33] Its
appeal to an aroused civic sense may have been an echo of classical republican preoccupations;[34] it certainly represented the apotheosis of the
mugwump point of view. E. L. Godkin's son had no doubt that his father
would have approved of Steffens's *The Shame of the Cities* – "He was, as you
know, a great believer in attacking the wicked and not confining oneself
to denunciations of wickedness, and the former is what you are doing."[35]
The common theme of early muckraking, as S. S. McClure wrote in the
editorial that marked the self-conscious emergence of the movement, was
"the American Contempt of Law."[36] Its indictments, while specific, were
not confined to any particular section of society – Baker's first muckraking article exposed the misdeeds of union labor[37] – and its prescriptions
called for the upholding, not the reform, of traditional legal and moral
codes. Even Russell, in a survey of the origins of several great fortunes,

Baker, 6 May 1916, Ray Stannard Baker Papers, ser. 2, box 95. A letter in support of Brandeis
from citizens of New York to Senator William Chilton, chairman of the subcommittee of the
Judiciary Committee holding hearings on the nomination was signed by Holt, Howe, Lippmann, Kellogg, and Amos Pinchot among many others. Amos Pinchot to Paul U. Kellogg, 28
Feb. 1916, Amos Pinchot Papers, box 25. See also Steel, *Lippmann*, p. 101.

33 *Progressive Democracy* (New York, 1914), p. 5.
34 See McCormick, "The Discovery That Business Corrupts Politics," p. 252; Robert Kelley
"Ideology and Political Culture from Jefferson to Nixon," *American Historical Review*, 82 (June
1977), pp. 531–62 at p. 549.
35 Lawrence Godkin to Steffens, 1 Apr. 1904, Lincoln Steffens Papers, reel 1.
36 *McClure's*, 20 (Jan. 1903), p. 336.
37 "The Right to Work," ibid., pp. 323–36.

appropriately entitled *Lawless Wealth,* concluded that "it is the *fraudulent* stock issue and the *unfair* stock manipulation that from the fund that should be for all draw the useless and senseless hoards of the few."[38] In his early years as editor of *Collier's Weekly,* Hapgood remained firmly in the mugwump tradition. He was "most happy supporting fighters against graft such as Joseph Folk and William Travers Jerome," and he first caused a sensation with an outspoken attack on a scandal sheet, *Town Topics,* that purveyed gossip about the private lives of members of New York society.[39]

By the second decade of the twentieth century, this civicist and essentially moralistic viewpoint had been transcended, and in some cases strongly repudiated, by that substantial proportion of these publicists whose political starting point it had been. The change in their outlook was usually gradual, and there were naturally differences in its nature and extent in individual cases, but the general tendency was toward attributing corruption and other evils to "the system" itself rather than individual wrongdoing and particular abuses, and a consequent shift from a combination of specific denunciations and generalized "uplift" to the advocacy of a broad program of social and economic reform.[40] "I am not seeking proof of crime and dishonesty," Steffens explained to Theodore Roosevelt in 1908. "What I am after is the cause and the purpose and the methods by which our governments, city, state and federal, is [*sic*] made to represent not the common, but the special interests; the reason why it is so hard to do right in the U.S."[41] Being in politics, Howe had concluded a few months earlier, compelled one "to revise all of the simple Sunday school morals of his childhood," as it was clear that "the vulgar grafter" was "so much less dangerous and cost the state so little in comparison with the fellows who go wrong on every question through class instinct or party expediency."[42]

This process of "unlearning" the truths of their upbringing and education was to form a major theme in the autobiographies of Howe and Steffens, but a somewhat similar evolution can also be traced in the views of Baker, Hapgood, and Russell, and, to a lesser extent, in those of Rowell, White, and Creel.[43] It brought these men closer to the perspec-

---

[38] *Lawless Wealth: The Origin of Some Great American Fortunes* (New York, 1908), p. 267. My italics.
[39] Marcaccio, *The Hapgoods,* pp. 81, 89–96.
[40] See Croly, *Progressive Democracy,* pp. 10–11.
[41] Steffens to Theodore Roosevelt, 6 May 1908, Steffens Papers, reel 5.
[42] Howe to Steffens, 29 Feb. 1908, Steffens Papers, reel 2.
[43] Howe, *Confessions,* pp. 317, 53–5, 75–9, 83–112, 115–16, 168–81; *The Autobiography of*

tive of such radicals as the Single Taxers, Socialists, and former Populists. It was presumably not the "good government" variety of progressivism that White had in mind when he recalled that "the Insurgents caught the Populists in swimming and stole all of their clothing except the frayed underdrawers of free silver."[44] At the same time, this development in their thinking separated these publicists from those of their fellow muckrakers who retained a more conservative point of view. Ida Tarbell, for example, lamented that she had difficulty explaining to "my reforming friends" that "I had no quarrel with corporate business so long as it played fair . . . I had no quarrel with men of wealth if they could show performance back of it."[45]

In her dissent, Tarbell touched on the heart of the matter. For the pre-war progressive consensus rested on an objection to the existing distribution of wealth in America, regardless of the means by which particular riches were acquired. This concern was shared by Socialists, Single Taxers, New Nationalists, and those not firmly identified with any particular brand of reform. The documentation and vivid depiction of poverty was a central element in the socialist indictment, and it was customarily contrasted with extremes of wealth. "The cruel and anomalous contrast of idle men and toiling children must disappear," declared Spargo.[46] Others supplemented rhetoric with statistics. "Seventy per cent of the wealth in America is in the hands of a small group, forming less than nine per cent of the population," claimed Amos Pinchot, in a relatively conservative estimate.[47] The situation with respect to income was little better. In 1910, Howe calculated that "the annual wealth produced in America amounts to $1,170.20 for every family of five, which is just about two

Lincoln Steffens (New York, 1931), pp. 469, 477–81, 492–4, 518–20, 522–3, 528–34, 567–75, 595–7. See also Semonche, *Ray Stannard Baker*, pp. 211–15; Marcaccio, *The Hapgoods*, pp. 82, 108; Everett, "Chester Harvey Rowell," pp. 292, 306–7, 359–60, 391–2; *The Autobiography of William Allen White* (New York, 1946), pp. 215–17, 233–4, 366–9, 486–8.

[44] Quoted in Kenneth W. Hechler, *Insurgency: Personalities and Politics of the Taft Era* (New York, 1940), pp. 21–2.

[45] Tarbell, *All in the Day's Work*, p. 296. In the immediate pre-war period, Miss Tarbell was chiefly an enthusiastic advocate of the efficiency movement. Besides its application to housework, she was particularly interested in its implication that employers and employees shared a common interest. See "The Cost of Living and Household Management," *Annals [of the American Academy of Political and Social Science]*, 48 (July 1913), pp. 127–30, and *New Ideals in Business* (New York, 1916).

[46] Spargo (with George Louis Arner), *Elements of Socialism* (New York, 1912), p. 208. See also Russell, *Why I Am a Socialist* (New York, 1910), pp. 100–5.

[47] Notes for a speech at the Daily Temple, New York, 17 Apr. 1914, Amos Pinchot Papers, box 16. In 1917, Howe wrote that two percent of the population owned 65 percent of the wealth. *The High Cost of Living* (New York, 1917), p. 23.

and a half times the average wealth as ascertained by the census," and concluded, "there is, therefore, wealth in abundance were it justly distributed."[48] The same point was emphasized by Weyl, who believed that "the motive force of our modern ethics of social improvement reveals itself in a sense of disequilibrium between social wealth and a residual misery of large sections of the population."[49]

Naturally, the various schools of thought differed in their diagnoses of this state of affairs, and in their remedies. Thus, to Single Taxers like Howe and Post, the reason why "the few receive more than they can possibly earn, while the millions receive less than they absolutely need" was the monopolization of land.[50] Without being such faithful disciples of Henry George, others, too, believed that "the bottom of the trouble," as Amos Pinchot put it, was that the "natural resources and raw materials themselves are so cornered and controlled by a small monopolist group."[51] On the other hand, to Socialists, such as Spargo and Walling, economic inequality was inherent in the nature of capitalism. Walling saw "Socialist reform as infinitely more important than progressive reform, because it alone would lead at the present moment directly towards a better distribution of income and opportunity", which he saw as "crucial" for democracy and "by far the most important phase of the movement towards Socialism."[52] None of these publicists specified an ideal distribution of the national income, though one or two hazarded some vague criteria. Thus to Baker, "the essential idea in radical public opinion" was "that no man should be allowed to have what he does not earn."[53] The degree of economic equalization they would have thought desirable doubtless varied from individual to individual, but this mattered less than that their common objection to what Weyl called "our crassly unequal distribution"[54] provided both a basis for criticism of the status quo and a sense of direction for a reform program.

[48] *Privilege and Democracy*, p. 273. See also Creel, "What the Industrial Commission Discovered," *Pearson's*, 35 (Mar. 1916), pp. 194–5.

[49] *New Democracy*, p. 197. See also Lippmann, *Drift and Mastery*, pp. 68–76.

[50] Howe, *Privilege and Democracy*, p. 186. See also pp. 29–45, 161–200; Louis F. Post, *Social Service* (London, 1910), p. 329.

[51] "The Cause of Industrial Unrest," Testimony before the Commission of Industrial Relations, 30 Jan. 1915, Amos Pinchot Papers, box 224. See also Hapgood, *Industry and Progress* (New Haven, 1911), pp. 81–4.

[52] Walling, *Progressivism – and After*, pp. ix, 80–1, 311–13.

[53] Baker, Notebook 12, Nov. 1916, pp. 44–8, R. S. Baker Papers. See also Croly, *Promise of American Life*, pp. 201–6; Spargo, *Applied Socialism: A Study of the Application of Socialist Principles to the State* (New York, 1912), pp. 204–5; Steffens, "Equality of Opportunities, Not of Incomes," *Public*, 17 (30 Jan. 1914), p. 113.

[54] *New Democracy*, p. 146.

The central importance of this issue became apparent when these publicists felt the need to define their political objectives. It was, for example, the ultimate justification for Croly's call for the repudiation of the tradition of economic individualism. "The automatic fulfillment of the American national Promise is to be abandoned, if at all, precisely because the traditional American confidence in individual freedom has resulted in a morally and socially undesirable distribution of wealth," he wrote in his ponderous, careful style. "The prevailing abuses and sins, which have made reform necessary, are all of them associated with the prodigious concentration of wealth, and of the power exercised by wealth, in the hands of a few men." The proposition "that the national interest of a democratic state is essentially concerned with the distribution of wealth" played a larger part in the argument of *The Promise of American Life* than has usually been appreciated.[55] In a very different idiom, White expressed a similar point of view. "All the club-footed gods have been at work piling up wealth, but piling it up inequitably," he declared in 1907. Now the need was to "attack that pile of wealth, and distribute it fairly among the people of the next generation and the next."[56] When in his *Autobiography*, White attempted to explain progressivism, this was the issue that he concentrated on. "Our social philosophy simmered down to this: The national income must be shifted so that the blessings of our civilization should be more widely distributed than they were . . . And the shift or redistribution of national income should be achieved by using government where necessary as an agency of human welfare."[57] "The Progressive Movement," agreed Amos Pinchot, "deals chiefly with a more just distribution of wealth." "The whole political question in America," he wrote on another occasion, "seems one of making the poor man richer and the rich man poorer. That is all there is to it."[58]

Progressive values

Pinchot's crude definition of the issue has the virtue of clarifying the political battle lines in the early twentieth century. It provides a better

[55] *Promise of American Life*, pp. 22–23, 367. See also pp. 11, 25, 59, 116, 139, 205, 380.
[56] White to Scott Hopkins, 7 June 1907, quoted in Johnson, *William Allen White's America*, pp. 213–14.
[57] White, *Autobiography*, pp. 487–8.
[58] Amos Pinchot pamphlet, "What's the Matter with America," p. 37; AP to E. W. Scripps, 11 Sept. 1914, Amos Pinchot Papers, boxes 225, 18. See also Chester Rowell, "Progressivism: What It Means to the Future Republicanism," *San Francisco Examiner*, 20 Nov. 1916.

single indicator of the difference between progressives and conservatives than the argument over the extent to which the government should intervene in economic and social life. The two questions were linked, of course, in that redistribution of wealth would inevitably require some action by government, and the doctrine of laissez-faire certainly constituted a powerful element in the defence of the status quo. However, progressives differed over the precise nature and scope of the role government should play, while far from all the new activities that government actually undertook in this period were even designed to reduce economic inequalities, let alone did so in practice.[59]

Nonetheless, the pre-war progressive consensus, as it appeared in the writings of these publicists, went deeper and extended rather more widely than this single issue. It also involved a considerable measure of agreement on many aspects of a reform program, similar attitudes to the possibilities and methods of progress, and a shared commitment to certain fundamental values. These values, which like most powerful ones were not thoroughly systemized, were derived from two major traditions in the culture — Protestant Christianity and the national ideology of republicanism and democracy. These were, of course, the orthodoxies of early twentieth-century America and for many provided legitimation of the status quo, but for progressives some of the ideals embodied in these traditions constituted both a reproach to the existing state of affairs and a guide to the shape of a better alternative.

There is much evidence of the pervasive influence of social Christianity upon progressivism.[60] For many, doubts about the theological claims of Christianity seem to have intensified commitment to its ethics. "My root belief," Baker wrote to a Catholic friend, is "that the purpose of human life here is to grow in love. . . . I believe that the life and doctrine of Jesus are the nearest expression we have of that love. . . . But I am not deeply concerned about any life beyond this."[61] The social and political implications of Christianity have been variously interpreted, but for these progressives the most important doctrine was that of human brotherhood and the chief injunction was the "golden rule."[62] Thus, the selfishness of

---

[59] This would be largely true, for example, of the Federal Reserve Act. There was very little interest shown by any of these publicists in banking reform.

[60] This point has been more fully developed by Robert M. Crunden in his recent study of a different, though marginally overlapping, cast of characters. See *Ministers of Reform: The Progressives' Achievement in American Civilization 1889–1920* (New York, 1982).

[61] Baker to Norman F. Woodlock, 2 July 1912, R. S. Baker Papers, ser. 2, box 94.

[62] See, for example, Hapgood, *Industry and Progress,* pp. 39–40; Howe, *The City: The Hope of*

economic individualism and class feeling was condemned, in favor of what Baker called "faith in the common action and self-sacrifice for the common conquest of natural difficulties."[63] The most famous example of such an attitude was, of course, Steffens's attempt to make the golden rule practical politics in the McNamara case, following his reading of the New Testament, "without reverence, with feet up on the desk and a pipe in the mouth, as news."[64] No one was more scornful of Steffens's *naiveté* on this occasion than Creel, but he, too, invoked "the teachings of the Nazarene" when defending his administration of the Denver police department.[65] Spargo claimed that there was "a very real kinship and affinity between Christianity and Socialism" and, like the Populists earlier, saw radical implications in the Pauline injunction, "if any would not work, neither should he eat."[66]

Such appeals to the ethics of Christianity were often accompanied by a hostility to organized religion, which was commonly seen as a defender of the established order. Thus, Steffens made much of the opposition of the churches in his account of the McNamara affair, Post defined his life-long faith as "the democracy that Jesus taught and so many of his worldly disciples despise," while even the more pious Baker confessed to his father that his investigations preparatory to writing *The Spiritual Unrest* had left him in a skeptical frame of mind: "Sometimes I think the churches, as at present organized, hinder rather than help the spread of Christianity."[67] Amos Pinchot's conclusion was characteristically less temperate. "The churches are no longer Christian. They represent wealth, power and the right of exploitation of the common people," he wrote in 1915. "I don't see any immediate hope in the churches."[68]

In view of this equivocal attitude toward authorized interpretations of the gospel, the explicit teachings of Christianity may have been a less significant influence on many of these men than those more subtle conse-

Democracy (New York, 1905), p. 220: Russell, *The Uprising of the Many* (London, 1907), p. 276; White, *The Old Order Changeth: A View of American Democracy* (New York, 1910), pp. 3–4, 63–4.

63 Notebook 14, Sept. 1917, pp. 33–5, R. S. Baker Papers.

64 Steffens, *Autobiography*, pp. 525, 659–89.

65 Creel, *Rebel at Large*, pp. 98–9, 107.

66 Spargo, *Applied Socialism*, p. 309; "Socialism as a Cure for Unemployment," *Annals*, 59 (May 1915), p. 160. Baker was another who felt there was a connection between Christianity and Socialism. "What Christians are trying to arrive at deductively the socialists are trying to arrive at inductively." Notebook 2, May 1914, pp. 95–6, R. S. Baker Papers.

67 Steffens, *Autobiography*, pt. 4, chap. 6, "The Churches Decide against Christianity"; Post, unpublished manuscript, "Living a Long Life Over Again" (renumbered), p. 409, Post Papers; Baker to J. S. Baker, 2 May 1909, quoted in Bannister, *Baker*, p. 138.

68 Pinchot to Edwin Jennings, 12 Apr. 1915, Amos Pinchot Papers, box 20.

quences of a Protestant upbringing to which Hofstadter drew attention in *The Age of Reform.*[69] Certainly, several of them seem to have suffered from feelings of guilt that could only be assuaged by a commitment to reform. Howe in his memoirs explained how he felt the need "to justify my training, my sense of responsibility to the world."[70] "Today wealth puts a man in an attitude of apology," observed Hapgood, who argued that he who devoted his life to reform would enrich it.[71] Moreover, one did not have to be conspicuously blessed by riches in order to be purged of complacency by the extremes of social distress. "Well enough I knew and at times admitted that if I had been born and reared in such conditions I should have been a drunkard or a criminal or both," wrote Russell of the slums of New York.[72] It seemed that their own comfort rested on the sufferings of others. "The very food we eat, the clothes we wear, the simplest necessities of life with which we provide ourselves, have their roots somewhere, somehow, in exploitation and injustice," declared Bourne. "We are all tainted with the original sin; we cannot escape our guilt. And we can be saved out of it only by the skill and enthusiasm which we show in our efforts to change things."[73] White, who interpreted the whole issue between conservatives and progressives as "the commonplace conflict between egoism and altruism," felt that "the movement in our national politics toward the more equitable distribution of our common wealth is from the Puritan's conscience," arising from "a conviction of past unrighteousness."[74] Altogether, it is not surprising that some of these men likened the apparent upsurge in reform sentiment to "a great religious revival" or "evangelical uprising."[75]

Yet religion was certainly no more important than patriotism as a source of authority for the values these publicists proclaimed. Few themes were more common in their writings than that progressive reform was in the mainstream of the national tradition, a movement to redeem "the promise of American life." "The obvious reflection about reform movements in America," wrote Russell, who was proud of his abolitionist and antimonopoly background, "is that if they have merit they consciously or

[69] *Age of Reform*, pp. 205–14.
[70] Howe, *Confessions*, pp. 75–6.
[71] Hapgood, *Industry and Progress*, pp. 2–3, 122–3.
[72] Russell, *Bare Hands and Stone Walls*, p. 90.
[73] Bourne, *Youth and Life* (London, 1913), pp. 303–4.
[74] White, *The Old Order Changeth*, pp. 69, 167, 30.
[75] Baker, *American Chronicle*, pp. 258–9; White, *Autobiography*, p. 430.

unconsciously seek to complete the ideals of the Revolutionary fathers. The fathers started; it is for the sons to go on."[76] "The old progressive spirit of our forefathers is once more aroused," declared Amos Pinchot in 1912. "America's purpose will be fulfilled."[77]

The aspects of the national heritage that were cherished were those that generations of liberals have celebrated – the liberating discovery of a New World, the ideology of the revolution, the abundance of free land, and the dreams of immigrants. "America is free from the tyranny of the past," claimed Howe, echoing Goethe's classic lines. "No worn-out institutions cramp and confine our imaginations. There are no such fearful feudal burdens as the old world staggers under."[78] Several looked back for inspiration to "the stately, sounding phrases of the Declaration of Independence," "the sublime abstractions that Jefferson moulded into form," while lamenting that "we have allowed the Declaration to remain a mere declaration" and that "America no longer teaches democracy to an expectant world."[79]

This sense of a decline fitted naturally with that old assumption which Frederick Jackson Turner had made the basis of his "frontier thesis." "It is the free public lands of the West that have made us free," wrote Howe. "A people's destiny is determined by its economic environment and the relation of the people to the land is the controlling influence of all else."[80] This way of thinking came naturally to those of a Single Tax or anti-monopoly inclination. "Up to now there has been superior opportunity, not because of our institutions, but because of our enormous undeveloped natural resources, which have given a better chance for labor to earn a living than in older countries, where the resources are already largely exhausted," argued Amos Pinchot. "Before the public lands were exhausted there was little or no unemployment or industrial oppression in

---

76 Russell, *Bare Hands and Stone Walls*, p. 340. See also Russell's introduction to Caro Lloyd, *Henry Demarest Lloyd: A Biography* (New York, 1912), pp. vi–vii. Russell's fellow Socialist, Walling, was bolder in seeking to appropriate the liberal tradition. "We are the only true followers of Danton, of Thomas Jefferson and of Lincoln," he wrote in 1910. "Those who have read the papers of these immortal and revolutionary Democrats cannot doubt for a moment that all three of them would be Socialists if they were living out their young manhood to-day." "Socialism and Liberty," ca. 1910, in Walling, ed., *Walling: A Symposium*, p. 100.

77 "What's the Matter with America," pp. 37–8, Amos Pinchot Papers, box 225.

78 Howe, *The British City: The Beginnings of Democracy* (New York, 1907), pp. 344–5.

79 Weyl, *New Democracy*, pp. 2, 20; Creel, *Wilson and the Issues* (New York, 1916), pp. 147, 149; White, *The Old Order Changeth*, pp. 33–4. See also Steffens, press release Nov. 1906, Steffens Papers, reel 4.

80 Howe, *Privilege and Democracy*, pp. 18, 25.

this country."[81] Under the influence of the Mexican Revolution, Steffens even claimed in 1916 that "the American working man is all wrong in clamoring for nothing but higher wages. Land is what he needs."[82] Perhaps not surprisingly, the economic determinism of this view of history also had some appeal to socialists. Thus, although Walling believed that the United States had bypassed rather than solved the problems inherent in capitalism, he admitted that "the empire of free or cheap lands made it possible to hold the view that already we had practically abolished hereditary privilege."[83] Even Croly, who, like Weyl and Lippmann, was more inclined to stress the negative aspects of the frontier inheritance, was prepared to admit the beneficent effects of free security and free land – "had it not been for the Atlantic Ocean and the virgin wilderness, the United States would never have been the Land of Promise . . . in which men were offered a fairer chance and a better future than the best which the Old World could afford."[84] That view of America had originated with what Creel bombastically called "the hopes and aspirations of those who first sought refuge in the New World from the oppressions of the Old."[85] So, Croly insisted, "an America which was not the Land of Promise, which was not informed by a prophetic outlook and a more or less constructive ideal, would not be the America bequeathed to us by our forefathers. In cherishing the Promise of a better national future the American is fulfilling rather than imperiling the substance of the national tradition."[86]

As to the nature of the promise, Croly had no hesitation in characterizing it. Unlike the states of Europe, "the American nation is committed to a purpose which is not merely of historical manufacture," he wrote. "It is committed to the realization of the democratic ideal. . . . The moral and social aspiration proper to American life is, of course, the aspiration vaguely described by the word democratic."[87] The value attached to "democracy" by these progressive publicists is indicated by the titles and subtitles of many of their books – *Progressive Democracy, The City: The Hope of Democracy, Democracy and Privilege, An Experiment in Democracy, The*

[81] AP to William H. Ingersoll, 14 Mar. 1916; "Labor and the Future," address in Denver, Colo., 31 July 1915, Amos Pinchot Papers, box 24, Subject File 55.
[82] Speech in St. Paul, Minn., 9 Nov. 1916, Steffens Papers, Scrapbook 3, p. 52.
[83] Walling, *Progressivism – and After*, pp. 319–20.
[84] Croly, *Promise of American Life*, pp. 7–8. Also, pp. 13–14.
[85] Creel, *Wilson and the Issues*, p. 151.
[86] Croly, *Promise of American Life*, p. 3.
[87] Ibid., pp. 6, 17.

Struggle for Self-Government, The New Democracy, A View of American Democracy.[88] In view of the authority and appeal of the word, we need to explore a little further what they saw as its meaning.

Its core, of course, was the idea of self-government, the insistence that political authority rested with the whole body of the people. "I look at the government merely as machinery, devised by the people, through which the public will, whatever it may be, shall be accomplished," Amos Pinchot explained to a conservative correspondent.[89] These writers generally seem to have assumed that to take part in the government of one's society was a basic human right, as when Baker wrote that "it is because we have a passionate desire to emphasize the value of women as human beings that we wish to have them vote."[90] But they were also prepared to argue that democracy was not only the right but the best form of government. They believed, with Russell, in "the immense potency of a purely democratic form of government to do away with the ills that beset us." This involved faith in the judgment of the electorate. Russell, characteristically, was unequivocal: "When the masses of people anywhere understand any cause they never fail to do justice."[91] Rowell showed a little more scholarly caution. "The collective voice of the people," he wrote to Croly, "is likely to show more wisdom than can be attributed to an average individual voter."[92] After being defeated in a bid for another term as mayor, Tom Johnson may not have been entirely consoled by Steffens's assurance that "in the long run the people will go right more surely than any individual or set of individuals."[93] The reason, Steffens explained on another occasion, "seems to be, not that the people are better than their betters, but that they are more disinterested; . . . they are free to be fair." Theirs was a moral wisdom. "The American people seem not to know the difference between clean streets and dirty streets, but they do know the difference between hypocrisy and sincerity, between plutocracy and democracy."[94] "We believe," Baker wrote in his notebook, "that

---

88 Croly, *Progressive Democracy* (New York, 1914); Howe, *The City: The Hope of Democracy; Privilege and Democracy; Wisconsin: An Experiment in Democracy* (New York, 1912); Steffens, *The Struggle for Self-Government* (New York, 1906); Weyl, *The New Democracy;* White, *The Old Order Changeth: A View of American Democracy.*

89 AP to William H. Ingersoll, 14 Mar. 1916, Amos Pinchot Papers, box 24.

90 Notebook 13, Feb. 1917, pp. 12–16, R. S. Baker Papers.

91 Russell, *Uprising of the Many*, p. 344; *Why I Am a Socialist* (New York, 1910), p. 134.

92 Rowell to Herbert Croly, 9 Nov. 1914, Rowell Papers.

93 Steffens to Tom L. Johnson, 1 Sept. 1909, *Steffens Letters*, I, p. 223.

94 Steffens, *Upbuilders* (New York, 1909), pp. xi, 86. Also p. 282.

there is a curious mystic something in the united action of men which infallibly reaches the right conclusions."[95]

Generally, however, these men were much more hard-headed than this suggests about the reality of modern democracy. They had few illusions about the sources of public information, as muckraking exposures of the press had demonstrated.[96] "The development of the organized news service has now reached such a stage," wrote Russell, "that a single influence can sway or poison the minds of literally millions of readers around the world."[97] "Appeals to the primitive passions always get quicker action than appeals to the mind," Creel observed.[98] At best, as Weyl conceded in a fairly sanguine analysis of "the plutocracy and public opinion," there could be little doubt that "public opinion is at times still confused and self-contradictory, or else uninformed, dwarfed, and hysterical, and occasionally it degenerates into mob opinion."[99] Like White, most of these writers had absorbed a liberal fear of "the tyranny of the mob."[100]

Nevertheless, the general tenor of their comments on public opinion in the pre-war years was positive. "It is daily becoming more powerful and beneficent," concluded Weyl. "It cannot be bribed. It cannot be stifled. To overcome it, the people must be fooled, and, year by year, it is becoming more difficult to fool them."[101] The answer to the possibly corrupting influence of the press, it was agreed, was not censorship but education. "The task of intelligence is to dig new wells of information that may be kept free from poison, filth and stagnancy," wrote Creel, as he recommended making the public schools "a headquarters for citizenship, an all-year-round meeting-place of the community."[102] "As the matter now stands, we are a people from the sixth grade," declared White. "And the problem of democracy is . . . what will our schools do for us."[103] Indeed, one of the principal justifications for devolving more responsibility on to the people was that this itself would be an educative process. Thus, Howe argued that the initiative and referendum would

[95] Notebook 13, Feb. 1917, pp. 12–16, R. S. Baker Papers.
[96] See, for example, Harvey Swados, *Years of Conscience: The Muckrakers* (New York, 1962), pt. 9; Semonche, *Ray Stannard Baker*, pp. 135–6.
[97] Russell, *Why I Am a Socialist*, p. 130.
[98] Creel, "The Man Hunt," *McClure's*, 48 (Nov. 1916), p. 34.
[99] Weyl, *New Democracy*, p. 137.
[100] White, *The Old Order Changeth*, p. 65.
[101] Weyl, *New Democracy*, p. 137.
[102] Creel, "The Man Hunt," p. 34. See also AP to Abraham L. Shongut, 25 July 1916, Amos Pinchot papers, box 24.
[103] White, *The Old Order Changeth*, p. 228.

serve as "a training-school for democracy."[104] "The electorate must be required as the result of its own actual experience and unavoidable responsibilities," wrote Croly sternly, "to develop those very qualities of intelligence, character, faith and sympathy which are necessary for the success of the democratic experiment."[105]

"Because it allows people to think for themselves and teaches them to govern themselves by governing themselves," concluded Amos Pinchot, "democracy, after all, with all its mistakes and inefficiency, is the wiser plan." This view was rejected, in Pinchot's opinion, by those conservatives who "stand for the idea that the people should be governed by a small group of efficient, powerful personages, who will tell the people what to think and what to do and make them do it."[106] It was, however, endorsed by all these progressives, even those whose interest in efficiency has sometimes been interpreted as a sign of antidemocratic inclinations.[107] Thus Croly made it clear that "if the choice had to be made," he would prefer "a relatively inefficient but entirely popular government" to "one which was highly efficient but alien to popular sentiment."[108] Similarly Lippmann, though as a pupil of Graham Wallas skeptical of the rationality of electorates, was firm in his defence of democracy. It was, he argued in *A Preface to Politics*, the best means of discovering those desires and drives that it was the task of statesmanship to satisfy or sublimate. "Voting does not extract wisdom from multitudes: its real value is to furnish wisdom about multitudes," and so, "in a rough way, and with many exceptions, democracy compels law to approximate human need."[109] Nor did the socialists among these publicists discount the value of political democracy. "I consider them to be more important than all other reforms put together," Walling wrote in 1910 of the "Referendum, Recall, Proportional Representation and other democratic reforms."[110] Although he later expressed some misgivings about "the possibility of a privileged *majority* . . . the nightmare of every democrat for whom democracy is more than an empty political reform,"

---

[104] See Rush Welter, *Popular Education and Democratic Thought in America* (New York, 1962), pp. 246–50. Quotation on p. 248. See also Weyl, *New Democracy*, p. 310.

[105] *Progressive Democracy*, p. 279. See also *Promise of American Life*, pp. 340, 405.

[106] AP to Samuel Seabury, 16 Sept. 1916, Amos Pinchot Papers, box 25.

[107] For example, Samuel Haber, *Efficiency and Uplift: Scientific Management in the Progressive Era, 1890–1920* (Chicago, 1964), pp. xi–xii.

[108] Croly, *Progressive Democracy*, p. 325. See also pp. 230–1, 237, 262–6, 307–8, 315, 323–5; Forcey, *Crossroads of Liberalism*, pp. 155–7. Croly also approved the referendum and the recall in *Promise of American Life*, pp. 327–8, 332–3.

[109] Lippmann, *Preface to Politics*, pp. 90–1.

[110] Walling to George H. Shibley, 9 Mar. 1910, Walling Papers.

Walling was utterly opposed to any suggestion of elitism.[111] Characteristically less interested in complexities, Spargo simply insisted that "politically, the organization of the Socialist state must be democratic. Socialism without democracy is as impossible as a shadow without light."[112]

These progressives, then, were firmly committed to popular government, but they also agreed that the true meaning of democracy involved more than this. Thus, both Amos Pinchot and Weyl contrasted "real democracy" with "political democracy," "the mere right to vote."[113] "Democracy does not mean merely government by the people or majority rule, or universal suffrage," explained Croly. Rather, it was the pursuit of "results of moral and social value . . . which converts democracy from a political system into a constructive social idea."[114] What were these, the substantial rather than the procedural, marks of democracy?

The first involved equality among individual citizens. Equality of political rights was, of course, implied in the narrowest definition of democracy, but the principle was generally agreed to have wider application. "All Americans," Croly observed, "whether they are professional politicians or reformers, 'predatory' millionaires or common people, political philosophers or schoolboys, accept the principle of 'equal rights for all and special privileges for none.'"[115] Croly's animadversions on its inadequacy as a guide to policy should not be mistaken for repudiation of the principle. On the contrary, he insisted that "there is no room for permanent legal privileges in a democratic state. . . . It ceases to be a democracy, just as soon as any permanent privileges are conferred by its institutions or its laws; and this equality of right and absence of permanent privilege is the expression of a fundamental social interest."[116] There would be no dissent among these publicists from that proposition.

The absence of privilege was supposed to ensure equality of opportunity. For most of these writers this remained a central feature of the American creed. At the time the nation had been born, according to Amos Pinchot,

---

[111] Walling, *Socialism As It Is: A Survey of the World-Wide Revolutionary Movement* (New York, 1912), p. 45. See also *Progressivism – and After*, pp. 121, 134, 244.

[112] Spargo, *Socialism: A Summary and Interpretation of Socialist Principles* (New York, 1906), p. 215. See also Spargo, *Applied Socialism*, p. 69; Russell, *Uprising of the Many*, pp. xi, 344.

[113] AP to William H. Ingersoll, 14 Mar. 1916, Amos Pinchot Papers, box 24; Weyl, *New Democracy*, p. 164.

[114] Croly, *Promise of American Life*, pp. 207, 17.

[115] Croly, *Promise of American Life*, p. 151.

[116] Ibid., pp. 180–1.

"the new spirit of democracy . . . burst upon the world, proclaiming the doctrine of equality of opportunity for human beings."[117] For Howe, "the law of nature is the law of equal opportunity."[118] It was characteristic of those who had been influenced by the ideas of Henry George to stress the need to "equalize opportunities," as Steffens did to Theodore Roosevelt, since it was fundamental to their point of view that monopoly represented privilege.[119] But the goal was also important to New Nationalists. "The democratic principle requires an equal start in the race," wrote Croly. "The purpose of a democratic nation must remain unfulfilled just in so far as the national organization of labor does not enable all men to compete on approximately equal terms for all careers."[120] "In a socialized democracy," Weyl agreed, "the fullest conceivable opportunities would be accorded to all."[121] The socialists among these publicists not only endorsed this most traditionally American ideal but presented it as the best justification for their own position. "Equal opportunity for children, indeed, promises to be the first principle likely to secure general acceptance which passes beyond the program of the 'Progressives,'" observed Walling. "The principle is irresistible in its justice and can only be covertly fought."[122] "Democracy implies the abolition of all privileges based upon birth or possession, of all class restrictions and distinctions," argued Spargo. "Formal equality, whether of political power, legal status, or educational opportunity, does not constitute democracy. So long as economic exploitation is possible, democracy is an unrealized dream."[123]

These socialists further narrowed the gap between themselves and non-socialist progressives by emphasizing that it was equality of opportunity to which they were committed, not "equality of remuneration, regardless of the nature of the service performed" – that, declared Spargo scornfully, "had been advocated by only a few extremists of the Utopian school."[124] The same point was emphasized by Steffens in the *Public* and by Amos

[117] "What's the Matter with America," p. 3, Amos Pinchot Papers, box 225.
[118] Howe, *The British City*, p. 305.
[119] Steffens to Theodore Roosevelt, 20 June 1908, *Steffens Letters*, 1, p. 200. See also Norman Hapgood "The Spirit of the Administration," *Independent*, 86 (22 May 1916), p. 278.
[120] Croly, *Promise of American Life*, pp. 181, 417.
[121] Weyl, *New Democracy*, pp. 352–3. See also Lippmann, *Drift and Mastery*, p. 138.
[122] Walling, *Progressivism – and After*, p. 107.
[123] Spargo, *Social Democracy Explained: Theories and Tactics of Modern Socialism* (New York, 1918), p. 58. See also Russell, *Lawless Wealth*, pp. 243, 266, and *Uprising of the Many*, pp. 92, 356.
[124] Spargo, *Applied Socialism*, p. 113. Also pp. 204–5; *Socialism*, p. 236; *Elements of Socialism*, p. 208; Walling, *Socialism As It Is*, pp. 432–5.

Pinchot, as well as by Croly and Weyl.[125] This did not, however, do much to moderate their criticism of the status quo since the disparities of wealth so evident in early twentieth-century America could not easily be attributed solely to differences in ability and effort. "The princely fortunes which have come into existence during the past few years," wrote Howe, "are not traceable to thrift, intelligence or foresight on the part of their owners any more than the widespread poverty of the masses of people is due to the lack of these virtues on their part."[126] "Under a legal system which holds private property sacred there may be equal rights, but there cannot possibly be any equal opportunities for exercising such rights," Croly pointed out. "It is as if the competitor in a Marathon cross country run were denied proper nourishment or proper training, and was obliged to toe the mark against rivals who had every benefit of food and discipline."[127]

If equality among individuals was part of the wider meaning of democracy for these writers, so too, was cooperation between them. "Today," wrote Weyl, "no democracy is possible in America except a socialized democracy, which conceives of society as a whole and not as a more or less adventitious assemblage of myriads of individuals."[128] He, like Howe and Lippmann, saw signs of "a new social spirit" of fraternity and altruism.[129] This was the heart of progressivism for such men as Baker and White. There was, Baker noted, "a greater sympathy among the poor and that is why the democratic spirit boils up from underneath."[130] White dissented from the observation but accepted the definition. "Democracy is the altruism of all classes," he wrote. "The democratic movement is by no means – or even largely – confined to the poor."[131] Indeed, for White, as for the *Public,* "the struggle between democracy and capital" was "a struggle in every man's heart between the unselfish and the selfish instincts of his nature."[132] It will be seen that in this sense what, as Baker

[125] Steffens, "Equality of Opportunities, Not of Incomes," p. 113; AP to Mrs. J. Borden Harriman, 17 June 1915, Amos Pinchot Papers, box 21; *Pinchot's History,* ed. Hooker, p. 62; Croly, *Promise of American Life,* pp. 201–6; Weyl, *New Democracy,* p. 352.

[126] Howe, *Privilege and Democracy,* p. 232.

[127] Croly, *Promise of American Life,* p. 181.

[128] Weyl, *New Democracy,* p. 162.

[129] Ibid., pp. 160–3; Howe, *The City,* p. 30; *The British City,* pp. 340–1; Lippmann, *Drift and Mastery,* pp. 142–3.

[130] Notebook 12, Dec. 1916, p. 118, R. S. Baker Papers. See also Russell, *Uprising of the Many,* p. 356.

[131] White, *The Old Order Changeth,* p. 160.

[132] Ibid., pp. 6, 37; *Public,* 9 (21 Apr. 1906), p. 53.

confessed, "we vaguely call democracy"[133] was virtually indistinguishable from their understanding of Christian doctrine, and the parallel was occasionally drawn. "The progressive democratic faith, like the faith of St. Paul," Croly wrote, "finds its consummation in a love which is partly expressed in sympathetic feeling, but which is at bottom a spiritual expression of the mystical unity of human nature."[134]

The justification for adding this social and ethical dimension to democracy was that it was seen as intimately connected with its political meaning. On the one hand, Weyl argued that "all the inspiring texts of democracy fall into nonsense or worse when given a strict individualistic interpretation" – by which individuals might withhold obedience or taxes whenever they personally did not give their consent.[135] On the other hand, there was a general belief that the responsibility of self-government imposed an internalized discipline upon the unrestrained pursuit of self-interest and thus promoted moral development. "Democracy seems to make for morals in most of the great departments of our lives," noted Hapgood.[136] "Democracy deals with inner things," Baker reflected. "It is a spiritual principle. *Self*-government."[137] "The democratic theory," explained Steffens, "is founded on the expectation that self-government, by its very abuses, will tend gradually to develop in all men such a concern for the common good that human nature will become intelligent and considerate of others."[138]

The "common good" or the "general welfare" was, indeed, frequently invoked. The *Survey,* for example, had long seen its "special task" as "to discover and to report as accurately as we can what financier and trade unionist, philanthropist and social worker, scientist and merchant, and all others, are doing for the common good."[139] That the promotion of the

---

[133] Notebook 13, Feb. 1917, pp. 12–16, R. S. Baker Papers.

[134] Croly, *Progressive Democracy*, p. 427. See also Baker to Norman F. Woodlock, n.d. [July 1912], R. S. Baker Papers, ser. 2, box 94.

[135] Weyl, *New Democracy*, p. 163.

[136] Hapgood, *Industry and Progress*, p. 120.

[137] Notebook 9, 3 Mar. 1916, p. 42, R. S. Baker Papers. In his youth, Baker had been impressed by Benjamin Kidd's description in *Social Evolution* of Democracy as "the crowning result of an ethical movement in which qualities and attributes which we have been all taught to regard as the very highest of which human nature is capable find the completest expression they have ever reached in the history of the race." *American Chronicle*, p. 59.

[138] Steffens, *Upbuilders*, p. 278.

[139] Edward T. Devine, lead editorial, *Charities and the Commons*, 19 (14 Jan. 1908), p. 1305a. Quoted in Chambers, *Kellogg and The Survey*, p. 29. "Soldiers of the Common Good" was the title of the series of articles by Russell in *Everybody's* magazine that formed the basis of *Uprising of the Many*.

common good was the proper object of a democracy was generally accepted; in *The Promise of American Life,* Croly seemed to imply that it was a
defining characteristic. After expressing doubts whether the decisions and
actions of "any chance majority which happens to obtain control of the
government" were "inevitably and unexceptionally democratic," he insisted that "the people are not Sovereign as individuals. . . . They become Sovereign only in so far as they succeed in reaching and expressing a
collective purpose."[140] This exaltation of the Common Good has reso-
nances of an Idealist political philosophy, but its content was generally
conceived in down-to-earth terms, largely reducible to individual satisfactions. Moreover, in weighing the relative claims of such satisfactions,
there was a general readiness to proceed in a straightforward, Benthamite
way, with every person counting as one and none as more than one. Weyl,
for example, took it for granted that "a masterpiece of art in a private
gallery, seen by a hundred people, gives less pleasure than would the same
masterpiece in a public gallery seen by a million people."[141] The "greatest happiness of the greatest number" could, after all, be plausibly seen as
the public purpose implied by the Declaration of Independence. Even
Croly, for all his interest in the exceptional individual, accepted that the
national tradition required meeting the demand of "the mass of the
population" for "more generalized opportunities." "The implication was
and still is," he wrote, "that by virtue of the more comfortable and less
trammeled lives which Americans were enabled to lead, they would constitute a better society and would become in general a worthier set of
men"; and so, "just because our system is at bottom a thorough test of the
ability of human nature to respond admirably to a fair chance, the issue of
the experiment is bound to be of more than national importance."[142]

Progressives and progress

The recognition that their ideals were in many ways "familiar and traditional" has given rise to the view that the Progressives were essentially
"backward looking" – guided by "less a utopian vision than a memory."[143] It is not surprising that this view can be traced back to John
Chamberlain's *Farewell to Reform* (1932) and other works written from a
Marxist perspective, since the dichotomy between backward looking and

[140] Croly, *Promise of American Life,* p. 280. See also p. 207.
[141] Weyl, *New Democracy,* p. 145.
[142] Croly, *Promise of American Life,* pp. 207, 12, 13.
[143] Hofstadter, *Age of Reform,* p. 215; Graham, *Encore for Reform,* p. 89.

forward looking makes most sense if one assumes the course of history to be both unilinear and homogeneous.[144] If one abandons such Whig interpretations – whether of a Marxist or modernization variety – it no longer seems a natural way of categorizing different viewpoints. In the early twentieth century, was the advocate of a class-based socialism more forward looking than the prophet of corporate capitalism? There are usually alternative visions of the future; and none of them is likely to involve a repudiation of all aspects of the past.

Certainly, there are times when progressive publicists appear to be looking back nostalgically to what Hofstadter described as "a preponderantly rural society with a broad diffusion of property and power."[145] While denouncing "the growing slums in great cities, the millions of lives there without light, hope or opportunity," Russell deplored "the gradual expropriation of the farmer, the steady decline in the number of farm owners, the steady increase in the number of farm tenants."[146] Of "the vagabond, the sick, the destitute, the prostitute, the flotsam and jetsam of the community," Howe wrote, "the country does not breed this class." The tenement was "a sort of social gangrene," a sad mockery of the true American home, "the basis of our citizenship."[147] Others lamented what they saw as the effects of industrialism on the quality of work. Hapgood observed that modern production "often makes of the laborer a mere attendant to a machine. It takes away the variety, companionship and personal significance of the old days when one article was entirely manufactured by the workman, who thus, a creator, saw his work take living form beneath his touch."[148] Bourne more broadly condemned "the crude malignity of modern life."[149]

"Nations make their histories to fit their illusions. That is why reformers are so anxious to return to early America," wrote Lippmann scornfully. "We find it very difficult to remember that there were sharp class divisions in the young Republic, that suffrage was severely restricted, that the Fathers were a very conscious upper class determined to maintain their privileges."[150] However, it was not generally eighteenth-century America

[144] John Chamberlain, *Farewell to Reform: The Rise, Life and Decay of the Progressive Mind in America* (New York, 1932), especially pp. 142–3, 310–11, 323–4.

[145] Hofstadter, *Age of Reform*, p. 215.

[146] Russell, *Uprising of the Many*, pp. vii, viii.

[147] Howe, *The City*, pp. 34–5, 212, 211.

[148] Hapgood, *Industry and Progress*, pp. 65–6.

[149] Bourne, *Youth and Life*, pp. 309–10.

[150] Lippmann, *Drift and Mastery*, p. 101. Lippmann's acceptance of the revisionist historiography of J. Allen Smith and Charles Beard, evident here, was common to the *New Republic* group. See Forcey, *Crossroads of Liberalism*, pp. 76, 157.

that these progressives had in mind when they summoned the past to rebuke the present, but something more recent and western. "The great teaching of my youth on the frontier had been the incomparable preciousness, the value, of a man," recalled Baker. "What I found in Chicago, or seemed to find, was a cheapening of human beings."[151] Even Croly and Weyl, though it was the burden of their argument that the individualism of the tradition was outmoded, wrote approvingly of the democracy of the Jacksonian period – whose "community of feeling" Croly rather quaintly compared to "the sense of good-fellowship which pervades the rooms of a properly constituted club."[152]

However, there was no question of these writers – who, after all, thought of themselves as "progressives" – wishing to put the clock back. On the contrary, they showed a very positive attitude to scientific· and technological advance,[153] to economic progress, and even to urbanization. None of them expressed more concern about the decline of the yeoman farmer and the rise of farm tenantry than Howe,[154] yet it was he who entitled his first book *The City: The Hope of Democracy*. "The city has brought us whatever sense of social responsibility we now have," he wrote. "The humanizing forces of today are almost all proceeding from the city." The influx of population to urban centers he saw as more than a response to economic pressures: "It is but part of man's desire for a larger life, for freer social intercourse, for amusement." As for what Howe called "the advance in civilization which has made all nature tribute to man's energy," it was seen as offering the promise of a better life for all.[155] It was true, Hapgood conceded, that "the individual can never again in the United States change his social and business standing as readily as he has been able to do among the virgin resources, sparse population, and smaller units of the past. . . . He should, however, if our brains and hearts act well, have for his labor a greater product, which should mean more time for thought and reading, pleasanter surroundings for his work, longer and

[151] Baker, *Native American: The Book of My Youth* (New York, 1941), p. 288.

[152] Croly, *Promise of American Life*, p. 61; Weyl, *New Democracy*, pp. 18–21.

[153] See Baker, *Native American*, pp. 158–9, 334–5; Stein, "Lincoln Steffens," pp. 9, 16; Everett, "Chester Rowell," pp. 102, 357–8; Hapgood, *Industry and Progress*, pp. 78–9; White, *The Old Order Changeth*, p. 161; Croly, *Progressive Democracy*, p. 404; Bourne, *Youth and Life*, p. 167 and, especially, Lippmann, *Drift and Mastery*, chaps. 14–16.

[154] For example, Howe, *Privilege and Democracy*, especially chaps. 6–7, and "The Problem of the American Farmer," *Century*, 94 (Aug. 1917), pp. 625–32.

[155] Howe, *The City*, pp. 27–8, 24, 42. On another occasion, Howe pointed out that as a result of modern refrigeration, "even the poorest dine on foods that were unknown a century ago." *High Cost of Living*, p. 53.

better schooling for his children."[156] No one was more impressed by the beneficent potential of economic progress than Weyl. Influenced by his mentor, Simon N. Patten, Weyl argued that the industrial revolution had enabled men to escape the age-old economy of "poverty, pain, and deficit," and hence made democracy for the first time a realizable ideal. "Without an excess of wealth no democracy on a large scale was possible, however much men might dream dreams or voices cry aloud in the wilderness," for "until the material problems which beset mankind are solved; until misery, disease, crime, insanity, drunkenness, degeneration, ignorance, and greed – which are the offspring (as also the parents) of poverty – are removed (and their removal costs money), humanity will not be able to essay the problems of mind and of social intercourse." Writing fifty years before J. K. Galbraith, Weyl observed that "never in history has there been a social surplus equal to that of America today," and that now there existed "the possibility of giving a full life to all the people."[157]

At the heart of much of the progressive case, of course, was the insistence that this possibility had not been realized. In spite of the "enormous advances in science and industry," Amos Pinchot complained, "the average wage-earner of today lives in, or on the brink of, extreme poverty. He is infinitely worse off than he was in colonial times, or even fifty or a hundred years ago."[158] Any nostalgia here, however, was for "a broad diffusion of property and power" rather than "a preponderantly rural society."[159] "It is difficult to believe," Howe observed sarcastically, "that the revolution in industry which has increased the productive power of the world a thousand-fold should of necessity leave an increasing proportion of mankind worse off than they were before."[160] White's view was broadly similar. "The nineteenth century will be known as the century made marvelous by the use of steam," he wrote. "Our problem in this century must be the socialization of steam; and incidental to that will be the control of capital." He derived confidence from the reflection that "the history of man has been a story of the socializing of human inventions, taking them from the few who received homage and taxes for them, and

[156] Hapgood, *Industry and Progress*, p. 86.
[157] Weyl, "Democracy and the Social Surplus," *New Democracy*, chap. 13. Quotations are on pp. 191, 193, 203, 201, 200. For similar arguments, see Lippmann, *Drift and Mastery*, pp. 140–1; *Public*, 20 (12 Jan. 1917), p. 29.
[158] "What's the Matter with America," p. 28, Amos Pinchot Papers, box 225.
[159] Cf. Hofstadter, *Age of Reform*, p. 215.
[160] Howe, *The City*, p. 42.

distributing the inventions and the blessings they brought among all the people."[161]

White's optimism here might seem to support the view that these publicists "believed in the inevitability of progress."[162] However, the more reflective of them carefully distanced themselves from this idea, which they realized could easily be taken to have politically conservative implications. "It is a peculiarly paralyzing, narcotizing theory that teaches that mankind on the whole and in the long run necessarily goes forward," Walling observed. "Pragmatism and Socialism point out, on the contrary, that, on the whole and in the long run, mankind has every opportunity to go forward, but that the result depends largely, though within limits on mankind."[163] Croly, too, had emphasized the need to abandon the "optimistic fatalism" that had led Americans to assume that the national Promise was "destined to automatic fulfillment."[164] "The success of a thoroughgoing democracy," he wrote later, "is not to be prophesied. It is to be created."[165] "In the real world," Lippmann concluded, "destiny is one of the aliases of drift."[166]

In this period, the most intellectually fashionable versions of destiny were associated with some type of evolutionary theory, and many of these publicists adopted in response what Eric Goldman has called "Reform Darwinism," stressing the role of mind and conscious purpose in the evolutionary process.[167] "We are chiefly interested, not in the 'origin of species' in nature, but in the destiny of species under man," wrote Walling. "Our affair is not with the evolution of life and its adaptation to the natural environment, but with the evolution of man and the adaptation of life to his purposes."[168] Older kinds of fatalism were abandoned rather than attacked. "Once in the face of extensive evil we talked about the will of providence," Hapgood recalled. "Now we mitigate the evil."[169]

[161] White, *The Old Order Changeth*, pp. 5, 233, 231.

[162] David W. Noble, *The Paradox of Progressive Thought* (Minneapolis, 1958), pp. 36–7. Noble attributes this view, without supporting citation, to the editors of the *New Republic*.

[163] Walling, *The Larger Aspects of Socialism* (New York, 1913), pp. 55–6. Spargo also repudiated "the old fatalistic cry that Socialism is inevitable as a result of economic development without regard to our willingness or otherwise." Friedberg, "Marxism in the United States," p. 47.

[164] Croly, *Promise of American Life*, pp. 21, 20.

[165] Croly, *Progressive Democracy*, p. 173.

[166] Lippmann, *Drift and Mastery*, pp. 105–6.

[167] Eric F. Goldman, *Rendezvous with Destiny: A History of Modern American Reform* (New York, 1953), pp. 93–4.

[168] Walling, *Larger Aspects of Socialism*, p. 86. See also Bannister, *Baker*, pp. 100–1, 133–6; Bourne, *Youth and Life*, p. 308; Steffens to Laura Steffens, 18 July 1916, *Steffens Letters*, 1, p. 378.

[169] Hapgood, *Industry and Progress*, p. 41.

Hapgood's declaration implied that evil was not due entirely to original sin, and this essential precondition of a faith in the possibility of social improvement was explicitly emphasized by many of these progressives. Corruption, poverty, vice, crime, and disease "are traceable to our Institutions, rather than to the depravity of human nature," Howe insisted. "Their correction is not a matter of education or of the penal code" but of economic and social reform.[170] Countless denunciations of slums and other social abuses stressed the effects of environment in moulding character. "It is conditions, not solely the devil in us, that makes men bad," Steffens concluded. "Human nature is all right. It's something else that's wrong; the laws mostly."[171] While rebuking Steffens for pushing this argument a little too far, Rowell did not dissent from the premise: "We need legislative and economic reform. But we need preachers and jails too."[172] Some uncertainty about the malleability of human nature was perhaps excusable; Croly, for one, seemed to oscillate on the subject. The bold declaration that "democracy must stand or fall on a platform of possible human perfectibility" followed shortly on his admission that "human nature is composed of most rebellious material, and . . . the extent to which it can be modified by social and political institutions of any kind is, at best, extremely small."[173]

Interestingly, the limits of human perfectibility that Croly was most immediately concerned with derived not from religious doctrine but from genetic determinism. "The most effectual of all means" of improving human nature in his view would be by "improving the methods by which men and women are bred." He had earlier speculated that "a really regenerated state government . . . might conceivably reach the conclusion that the enforced celibacy of hereditary criminals and incipient lunatics would make for individual and social improvement even more than would a maximum passenger fare on railroads of two cents a mile."[174] Such ideas were current at the time and were endorsed by Spargo, Weyl, and some writers in the *Survey,* were briefly entertained by Baker, and roundly condemned by Walling.[175] However, even Weyl warned that it

---

[170] Howe, *The City,* p. vii. Also, p. 296. This is a recurrent theme in Howe's writings. See also *The British City,* pp. 338–9; and *Privilege and Democracy,* p. 31.

[171] Steffens, "An Apology for Graft," *American,* 66 (June 1908), p. 130; Steffens to Allen H. Suggett, 25 July 1916, *Steffens Letters,* 1, p. 380.

[172] Rowell to Steffens, 1 Aug. 1908, Steffens Papers, reel 4.

[173] Croly, *Promise of American Life,* pp. 400, 399. See also Weyl, *New Democracy,* pp. 326–7.

[174] Croly, *Promise of American Life,* pp. 400, 345–6.

[175] Spargo, *Applied Socialism,* pp. 259–60; Weyl, *New Democracy,* pp. 335–6; *Survey,* 33 (24, 31

was only "extreme cases in which we may act" and that "with our present knowledge we cannot go too far in this direction. We can no more trust ourselves with any absolute dominion over life and death than we could trust the medieval scribes with the preservation of classical literature." For Weyl, eugenics was at most a very minor element in comparison with "the advancement and improvement of the people . . . through a conservation of life and health, a democratization of education, a socialization of consumption, a raising of the lowest elements of the population to the level of the mass."[176] "The defective mentally or morally will have the devil's own time keeping up with the procession," White admitted, but "the average man, well-equipped physically and mentally, need not fear in a generation or so to sink into what is called poverty. We will stop that . . . by changing the environment of those who work with their hands."[177]

Once again, White's optimism is striking, but it reflected the generally optimistic outlook of these publicists in the pre-war years. This, too, may be linked to the impression made by the speed and scale of scientific and technological advance. The great extension of control over the material environment seems to have left this generation unawed by the intractable inertia of complex, deep-rooted social mores and institutions. "To the creative imagination," Lippmann asserted, "fact is plastic, and ready to be moulded by him who understands it."[178] In the *Survey*, Vida Scuder recommended to social workers "the bold thinking on large lines" of H. G. Wells.[179] " 'Man is the maker of the Universe.' Here is the principle which underlies both modern science and philosophy and the modern social movement," wrote Walling, to whom the industrial revolution was sufficient refutation of the view that social evolution necessarily moved at a glacial pace.[180] Furthermore, as we have seen, material progress was itself a positive factor. It had apparently generated the "great social surplus" that in Weyl's view had made "a real democracy . . . possible" (though, he warned, "not inevitable").[181] "The dynamics for a splendid human civilization are all about us," Lippmann declared, as he compared

Oct. 1914), pp. 91, 115–16; Bannister, *Baker*, p. 101; Walling, *Larger Aspects of Socialism*, p. 79.
[176] Weyl, *New Democracy*, pp. 335–6, 320.
[177] White to W. H. Sikes, 9 Mar. 1916, White Papers.
[178] Lippmann, *Drift and Mastery*, p. 173.
[179] *Survey*, 32 (29 Aug. 1914), p. 548.
[180] Walling, *Larger Aspects of Socialism*, pp. 5, 61–3.
[181] Weyl, *New Democracy*, pp. 206–7.

"this age" with "Athens in the Fifth Century B.C.," and speculated that the "liberation" was "due to the great surplus of wealth."[182] "Radicalism is often ascribed to misery," wrote Giddings in the *Independent*, "but . . . it is in fact a product of surplus energy and surplus wealth."[183]

The apparent vindication of this generalization by the growth of reform sentiment abroad as well as at home was the other chief basis for optimism about the course of events. Howe, to whom the twentieth century promised "a movement for the improvement of human society more hopeful than anything the world has known," was confident that in Europe "a generation is bound to see something like socialism even if the socialists do not come into power."[184] "A general heightening of the moral tone can be seen everywhere," Hapgood observed in 1910, while a few years later Baker enthused over the "wonderful enlargement of the sense of brotherhood throughout the world," shown "in the vast humanitarian movements."[185] "It is but dawn in the new day of spiritual awakening," declared White. "In all the heavens, the sea, and the earth this movement has no other prototype except the miracle of growth that we pass by unnoticed every day of our lives."[186] "How wonderful everything is!" exclaimed Baker in 1913. "Such changes everywhere in evidence – such a time of hot life, of real questioning of institutions, of the break up of the old loyalties and the setting up of new."[187]

Goals and policies

If these publicists, while often consciously distancing themselves from the idea of the inevitability of progress, were not only insistent upon its possibility but also optimistic about the prospects for substantial advance in the foreseeable future, the question remains: What exactly did they wish to see done? It is not possible to set out a program of specific measures to which they were all committed, partly because at this level there were significant differences between them, but also because the emphasis in most of their writing was on general principles rather than

---

[182] Lippmann, *Preface to Politics*, pp. 237–8.
[183] *Independent*, 87 (14 Aug. 1916), p. 213.
[184] Howe, *The City*, p. 301; Howe to Steffens, 22 July 1909, Steffens papers, reel 2. See also Steffens to Brand Whitlock, 24 Nov. 1909, *Steffens Letters*, 1, p. 231; "What's the Matter with America," p. 37, Amos Pinchot Papers, box 225.
[185] Hapgood, *Industry and Progress*, p. 121; Baker to Norman F. Woodlock, 8 Sept. 1913, R. S. Baker Papers, ser. 2, box 94.
[186] White, *The Old Order Changeth*, pp. 253, 61.
[187] Notebook M, 21 Jan. 1913, p. 54, R. S. Baker Papers.

detailed proposals. Nevertheless, there was much agreement upon the directions that change should take, as can be seen by briefly reviewing their ideas about constitutional and political reform and about the desirable shape of government intervention in economic and social life.

All of these publicists were in favor of at least some of the reforms in what White called "our machinery for self-government" that are generally associated with the progressive movement – direct primaries, the initiative, referendum and recall, municipal "home rule" often combined with the adoption of a commission or city-manager form of government, and some restriction of the power of the judiciary over legislation.[188] Traditionally, such reforms have been interpreted in the simple terms in which they were usually advocated – as means to increase the power of "the people" and to attack the dominant position of special "interests." More recently, they have been seen as constituting an important element in the transition from a nineteenth-century political system in which the parties and the courts played the central roles to the new "bureaucratic" order of the twentieth century.[189] In some accounts, this transition is regarded as antidemocratic in tendency, with decision making being shifted further from "the grass-roots" and placed in the hands of specialized "experts" governing in the name of "efficiency."[190] The early twentieth century witnessed not only a weakening of party loyalties but also a decline in the proportion of the electorate who voted. This shrinking of the "political universe," it is sometimes suggested, was in fact the tacit goal of the reforms of the progressive era.[191]

There is no doubt that most of these writers shared in the enthusiasm for efficiency characteristic of their generation, and that they respected the claims of expertise in government as in other fields. One aspect of the American democratic tradition they did not endorse was the Jacksonian

---

[188] In addition to the references in nn. 195–202 below, see Semonche, *Ray Stannard Baker*, pp. 235–6; Creel Scrapbook, 25 Mar. 1914, Creel Papers; Kuehl, *Hamilton Holt*, pp. 52–4; Howe, *The City*, pp. 160–71; Rowell, "Progressivism: What It Means to the Future Republicanism," *San Francisco Examiner*, 20 Nov. 1916; Spargo, *Socialism*, pp. 215–16; Walling to George H. Shibley, 9 Mar. 1910, Walling Papers; Walling, *Socialism As It Is*, pp. 148–50.

[189] Richard L. McCormick, "The Party Period and Public Policy: An Exploratory Hypothesis," *Journal of American History*, 66 (Sept. 1979), pp. 295–8; Stephen Skowrenek, *Building a New American State: The Expansion of National Administrative Capacities, 1877–1920* (Cambridge, England, 1982).

[190] See, particularly, Samuel P. Hays, *American Political History as Social Analysis* (Knoxville, Tenn., 1980), chaps. 6–8, 10–11.

[191] Walter Dean Burnham, "The Changing Shape of the American Political Universe," *American Political Science Review*, 59 (Mar. 1965), pp. 7–28; *Critical Elections and the Mainsprings of American Politics* (New York, 1970), chap. 4.

doctrine that Baker called "the fallacy that all men are equal to *anything* – any task."[192] "Our most grievous lack, as a people," agreed Rowell, "is our ignoring of experts, and our fiction that 'any man is fit for any job.'"[193] For several of these men, as for earlier reformers, the British civil service, staffed by career professionals selected on merit, was a model for the "body of expert administrative officials" that American governments needed.[194]

However, to assume that this respect for efficiency and expertise indicates a covert hostility to democracy is to ignore other, more central, aspects of these progressives' political outlook. The first is their commitment to popular control of the political process, which was frequently and emphatically reiterated. "The important thing, the permanent thing," White declared, "is the growth of democratic institutions – the broadening and deepening of the power of the people as shown by the adoption of the secret ballot, the purification of the party system, the spread of the direct primary, and the popular acceptance of the initiative and referendum and the recall."[195] Such democratic procedures were advocated even when it was foreseen that they might obstruct the cause of reform. "Conservative groups will naturally use these tools for preventing changes as radicals use them for hastening them," wrote Baker. "This is why democracy with its referendum, initiative and recall is so safe a method of government for human society."[196] Weyl judged the "tendency" of the referendum to be "somewhat conservative," but nonetheless strongly advocated it.[197] Croly's insistence on the crucial contribution to society of "exceptionally able individuals"[198] might lead one to expect him to have greater reservations about entrusting power to the people. However, not only did he explicitly rank the claims of "popular government" above those of efficiency, as we have seen, but he argued that "representative government of any type becomes in actual practice a species of class government" and that with modern communications "pure democracy," as exemplified by the New England town meeting, "becomes not merely possible, but natural and appropriate."[199]

192 Notebook 5, 4 June 1915, p. 93, R. S. Baker Papers. See also Weyl, *New Democracy*, pp. 56–7.
193 Address to the American Association for the Advancement of Science, 17 June 1919, Rowell Papers.
194 Croly, *Progressive Democracy*, pp. 355–6. See also *Independent*, 87 (21 Aug. 1916), pp. 257–8.
195 White, *The Old Order Changeth*, p. 246.
196 Baker to Norman F. Woodlock, 8 Sept. 1913, R. S. Baker Papers, ser. 2, box 94.
197 Weyl, *New Democracy*, pp. 309–10.
198 Croly, *Promise of American Life*, chap. 13.
199 Croly, *Progressive Democracy*, pp. 262–5; see above n. 108.

Even those measures that might seem designed to narrow the role of the electorate in government, such as the reduction in the number of elected officials, could be plausibly defended on the basis of a more realistic appreciation of the way politics actually worked. "Experience has shown," wrote Lippmann in the spirit of Wallas, "that a seven-foot ballot with a regiment of names is so bewildering that a real choice is impossible."[200] The result, in the real world, was blind party loyalty. "The American voter, as confused as a child at a four-ringed circus," wrote Weyl, "seeks to answer a dozen questions and decide among a hundred candidates, not by writing a three-volume book, but by putting his mark under the Republican or the Democratic emblem."[201] Like Croly and Lippmann, Weyl was indeed critical of the existing two-party system, but his sympathy for the idea of proportional representation implied that he envisaged some alternative, doubtless more ideologically focused, political groupings.[202]

Furthermore, it needs to be remembered that for these progressives democracy meant more than simply the maximum level of political participation; it involved what was done as well as how it was done. To some, constitutional reforms were of secondary importance. Without an attack on "the monopoly principle," Amos Pinchot wrote, "we may change the political machinery as much as we please" without making "the slightest improvement in conditions."[203] To others, they were essentially instrumental. "The 'I & R' is nothing but a tool," Steffens declared. "It is worth while only as it can be used to change the 'conditions that make men do bad things.'"[204] The view that the chief value of such political changes was that they opened the way to more substantive advance was shared by writers who also advocated them on grounds of principle. "Each one of these movements," wrote White of the standard progressive electoral reforms, "is a leveling process, a tendency to make money, capital, property, wealth, or financial distinction count for nothing save as an indirect influence in the ballot box."[205] "The chief object of direct prim-

[200] Lippmann, *Preface to Politics,* p. 54.

[201] Weyl, *New Democracy,* p. 306.

[202] Ibid., p. 316. See also Croly, *Progressive Democracy,* pp. 343–9; Lippmann, *Preface to Politics,* pp. 195–8; *New Republic,* 1 (30 Jan. 1915), p. 5; Steffens, *Upbuilders,* p. 302.

[203] AP to Charles Ferguson, 8 Nov. 1915. On another occasion, however, Pinchot urged the importance of "the direct voting principle in all elections" on the grounds that "when the direct vote is accomplished fact throughout the country, prosperity, a better distribution of wealth, etc. will be merely dependent on popular education." AP to Gifford Pinchot, 3 Apr. 1915, Amos Pinchot Papers, boxes 22, 16.

[204] Steffens, *Upbuilders,* p. 319. See also Howe to Steffens, 29 Feb. 1908, Steffens Papers, reel 2.

[205] White, *The Old Order Changeth,* p. 50.

aries and of other proposals for the democratization of the party," Weyl explained, "is to break up the alliance between corrupt business and corrupt politics."[206] Croly believed that "direct democracy . . . has little meaning except in a community which is resolutely pursuing a vigorous social program."[207]

Several aspects of these men's thinking about political reform can, indeed, best be understood in the light of these broader goals. A concern with the efficiency of government was, as Weyl pointed out, a natural concomitant of a desire to extend its functions.[208] Similarly, the stress on the importance of leadership, which was manifested not only in proposals to strengthen the authority of elected executives at all levels of government but also in a fascination with individual personalities, need not necessarily reflect either elitist or authoritarian predispositions.[209] It is also, as the attitudes of later generations of liberals have tended to confirm, a natural stance for those who favor reform and who recognize the need under the American political system for a constituency to be aroused and mobilized, and for specific measures to be framed, propelled through the legislative process, and effectively implemented.

When in 1916 Rowell was asked to give an account of progressivism, he wrote that, although the first requirement was "political democracy," "primarily the job is a larger measure of industrial justice and of social democracy," which would involve "the new government task of better distributing the material and immaterial benefits of modern knowledge, invention and organization."[210] The essence of the progressive point of view was that the new conditions and problems of American life, of which the maldistribution of income was a central feature and symptom, called for an extension of the role of government involving both the direct

---

206 Weyl, *New Democracy*, p. 300.
207 Croly, *Progressive Democracy*, p. 270.
208 Weyl, *New Democracy*, p. 311.
209 For proposals to strengthen the authority of executives, see Howe, *The City*, pp. 178–86; Croly, *Promise of American Life*, pp. 330–40, and *Progressive Democracy*, pp. 312–13; Lippmann, *Preface to Politics*, p. 54; *New Republic*, 1 (28 Nov. 1914), p. 7.

On the importance of leadership generally, and the contribution in particular of Theodore Roosevelt, see Howe, *The British City*, pp. 362–3; Steffens, *Upbuilders*, pp. 318–19; White, *The Old Order Changeth*, p. 146; Baker, *American Chronicle*, pp. 249–60; Croly, *Promise of American Life*, pp. 168–70, 441, 449; Lippmann, *Preface to Politics*, pp. 15, 23, 78, 222–3. The one dissenter from this point of view was Walling, who argued that the exaltation of individuals was undemocratic and moreover that "leaders" were usually corrupted into betraying the Socialist cause. See *Socialism As It Is*, p. 179, and *Progressivism – and After*, pp. 220–2.
210 "Progressivism." Similarly, Benjamin P. De Witt, in the earliest history of progressivism, *The Progressive Movement* (1915), pp. 244–5, viewed "such preliminary measures as the initiative, referendum, recall, direct primaries and others" as means to an end and asserted "that the social phase of the progressive movement in the state is by far the most important."

provision of social services and greater control over private economic activity.

That government ought to assume greater responsibilities in the general field of social welfare was a common theme in the writings of these men. These were demands for laws to regulate working and housing conditions, for the extension and improvement of education, and for some measure of social insurance.[211] The latter, which was widely supported with respect to industrial accidents, was also proposed for various forms of disability and dependency, old age, and unemployment. The case for such reforms was commonly based on an evocation of the conditions they were designed to ameliorate. Thus it was to combat "industrial exploitation which will seem infinitely hideous to our descendants" that the *New Republic* advocated minimum wage laws for women.[212] To relieve "the overwhelming mass of human misery" revealed, according to Devine in the *Survey*, by an investigation into the circumstances of widows with dependent children in New York, "a liberal, inexpensive and safe system of social insurance" was needed.[213] The constitutional location of responsibility for most of these matters at the state or local level was not in general questioned, though the need for national action on the issue of child labor was widely accepted, and some called for a federal system of employment bureaus or labor exchanges. But even Croly, the prophet of nationalism, shared the view, often advanced by Howe, that "in all probability, the American city will become in the near future the most fruitful field for economically and socially constructive experimentation; and the effect of the example set therein will have a beneficially reactive effect upon state and Federal politics."[214] Here again, these progressives may be seen as anticipating later "urban liberalism."

However, Croly did view some matters as the exclusive province of the

---

[211] Hapgood, *Industry and Progress*, pp. 14, 21, 27, 34–5, 104–5; Howe, "Unemployment: a Problem and a Program," *Century*, 89 (Apr. 1915), pp. 843–8; Weyl, *New Democracy*, pp. 68, 320–47; Hamilton Holt to Franklin Giddings (on the reforms "*The Independent* stands for"), 26 Apr. 1913, Giddings papers; *Survey*, 32 (4 Apr., 23 May 1914), pp. 23–9, 223, and 33 (6 Feb. 1915), pp. 503–4; *New Republic*, 1 (5 Dec. 1914, 23 Jan. 1915), pp. 4, 10; "What's the Matter with America," pp. 33–4, Amos Pinchot Papers, box 225; "Preparedness," *Public*, 19 (4 Feb. 1916), p. 111; Creel, "The Hopes of the Hyphenated," *Century*, 91 (Jan. 1916), pp. 350–63; Semonche, *Ray Stannard Baker*, pp. 213–14; Everett, "Chester Rowell," pp. 359, 388–9; Cheslaw, "intellectual Biography," pp. 154–5; White to George Perkins, 13 May 1915, and to Charles F. Scott, 27 Nov. 1916, White Papers.
[212] *New Republic*, 1 (23 Jan. 1915), p. 10.
[213] *Survey*, 32 (4 Apr. 1914), pp. 23–29.
[214] Croly, *Promise of American Life*, p. 349. See also Howe, *The City*, pp. 7–8; and *The British City*, pp. 339–41.

central government, specifically "the regulation of commerce, the control of corporations, and the still more radical questions connected with the distribution of wealth and the prevention of poverty."[215] This last involved the issue of taxation, on which these writers were often radical in principle if rarely anticipating mid-twentieth-century rates. Many, even among those who did not envisage it as the *single* tax, strongly supported taxation of the income accruing from increasing land values.[216] The taxation of private or corporate income was widely approved, and inheritance taxes were especially favored since second-generation millionaires had not only not earned their fortunes but were judged less qualified to dispose of them. "Men who inherit great wealth and are brought up in extravagant habits nearly always spend their money on themselves," Croly observed disapprovingly.[217] Howe stressed "that the burdens of taxation in the United States are more unjustly distributed than in the other great powers" because a higher proportion of revenue was derived from indirect taxes.[218] Weyl argued that taxation should no longer "be levied for the sole purpose of raising government revenues," but should be regarded "as a means of changing the currents and directions of distribution."[219]

The role of government in "the regulation of commerce" and "the control of corporations" raised much more directly than did questions of taxation or social welfare those issues that divided the different schools of reform thought. Nevertheless, even here, at the programmatic level there remained a fair measure of common ground, which again would be highlighted by a contrast with the views of conservative upholders of laissez-faire. From this perspective, there is no reason to question Weyl's conclusion that "the most characteristic feature of the industrial program of the democracy . . . is the emphasis which is laid upon the state in industry."[220] Progressives of all types, indeed, looked favorably upon an extension of outright public ownership. This was especially true, of course, of the municipal ownership of public utilities, which had long been advocated by reformers like Howe and Steffens as the only means of preventing

---

215 *Promise of American Life*, p. 350.
216 Ibid., pp. 380–1; Weyl, *New Democracy*, p. 295; Lippmann, *Drift and Mastery*, pp. 69–70; Baker, Notebook 12, Nov. 1916, pp. 44–8, R. S. Baker Papers; *Independent*, 88 (2 Oct. 1916), p. 8.
217 *Promise of American Life*, p. 382.
218 "Memorandum on New Sources of Federal Revenue," enclosed in F. C. Howe to O. G. Villard, 1 Oct. 1915, Villard Papers, file 17.
219 *New Democracy*, p. 297.
220 Ibid., p. 278.

corruption as well as of securing efficient and economical public services. However, there was also a wide measure of support among progressive publicists and journals for government ownership of the railroads.[221] A particularly energetic advocate of this cause was Amos Pinchot, who, like the Single Taxers, saw the public ownership of natural monopolies and natural resources as a central element in a program to restore real competition in the rest of the economy.[222] This principle, which had a broad appeal, could also encompass coal mines, and during the serious labor troubles in Colorado in 1914, Holt and Weyl were among those who joined Pinchot in advocating government ownership as the only solution.[223] For most of these men, the dividing line between the private and the public sphere was a matter not of principle but of pragmatic judgment and experiment. "For some industries you may have to use public ownership, for others the co-operative society may be best, for others the regulating commission," explained Lippmann. "It will depend on the nature of the industry which instrument is the more effective."[224] "There is no general principle which makes public ownership either better or worse than private ownership," Rowell had concluded some years earlier. "Whichever works best in a particular instance is best in that instance."[225] It might be assumed that for socialists a principle did exist, but the perspective of men like Spargo and Russell was not very different from that of other reformers. "Socialism by no means involves the suppression of all private property and industry," Spargo insisted. "Only when these fail in efficiency or result in injustice and inequality of benefits does socialization present itself."[226]

The recognition that, as Weyl put it, "the necessity of preserving the highest possible industrial efficiency" imposed "certain definite limits . . . to an extension of government ownership"[227] was reinforced for

[221] Croly, *Promise of American Life*, pp. 376–7; Steffens in *Chicago Examiner*, Nov. 1906, cited in Cheslaw, "Intellectual Biography," pp. 181–2; Howe, *Privilege and Democracy*, pp. 283–92; Amos Pinchot, "The Cost of Private Monopoly to Public and Wage-Earner," *Annals*, 48 (July 1913), p. 185; White to Hiram Johnson, 23 Nov. 1914, White Papers; Creel, "Can a Democratic Government Control Prices?" *Century*, 93 (Feb. 1917), p. 610; Rowell to E. B. Osborne, 31 July 1915, Rowell Papers; *Public*, 17 (6 Nov. 1914), p. 1063; *New Republic*, 1 (19 Dec. 1914), pp. 8–9; *Independent*, 89 (5 Feb. 1917), p. 204.

[222] See, for example, Amos Pinchot, "The Biggest Thing between You and Prosperity," *Pearson's*, 39 (Sept. 1915), pp. 225–40; Howe, *The City*, p. 119; *Public*, 17 (6 Nov. 1914), p. 1063.

[223] AP to Gilson Gardner, 15 July 1914, Amos Pinchot Papers, box 17.

[224] *Drift and Mastery*, p. 99. See also Croly, *Promise of American Life*, pp. 378–9.

[225] *Fresno Republican*, 4 May 1899, cited in Everett, "Chester Rowell," p. 380.

[226] *Socialism*, p. 220. See also *Applied Socialism*, pp. 119–20; Russell, "No More Foes Without – and None Within," *Pearson's*, 33 (June 1915), p. 699.

[227] *New Democracy*, p. 287.

many by misgivings about the growth of bureaucracy. This was, of course, a central element in the Single Tax philosophy. "The choice is not between competition and something better. It is between competition and bureaucratic regulation," declared Post who even feared that Theodore Roosevelt's policies as president were leading toward "a regime of state socialism radiating from the national capital."[228] For Howe, one of the virtues of municipal socialism was that "with the unit reduced to the city, and with its functions determined by popular control as is done in the New England town meeting, the dangers from bureaucratic or distant control are reduced to a minimum."[229] Anxieties of a similar sort were expressed by some of those more favorably disposed to collectivism. Indeed, Lippmann's journey away from his youthful socialism may have owed something to his fear that it had "within it the germs of that great bureaucratic tyranny which Chesterton and Belloc have named the Servile State."[230] However, one of the few points on which Spargo and Walling agreed was that, as Spargo plainly put it, "modern Socialism is not an attempt to create a great bureaucracy; . . . it has no more in common with such monstrous exaggerations of centralized government as described in Bellamy's *Looking Backward* and mechanical Utopias of its kind than with sunworship or alchemy."[231] As so often, Walling took an extreme position. "Socialism, in its aversion to all artificial systems and every restriction of personal liberty is far more akin to the individualism of Herbert Spencer than it is to the 'State Socialism' of Plato," he concluded.[232]

This sensitivity to the danger of a collectivist state becoming oppressive is one indication that repudiation of the principles of laissez-faire did not necessarily imply abandonment of the strong attachment to individual freedom that was such a central element in the American tradition. It is true that there were discernible differences among these writers in the degree and nature of their concern for this value. The pragmatists and nationalists of the *New Republic* did not care for the language of rights. In *The Promise of American Life*, Croly observed that "it is in the nature of

---

228 Post, *Social Service* (London, 1910), p. 337; *Public*, 5 (30 Aug. 1902), p. 321, quoted in Stuart Portner, "Louis F. Post: His Life and Times" (Ph.D. dissertation, University of Michigan, 1940), p. 184.

229 *The City*, p. 303. See also Steffens, "Equality of Opportunities, Not of Incomes," p. 113.

230 *Preface to Politics*, p. 201. See also *Drift and Mastery*, p. 171.

231 Quoted in Friedberg, "Marxism in the United States," p. 304. See also Spargo, *Socialism*, pp. ix, 239, and *Applied Socialism*, p. 121.

232 *Socialism As It Is*, p. 436; "Socialism and Liberty" [c. 1910] in Walling, ed., *Walling: A Symposium*, p. 98. See also "State Socialism and the Individual," *New Review*, 1 (May, June 1913), pp. 506–15, 579–83.

liberties and rights, abstractly considered, to be insubordinate and to conflict both one with another and, perhaps, with the common weal." He made this point in the context of a criticism of the abolitionists, and it was on questions concerning race that some of these men were least sensitive to civil liberties and civil rights. Croly himself not only flatly affirmed that "the negroes were a race possessed of moral and intellectual qualities inferior to those of the white men" but also attributed "the prevalence of lynching in the South" largely to the ease with which murderers escaped punishment in the courts.[233] Some seem to have feared that too great a cultural heterogeneity, combined with the implacable reality of racial consciousness and animosity, would constitute a further obstacle on the path to that egalitarian and cooperative democracy which they envisioned. This was the position of Weyl, who frankly proposed to evade the issue of negro suffrage as a lost and in some ways dubious cause,[234] and observed that "if today our ten million American Negroes resided, not in the United States, but in a contiguous territory, asking for admission into the Union, it is extremely improbable that the mass of white men would permit the annexation." A similar attitude is evident in Weyl's views on immigration, which he not only wanted to restrict in order to counter its depressing effects on conditions of labor but to limit to "people especially selected for their adjustability to American conditions."[235] Rowell, too, was in favor of selective immigration restriction – specifically, as a Californian, Asiatic exclusion – but on slightly different grounds. Recognizing that discrimination of the kind that negroes and orientals suffered was unjust, he also saw it as an inevitable consequence of a racial prejudice that was natural and ineradicable. "It is hard enough," he wrote to a Japanese publisher, "to teach our people to treat with just consideration even the Japanese who are here, though these are few in numbers and are doing no harm to anybody. If we had enough Japanese to present a real problem, it is a problem which our people would refuse to deal with on any terms of justice, and no amount of leadership could induce them to do so."[236]

Others, however, were much more militant in their defense of civil rights and civil liberties. As we have seen, Russell, Steffens, and Holt as

---

[233] Croly, *Promise of American Life*, pp. 79, 81, 318.
[234] "We look at the Negro vote in Philadelphia and Cincinnati, and wonder whether it is worth while to lay aside other problems to secure a Negro vote in Atlanta and Charleston." *New Democracy*, p. 343.
[235] Ibid., pp. 345, 347.
[236] Rowell to K. K. Kakawami, 11 Dec. 1914, Rowell Papers. See also Everett, "Rowell," pp. 393–428.

well as Walling were involved in the founding of the NAACP in 1909, and in 1915 both Baker and Amos Pinchot accepted official positions in the organization.[237] While, like most Socialists, favoring some restriction of immigration, Spargo led the opposition to Asiatic exclusion at the party's 1910 Congress.[238] Civil liberties issues in the prewar years generally involved radical groups, notably the Industrial Workers of the World (IWW), and some of these men were directly involved in the defence of free speech. Steffens helped to organize a Free Speech League, and in a debate with Erman J. Ridgway of *Everybody's* magazine in 1911 argued strongly against any form of censorship.[239] As police commissioner in Denver, Creel came under strong attack for permitting IWW meetings to proceed without interference.[240] Amos Pinchot was a leading member of the Labor Defense Council that emerged from the Colorado troubles of 1913–14, and he contributed to the legal expenses not only of accused IWW leaders but of the *Masses* in a libel case "for the sake of general free expression."[241] Those of an antimonopoly or Single Tax persuasion were likely to have a particularly strong concern for individual rights, as the *Public* indicated when it declared that "laws and local ordinances interfering with freedom of speech or of the press" ought not to be obeyed,[242] but progressives of a more collectivist inclination also cherished the values of traditional liberalism. Reporting on a meeting of the American Sociological Society, Kellogg observed that "the enduring force of abstract rights, set up as bulwarks against tyranny and oppression, could not have been better illustrated than by the tenacity with which the discussion of these twentieth century sociologists clung to familiar lines – on free assemblage, free speech, freedom of the press and freedom of teaching."[243] Concern for "the old freedoms" may also be discerned in the reluctance of some to accept the need for a *compulsory* system of social insurance as well as in opposition to prohibition, Sabbatarian laws and "sumptuary legislation".[244] Even Croly conceded that "individual free-

---

237 See the concluding remarks of Chapter 2; Semonche, *Ray Stannard Baker*, pp. 207–8; AP to May Childs Nerney, 1 Feb. 1915, Amos Pinchot Papers, box 19.

238 Friedberg, "Marxism in the United States," pp. 128–30.

239 Stein, "Lincoln Steffens," pp. 134–5; Cheslaw "Intellectual Biography," pp. 189–90.

240 *Rebel at Large*, p. 103.

241 AP to Edward P. Costigan, 30 Dec. 1916; to Mark Sullivan, 9 June 1914; to George F. Porter, 14 Jan. 1914, Amos Pinchot Papers, boxes 25, 17, 16.

242 *Public*, 17 (18 Dec. 1914), p. 1207.

243 "The Old Freedoms Discussed by Twentieth Century Sociologists," *Survey*, 33 (9 Jan. 1915), pp. 406–12a.

244 Hapgood, *Industry and Progress*, pp. 34–5, 75; Baker, Notebook 13, Apr. 1917, p. 130, R. S. Baker papers; Howe, *The City*, p. 166; Lippmann, *Preface to Politics*, pp. 31–44, 152–3; Weyl, *New Democracy*, p. 353.

dom is important" and condemned "an illiberal puritanism," while Walling had no doubt "that whole departments of restrictive legislation directed against individual liberty would at once be repealed by any Socialist government."[245]

This assumption that traditional liberal values would in no way suffer from the abandonment of economic individualism was widely shared. Thus, Weyl argued that "what is often interpreted as a limitation of freedom is in effect an increase of liberty, through the protection of some individuals from the hitherto permitted aggressions of others."[246] The growth of cooperation in place of competition, Baker assured one of his conservative friends, "will never overturn the liberties of men or suppress free speech or make a free press impossible."[247] Characteristically, White pinned his faith on the racial heritage of the Anglo-Saxon. "The fact that the surrender to the state of many of the things of life which individuals have hitherto enjoyed, has proved harmful to the Latin races, proves nothing as to the American people," he observed. "They have an extra supply of individualism, of love of personal liberty, and will guard the liberties they surrender as closely as those they hold."[248] In *A Preface to Politics,* Lippmann was confident it would be possible to develop "the productive state" while abolishing "the repressive." "Without the Jeffersonian distrust of the police we might easily grow into an impertinent and tyrannous collectivism: without a vivid sense of the possibilities of the state we abandon the supreme instrument of civilization."[249] The new liberalism would preserve the best of the old.[250]

The way forward

"The New Liberalism" was in these years a term more current in British than in American politics, and setting these American progressives in an international context helps further to define their position, particularly with respect to the means by which they expected their goals to be achieved. The comparisons they themselves drew serve to emphasize again

---

[245] Croly, *Promise of American Life,* pp. 178, 150; Walling, *Socialism As It Is,* p. 434. Spargo, too, promised that "in the socialist state, liberty will continue to grow." *Applied Socialism,* p. 160.

[246] *New Democracy,* pp. 353–4.

[247] Baker to Norman F. Woodlock, 8 Sept. 1913, R. S. Baker papers, ser. 2, box 94.

[248] "The Kansas Conscience," *Reader,* Oct. 1905, pp. 488–93, cited in Johnson, *White's America,* p. 149.

[249] *Preface to Politics,* pp. 200–2.

[250] On "the new liberalism," see Forcey, *Crossroads of Liberalism,* pp. xiii–xiv.

that for them the key issue was the extension of the role of government in order to reduce economic inequalities. Several observed that in this respect the United States was the most backward of the industrial nations. After a transatlantic trip in 1910, Steffens concluded that European liberals and radicals were "way ahead of us."[251] "The things which I am trying to get support for in this country are only the things which have been adopted for decades in Germany and England," Amos Pinchot explained. "They are only such rational and sensible measures as must always be applied to such conditions as generally spring up in countries where reckless and thoughtless commercialism has ruled for a long time."[252] "If there are any standpatters left outside of America, they have hidden where nobody can find them," Rowell concluded in 1915. "It is only in America that there is any considerable body of men, educated enough to express themselves, who still believe that there is any possibility of maintaining or reviving eighteenth-century individualism and its once-plausible maxims."[253]

In European countries the enemies of laissez-faire were politically very diverse, including as they did both conservative nationalists and revolutionary socialists. Within this range, nearly all these publicists identified themselves with "new liberals" or revisionist socialists, groups that they generally did not much distinguish. Not surprisingly, it was the British political scene they were most familiar with.[254] "The liberalism of the middle of the century is being Fabianized," observed Howe, who, like Steffens, was keen to attend a Fabian Society meeting when visiting Britain.[255] Apart from Walling, who after resigning from the society in 1907 became a fierce critic of its leaders,[256] progressives of all types saw the Fabians as an attractive model. Through Wallas, Lippmann joined the society in 1909, and given the nationalist collectivist outlook of Croly and Weyl, it was not surprising that the *New Republic* seemed to another of its

---

251 Steffens to Allen H. Suggett, 22 Oct. 1910, *Steffens Letters*, 1, p. 252.
252 AP to Henry Lane Eno, 20 July 1914; also AP to George F. Porter, 25 Feb. 1915, Amos Pinchot Papers, boxes 17, 19.
253 *Fresno Republican*, 9 Sept. 1915.
254 These points are made in the most recent and discriminating study of the relationship between American progressives and European radicalism, Melvyn Stokes, "American Progressives and the European Left," *Journal of American Studies*, 17 (April 1983), pp. 5–28. See Arthur Mann, "British Social Thought and American Reformers of the Progressive Era," *Mississippi Valley Historical Review*, 42 (Mar. 1956), pp. 672–92; Kenneth O. Morgan, "The Future at Work: Anglo-American Progressivism 1890–1917," in *Contrast and Connection, Bicentennial Essays in Anglo-American History*, ed. H. C. Allen and Roger Thompson (London, 1976), pp. 245–71.
255 *The City*, p. 137; Howe to Steffens, 24 Nov. 1909, Steffens Papers, reel 2.
256 *Progressivism – and After*, pp. 241–6; *Socialism As It Is*, pp. 155–64.

editors to constitute a "special semi-Fabian world,"[257] but Amos Pinchot, too, evidently saw no inconsistency in recommending as examples both the Liberalism of Lloyd George and the Fabian Society, which he described as "the finest thing that has been done along that line and the foundation of the progressive movement in England."[258] "Most of the American Progressives occupy a position similar to that of the English Fabians," White wrote in the spring of 1917. "They are for the gradual evolutionary smash of the present capitalistic system, and they want the smash to come not as a blow-up, but in a sort of Mendelian evolution."[259]

As White made clear, it was not the elitism excoriated by Walling that drew these progressives to the Fabians so much as the stress on gradualism. Howe, for example, foresaw each city expanding its activities "only in response to the developing demands of the community; it will assume new burdens only as it justifies its abilities to perform them." Thus "each city will be an experiment station, offering new experiences to the world."[260] The idea that social reform should be experimental was widely accepted; the triumphs of science testified to the virtues of what was seen as its method.[261] The accumulation of firmly established, objective facts was the first requirement, and several of these writers, including both muckrakers and investigators for the *Survey,* saw themselves as contributing to this task. Thereafter, policies should be, as the *Survey* urged, "amended and reamended and amended again" in the light of experience.[262] "The more intelligent men become the more soundly practical they become," Baker wrote. "As in the past progress is going to take place only as the result of infinite experimentation."[263] The comparison with science, and the ever-present consciousness of evolution, implied that this process would never cease. "The kingdom of heaven on earth is always a

[257] Steel, *Lippmann,* p. 43; Francis Hackett, "Publicist and Radical" in [Brubaker, ed.], *Weyl: An Appreciation,* p. 95. See also Lippmann Diary, 14, 17, 20 July 1914, Lippmann Papers; Lippmann, *Preface to Politics,* pp. 57–9; Weyl, *New Democracy,* pp. 182–3.

[258] AP to Mrs. George Bernard Shaw, 6 Jan. 1915, Amos Pinchot Papers, box 19. Also AP to Julius S. Grunow, 25 July 1914, and to Hugh O'Neill, 4 Dec. 1914, ibid., boxes 17, 18. "The Failure of the Progressive Party," *Masses,* 6 (Dec. 1914), pp. 9–10.

[259] White to Effie June Franklin, 13 Mar. 1917, White Papers.

[260] *The City,* p. 303.

[261] For admiration for the method as well as the achievements of science, see the references in n. 153. See also David A. Hollinger, "Science and Anarchy: Walter Lippmann's *Drift and Mastery,*" *American Quarterly,* 29 (Winter 1977), pp. 463–75.

[262] *Survey,* 33 (17 Oct. 1914), p. 73.

[263] Baker to Norman F. Woodlock, 8 Sept. 1913, R. S. Baker Papers, ser. 2, box 94. See also Croly, *Promise of American Life,* pp. 346–7.

permanent, unchanging, perfect and unutterably stupid place," complained Weyl. "Utopias break down because they represent attainment, fulfillment. But society does not strive toward fulfillment, but only towards striving."[264]

Such an approach was obviously antithetical to that which looked forward to a decisive, transforming, revolution. Indeed, when the possibility of a violent upheaval figured in the writings of these men, it was almost invariably as a threat of what was likely to happen in the absence of reform. "We must suffer if we do not change our ways," warned White, as he prophesied that the "millions, bound to machines, working automatically for long hours . . . at small wages . . . taken from school at the end of infancy" would "visit upon this nation a terrible vengeance for its criminal neglect of their cause."[265] Before taking it as a uniquely candid revelation of their own motives, one needs to appreciate that this line of argument served a tactical purpose. Thus it was to a conservative relative that Amos Pinchot wrote that "what I am trying, in a humble way, to help do, is to prevent violence, disorder and misery by getting people to see the justice of the average man's demand for a better economic position in this country, and the utter futility of denying or ignoring this demand."[266] Although the socialists among these publicists were less ready to repudiate the idea of revolution, the outlook of Spargo and Russell did not much differ from that of other reformers. "The Social Revolution is not a sanguinary episode which must attend the birth of a new social order. It is a long period of effort, experiment and adjustment, and is now taking place," explained Spargo, who elsewhere raised the bogy of "anarchistic vengeance" as the dire alternative to socialism.[267] Even Walling, who explicitly insisted that the gains of revolutions exceeded their costs, assured his readers that "this does not mean that Socialists suppose that all progress must await a revolutionary period."[268]

There appeared to be a more substantial difference between socialists and non-socialists on the related question of the desirability of class con-

264 *New Democracy*, p. 354.
265 *The Old Order Changeth*, p. 191. See also Lippmann, *Preface to Politics*, pp. 25, 211–14, 236–7; *Harper's Weekly*, 60 (27 Feb. 1915), p. 193; Creel, "Making Vagrants," *Pearson's*, 34 (Sept. 1915), pp. 302–10; Rowell, "Progressivism."
266 AP to Henry Lane Eno, 20 July 1914, Amos Pinchot Papers, box 17. On this general point, see Rhodri Jeffreys-Jones, *Violence and Reform in American History* (New York, 1978), especially pp. 6–7, 34.
267 *Applied Socialism*, p. 128; *Socialism*, p. 144. See also Russell, "No More Foes Without – and None Within," *Pearson's*, 33 (June 1915), p. 699.
268 *Socialism As It Is*, pp. 242–3.

sciousness and class conflict. The doctrine of class war was generally deplored and repudiated, not least by some, such as Baker, Steffens, and Weyl, otherwise attracted to socialism.[269] "It is not a struggle of classes, not in America," White insisted. "It is a contest in the heart of the common people."[270] Writing from Paris in 1914, Bourne fumed that to see this "kind of sentimental mawkishness" as the route to "social salvation" was "to pervert the whole issue, which is one so largely of class-relations and institutions." "My social philosophy," he concluded, "is working around to a paradoxical desire for Tolstoyan ends through Nietzschean means: socialism, dynamic social religion, through the ruthless application of scientific materialism."[271] However, on closer examination, there is a less stark contrast between the attitudes to class consciousness of socialists and other reformers. Many of the latter recognized that working-class militancy could spark the sometimes sluggish engine of progress, while socialists were aware that its outlook was often closer to that of its capitalist opponents than to the spirit of "the cooperative commonwealth." "So long as the poor are docile in their poverty, the rest of us are only too willing to satisfy our consciences by pitying them," Lippmann observed.[272] In the same vein, the *New Republic* attributed the failure to cure unemployment to the fact that "the unemployed, the victims of the bungling, have not made themselves felt as a social force."[273] Even Baker insisted to Theodore Roosevelt in 1908 that *"class action is a condition now existent:* a mode of progress which cannot be at present dispensed with."[274] Walling, however, while scornful of the faith placed by "non-Socialist reformers" in social harmony, enlightenment, and altruism,[275] was fiercely opposed in the pre-war years to the idea of a labor party. "A 'class-conscious' worker engaged in a 'class struggle' to advance the interests of his class without any further aim is exactly the opposite to a Socialist," he declared. "He is a reactionary doing all in his power to restore the regime of status or class."[276]

[269] Baker to Norman F. Woodlock, 8 Sept. 1913, R. S. Baker Papers, ser. 2, box 94; Cheslaw, "Intellectual Biography," pp. 165–70, 180–2; Weyl, *New Democracy,* chap. 12.
[270] *The Old Order Changeth,* pp. 6–7.
[271] Bourne to Alyse Gregory, 18 Mar. 1914, Bourne Papers, reel 1.
[272] *Preface to Politics,* p. 208.
[273] *New Republic,* 2 (20 Feb. 1915), p. 56.
[274] Baker to Theodore Roosevelt, 8 June 1908, cited in Bannister, *Baker,* p. 128.
[275] *Socialism As It Is,* pp. 15, 19, 32–5.
[276] *Larger Aspects of Socialism,* p. xiii. See also Walling to Eugene Debs, 14 Dec. 1909; to H. M. Hyndman, 19 Feb. 1910, Walling papers. Characteristically, Spargo sought through the power of assertion to bridge not only the gulf between socialism and progressivism but also that between

This perspective accounts for much of the ambivalence toward organized labor. Of course, attitudes to labor disputes varied, though in ways that seem to have reflected temperamental differences at least as much as ideological or programmatic ones: Weyl, Howe, Steffens, and Amos Pinchot were instinctively more sympathetic to strikers than Rowell, White, or even Baker. In their general approach, however, there was again a good deal of common ground. The principle of collective bargaining was generally accepted,[277] though in the case of some Single Taxers only as a necessary implication of the regrettable existence of monopolies and other large corporations.[278] At the same time, sympathy for labor unionism was often qualified by commitment to other, broader, principles. The first was concern for the poor. Although Croly insisted on the qualitative superiority of union to nonunion labor in arguing that governments should discriminate in favor of the former,[279] the apparent elitism of the American Federation of Labor (AFL) offended many. "Unions composed exclusively of skilled workers, as many of the present ones, operate against the interests of the less skilled," observed Walling.[280] Kellogg and the *Survey* deplored the AFL's opposition to wages and hours legislation and other social welfare measures.[281] Indeed, Kellogg found himself more drawn to the IWW, as did a number of these publicists, particularly at the time of the 1912 Lawrence strike.[282] The other significant constraint on progressive support for trade unionism was the commitment to the supremacy of the common good, which involved the general interest in industrial peace. This principle could lead to authoritarian conclusions as was illustrated by Spargo's prediction that "the attitude which the

the goal of a classless society and the route of class conflict. "The Socialists," he claimed, "by placing the class struggle in its proper place as one of the great social dynamic forces, have done and are doing more to allay hatred and bitterness of feeling . . . than any other body of people in the world." *Socialism*, p. 144.

277 For example, Croly, *Promise of American Life*, pp. 386–91; Hapgood, *Industry and Progress*, pp. 23, 41–57; Weyl, *New Democracy*, pp. 292–3; Lippmann, *Drift and Mastery*, chap. 5; Amos Pinchot, "Why Violence in Bayonne?" *Harper's Weekly*, 61 (7 Aug. 1915), p. 126; Creel, "A Way to Industrial Peace," *Century*, 90 (July 1915), pp. 433–40; Baker Notebook 14, pp. 91–8, R. S. Baker Papers; Everett, "Rowell," pp. 381–7.

278 *Public*, 6 (13 June 1903), p. 144; 17 (13 Nov. 1914), pp. 1084–5.

279 *Promise of American Life*, pp. 386–96.

280 *Socialism As It Is*, p. 357.

281 Kellogg, "Immigration and the Minimum Wage," *Annals*, 48 (July 1913), pp. 66–77; John A. Fitch, "The Eight-Hour Day," *Survey* 33 (19 Dec. 1914), p. 323.

282 Kellogg, "Immigration and the Minimum Wage," p. 73. See also Forcey, *Crossroads of Liberalism*, pp. xxiv, 73, 157–8, 161, 165–6; Pinchot, *History*, ed. Hooker, pp. 62–3; Bannister, *Baker*, p. 136; Walling, *Socialism As It Is*, p. 372; "Industrialism or Revolutionary Unionism," *New Review*, 1 (11 Jan. 1913), pp. 45–51; Creel Scrapbook, 25 Mar. 1915, Creel Papers; Steffens to Allen and Lou Suggett, 10 Dec. 1915, *Steffens Letters*, 1, p. 364.

labor unions of today very properly take in industrial conflicts would not be tolerated if adopted against the State. In self-protection the State would be obliged to treat as treasonable, acts which are perfectly proper and justifiable when directed against individual or corporate employers."[283] However, it also inspired the *Survey*'s campaign for the establishment of the Commission on Industrial Relations, whose report was taken by Creel to have demonstrated "the truth of labor's claim that it has been cheated, robbed, oppressed and stripped of supposed rights."[284] Most of these writers suggested that the only real answer to the labor question was "industrial democracy," but the meaning of this vague slogan was rarely spelled out, though it commonly implied some form of workers' representation or co-partnership.[285]

On the whole, then, hopes of progress rested less on class conflict than on a general growth of enlightenment and community feeling. This focused attention on the attitudes of those on the other side of industry and here, too, a certain ambivalence is apparent. As the beneficiaries as well as the upholders of the inequalities generated by unreformed capitalism, businessmen were, of course, the targets of much criticism and denunciation. However, some even of those most insistent that under the existing "system" businessmen were the source of corruption occasionally thought that their undoubted effectiveness might be enlisted in the cause of reform. "I should like to see a really big business man who had the support of his class tackle the problem of the city and see what he would do with it," Howe wrote to the like-minded Steffens. "Some times I think there is nothing to hope from the business men, sometimes I think nothing will be done for some years except through them. They are being changed along with the rest of us only they are about ten or a score of years

[283] *Applied Socialism*, p. 216. This statement was cited by Walling as evidence of the tyrannous character of state socialism. *Progressivism – and After*, p. 232. But others also suggested that there might have to be legal limits to the power of unions. See Croly, *Promise of American Life*, pp. 390–7; Lippmann, *Drift and Mastery*, p. 65; *New Republic*, 5 (29 Jan. 1916), p. 320; *Independent*, 87 (21 Aug., 4 Sept. 1916), pp. 255–7, 324–5, ad 88 (2 Oct., 11 Dec. 1916), pp. 6, 437–8.

[284] Kellogg, "Statement before U.S. Commission on Industrial Relations, 1915," Kellogg Papers; Chambers, *Kellogg and The Survey*, pp. 49–50; Creel, "What the Industrial Commission Discovered," *Pearson's*, 35 (Mar. 1916), p. 201.

[285] For example, Hapgood, *Industry and Progress*, pp. 39–40, 109–10; Croly, *Progressive Democracy*, chap. 18; Weyl, *New Democracy*, pp. 276–9, 291–3; Lippmann, *Preface to Politics*, pp. 55, 214–16; Spargo, *Socialism*, pp. 225–7; Walling, *Progressivism – and After*, p. xix; Amos Pinchot to George F. Porter, 16 Feb. 1915, Amos Pinchot papers, box 19; White to George Perkins, 13 May 1915, White Papers; Devine, "Philanthropy and Business," *Survey*, 32 (6 June 1914), pp. 263–5; *New Republic*, 1 (19 Dec. 1914, 30 Jan. 1915), pp. 10, 8–10. For the wider debate about the meaning of the term, see Milton Derber, *The American Idea of Industrial Democracy 1865–1965* (Chicago, 1970).

in arrears."[286] Others, notably the *New Republic* group, were encouraged by the rising importance in business of technical experts and salaried administrators skilled in "scientific management" in place of the old-style, buccaneering capitalists. "The Napoleons of business are being succeeded by the Von Moltkes," Croly noted with satisfaction.[287] This was expected to lead to the taming of the spirit of commercialism by that of professionalism. Thus, Lippmann predicted that "it will make a world of difference if the leadership of industry is in the hands of men interested in production as a creative art instead of as brute exploitation."[288] Such hopes reinforced the conviction that, as Weyl put it, "social cooperation, which is the goal of democracy, is also its weapon."[289]

This account of the views of a group of the most prominent progressive publicists in the years before the First World War has focused upon the common elements in their thought. Some of these, of course, such as commitment to the national democratic tradition, respect for Christian ethics, or concern for civil liberties, could also be found among Americans of a more conservative persuasion, but the way they were combined with others constituted a distinctively progressive consensus. The general character of this political outlook surely suggests that the comparison several of these men themselves drew with European social democrats or new liberals was not misplaced.[290] There were, it is true, some particularly American aspects to their thought – the anxiety over the issue of monopoly, the serious attention paid to the mechanisms of popular government, and possibly greater reservations about the growth of state power. But several of the specific programs they recommended – particularly in such fields as social insurance and municipal ownership of public utilities – were frankly derived from European precedents, and the basic commitment to using the power of government to achieve a less unequal distribution of wealth was the same.

There were also, of course, considerable differences within this group of progressives. As we have seen, these did not fall along any single line of

---

[286] Howe to Steffens, 24 Nov. 1909, Steffens Papers, reel 2.
[287] *Progressive Democracy*, p. 398. On the enthusiasm with which some progressives embraced scientific management, see Haber, *Efficiency and Uplift*, especially chap. 5.
[288] *Preface to Politics*, p. 48. See also *Drift and Mastery*, pp. 35–44.
[289] *New Democracy*, p. 270.
[290] See, especially, Peter F. Clarke, "The Progressive Movement in England," *Transactions of the Royal Historical Society*, 5th ser., vol. 24 (1974), pp. 159–81, and *Liberals and Social Democrats* (Cambridge, England, 1978).

cleavage, and, indeed, differences of temperament, including those in the strength of their commitment to change, were as likely as more ideological ones to determine individual responses to particular issues. It could well be argued, however, that the conflicts between the various schools of reform thought were of less fundamental significance than the tensions within the structure of beliefs that was generally shared. Some of these were explicitly recognized, such as the dangers that a collectivist state might diminish individual freedom or escape democratic control. Less attention was paid to the possible conflicts between these latter two values themselves – though Lippmann casually prophesied "a tyranny of the majority for which minorities will have to be prepared."[291] But one dilemma was almost never confronted in the pre-war years. It can perhaps be expressed in terms of their double commitment to democracy – as a political process and as a social ideal. For the confidence that the two were necessarily connected could in the long run only be sustained if a majority of the electorate chose to support the sort of reforms advocated by these publicists.

[291] *Drift and Mastery*, p. 55.

CHAPTER 4

War in Europe

First reactions

On August 3, 1914, Charles Edward Russell was on board ship, bound for an international Socialist conference in Vienna, when a wireless message was received telling of the outbreak of war between France and Germany. "Deluge come at last," he wrote in his diary. "No wonder we have no appetite at the captain's table."[1] As his note implies, Russell himself was distressed but not surprised by the news. Frequent visits to Germany had bred in him a lively apprehension of that country's militarism; in an article published in 1912 he warned that the German war party dreamed of seizing an Atlantic port from Holland or France,[2] and a year later he "offered to two magazine editors an outline indication of the coming storm, including the invasion of Belgium," only to be "laughed to scorn."[3]

This dismissive reaction was much more typical of American attitudes to international affairs in the pre-war years than Russell's alarmed premonitions. In common with the majority of their fellow countrymen, most of these progressive publicists had shared an outlook on world politics in which inattention was combined with optimism. Even Lippmann, who was to write so much on the subject over so many years, could "not remember taking any interest whatsoever in foreign affairs until after the outbreak of the First World War." On his way at the time to the Alps for a walking holiday, Lippmann recalled "being astonished and rather annoyed when I went to the railroad station and found that the German border was closed because Belgium had had an ultimatum."[4] "Few of us knew or cared about 'international relationships'," Baker was to recall.[5]

---

[1] Diary no. 1, 3 Aug. 1914, Russell Papers; Russell, *Bare Hands and Stone Walls*, p. 264.
[2] "The Heir of the War Lord," *Cosmopolitan*, 52 (Mar. 1912), pp. 464–8.
[3] *Bare Hands and Stone Walls*, p. 263. For Russell's earlier dissent from "the optimistic philosophy" that war was declining or becoming more humane, see *Why I Am a Socialist*, pp. 114–18.
[4] Lippmann, *U.S. Foreign Policy: Shield of the Republic* (Boston, 1943), pp. x–xii.
[5] Baker, *American Chronicle*, p. 298.

Of those few, most had some involvement with the peace movement, which was particularly strong and active in pre-war America.[6] Holt, a founder-member of the New York Peace Society, had been for some years propounding his scheme for a Federation of the World on public platforms as well as in the columns of the *Independent*.[7] Some social reformers saw the peace movement, which was lavishly financed by Andrew Carnegie and supported by prominent conservatives, as a distraction from the more pressing battle against domestic evils,[8] but in June 1914 the American Association for International Conciliation published an essay by the young radical Randolph Bourne condemning "militarism" as an unhealthy and undemocratic social institution that had lost its original functional justification. "Even in Europe none of the great civilized nations has seen war within its boundaries for more than forty years," he noted. "The fact can no longer be blinked at; the military game is up."[9] This was an extreme statement but a more moderate optimism was widespread. Thus Weyl, in a casual aside in *The New Democracy*, suggested that international peace would be an incidental benefit from economic progress for "in the last analysis, the wars of all the ages have been wars of poverty."[10] In this climate of opinion, it is not surprising that liberal journals, like the American press generally, failed to attach much significance to the Sarajevo crisis. As late as July 31, 1914, the *Public* attributed talk of a general war in Europe to "the fertile imagination of sensational newspaper correspondents."[11]

Few among this group of publicists could claim to have been more farsighted about the likelihood of a major war. Apart from Russell,

---

[6] Of the large literature on the peace movement, see particularly David S. Patterson, *Toward a Warless World: The Travail of the American Peace Movement, 1887–1914* (Bloomington, Ind., 1976); and C. Roland Marchand, *The American Peace Movement and Social Reform, 1898–1918* (Princeton, N.J., 1972).

[7] Kuehl, *Holt*, chaps. 5–7.

[8] Paul U. Kellogg, "Of Peace and Good Will," *American*, 71 (Apr. 1911), pp. 739–45. "We had, prior to August, 1914, ignored the threat of war, ignored the movements to prevent it and ignored the human consequences bound up in both," Kellogg was later to admit. "The Fighting Issues," *Survey*, 37 (17 Feb. 1917), p. 572.

[9] "The Tradition of War," *International Conciliation* (New York), no. 79 (June 1914), pp. 8–10, 12–13.

[10] *New Democracy*, p. 261.

[11] *Public*, 17 (31 July 1914), p. 721. See also *Independent*, 79 (20 July, 3 Aug. 1914), pp. 83–4, 149–50. No comment on or news of the European crisis appeared in *Harper's Weekly* until after the Austrian ultimatum. See *Harper's Weekly*, 59 (8 Aug. 1914), p. 121. For more general press reaction to the outbreak of war, see Edwin Costrell, *How Maine Viewed the War* (Orono, Maine, 1940), p. 32; Cedric C. Cummins, *Indiana Public Opinion and the World War, 1914–17* (Indianapolis, Ind., 1945), p. 5.

Rowell had also retained from his period in Europe in the 1890s a sense of the depth of Franco-German hostility, and Walling had expressed the conventional socialist expectation that "racial and nationalistic conflicts" might be "the last defence of the ruling classes."[12] The most explicit pessimist, however, was Croly, who in *The Promise of American Life* had insisted that the strength and significance of "the existing rivalries and enmities among European states must not be under-estimated" and had argued that "peace will prevail in international relations, just as order prevails within a nation, because of the righteous use of superior force – because the power which makes for pacific organization is stronger than the power which makes for a warlike organization." Until this was the case, Croly prophesied, nations would try "again and again the dangerous chances of war" so that "the probabilities are that . . . the road to any permanent international settlement will be piled mountain high with dead bodies, and will be traveled, if at all, only after a series of abortive and costly experiments."[13]

While the existence of these and a few other warning voices did not perceptibly disturb the prevailing complacency and indifference about world affairs, the events of August 1914 shattered both. The shock with which Americans responded to the outbreak of the First World War reflected not only their innocent optimism but also their underlying sense of involvement with the old world. For some of these publicists, the reality of this involvement was manifest in the most concrete way, by their physical presence; as well as Russell and Lippmann, Bourne, Hapgood, and Steffens were in Europe in August 1914. A few were soon caught up emotionally in the cause of one of the belligerent countries. This was particularly true of Russell, who was immediately consumed by anxiety about the fate of the sister republic to which he had long had a sentimental attachment. "Will there be any France when all this is done?" he wondered. "Never thought before of a world without France."[14]

The chief form that the sense of involvement took, however, was distress at the very fact of the war itself and its consequences for Europe as a whole. "This civilization that I have been admiring so much seems so palpably about to be torn to shreds that I do not even want to think about

---

[12] Everett, "Chester Rowell," p. 104; Walling "Why a Socialist Party?" *New Review*, 2 (July 1914), p. 403.

[13] *Promise of American Life*, pp. 264, 312, 307.

[14] Diary, 3 Aug. 1914, Russell Papers. Russell had dedicated his volume of verse *The Twin Immortalities and Other Poems* (Chicago, 1904) to the president of the French Republic and had begun the volume with a dedicatory poem to "O Queen, my France."

Europe until the war is over," wrote Bourne from the ship carrying him back to America.[15] On a "quiet peaceful summer day" in Amherst, Massachusetts, Baker read the news of war "with intense sadness of heart," noting in his diary, "these are our brothers who suffer."[16] Sisters, too, Rowell reminded his Californian readers, as he evoked "the tears of women, mostly ignorant and helpless peasant women" as "the men of their families have been called away to war, in unknown regions, against an unknown foe, as a part of an incomprehensible catastrophe."[17] For sensitive and humane men, imagining the horrors of the war was a torment: Weyl, apparently, slept little for weeks.[18] "If civilized Europe were holding back India, for example, it would be comprehensible," observed *Harper's Weekly.* "But for Germans and French, with a whole complex and delicate civilization in common, to be using huge death engines to mow down men and cities, is so unthinkable that we go about in a daze, hoping to awake from the most horrid of nightmares."[19]

These were initial reactions, but the reports that came from the battlefronts during the first year of the war did nothing to mitigate the abhorrence with which most of these men regarded the whole business. In London, Russell witnessed personally the "excruciating sight" of "the poor maimed fellows being carried from the ambulances" and concluded that "war is sheer insanity."[20] White agreed that "the world is mad" and insisted that "there is no such thing as civilized warfare" for "war always is bestial, cruel, insane."[21] After "the most terrible year since the world began," Rowell declared that "all the crimes and all the blunders since Cain slew Abel and Eve ate the forbidden fruit, do not together equal the score of that month of madness, from June 28 to August 1, 1914."[22]

Such extravagant denunciations were somewhat suspect in the offices of the *New Republic,* where Lippmann insisted that "it is not enough to hate war and waste, to launch one unanalyzed passion against another,"[23] and

---

[15] To Alyse Gregory, 25 Aug. 1914, Bourne Papers, box 1, reel 1.

[16] Notebook 3, 2 Aug. 1914, pp. 70–2, R. S. Baker Papers.

[17] *Fresno Republican,* 5 Sept. 1914.

[18] [Brubaker, ed.], *Walter Weyl,* p. 72.

[19] *Harper's Weekly,* 59 (12 Sept. 1914), p. 241.

[20] Diary 2A, 13 Sept. 1914, Russell papers; "The Inside of the European Madhouse: A Narrative," *Pearson's,* 32 (Dec. 1914), p. 733.

[21] *Emporia Gazette,* 10, 15 May 1915.

[22] *Fresno Republican,* 1 July 1915.

[23] "Force and Ideals," *New Republic,* 1 (7 Nov. 1914), p. 7. Authorship of this unsigned editorial is identified in Arthur M. Schlesinger Jr., ed., *Walter Lippmann: Early Writings* (New York, 1970), pp. 3–6.

Croly became impatient with "the invectives of the dogmatic pacifists."
"The voluntary sacrifice by so many million men of the affections, associations and ambitions which make up the stuff of their personal lives," he
wrote in August 1915, "the voluntary acceptance of the certainty of
suffering and the strong probability of death, imposes itself on the imagination and subdues the judgment. Rather silence than a sermon."[24]
Nevertheless, the *New Republic* itself unequivocally condemned war as
"murderous, damned nonsense," "the sum of all villainies," "insane,
brutal, hideous,"[25] and it blamed the belligerent powers when the Turks
resorted to massacres again. "The tortured Armenians are a reminder of
what a price the makers of their war are asking us to pay. By embroiling
the western world in what is essentially a civil war they have let loose
anarchy in all the ends of the earth."[26]

The war and progress

The relapse to barbarism was, indeed, a common theme and one with
obvious implications for pre-war optimism and a belief in progress.
"There is a calamity in this warfare which is more permanently terrible
than any of the surface incidents of the struggle," wrote the Reverend
John Haynes in the *Survey*. "Suddenly, as in the wink of an eye, three
hundred years of progress is cast into the melting-pot. Civilization is all at
once gone, and barbarism come."[27] "We have been led to think that the
red Indian was a savage," Russell observed bitterly. "Well, I'd like to go
to the Rosebud Agency and gather together a band of red Indians to take
to Europe to teach the white man what is civilization."[28]

Even technological development was now seen to be a mixed blessing.
Russell described in graphic detail the contributions of science to warfare –
"poisoned wells, asphyxiating gas bombs that kill 10,000 at once, shrapnel
that sends shell like rain; 'Busy Berthas' that with one shell can raze a stone
building and bury two hundred men underneath . . . ; barbed wire fences
fitted with heavy dynamos so that men charging through, upon cutting the
wires are instantly killed."[29] Rowell pointed out that long-range artillery

[24] "The Meaning of It," *New Republic,* 4 (7 Aug. 1915), p. 11.
[25] *New Republic,* 2 (13 Feb., 20 Mar. 1915), pp. 36–7, 166–7.
[26] Ibid., 4 (9 Oct. 1915), p. 245.
[27] *Survey,* 32 (26 Sept. 1914), p. 629. See also *Independent,* 80 (23 Nov. 1914), p. 267.
[28] "In the Shadow of the Great War," *San Francisco Bulletin,* 30 Oct. 1915.
[29] Ibid.

had dehumanized war and made the infliction of suffering psychologically as well as physically easier, for "there is no sentiment in a parabola and there is no consideration for an enemy who cannot be seen but has to be computed."[30] As the war came to demonstrate the malign potentialities of such inventions as the submarine and the airplane, there seemed to be no escape from Baker's sad conclusion that "we have produced the mechanical tools faster than the spiritual power which enables us to use them."[31]

To conservative critics both at the time and since, the appalling nature of the First World War has seemed to discredit the optimistic assumptions on which pre-war progressivism was based.[32] It certainly induced some defensiveness. "The strong young men are dying in the trenches and the high prophetic hopes of human brotherhood are withering in the pestilential atmosphere of revengeful hate," Devine wrote. "Surely, we who believed this impossible, and still believe it indefensible, must have been living in a fool's paradise."[33] "Hitherto forward-facing, stout-hearted men and women are apologizing to each other for having held higher hopes and more advanced ideals than the stern, hard facts of war seem to have justified," reported Graham Taylor in the *Survey*.[34] The need to reconsider assumptions and commitments was often proclaimed. In a *New Republic* editorial, Bourne self-critically castigated the "mental unpreparedness" that had envisaged mankind evolving inevitably toward social democracy in an industrialized, cosmopolitan world.[35] "One thing is certain," Hapgood declared. "A person whose business it is to formulate ideas about political, economic, spiritual movements, will for many, many years be compelled to re-examine himself and his creed, in view of what humanity is doing with itself in 1915."[36]

None of these men took the challenge presented by the war more seriously than Ray Stannard Baker, who recorded his observations, feel-

---

[30] *Fresno Republican*, 23 Feb. 1915.

[31] Notebook 12, 4 Feb. 1917, pp. 154–5, R. S. Baker Papers. See also *Emporia Gazette*, 27 Nov. 1915.

[32] For example, George Santayana, "Liberalism and Culture," *New Republic*, 4 (4 Sept. 1915), pp. 123–5; Henry F. May, *The End of American Innocence: A Study of the First Years of Our Own Time 1912–1917* (New York, 1959), p. 361.

[33] "Humanity, Security and Honor," *Survey*, 34 (7 Aug. 1915), p. 431.

[34] "World Salvage," *Survey*, 35 (29 Jan. 1916), pp. 525–6.

[35] *New Republic*, 4 (11 Sept. 1915), pp. 143–4. For identification of this unsigned editorial, see Forcey, *Crossroads of Liberalism*, p. 343. See also Weyl, *American World Policies* (New York, 1917), p. 1.

[36] "When Will the War End?", *Harper's Weekly*, 60 (5 June 1915), p. 532.

ings, and thoughts extensively in his notebooks.[37] In May 1914, he had written confidently that "we may take our stand firmly upon this fundamental proposition: that the impulses of men toward good are stronger, more numerous than those toward evil: that the progress of men through the ages has ever been upward."[38] His immediate response when war broke out was that "we are not yet a civilized race."[39] After a year, during which "reading the papers these days it actually seems as though the world has gone stark mad," he confessed that "this war makes one feel his ignorance and impotence."[40] When, in October 1915, he resigned from the *American Magazine,* he drafted a letter to the editor, J. S. Phillips, explaining that "since this war began, it seems to me I've been more unsettled in my own mind than ever before in my life. Every solid thing seems to have gone into the melting pot, things that I've done and thought in the past seem worthless and feeble and the only way out seems to be to get somewhere, somehow, a new orientation, and a new grip on things."[41]

Baker's agony of spirit might well seem to vindicate Henry F. May's conclusion that "perhaps the most important victim of war was practical idealism."[42] However, not many were as deeply affected by the war's implications as Baker, who was in any case at a low point in these years for other reasons.[43] Indeed, the truth is that the Great War, at least during the period of American neutrality, did not produce significant modifications in the political outlook of any of these publicists. Almost invariably, the articles that began with a declaration of the blow dealt to pre-war assumptions concluded on an upbeat note, if sometimes a slightly chastened one. "May it not be that this calamity, like every calamity, will work at last to final and universal good?" asked Holmes. "And when, years hence, the works of civilization are restored and the voice of the social worker is again heard in the land, may it not be that he will see a

---

[37] The evolution of Baker's thinking on the war's implications for progressive assumptions can be traced in the following entries: Notebook 3, pp. 67–72, 85–6, 118–19; Notebook 4, 11–12, 14, 70–4, 56–7; Notebook 5, 75–6, 104–13, 152; Notebook 6, 144–5, 195; Notebook 7, 13–14, 46, 51–4, 74–6, 91, 95, 122–3; Notebook 8, 26; Notebook 9, 2–4, 87, 95; Notebook 10, 120–1, 130–1; Notebook 11, 12–13, 147; Notebook 12, 78–81, R. S. Baker Papers. See also Semonche, *Ray Stannard Baker,* pp. 286–97.

[38] Notebook 2, p. 92, R. S. Baker Papers.

[39] Notebook 3, 2 Aug. 1914, p. 67, ibid.

[40] Notebook 7, 20 Aug., 8 Sept. 1915, pp. 74–91, ibid.

[41] Notebook 7, 8 Sept. 1915, p. 95, ibid. The war was certainly not the only reason for Baker's resignation. See Semonche, *Ray Stannard Baker,* pp. 276–9, and below.

[42] May, *End of American Innocence,* p. 361.

[43] See Semonche, *Ray Stannard Baker,* pp. 258, 276–82.

changed world, wherein his task is easy?"[44] "Whatever its brutal cost in life and blood and spirit, war has thrown a lance on the shield of complacency, of letting things be as they are," Kellogg observed.[45]

The war in Europe did not therefore induce a pessimistic fatalism in these progressives, a sense that human nature was unredeemable, hopes of reform futile in the face of original sin. The reasons why this was so may have been partly circumstantial. Despite the attention they devoted to it, in private letters and journals as well as published articles and books, and notwithstanding their unquestionable feelings of involvement, the war remained for most of these men a secondhand experience and a comparatively distant event. Lippmann may well have been right when he wrote to Graham Wallas that "we are too far away here to dwell long on the human horror of it."[46] Certainly, an impression of remoteness from the realities of the western front is conveyed by the attempts of some to minimize the significance of the war for a belief in progress. In August 1914, White had seen it as "only a passing madness," arguing that "war is cataclysmic, cutting athwart, for the time being, the normal course of the evolution of society."[47] Later, he had found it "one comfort anyway" that "the poor devils whose bodies are torn by ripping bullets or bursting shrapnel have the benefit of scientific surgery."[48] Evidence of moral progress, too, was occasionally discerned even in the attitudes of the belligerents. "Every nation is apologizing for the war," Rowell claimed. "The whole world is now ashamed of most things it is doing" whereas "there was a time when fighting was the only occupation worthy of a gentleman."[49] "There is no evidence that cruelties, outrages and the breaking of oaths has ever provoked so much or so violent recoil as in the last eighteen months," the *Independent* observed. "It is not unwarranted, we think, to see in these moral reactions of the war evidence that the human race really has made progress in other than material ways."[50] Giddings, who had invested heavily in the proposition, concluded that "the pre-

[44] *Survey*, 32 (26 Sept. 1914), p. 630.
[45] Report to annual meeting of Survey Associates, Oct. 1914. Cited in Chambers, *Kellogg*, p. 68. "It is not the fond assurances of fifty years, but the insanities of the hour . . . that are a fatuous delusion," Devine insisted. *Survey*, 34 (7 Aug. 1915), p. 432. See also Graham Taylor, "World Salvage," *Survey*, 35 (29 Jan. 1916), pp. 525–6.
[46] WL to Graham Wallas, 5 Aug. 1915. Lippmann papers, box 33, folder 1244.
[47] *Emporia Gazette*, 25 Aug. 1914.
[48] Ibid., 16 Sept. 1914.
[49] "World Ashamed," *Fresno Republican*, 4 Mar. 1915.
[50] *Independent*, 84 (8 Nov., 4 Oct. 1915), pp. 212–13, 6.

sumption of rational control in human affairs has been foreshortened, but
not painted out."[51]

There was also intellectual justification for the refusal to abandon the
essential elements of the progressive worldview in the face of the European
war. Evil and suffering did not of themselves invalidate progressivism –
on the contrary, its existence had always been the spur – as long as belief
in the possibility of amelioration was retained. Moreover, as we have seen,
these advocates of reform had generally insisted that progress was not
inevitable, but dependent on human effort and the growth of enlightenment. The "mental unpreparedness" of Americans, according to Bourne,
showed that "our background of contemporary Europe" had been "that
most perilous of things – a field where a benevolent destiny was working
itself out unaided." The war, Bourne claimed, tested the reality of the
pragmatism professed by young progressive intellectuals. "We can put
our ideals behind us and turn and worship them or we can put them ahead
of us and struggle towards them. . . . We do not need to surrender. But
we emphatically need to understand."[52] When eventually, after two and a
half years, Baker came to sum up the results of his meditations on the
meaning of the war, his conclusions, for all the difference of idiom, were
very similar to Bourne's. It was not "enough to have the mere lakadaisacal
[*sic*] faith that Good Prevails. That sentimental optimism is as bad as the
sentimental pessimism which washes its hands or mourns feebly of a world
too bad to bother with. There must be more than faith: there must be
stout works!" But "shall we be hopeless and discouraged because the work
is unfinished? Are we not working on it? Are we not doing our best?"[53]

Causes of war – and cures

The war in Europe, then, appalling as it was, did not necessarily discredit
the intellectual premises of pre-war progressivism. Indeed, it could be
seen as confirming them if the war was viewed not so much as a manifesta-

---

[51] "Introduction" to Randolph S. Bourne, ed., *Towards an Enduring Peace: A Symposium of Peace Proposals and Programs, 1914–1916* (New York, n.d.), p. ix.

[52] "Mental Unpreparedness," *New Republic*, 4 (11 Sept. 1915), p. 144. As early as September 1914, Bourne had written, "I find myself bracing against the war . . . , using my energy not in despair or recrimination, but only in an attempt to understand. While the clock of the world has stopped, we can learn many useful things, and at least look forward to the momentous readjust-ment." Bourne to Alyse Gregory, 28 Sept. 1914, Bourne Papers, box 1, reel 1.

[53] Notebook 12, December 1916, pp. 78–81, R. S. Baker Papers.

tion of the "old Adam" in man as a product of the old order in Europe. Such an interpretation came naturally to most Americans, as was indicated by many of the initial reactions to its outbreak. The phenomenon of militarism, and indeed the whole structure of international power politics, was widely regarded as an outgrowth of the essentially feudal social order that characterized the "Old World." To a striking extent, blame for the conflict was at once attached to those at the apex of the social order, the hereditary monarchs themselves. "It is autocracy that is at bay – the whole infamous theory of the divine right of kings that now has the sword at its throat!" declared Creel, while the *Public* called for "vengeance upon the crowned hellions who use men as pawns and nine-pins."[54] Russell traced the effects of intermarriage among royal houses in breeding "this race of lunatics and degenerates" to which "the nations of Europe, with three exceptions, have committed their destinies."[55] In denouncing the "demon dynasts," however, none outdid Franklin Giddings in the *Independent*. "Mad with the lust of power, drunk with their own egotism, the Head Devils have signed their own doom," he prophesied in the first week of the war. "The monarchs must go – *and go they will.*"[56]

In the case of Giddings, as with Russell and Creel, the attack on hereditary monarchy gathered force from partisanship in the European conflict. For these men and many others, the prime responsibility for the war lay with the emperors of the Central Powers, particularly Kaiser Wilhelm II, "this crowned throwback to the Middle Ages," "the War Lord" himself.[57] Nor, of course did one have to be very radical in the American political context to attack an institution repudiated by the United States in 1776, and the outbreak of war in Europe was taken by commentators of various political persuasions to vindicate the republican principle.[58] However, progressives were particularly inclined to empha-

---

[54] Creel, "The Ghastly Swindle," *Harper's Weekly*, 59 (29 Aug. 1914), p. 197; "Judgment Time for 'Crowned Criminals,'" *Public*, 17 (21 Aug. 1914), p. 798.

[55] "This King and Kaiser Business," *Pearson's*, 33 (Jan. 1915), p. 34. Also "As to Making Peace," *New Review*, 3 (Jan. 1915), p. 21.

[56] "Whom the Gods Would Destroy," *Independent*, 79 (10 Aug. 1914), p. 195. Holt thought this editorial "the greatest printed in *The Independent* since I have known it." Holt Papers. The *Independent* regularly reverted to the theme. See *Independent*, 79 (24 Aug. 1914), pp. 259–60; 81 (22 Mar. 1915), pp. 407–9; 87 (4 Sept. 1916), p. 327; 89 (15 Jan., 26 Mar. 1917), pp. 89–90, 523; 96 (23 Nov. 1918), p. 239.

[57] Creel, "The Ghastly Swindle," p. 197. See also "After the War: A Forecast," *Independent*, 79 (24 Aug. 1914), pp. 259–60; Russell, "The Heir of the War Lord," *Cosmopolitan*, 52 (Mar. 1912), pp. 464–8.

[58] See, for example, "The Responsibility for War," *Nation*, 99 (6 Aug. 1914), p. 151; "American Doctrines Not Outworn," *American Review of Reviews*, 50 (Sept. 1914), pp. 268–9.

size the argument that the war was due to the lack of democracy in Europe, though many did not confine their indictment to the German emperor, spreading the blame more widely, both within and between the belligerent countries. Some of those who pointed out that in none of the nations at war had the people been consulted before the decision was taken may well have been moved by a desire to challenge the presumption of German war guilt,[59] but this was certainly not always the case. Russell and Hapgood, for example, were both firmly pro-Ally in their sympathies, yet in England in the early weeks of the war each was impressed by the way the country had been presented with a *fait accompli*. "It is a mighty unpopular war," Russell observed. "It was forced upon the nation without the nation's will, consent or interest" by "a council of ministers appointed by the king," and "there is not the slightest indication that anybody outside of the governing classes gives a hoot about it."[60] "How little the ruling class in some of these kingdoms represent the millions who toil and wait and whose only privilege in great affairs of state is to struggle and starve and die," noted Hapgood.[61] A week later, Hapgood wrote that "nations set about murdering each other at the behest of a few rather stupid men."[62] "In Great Britain, as in Prussia the people do not really rule," explained Howe, as he sought to answer the question, "why war?" "The rule is still in the hands of the old feudal nobility, whose political and economic privileges remain only less sacred than they were in an earlier age." Particularly was this true in the field of foreign policy, where "aristocracy controls the foreign office and enjoys an exclusive place in the diplomatic service."[63]

This traditional American condemnation of the European class system, sometimes focused on the "flunkyism" of professional diplomats,[64] was often supplemented by interpretations of a more modern and cosmopolitan provenance. For several years, socialist publicists had been propounding what Russell called "the standard theory of the unconsumed surplus" as an explanation of imperialism and war,[65] and most of them unhesitatingly applied it to the European conflict. "The reason why we had

---

[59] For example, Samuel Danziger, managing editor of the *Public*. See "Popular Government and War," *Public*, 17 (11 Sept. 1914), p. 866.
[60] Diary 2A, 13 Sept. 1914, Russell Papers; "This King and Kaiser Business," p. 38.
[61] "In London," *Harper's Weekly*, 59 (22 Aug. 1914), p. 177.
[62] "Religion and Guns," *Harper's Weekly*, 59 (29 Aug. 1914), p. 202.
[63] *Why War?* (New York, 1916), pp. 19, 59.
[64] *Public*, 17 (2 Oct. 1914), pp. 938–9.
[65] *Why I Am a Socialist*, pp. 118–20.

this war," Russell stated, was that under capitalism "the working people, who constitute the overwhelming majority of the population, do not receive enough in wages to enable them to buy back the product of their own toil," and therefore industrial nations had been forced into "a ruthless struggle for markets in regions like South America, Africa, the Orient, wherever was still left a country that consumed more than it produced."[66] Walling, however, soon came to feel that the way most Socialists in the belligerent countries rallied to their nation's cause compelled some reconsideration of the assumption that only capitalists had a stake in international economic conflicts. He took issue with the theory of "the surplus," observed that "the chief feature of imperialism is not exports but investments in backward countries," and argued that "the great financial interests . . . are largely internationalist." Characteristically heretical, he concluded that "the economic nationalism of the workers and of the small capitalists, and not the imperialism of the large capitalists, is the chief cause of the present war and is likely to be the sole cause of the next war." Such a perspective gave Walling another stick with which to beat his bête noire, state socialism, but it did not lead him to abandon the view that "this war is an economic conflict" for the control of "certain foreign markets."[67]

The theory that the war had its root in the rivalries generated by capitalist imperialism was by no means confined to socialists, though the nature of the connection was diversely interpreted. Howe, who wrote on the subject extensively, acknowledged his debt to the English radical economist, J. A. Hobson.[68] Like Hobson, Howe attributed imperialism not to the inescapable need of capitalist economies to find export markets for their "surplus" production, but to the political influence of the special interests who profited from investments in underdeveloped countries. Because the "ruling class at home . . . is also the owning and investing class," the doctrine had been established that "the flag follows the inves-

66 "Will You Have Peace or War?", *Pearson's*, 33 (Mar. 1915), pp. 327–30. See also "In the Shadow of the Great War," *San Francisco Bulletin*, 30 Oct. 1915; Spargo speech in Tacoma, Wash., 18 Mar. 1917, Spargo Papers, box 1.

67 "The Remedy: Anti-Nationalism," "A Criticism of Kautsky," *New Review*, 3 (Feb. 1915), pp. 77–83, 101. See also "The Great Illusions," *New Review*, 3 (1 June 1915), pp. 49–50; "Socialists and the War," Address to the Public Forum, New York, June 1915, Walling Papers.

68 "The Flag and the Investor," *New Republic*, 7 (17 June 1916), p. 171. On the distinctive character of Hobson's theory of imperialism, see Peter Clarke, *Liberals and Social Democrats* (Cambridge, England, 1978), pp. 90–9; and Eric Stokes, "Late Nineteenth-Century Colonial Expansion and the Attack on the Theory of Economic Imperialism: A Case of Mistaken Identity?" *Historical Journal*, 12 (June 1969), pp. 285–301.

tor and backs up his private contracts." This had "created the new issues which are responsible for the tension, the suspicions, the imbroglios of recent years," and, abetted by the sinister influence of munitions manufacturers, had given rise to the armed alliances now tearing Europe apart. "The real cause of the war is to be found far back of the summer of 1914; it is to be found in the new economic and financial forces set in motion in the closing years of the last century," Howe concluded. "It is the struggle of high finance bent on the exploitation of weaker peoples that has turned Europe into a human slaughter-house and arrayed 400,000,000 peaceful people against one another in a death struggle."[69]

The *New Republic,* which printed some of his articles, commented editorially that "Mr. Howe's main thesis, that competition for investment opportunities is at bottom responsible for most of the aggression and international strife that have occurred since 1880, will be disputed by hardly anyone who has made a realistic study of recent history."[70] Not only the magisterial tone but also the substance of this remark suggests it was penned by Lippmann, who from the first days of the war had felt that "my own part in this is to understand world-politics."[71] "Feeling at every point how much of a novice I was,"[72] he nonetheless published in 1915 a book analyzing "the stakes of diplomacy." In this he confidently asserted that "out of the clash of imperialist policies modern war arises," though he saw it as being "fought not for specific possessions, but for that diplomatic prestige and leadership which are required to solve all the different problems on one's own terms."[73] Lippmann had had "a long talk" with Hobson in September 1914, but his adherence to "the theory of world exploitation" antedated this and probably owed more to his residual socialism.[74] It was in the Socialist *New Review,* in response to a critic, that he reiterated his views that "if the world consisted of nothing

69 Howe, *Why War* (New York, 1916), pp. 107, 80. vii, viii. See also "Reservoirs of Strife: The Distribution of Wealth in Relation to the Invisible Causes of War," *Survey,* 33 (6 Mar. 1915), pp. 614–15; "Responsibility for War," *Public,* 18 (25 June 1915), pp. 622–3; "The Flag and the Investor," pp. 170–1; "Democracy or Imperialism – The Alternative That Confronts Us," *Annals,* 66 (July 1916), pp. 254–7.

70 *New Republic,* 7 (17 June 1916), p. 161.

71 Diary, 5 Aug. 1914, p. 20, Lippmann Papers. In fact, in *The Promise of American Life* (pp. 260–1), Croly had argued that "colonial expansion by modern national states is to be regarded, not as a cause of war, but as a safety-valve against war."

72 WL to Graham Wallas, 18 Dec. 1915, Lippmann Papers, box 33, folder 1244.

73 *The Stakes of Diplomacy* (New York, 1915), pp. 166, 108.

74 Some days before his talk with Hobson, Lippmann had, in conversation with Alfred Zimmern, "argued the theory of world exploitation as against his exaggerated racialism and nationalism." Diary, 10, 14 Sept. 1914, pp. 24–5, Lippmann papers.

but Germany and France, rivalry would disappear as it has between New York and New Jersey. It is the prizes outside of both Germany and France which set them at each other's throats."[75] Lippmann's *New Republic* colleague, Weyl, also argued that it was "the desire for imperialistic expansion" that led to "an irrepressible conflict between England and Germany, in short, to a world war," although his own analysis of the economic motive for imperialism stressed the simple need for resources of food and raw materials from the tropics at least as much as the desire for export markets and investment income. "Imperialism from an economic point of view," he bluntly asserted, "is in the main a foreign political control to make the 'niggers' work."[76]

Although few devoted as much attention to the subject as Howe, Lippmann, and Weyl, and most were surely not attuned to the different economic interpretations of imperialism, the general idea that, as Steffens put it, the war "was caused and directed by the conflicts of the various imperial expansions" became widely current in progressive circles.[77] In theoretical terms, there was clearly a gulf between such explanations of the war and those that attributed it to the persistent power of feudal institutions and attitudes but, as we have seen, writers like Russell and Howe cheerfully combined them. "Commercialism has found in the monarchical idea its powerful bulwark and chief asset," Russell declared.[78] The conflation of these rather different analyses perhaps indicates that the main concern of progressive publicists was to emphasize that the war was caused by remediable social institutions rather than by the unregenerate character of common humanity. "It matters little whether militarism, monarchism or commercialism is most to blame," The *Independent* observed. "The cardinal fact never to be forgotten is this: The war was precipitated by a handful of captains, kings and cabinet officers. It was not a people's war."[79] "There is no evidence that the millions of small

[75] *New Review*, 4 (1 Jan. 1916), pp. 21–2. See also WL to Professor Amos, 24 July 1916, Lippmann Papers, box 2, folder 58.

[76] *American World Policies*, pp. 115, 85–95. Quotation on p. 85.

[77] Steffens, *Autobiography*, pp. 712–13. See also Steffens to Mrs. J. James Hollister, 1 July 1916, *Letters*, 1, pp. 374–5; "President Wilson's Mexican Policy" [1916], Steffens Papers, reel 9; *Public*, 17 (16 Oct. 1914), pp. 993–4; Amos Pinchot, "American Militarism," *Masses*, 6 (Jan. 1915), p. 9; Giddings, "Introduction" to Bourne, ed., *Towards an Enduring Peace*, p. viii; Kellogg, "A Bill of Particulars: Items in an International Policy for America," *Nation*, 103 (3 Aug. 1916), sec. 2, p. 1.

[78] "This King and Kaiser Business," p. 36. See also Howe, *Why War*, p. 19.

[79] *Independent*, 87 (31 July 1916), p. 143. See also *Fresno Republican*, 31 Jan. 1915; *Public*, 17 (16 Oct. 1914), pp. 993–4.

agriculturists wanted war. Nor is there any evidence that the masses of industrial workers, organized or unorganized, wanted it," the *New Republic* reminded its readers in August 1915. "The fomenters of war were the elite – the military officers, journalists, authors, politicians, lawyers and the gilded youth who had emptied the cup of civil enjoyment and yearned for primitive emotions: a small minority, but a minority including all who govern and command, and many who write and agitate."[80] "The indictment is against the ruling classes, not against the people," Howe insisted.[81]

This perspective led naturally to the hope that the indictment would be pressed. Although some of these publicists expressed the time-honored view that the desire to avert domestic discontent had provided one motive for the war,[82] this was not apparently incompatible with the expectation that it would discredit existing regimes. Several of the earliest comments, most of which not only held the governments of the Central Powers primarily responsible but anticipated their defeat, saw here what *Harper's Weekly* called "the one star of hope that hangs on the smoke blackened horizon."[83] "If the war leads to a general overthrow of governments by peoples, may it not be worth the price?" asked Walling, who later observed that "if governments are disorganized and revolutions begin, they may go far. Socialists have waited impatiently for just such a day as this."[84] For Walling, as for such other fierce opponents of the German regime as Giddings and Russell, the prospect of revolution was worth the prolongation of the war,[85] but it also beguiled those who viewed the European conflict more impartially. "Before this war is through all western Europe may be wrestling to shake dynastic militarism from the shoulders of the common life," Kellogg prophesied.[86] It was on the "theory . . . that the inevitable war would bring on the inevitable revolution"

[80] *New Republic*, 4 (7 Aug. 1915), p. 3.
[81] *Why War*, p. xi.
[82] Baker, Notebook 3, (2 Aug. 1914), pp. 67–70, R. S. Baker Papers; *Public*, 17 (28 August 1914), p. 817; Giddings to Kellogg, 13 Feb. 1915, Kellogg Papers, folder 308; Weyl, *American World Policies*, p. 137; *Independent*, 89 (26 Mar. 1917), p. 523.
[83] *Harper's Weekly*, 59 (22 Aug. 1914), p. 169. See also *Independent*, 79 (24 Aug. 1914), pp. 259–60; Creel, "The Ghastly Swindle," p. 197; *Harper's Weekly*, 60 (2 Jan. 1915), p. 1.
[84] "British and American Socialists on the War," *New Review*, 2 (Sept. 1914), p. 512; "The Real Causes of the War," *Harper's Weekly*, 59 (10 Oct. 1914), p. 347.
[85] Giddings to Kellogg, 13 Feb. 1915; Russell, "As to Making Peace," *New Review*, 3 (Jan. 1915), pp. 20–2; Walling, "Nationalism and State Socialism," *Publications of the American Sociological Society*, 10 (1915), p. 90.
[86] "Statement before U.S. Commission on Industrial Relations, 1915," p. 2, Kellogg Papers.

that in late 1914 Steffens went to Mexico to study the phenomenon more closely.[87]

"My theory was false, of course," Steffens rather surprisingly remarked in his *Autobiography*.[88] Certainly in the early years of the war, as the *New Republic* observed, Europe seemed to furnish "many indigestible facts for pacifist democrats."[89] To begin with, there was the evidence of popular enthusiasm for the war in most of the belligerent countries. "It made me very blue," Bourne had written from Dresden in July 1914, "to see the crowd of youths parading the streets long after midnight the other night, cheering for Austria and the war and singing 'Die Wacht am Rhein.' "[90] The virtually complete collapse of Socialist opposition to the war was a source of surprise and distress to many outside the ranks of the party, as Spargo noted with some satisfaction.[91] "If anything is certain about the war of 1914, it is that the impulse came from the peoples," Weyl concluded gloomily in November. "Each nation was willing to fight because it believed that it fought in self-defense."[92] Yet even this interpretation came under pressure the following summer when Italy, unthreatened, entered the war for gain and apparently in response to popular demand. "It looks as if the people were forcing a reluctant government," Russell noted in his diary at the time. "This doesn't jibe well with the previously entertained notions that the common people never want war and the capitalistic rulers always force war upon them."[93] "At the very moment when the world is being furnished with the most convincing of all demonstrations of the cost of the war, nations which have hitherto remained neutral are deliberately deciding to participate," the *New Republic* commented as Greece seemed about to follow Italy. "Secret diplomacy has not

[87] *Autobiography*, pp. 712–13; Ella Winter and Herbert Shapiro, eds., *The World of Lincoln Steffens* (New York, 1962), p. 1.
[88] *Autobiography*, p. 712.
[89] *New Republic*, 3 (19 June 1915), p. 159.
[90] RSB to Alyse Gregory, 30 July 1914, Bourne Papers, box 1, reel 1.
[91] See, for example, *Survey*, 32 (5 Sept. 1914), p. 561; *Public*, 17 (11 Sept, 27 Nov. 1914), pp. 867, 1130; *Independent*, 80 (21 Dec. 1914), pp. 468–9; *New Republic*, 4 (11 Sept. 1915), pp. 143–4. "Nobody seems to be disappointed at the failure of organized religion to prevent the war," Spargo observed. "On the other hand, men did expect great things of the Socialist movement." "Socialism and the War," *Ford Hall Folks*, vol. 3, no. 23 (21 Mar. 1915), Spargo Papers, box 1.
[92] *New Republic*, 1 (14 Nov. 1914), p. 25.
[93] Diary no. 3, 18 May 1915, Russell Papers. See also *Independent*, 82 (31 May 1915), p. 339. This was, of course, a misapprehension of the process by which Italy entered the war, which involved negotiations with both sides before the secret treaty of London with the Allies was signed in April 1915, and also complex internal political divisions. See Christopher Seton-Watson, *Italy from Liberalism to Fascism 1870–1925*, (London, 1967), pp. 413–50.

involved them in war, the consultation of public opinion has not kept them out."[94] Nor did the experience of war appear to produce the expected disillusionment and rebelliousness. Although simultaneous strikes in Britain's coal mines and the Krupps's munition plants in the summer of 1915 were seized on by White as a hopeful portent, candid observers felt increasingly forced to accept the *New Republic*'s verdict that "this is a people's war surely enough."[95] "There is no cleavage of sentiment between the German people and its rulers," the editors noted in October. "If any change has taken place, it is in the direction of deeper devotion to the imperial house and a revived toleration of the landed aristocracy."[96]

Such conclusions impelled reconsideration of the appeal of nationalism, and some attempts were made to explain the bellicosity of public opinion. Both Lippmann and Weyl stressed the basic nature of group consciousness and the important role of fear. "The fierce power of national feeling is due to the fact that it rises from the deepest sources of our being," Lippmann concluded. "When war breaks out, or threatening uncertainty, there is a swift retreat into our own origins. We become intensely aware of the earliest things with which we were associated; we love the security where we were born, we huddle to the people with whom we played as children."[97] For Croly, of course, it was not a surprise but a vindication of his pre-war views that "the national bond has proved to be infinitely stronger than that of church, class, economic interest, or cosmopolitan feeling."[98]

Taxed by a reader with the apparent contradiction between such judgments and the attribution of war to an "elite," the *New Republic* responded that "this is a people's war surely enough, but it is equally certain that the people had no hand in bringing it about."[99] Yet this distinction, which was quite commonly made,[100] did not take any account of the influence in times of crisis of the bellicose public opinion that was commented on so widely in the summer of 1914 and in Italy in 1915, and that Lippmann

94 *New Republic*, 3 (19 June 1915), p. 159.
95 *Emporia Gazette*, 16 July 1915; *New Republic*, 4 (21 Aug. 1915), p. 75.
96 *New Republic*, 4 (30 Oct. 1915), p. 324. See also Weyl, *American World Policies*, p. 141.
97 "Patriotism in the Rough," *New Republic*, 4 (16 Oct. 1915), pp. 277–9. This article was a slightly abbreviated form of what was later published as Chapter 5 of *The Stakes of Diplomacy*. See also Weyl, "Self-Defense and Self-Delusion," *New Republic*, 1 (14 Nov. 1914), pp. 25–6; *American World Policies*, pp. 111–15.
98 *New Republic*, 2 (13 Mar. 1915), pp. 142–3. See *The Promise of American Life*, especially pp. 142–3.
99 *New Republic*, 4 (21 Aug. 1915), p. 75.
100 See, for example, *Public*, 17 (11 Sept. 1914), pp. 867–8; Howe, "Reservoirs of Strife," *Survey*, 33 (6 Mar. 1915), p. 614.

claimed to discern in the United States itself during the *Lusitania* crisis. [101] The recourse to it was one of several indications that the conviction that, in Russell's words, "democracy means peace" was deep and persistent. [102] Lippmann himself reminded his readers that democracy involved more than merely majority rule. "Because a whole people clamors for a war and gets it, there is no ground for calling the war democratic," he insisted. "One might as well call the subjection of negroes democratic because the whole white South desires it." In reality "democracy is a meaningless word unless it signifies that differences of opinion have been expressed, represented, and even satisfied in the decision." [103] The *Lusitania* crisis set Lippmann to brooding about the problem of public opinion and foreign policy, which in its various aspects was to be for him a lasting preoccupation. [104] He concluded that there was a fundamental difference "between the psychology of domestic and of foreign politics" simply because "in domestic affairs we live with and know the men who disagree with us; in foreign affairs the opposition lives behind a frontier, and probably speaks a different language." As a result, "the average man meets almost nobody who disagrees with him" and so his opinions become more extreme and dogmatic, since "opposition is about the only incentive we have to practice reason and tolerance." The situation was exacerbated by newspapers, whose taste for sensationalism and temptation to appeal to "ignorance and distrust of the alien" made them "in the main instruments of irritation between peoples." [105] Nevertheless, at this time Lippmann retained the belief, common among progressives, that the answer to these problems lay in the extension of publicity and democratic control of foreign policy. [106]

Nor did the hope of popular revolutions in Europe easily die. In the same article in which it noted the patriotic solidarity of the German people, the

---

[101] In *The Stakes of Diplomacy*, Lippmann asserted that in May 1915 "it would have been difficult to find a person in the country anxious for peace who didn't also wish Congress to stay at home," so "to our surprise and humiliation some of us discovered that our desire for peace and our faith in democratic institutions conflicted" (pp. 16, 25). Lippmann seems to have misjudged the strength of antiwar feeling in Congress. See Arthur S. Link, *Wilson: The Struggle for Neutrality, 1914–1915* (Princeton, N.J., 1960), pp. 416–17, 439.

[102] Russell, "Who Made This War?" *Pearson's*, 32 (Nov. 1914), p. 516.

[103] *Stakes of Diplomacy*, pp. 47–8.

[104] Diary, 20 May 1915, pp. 31–5, Lippmann papers.

[105] *Stakes of Diplomacy*, pp. 50–1, 54–7.

[106] Ibid., pp. 196–204. To counter ignorance and misrepresentation, Steffens proposed a "small but popular" convention of representatives from California and Japan to "thrash out" the immigration issue. "California and the Japanese," *Collier's*, 57 (25 Mar. 1916), pp. 5–6, 32–36. See also Baker Notebook 3, Nov. 1914, pp. 118–19, Notebook 5, 1915, pp. 3–4, R. S. Baker papers; Russell, "This King and Kaiser Busines," p. 41; *Survey*, 33 (6 Mar. 1915), p. 631; *Emporia Gazette*, 16 July 1915; *Fresno Republican*, 25 Nov. 1915; Howe, *Why War*, pp. 340–1.

New Republic pointed out that the war was being largely financed through the issue of bonds but that, in due course, "the necessity of payment is inevitable; the government can only mitigate the resultant bitterness through granting the respective classes a fair share in determining the distribution of burdens. But this means constitutional reform. Barring the miracle of colossal military indemnities, autocratic government in Germany is doomed. Its downfall is written in the skies."[107] Nor would such difficulties be confined to Germany, the editors predicted on other occasions, for "in every country of Europe" the war was creating a class of privileged bondholders whose profits at a time of others' suffering could hardly fail to bring into question the whole institution of private property.[108] Once the excitement of war passed away, "all over Europe the people will be counting the cost" in human as well as material terms and "the result can hardly fail to be a measure of revolution".[109] This anticipation was widely shared. In the *Independent*, Holt pictured the scene dramatically: "First a murmur, then a rumble, then a roar, then – the Revolution, peaceful or bloody; and all the emperors and kings, all the autocrats and aristocrats, go."[110]

The durability of this basic view – that the war in Europe was fundamentally the product of an inegalitarian and undemocratic social order which would in the long run be weakened by it – doubtless owed much to the fact that it was congruent with the values and assumptions of pre-war progressivism. The analogy between domestic and international politics was drawn by several of these publicists. "Surplus wealth seeking privileges in foreign lands is the proximate cause of the war just as wealth seeking monopoly profits is the cause of the civil conflicts that have involved our cities and states," Howe declared.[111] The "essence of corrupt politics is control by selfish interests, big business," Baker noted in his diary, "and the remedies as we see clearly now after years of agitation is [*sic*] a more direct control by the people – more genuine self-government. The same is true in the Great World: only the trouble there is complicated by the presence of Royalty: the Big Political bosses of the Earth. Remedy

107 *New Republic*, 4 (30 Oct. 1915), pp. 324–6.
108 Ibid., 5 (27 Nov. 1915), pp. 82–4.
109 Ibid., 6 (26 Feb. 1916), p. 104.
110 *Independent*, 83 (20 Sept. 1915), p. 381. This unsigned editorial is attributed to Holt in the Holt Papers. See also Hapgood, "The Great Settlement," *Harper's Weekly*, 59 (12 Sept. 1914), p. 250; Howe, *Why War*, p. 333; Steffens, *Autobiography*, p. 713.
111 Howe, *Why War*, p. viii, also pp. 307–8. Steffens made the same comparison. See "Making Friends with Mexico," *Collier's*, 58 (25 Nov. 1916), pp. 6, 23; *Autobiography*, p. 713.

is the same: getting back to peoples."[112] "The simple truth," Weyl concluded, was "that the enemy of peace lies always this side of the frontier."[113]

This being so, it followed that the road to peace was in large part a familiar one to domestic reformers. From the earliest days of the war, it had been argued that measures ranging from free trade to woman suffrage would reduce the likelihood of international conflict,[114] but the central issues ramained the extension of democracy and the equalization of wealth. Contrasting France, Switzerland, Holland, and the Scandinavian countries on the one hand with Russia, Germany, Austria-Hungary, and Great Britain on the other, Howe claimed that "the countries of widely distributed wealth are the peaceful countries; the militarist countries are those in which the aristocracy still owns the land and wealth of the nation." Consequently, "no single measure would do more to promote peace and disarmament than the placing of taxes on wealth, incomes, and inheritances, so that the cost would be felt directly by the classes that rule in the warring nations of the world."[115] Weyl, too, called for higher, "sharply graduated," taxes, arguing that economic inequality led to imperialism as capital that could not be profitably absorbed by industries manufacturing for the home market sought opportunities abroad. It followed that "the demand of the workman for higher wages, shorter hours and better conditions is, whether the wage-earner knows it or not, a demand for international peace." Moreover, Weyl thought, a rising standard of living might psychologically "immunize" the population against jingoism. "A device, familiar to certain statesmen, is to divert the people's minds from domestic affairs by arousing animosity against the foreigner. Is it impossible to allay hatred of the foreigner by concentrating interest on home concerns?"[116] Lippmann traced a similar connection between social welfare and international peace when he suggested that "human life will become valuable as we invest in it. The child that is

---

[112] Notebook 5, 1915, pp. 3–4, R. S. Baker Papers. See also Lippmann, *Stakes of Diplomacy*, p. 198.

[113] "Self-Defense and Self-Delusion," *New Republic*, 1 (14 Nov. 1914), p. 26.

[114] *Independent*, 79 (17 Aug. 1914), p. 228; *Public*, 17 (21 Aug. 1914), pp. 793–4; *Survey*, 35 (6 Nov. 1915), pp. 148–50; *Harper's Weekly*, 61 (4 Dec. 1915), pp. 548–51. The *Public* claimed on one occasion that "were such conditions established in any country as would follow complete application of the Singletax no other policy would need to be thought of." *Public*, 17 (20 Nov. 1914), p. 1106.

[115] *Why War*, pp. 300–1, 307–8. See also "Reservoirs of Strife," *Survey*, 33 (6 Mar. 1915), pp. 614–15; "Responsibility for War," *Public*, 18 (25 June 1915), p. 623; *Public*, 17 (4 Dec. 1914), pp. 1153–4.

[116] *American World Policies*, chap. 14, at pp. 192, 188, 193.

worth bearing, nursing, tending and rearing, worth educating, worth making happy, worth building good schools and laying out playgrounds for, worth all the subtle effort of modern educational science, is becoming too valuable for the food of cannon. . . . Just so far as we can induce the state to sink money and attention in human beings, by just so much do we insure ourselves against idle destruction."[117] "Peace is a product of rational social relations and conditions," concluded Devine.[118]

War and reform

If the need for peace provided a further reason for progressive reform, so, too, did the course of the war. For, as we have seen, most of these publicists had become accustomed to arguing their case in terms of efficiency as well as other values, and in an intellectual climate in which a vulgarized Darwinism constituted a pervasive element it was natural to see wartime Europe as an evolutionary jungle wherein various methods of social organization were proving their comparative fitness to survive.[119] To Americans, the most prominent antagonists seemed to be Germany and Great Britain, and the general impression was soon formed that Germany, engaged with three powerful enemies, was faring remarkably well, while Britain was doing rather badly. "England has proved nothing but a house of cards," Russell commented scornfully, having noted that ten months after the outbreak of war her armies held little more than a twentieth of the length of the western front.[120] Her performance had been "disappointingly inefficient," the more sympathetic *Harper's Weekly* admitted.[121]

Russell, who spent several of the early months of the war in London, had no doubt about the causes of the British failure. The empire was paying the price of the class system and the policy of laissez-faire. Watching the drilling of new recruits in September 1914, he had been struck by

---

[117] "Life is Cheap," *New Republic*, 1 (19 Dec. 1914), p. 13.

[118] "Through Good Will to Peace," *Survey*, 35 (18 Dec. 1915), p. 335. For further comment along these lines, see *Public*, 17 (4 Sept., 16 Oct. 1914), pp. 842–3, 993–4, and 18 (11 June 1915), pp. 563–4; Russell, "Some Obscured Lessons of the War," *Pearson's*, 33 (Feb. 1915), pp. 164–6, 171.

[119] Unsurprisingly, it was Giddings who made this point explicitly. See "Leadership Versus Lordship," *Independent*, 79 (14 Sept. 1914), p. 363. This unsigned editorial is attributed to Giddings in the Giddings Papers.

[120] "In the Shadow of the Great War"; "Why England Falls Down," *Pearson's*, 34 (Aug. 1915), pp. 210–19.

[121] *Harper's Weekly*, 61 (25 Sept. 1915), p. 289.

the difference in height between the officers and the troops and by the poor appearance of the latter: "the dull eyes, the open mouths that seem ready to drool, the vacant expression, the stigmata of the slum – terrible sight." These "scarecrows and hollow chests" were "the results of the system that builds slums and produces fat-souled millionaires."[122] Nor was the quantity of these recruits any more impressive than their quality for "the masses have no interest in the war," considering it "a toff's war."[123] It was hardly surprising that British workers were lacking in a sense of patriotic identification: "[T]heir government had done nothing for them, why should they do anything for their government?"[124] In articles and speeches on his return to America, Russell drove home the moral that England's "real traitors have been her honored citizens that have drawn profits from the existing system; her best soldiers have been those that have stood up and denounced that system."[125]

Such an account of the reasons for Britain's difficulties accorded not only with the ideological presuppositions of these progressive publicists but with the impressions several of them had formed in the pre-war period. While "Europe is in a real ferment," Howe had reported to Steffens in 1909, "nobody can tell what is going to happen in England. The whole nation is so caste ridden it loves its crooked and imbecile nobility."[126] Earlier Howe had written that "everywhere in Great Britain there are symptoms of decay" as a result of "the abuses of privilege which centuries of feudal tradition has engrafted upon the people."[127] Croly, too, had concluded that "the diminished economic vitality of England must be partly traced to her tradition of political and social subserviency, which serves to rob both the ordinary and the exceptional Englishmen of energy and efficiency." This, he suggested, was the price of a nonrevolutionary history, for in the accommodation between the aristocracy and the middle classes, "each of them sacrificed the principle upon which the vitality of its action as a class depended, while both of them combined to impose subordination on the mass of the people." "Englishmen have, it is true, always remained faithful to their dominant political idea – the idea of freedom," he conceded, but "the English political and economic system is precisely an example of the ultimate disadvantage of basing national

---

[122] Diary 2A, 12 Sept. 1914, Russell Papers.
[123] Diary 2B, 15 Sept. 1914, and Diary 3, 24 May 1915, Russell Papers.
[124] "No More Foes Without – And None Within," *Pearson's*, 33 (June 1915), p. 694.
[125] "Why England Falls Down," p. 214.
[126] Howe to Steffens, 22 July [1909], Steffens Papers, reel 2.
[127] *The British City*, pp. 303, 300.

cohesion upon the application of such a limited principle."[128] These views were emphatically shared by Croly's young associate, Bourne, who after "three months of England" had felt profoundly alienated from "Anglo-Saxon civilization."[129] Reviewing Robert Tressall's *The Ragged-Trousered Philanthropists,* he wrote savagely that "England . . . has failed to secure for more than a minority of her people anything more than a filthy caricature of human life. Up through the beauty of park and palace rises the stench of proletarian poverty."[130]

It is thus not surprising that the *New Republic* regarded the failures of the British war effort as "retribution." "To their dismay," the editors wrote in July 1915, "the English are discovering that a business anarchy which never served any purpose, which was simply an individual struggle of caprice, habit, accident, privilege and speculation, cannot suddenly be transformed into an organization national in scope to serve a definite end."[131] A few months later, they attributed "the ill-success which has attended British military operations" to "too much confidence in the well-intentioned, well-born and well-dressed amateur."[132] This diagnosis was endorsed by the *Independent,* which cited British critics such as H. G. Wells for the judgment that "the officers corps had come to be regarded in England as a sort of social club for the sons of the rich and titled classes," and concluded that "the English have, in fact, taken altogether too much content in their habit of 'blundering thru.'"[133]

By contrast, *Harper's Weekly* noted in September 1915, "the Teutons have done marvels."[134] It would, of course, have been possible to attribute this success to the militarist culture that Russell had found so offensive in Wilhelmine Germany,[135] or to the advantages in war of an authoritarian regime. Weyl did suggest that "the startling capacity shown by the semi-autocratic government of Germany has been a shock and a challenge to more easy-going nations laboring with democratic machinery,"[136] but for the most part more congenial lessons were drawn.

---

128 *Promise of American Life,* pp. 230–9 at 236, 238, 238–9.
129 RSB to Edward Murray, 26 Dec. 1913, Bourne Papers, box 1, reel 1. See also to Mary Messer, 28 Dec. 1913, ibid.
130 *New Republic,* 1 (14 Nov. 1914), p. 25.
131 "Retribution," *New Republic,* 3 (3 July 1915), pp. 215–16.
132 *New Republic,* 5 (20 Nov. 1915), p. 54.
133 *Independent,* 84 (27, 13 Dec. 1915), pp. 504, 419.
134 *Harper's Weekly,* 61 (25 Sept. 1915), p. 289.
135 *Bare Hands and Stone Walls,* pp. 256–8.
136 "The Average Voter," *Century,* 90 (Oct. 1915), p. 901. Stoughton Cooley in the *Public* also attributed early German success to the initial advantages of an autocratic government but

"By far the most important part of preparedness for war is preparedness for peace as well," Giddings insisted in an *Independent* editorial. "The amazing strength that Germany has shown since the present war began" was a tribute to her conservation of natural resources and her educational and welfare systems.[137] Here again, the ground for such an interpretation had been laid by pre-war praise of these aspects of German life. The role of the state in the economy, the system of social insurance, and the character of municipal government had been held up as models by many American reformers. To Croly, the success of "Bismarck's whole scheme of national industrial organization" had furnished a telling argument against the economic rationale of laissez-faire.[138] "Eighteen months ago," recalled one writer in the *New Republic* in October 1915, "Germany was to the American state socialist what free America had been to the European liberal in the early nineteenth century – a country where the heart's desire had been enacted into law, a country where labor won comfort and security, where privileges and obligations were held in true correlation."[139] This was in a review of a book by Howe, which, after describing the wide measure of public ownership and the welfare, educational, and taxation systems, concluded that "Germany differs from other leading countries in the thought that has been given to the distribution as well as the production of wealth" and that "the experience of Germany disproves many of the arguments against the possibility of a socialist state."[140]

Howe had conceived and written most of *Socialized Germany* before the war, but when he sent a copy to Colonel House in September 1915 he noted that "it explains the efficiency of Germany at war."[141] "Two divergent ideas of the state have come into conflict in the present European war," he wrote publicly a few weeks later. "Confronting one another on the battle line are socialized Germany and individualistic England: the countries of the world which best exemplify the philosophy of state in-

expressed faith that British reliance on individualism would prove itself in the long run. "British Blundering," *Public*, 17 (20 Nov. 1914), p. 1108.

[137] "A Fundamental Preparedness," *Independent*, 83 (21 July 1915), p. 41. Authorship of this unsigned editorial is attributed in the Giddings Papers. See also Giddings, "The Larger Meanings of the War," *Survey*, 33 (7 Nov. 1914), pp. 143–4; *Independent*, 80 (30 Nov. 1914), pp. 305–6; *New Republic*, 4 (30 Oct. 1915), p. 323.

[138] *Promise of American Life*, pp. 249–51.

[139] *New Republic*, 4 (30 Oct. 1915), p. 343.

[140] Howe, *Socialized Germany*, pp. 324–5 and passim.

[141] Howe to House, 20 Sept. 1915, E. M. House Papers. During his visit in 1909, Howe had copiously reported "the enthusiasm one feels for the way the Germans do things." Howe to Steffens, 18 May 1909, 22 July [1909], Steffens Papers, reel 2.

terest in its people on the one hand, and of *laissez-faire,* 'every man for himself, and the devil take the hindmost' on the other. . . . Fifteen months of struggle have demonstrated the strength of the one, and the weakness of the other."[142] This argument infuriated Walling, whose hostility to state socialism was matched only by his yearning for German defeat,[143] but it was widely echoed among these publicists. "The one thing that is keeping Germany on the war map today, with civilization practically united against her," White explained to his Kansas readers, "is the fact that for the fifty years last past Germany has followed a consistent program which has made the living standard of the poor higher and has developed strong hard men to stand the impact of war."[144] The German people were prepared psychologically as well as physically to meet the sacrifices demanded by war, Weyl suggested, since "a policy which taxes the rich for the benefit of the poor establishes a certain unity in the commonwealth."[145] Even the pacifist-inclined were prepared to praise what Kellogg called "those deep-reaching policies for developing economic and human strength which, since the Franco-Prussian War, have fitted the Teutonic peoples to withstand all Europe in arms against them."[146] Amos Pinchot, too, recommended Howe's book and held up Bismarck as a model.[147] Nor did one have to sympathize with the German cause to concede that, in Baker's words, "Germany's method excellent if the end is wrong."[148] Indeed, Lippmann felt that "it is just this internal excellence of Germany which makes Belgium and the Lusitania unbearable outrages. . . . In some ways the worst effect of Germany's behavior has been to associate technical ability and effective national organization with heartlessness, with military vanity, and an imperious temper."[149]

The view that state socialism provided the key to Germany's military

---

[142] "Socialized Germany," *Pearson's,* 35 (Jan. 1916), p. 2.

[143] Walling perhaps struck home when he inquired "Is not the recommending of state-socialism as a means of achieving militaristic efficiency a strange position for a pacifist like Mr. Howe?" "The German Paradise," *Masses,* 8 (June 1916), p. 20. Walling's own explanation for Germany's success both in war and in industrial competition was "the great degree of parasitical wealth, idleness, and inherited control of industry which we see in the western European countries when compared with Germany." See "Nationalism and State Socialism," pp. 84–5.

[144] *Emporia Gazette,* 8 Apr. 1915.

[145] *American World Policies,* p. 143.

[146] Kellogg, "A Bill of Particulars," *Nation,* 103 (3 Aug. 1916), sec. 2, p. 1.

[147] AP to Ruth Hapgood, 4 Nov. 1915, Amos Pinchot Papers, box 22; "Preparedness," *Public,* 19 (4 Feb. 1916), pp. 110–11.

[148] Notebook 6, pp. 131–3, R. S. Baker Papers.

[149] *New Republic,* 6 (11 Mar. 1916), p. 158.

efficiency seemed to receive confirmation from what the *New Republic* called "the landslide into collectivism" in the belligerent countries.[150] "During the present war the nations that most hate socialism have in extraordinary ways adopted socialistic measures in both agriculture and manufactures," William Hayes Ward observed in the *Independent*.[151] Again, it was the British experience about which Americans were best informed and which most interested them. As early as September 1914, Graham Taylor in the *Survey* hailed the extension of government authority in the fields of insurance, requisitioning, and price-fixing and the vast increase of public spending as "the most constructive, or reconstructive, legislation ever enacted in any one week throughout the long history of the British Parliament."[152] It was the egalitarian implications of such measures that were most unequivocally welcomed, and progressive journals, particularly the *New Republic* and the *Survey,* printed several encouraging reports on the rise in the status of labor in wartime Britain.[153] "England really being disciplined!" noted Baker gleefully, as he stuck into his journal a clipping from the *New York Times* on the damage the war had done to the class system.[154] The most striking development, however, was the grant to the government of sweeping powers over the country's financial resources and economic life under the Defence of the Realm Acts. Such legislation "ten months ago would have been considered revolutionary," the *New Republic* observed, but "the government by assuming these additional functions has unquestionably become more socialized."[155] "War does immeasurable harm," *Harper's Weekly* commented, but this might be "a corresponding good."[156] "At a single stroke," Howe concluded, "a condition has been created beyond the dreams of socialism for many years to come."[157]

The Defence of the Realm Act has passed into popular memory more for its restrictions on personal freedom than as a milestone on the road to social democracy,[158] and American critics of collectivism naturally em-

[150] Ibid., 2 (10 Apr. 1915), pp. 249–50.
[151] *Independent,* 82 (28 June 1915), pp. 525–6.
[152] "Social Measures Prompted by the War," *Survey,* 32 (12 Sept. 1914), pp. 587–8.
[153] For example, *New Republic,* 2 (27 Mar. 1915), pp. 205–7; 4 (2 Oct. 1915), pp. 227–8; 7 (27 May 1916), pp. 75–7. Also *Survey,* 33 (6 Feb. 1915), pp. 503–4; 34 (3 Apr. 1915), pp. 1–2; 36 (30 Sept. 1916), pp. 638–9. See also Arthur Gleason, "The Social Revolution in England," *Century,* 93 (Feb. 1917), pp. 565–72.
[154] Notebook 7, Aug. 1915, pp. 55–7, R. S. Baker Papers.
[155] *New Republic,* 2 (10 Apr. 1915), p. 255.
[156] *Harper's Weekly,* 61 (3 July 1915), p. 3.
[157] "Immigration after the War," *Scribner's,* 58 (Nov. 1915), pp. 635–9 at 636.
[158] According to A. J. P. Taylor, "'Dora,' an elderly lady, became the symbol of restriction." *English History 1914–1945* (Oxford, 1965), p. 18n.

phasized the unattractive features of what the *Nation* called "this whole government regimentation in the countries at war." Not only had labor been directed and businessmen bullied, but bureaucratic management had given rise to "great waste and extravagance, and, in some instances, corruption." Fortunately it could be seen as a temporary evil like martial law, for, with the return of peace, "the old aspirations of the free spirit of the citizen will certainly reassert themselves."[159] The *Nation* in these years was to be numbered among the enemies of progressivism,[160] but its advocates, too, were quick to point out that "war socialism" by no means represented their ideal. "Though war shatters many theories like 'laissez-faire,' it places undisputed power in the hands of the ruling castes," the *New Republic* reminded its readers in April 1915, as it warned that democratic collectivism could not be imposed from above but would have to grow out of the peacetime cooperation of people pursuing various purposes.[161] Amos Pinchot had already concluded that "England is none too intelligent in abandoning to a great extent the idea of popular democratic co-operation."[162] Nor, of course, did German state socialism constitute any less ambiguous a model. A review of *Socialized Germany* in the *Survey* stated there were "serious questions as to the benevolence" of the system it described.[163] In fact, despite his enthusiastic tone, Howe himself had been quick to point out that "it is not the socialism to which the Social Democratic party aspires; it does not involve control by the working classes. It is the socialism of the ruling caste, the great estate owners and the capitalists."[164] In their pre-war observations on the German system, Croly, Baker, Russell, and Walling, as well as Howe, had stressed the lack of freedom and participation on the part of the ordinary citizen.[165]

[159] "Socialism in the War and After," *Nation*, 100 (1 Apr. 1915), p. 346.

[160] Under the editorship of Hammond Lamont (1906–9), Paul Elmer More (1909–14), and Harold de Wolf Fuller (1914–18), the *Nation* remained in the conservative, mugwump tradition of E. L. Godkin. Oswald Garrison Villard, who owned the paper, changed its political character when he took over the editorship in 1918, but in the pre-war years, he, too, was an uncompromising opponent of progressive reforms and agitation. See, for example, "Justice to Public Service Corporations," "Universities in a Democracy," "The Vanishing Progressives," *Nation*, 98 (26 Mar., 25 June 1914), pp. 319–20, 744–5; 99 (6 Aug. 1914), pp. 153–4. These unsigned editorials are attributed to Villard in Daniel C. Haskell, *The Nation: Index of Titles and Contributors, 1865–1917* (New York, 1951).

[161] "The Landslide into Collectivism," *New Republic*, 2 (10 Apr. 1915), pp. 249–50.

[162] AP to Gifford Pinchot, 22 Mar. 1915, Amos Pinchot Papers, box 20.

[163] *Survey*, 35 (26 Feb. 1916), pp. 643–4. See also Walling, "German State Socialism," *Intercollegiate Socialist*, 4 (Dec. 1915–Jan. 1916), pp. 10–12.

[164] *Socialized Germany*, p. 1.

[165] Croly, *Promise of American Life*, pp. 252–4; *Progressive Democracy*, p. 282; Baker, *Seen in Germany* (London, 1902), pp. 4, 15, 61–2, 91, 97–130; Russell, *Uprising of the Many*, p. 91; Walling, *Progressivism – and After*, pp. 23–7; Howe, *European Cities at Work* (New York, 1913), pp. 152, 243, 262, 360.

The war naturally served to strengthen the belief that Germany had "gone too far in the direction of leadership by government," "at too great a sacrifice of individual liberty."[166]

Yet such judgments were commonly accompanied by the observation that "we can learn from any successful nation, especially if its faults and merits are the opposite of ours."[167] In January 1915, White suggested to his friend Theodore Roosevelt that he take the opportunity of pointing out that German success was largely due to a system of industrial organization and social welfare similar to that advocated by the Progressive Party in 1912 – "You could inject a vast amount of social and industrial justice into the people rather hypodermically by working out such an article or series of articles."[168] The Colonel did not look with favor upon this proposal to enlist the armies of the Kaiser in the battle for the Lord, but a little later Rowell explained to a German-American correspondent that "probably two-thirds of the last Progressive platform consisted of a proposal to adapt to America governmental methods already in successful operation in Germany."[169] When in September 1915, Bourne attempted to find "American use for German ideals," "German organization, German collectivism" were among the elements of the culture he saw as fruitful, while insisting that these should be applied to the task of working out "a democratic socialized life."[170] Likewise, the economic planning undertaken by the belligerent governments was cited as a model, particularly in the early part of 1915 when a severe industrial depression brought the problem of unemployment to the fore. "Among the earliest measures for national defense taken in Germany, France and Britain were enabling acts authorizing the national and local administrations to protect and promote employment," the *Survey* recalled. "Is not the possibility suggested of mobilizing the greater reserves of forethought and reserve capital available in times of peace, to meet the same sort of emergency in a nation's industrial life?"[171] "The only real obstacle to effective action," the *New Republic* agreed, "is a short-sighted reluctance on the part of the

---

166 *Harper's Weekly*, 61 (28 Aug. 1915), p. 193; Giddings, "The Larger Meanings of the War," *Survey*, 33 (7 Nov. 1914), p. 144.
167 *Harper's Weekly*, 61 (28 Aug. 1915), p. 193. See also Giddings, "The Larger Meanings of the War," p. 144; *Harper's Weekly*, 61 (10 July 1915), p. 27, and 62 (29 Jan. 1916), p. 99; *Independent*, 83 (2 Aug. 1915), p. 139; *New Republic*, 4 (11 Sept. 1915), p. 142.
168 White to Theodore Roosevelt, 15 Jan. 1915, White Papers.
169 Rowell to P. Richert, 24 May 1916, Rowell Papers.
170 "American Use for German Ideals," *New Republic*, 4 (4 Sept. 1915), pp. 118–20.
171 "Unemployment in War and Peace," *Survey*, 33 (6 Feb. 1915), pp. 516–17. See also Spargo, "Socialism as a Cure for Unemployment," *Annals*, 59 (May 1915), pp. 157–64. The measures adopted by Germany for mitigating unemployment were cited as a model in Howe, "Unemploy-

government to increase the national debt in time of peace."[172] Further-more, the editors argued a few weeks later, the growth in production achieved by the countries engaged in the war showed that the American economy must be operating at least 10 percent below capacity. Such a waste of resources was indefensible when "we have millions of homes in which little children are growing up, underfed, improperly clad, to be-come a prey to disease and, often, consequently, to vice and crime."[173]

The boom generated by Allied war orders soon dispelled the problem of unemployment, but this did not stem the suggestions by progressive publicists that the United States had much to learn from the success of Germany and the experience of the belligerent countries. Thus Hapgood felt that the successful operation of the railroads by the British govern-ment "will hereafter be a strong answer to those who assume that national business will be less efficient than private business."[174] Indeed, one has the impression that as the months passed not only was this line of argu-ment adopted by some who had originally appeared unsympathetic to it,[175] but that the negative aspects of "war socialism" were less empha-sized. It is true that as late as March 1917, the *New Republic* admitted that "it is a grim collectivism which Europe has established," but this was overshadowed by the judgment that "on its administrative side socialism has won a victory that is superb and compelling," and the warning that "if we wish to compete with Europe after the war we must do the same sort of thing with our production, our labor and our distribution that Europe has done with hers."[176] Similarly in the *Survey,* Devine concluded that "this huge laboratory of trench and submarine and munition factory is trying out experiments pregnant with instruction for us." "The cen-tralized despotism made necessary by military extremity is, of course, no real precedent for industrial democracy," he wrote, "but it is none the less an effective indictment of much of the unsocialized proprietary industrial organization with which we are familiar."[177]

ment: A Problem and a Program," *Century,* 89 (Apr. 1915), pp. 845, 848; *Independent,* 81 (8 Mar. 1915), pp. 343–4.

172 *New Republic,* 2 (10 Apr. 1915), p. 250. For similar proposals, see Howe to J. P. Tumulty, 28 Sept. 1914, Woodrow Wilson Papers, ser. 2, box 117; *Harper's Weekly,* 60 (27 Feb. 1915), p. 193; Amos Pinchot, public letter to Mayor J. P. Mitchel [n.d., early 1915], Amos Pinchot Papers, subject file 22.

173 "Economic Reserves in Peace," *New Republic,* 3 (29 May 1915), pp. 83–4.

174 "Fighting and Freedom," *Harper's Weekly,* 60 (12 June 1915), p. 562.

175 For example, Amos Pinchot. See "Preparedness," *Public,* 19 (4 Feb. 1916), pp. 110–13.

176 "In the Next Four Years," *New Republic,* 10 (3 Mar. 1917), p. 124; "Republican Resurrection," *New Republic,* 9 (16 Dec. 1916), p. 173.

177 "Through Good Will to Peace," *Survey,* 35 (18 Dec. 1915), p. 337.

The domestic scene: the decline of progressivism

Yet, as Bourne lamented in September 1915, far from learning from this European experience, Americans had "taken the occasion rather to repudiate that modest collectivism which was raising its head here in the shape of the progressive movement in national politics."[178] The midterm elections of 1914, a defeat for the Democrats and a disaster for the Progressive Party, were generally acknowledged to constitute a "standpat victory."[179] The immediate response of some was to attribute this to the inadequate radicalism and intellectual weaknesses of the Democratic and Progressive campaigns. "The existing reaction seeks to discipline progressivism rather than destroy it," the *New Republic* asserted. "American public opinion most assuredly remains loyal to the idea of continuing forward movement."[180] But this confidence was hard to sustain. A full analysis of the results of direct legislation in the 1914 elections led the *New Republic* to conclude a few months later that "the ban of popular disapproval fell upon progressive proposals with deadly uniformity." The editors still insisted that "if a political democracy is to learn its business it must participate directly in the transaction of its business,"[181] but as time passed it became clear that they were having to struggle to maintain this faith. "Can we expect political wisdom when fifteen million voters, ignorant as well as wise, are intrusted with final sovereignty in this vast country of ours?" Weyl asked. "The election was surely discouraging enough," he admitted, but "in the course of years the voter does grow in intelligence and perception, as education spreads and better means of political expression are devised. . . . The retreat is never as far as the advance."[182] Others clung to this hope. "We are coming in, it seems to me, for a period of

---

[178] "American Use for German Ideals," *New Republic*, 4 (4 Sept. 1915), p. 118. Elsewhere he observed that "a few years ago there seemed to be a promise of a forward movement toward Democracy, led by battled veterans in a war against privilege. But how soon the older generation became wearied of the march! What is left now of that shining army and its leader?" "This Older Generation," *Atlantic Monthly*, 116 (Sept. 1915), pp. 385–91 at 391.

[179] *Harper's Weekly*, 59 (21 Nov. 1914), p. 481. See also *New Republic*, 1 (7 Nov. 1914), p. 3; *Independent*, 80 (16 Nov. 1914), pp. 221–2; *Public*, 17 (27 Nov. 1914), pp. 1135–8; Steffens to Allen H. Suggett, 4 Nov. 1914, *Letters*, 1, p. 348; White to James Garfield, 18 Nov. 1914, White Papers. Socialists, too, found the results discouraging. See Friedberg, "Marxism in the United States," p. 174.

[180] *New Republic*, 1 (16 Jan. 1915), p. 6. See also *Public*, 17 (13 Nov. 1914), pp. 1082, 1083; Amos Pinchot, "The Failure of the Progressive Party," *Masses*, 6 (Dec. 1914), pp. 9–10.

[181] *New Republic*, 2 (6 Mar. 1915), suppl.

[182] "The Average Voter," *Century*, 90 (Oct. 1915), pp. 901–7. Lippmann's doubts were already biting deeper. See "Insiders and Outsiders," *New Republic*, 4 (13 Nov. 1915), pp. 35–6; Diary, 19 Dec. 1915, pp. 45, 47, Lippmann Papers. Also, *New Republic*, 4 (14 Aug. 1915), pp. 34–5.

reaction, but I believe it will not last long," White wrote to Theodore
Roosevelt. "The reactionary wave is usually a quick wave, while the tide
of progress is slow and unsteady."[183] Moreover, there were, as Weyl
noted, "excuses for all these electoral indiscretions."[184] One was the
economic depression, for, as we have seen, sympathy for reform was often
associated with prosperity.[185] The vote had been "not abnormal but
abdominal," White quipped in 1914. "We may be back in the liberal age
again, even by 1916," Rowell wrote hopefully. "That depends on the
state of business."[186]

However, 1916 was to bring only further discouragement. "It seems as
though the nation was never so completely under the control of privileged
interests," Baker noted in his journal in April.[187] He was confirmed in
this view by the final death of the Bull Moose in June.[188] "With it must
die the present hope of converting a national party into a faithful agent of
progressive political and social ideals," lamented the *New Republic*.[189] It
was a bitter blow, particularly for those who had joined the party in 1912
and worked for it. "I feel as though I have had my face blown off and that
I can never turn to the world again," White wrote.[190] Weyl, grief-
stricken, spent hours on the telephone, talking it over.[191]

The collapse of the Progressive Party was not, of course, unheralded.
White himself admitted that "we have all known what was going to
happen for a year,"[192] and the *New Republic* pointed out that even before
Roosevelt declined its nomination, the party had adopted a platform that
failed "to utter one single conviction which need cause any uneasiness to
the established order."[193] The concentration on what Albert J. Beveridge
scornfully called "Americanism, preparedness, and a protective tariff"[194]
could reasonably be attributed not only to TR's desire to build a bridge
back to the Republican Party but also to the impact on American domestic politics of the war in Europe. The war was, indeed, the explanation

---

[183] White to Theodore Roosevelt, 24 Nov. 1914, White Papers.
[184] "Average Voter," p. 901.
[185] See "Progressives and Progress," Chapter 3. Cf. Hofstadter, *Age of Reform*, pp. 134–5.
[186] Rowell to Theodore Roosevelt, 6 Dec. 1914, Rowell Papers. See also *New Republic*, 2 (6 Mar.
      1915), suppl.
[187] Notebook 9, 3 Apr. 1916, pp. 69–70, R. S. Baker Papers.
[188] Notebook 11, [June 1916], p. 25, ibid.
[189] "The Progressive Party – an Obituary," *New Republic*, 7 (17 June 1916), pp. 159–61 at 161.
[190] To Victor Murdock, 19 June 1916, White Papers.
[191] [Brubaker, ed.], *Weyl*, p. 122.
[192] To Victor Murdock, 19 June 1916, White Papers.
[193] "The Progressive Party – An Obituary," p. 161.
[194] Beveridge to John C. Shaffer, 19 June 1916, Beveridge Papers.

most frequently invoked for the decline in support for progressivism. [195] No one expounded this thesis more often than White, who even before 1914 had more than once expressed the view that "only a war can shatter the sure advance of this movement of the people for distributive justice." [196] "The moral slump that came out of the ballot box was caused, to my notion, largely by the war," he wrote in January 1915, "first in making people afraid of their own righteous judgments and second by benumbing what judgments they had and making them less responsive to the pleas of suffering and injustice." [197] The connection was made in various ways. Sometimes it was suggested that the altruistic impulses upon which progressivism depended had been weakened by the opportunities the war provided for the pursuit of self-interest, [198] sometimes that they were stemmed by fear. [199] "Liberal ease" required an atmosphere of security, Lippmann suggested, but the war had sapped confidence and "like sheep in a shower we huddle about a leader." "A procession of reactionaries has returned from exile," he noted. "The old shibboleths are uttered without a blush, for all old things are congenial to us now. They promise rest in a world at war." [200]

Most commonly, however, it was claimed that the war had simply diverted people's attention from domestic evils. "The voter thought more of the ghastly trenches on the Aisne and the Vistula than of Mr. Cannon and Mr. Penrose," Weyl reasoned in 1915. [201] "We are obsessed by the war and its consequences," complained Devine. "No newspaper is free to give serious attention to other matters." [202] "This has been the most damnable year for publishers in a long time, and especially for radical publications," the business manager of the *Masses* wrote to Amos Pinchot. "I attribute this to the fact that the war has made the industrial and political evils that we complain of in this country look like thirty cents." [203] Pinchot himself had had articles on the government ownership of railroads and on prison

---

[195] In addition to the references in nn. 197–205 below, see, for example, Rowell to Theodore Roosevelt, 6 Dec. 1914, Rowell Papers; *New Republic*, 3 (3 July 1915), p. 218; Russell, "In the Shadow of the Great War"; Chambers, *Kellogg*, p. 57.

[196] *Autobiography*, p. 496; White to R. S. Baker, 28 Aug. 1913, R. S. Baker Papers, ser. 2, box 94.

[197] To Clinton Woodruff, 19 Jan. 1915, White Papers.

[198] Baker, "The One Idea," *New Republic*, 1 (5 Dec. 1914), pp. 20–2; White to F. Dumont Smith, 10 Jan. 1916, White Papers.

[199] *Emporia Gazette*, 27 Nov. 1915.

[200] *Stakes of Diplomacy*, pp. 7–9.

[201] "Average Voter," p. 901. See also *New Republic*, 1 (19 Dec. 1914), p. 3.

[202] "Civilization's Peril," *Survey*, 33 (6 Feb. 1915), p. 518. See also "The Reality of Peace," *New Republic*, 4 (30 Oct. 1915), pp. 322–3.

[203] Marlen E. Pew to AP, 7 July 1915, Amos Pinchot Papers, box 21.

conditions returned by editors with apologetic remarks about the pressure on space created by "war material," while another disappointed contributor protested that "such periodicals as Harper's should not beat the tom-toms over the battles in Flanders and Poland so loudly and so insistently as to permit plunderers at home to get away with the swag without being seen or heard."[204] "The whole trouble with our humanitarian platform, as I see it," White concluded in June 1916, "is that it hit war. Kaiser Bill blew it up. You cannot get humanitarian progress on the first page when human-itarian retrogression is occupying the headlines. You cannot get people interested in minimum wages and laws for hours of service and equitable railroad rates in the face of the news from Verdun."[205]

In August 1914, however, Croly had anticipated that the war in Eu-rope would create "a state of mind in which a political and social agitation will find its words more influential and more effective in modifying public opinion." He expressed the hope that it might prove "in the end an actual help to the 'New Republic,'" which was to be launched three months later.[206] This is one among several indications that progressive sentiment did not appear to be at floodtide even before the war in Europe broke out. "Frankly, I am not at all sure that a radical campaign in Pennsylvania is wise," Amos Pinchot had felt obliged to warn his brother, who was about to run for senator on the Bull Moose ticket.[207] Mark Sullivan, who had been renowned as a muckraking editor during his early years at *Collier's*, confessed in the summer of 1914 that "I am not as excited about reform as I was. . . . If my intuition tells me anything, it is that we are due for a period of digestion and a long period in which we shall try to assimilate the changes we have already effected."[208] For jour-nalists whose work had become identified with the cause of reform, this change in the perceived mood of the public affected not only their politi-cal hopes but also their professional careers. "For the first time in many years I could not find a publisher for some of the articles I cherished most deeply," recalled Baker, who was generally unhappy about his rela-tionship with the *American Magazine* after an article on the 1912 Lawrence

204 William Hard to AP, 19 May 1915; Henry J. Whigham to AP, 29 June 1915; Delos F. Wilcox to AP, 26 Dec. 1914, Amos Pinchot Papers. Steffens also complained that "the trouble really is that the editors can't see anything but war." To Laura Steffens, 3 Oct. 1914, *Letters*, 1, p. 346.
205 To Rodney Elward, 24 June 1916. Walter Johnson, ed., *Selected Letters of William Allen White* (New York, 1947), p. 169.
206 Croly to Learned Hand, 17 Aug. 1914, cited in Forcey, *Crossroads of Liberalism*, p. 223.
207 AP to Gifford Pinchot, 3 Feb. 1914, Amos Pinchot Papers, box 16.
208 Mark Sullivan to AP, 4 Aug. 1914, Amos Pinchot Papers.

strike had been effectively censored before publication.[209] Steffens's difficulty in having articles published in what he called "the middle-class
magazines" in the years preceding the war had a perceptible effect on his
confidence.[210] Of his famous muckraking, he wrote defensively in 1916:
"It is long ago now, and most people have forgotten it."[211]

Overall, little in the writings of these publicists suggests that the
European war significantly weakened American progressivism in any direct way. As far as their own attitudes were concerned, there is no doubt
that most of them were shocked by the occurrence of such a terrible
conflict in the civilized world, and that several felt an obligation to
reassess their more optimistic pre-war assumptions. However, none felt
compelled to modify the essential character of his political outlook. This
may have been partly because the events in Europe remained for most a
little remote, but it certainly reflected the fact that the most widely
accepted and persistently held interpretations of the war's causes served to
confirm their pre-war views, particularly the belief in democracy. Moreover, as we have seen, they also found, both in the need to secure peace
and in the apparent requirements for successful warfare, additional justification for the sort of collectivist and egalitarian economic and social
reforms they had been advocating. It is true that they themselves often
suggested that, for one reason or another, the war might be responsible for
a decline in the broader popular support for progressive reform, but these
claims were not very convincing, particularly in the light of evidence that
such support was not flowing strongly even before the war broke out.
However, there was one further respect in which the war impinged upon
American progressivism. This was by raising questions, of a potentially
serious kind, with regard to U.S. foreign policy. These questions not only
absorbed much of the attention and energies of progressive publicists
themselves but also could give rise to deep differences of opinion among
those who on domestic issues were broadly united.

[209] Baker, *American Chronicle*, p. 302; Semonche, *Baker*, chap. 10, especially pp. 260–3.
[210] Stein, "Lincoln Steffens," pp. 167–8; Steffens to Laura Steffens, 2 Jan. 1914, to Allen H.
 Suggett, 5 Nov. 1918, *Letters*, 1, pp. 332–3, 440.
[211] "Making Friends with Mexico," *Collier's*, 58 (25 Nov. 1916), p. 23.

CHAPTER 5

Foreign policy and the debate over intervention

The relationship between progressivism and attitudes to foreign policy has been a subject of dispute among historians. The controversy originated with a provocative essay by William E. Leuchtenburg in 1952 arguing that "imperialism and progressivism flourished together because they were both expressions of the same philosophy of government" and that progressives, "with few exceptions, ardently supported the imperialist surge or, at the very least, proved agreeably acquiescent."[1] The latter conclusion has been effectively challenged by scholars who have analyzed the attitudes of members of Congress, particularly progressive Republican senators, to those issues that Leuchtenburg took to be indicators of "imperialism" – increased naval and military appropriations and a firm defense of American neutral rights as well as U.S. intervention in Latin America.[2] In the face of such evidence, those who seek to reestablish Leuchtenburg's basic thesis have had to resort to a much broader definition of "imperialism," including not only colonialism and overseas military intervention but also commercial expansion and a belief in the universal relevance of "the American model" of republican democracy combined with capitalist economic development. This makes it possible to maintain that "despite the differences of approach among progressives, and the division over America's military actions in the world, there was an overriding agreement among them about America's future role in the world."[3] True though this doubtless is at some level of generality, it not only fails to identify any distinctively progressive attitude to foreign policy, but both minimizes and leaves unexplained differences of opinion about the partic-

---

[1] "Progressivism and Imperialism: The Progressive Movement and American Foreign Policy, 1896–1916," *Mississippi Valley Historical Review*, 39 (Dec. 1952), pp. 483–504 at 500, 483.

[2] Howard W. Allen, "Republican Reformers and Foreign Policy, 1913–17," *Mid-America*, 44 (Oct. 1962), pp. 222–9; Walter I. Sutton, "Progressive Republican Senators and the Submarine Crisis, 1915–1916," ibid., 47 (Apr. 1965), pp. 75–88; Barton J. Bernstein and Franklin A. Leib, "Progressive Republican Senators and American Imperialism, 1898–1916: A Reappraisal," ibid., 50 (July 1968), pp. 163–205.

[3] Gerald E. Markowitz, "Progressivism and Imperialism: A Return to First Principles," *Historian*, 37 (Feb. 1975), pp. 257–75 at pp. 257–9, 274–5.

ular policy choices that were confronted, debated, and decided in these years.[4]

That progressives were divided over such choices is evident. Historians have long recognized that in foreign even more than in domestic policy a gulf separated the followers of Theodore Roosevelt from the followers of William Jennings Bryan.[5] John Milton Cooper, Jr., has argued in a thoughtful article that during World War I a third approach emerged and became associated with Woodrow Wilson. The dichotomy between "the imperialist and anti-imperialist viewpoints" was supplemented by "a liberal internationalist outlook which combined features of both." This analysis, which is combined with the suggestion that these differences over foreign policy reflected "basic attitudes toward political power," constitutes a marked advance over attempts to establish a simple relationship between homogeneous entities labeled "progressivism" and "imperialism."[6] However, two problems remain at least partly unresolved. One is that the three broad categories are adequate neither to describe the full variety of progressive attitudes to foreign policy nor to predict positions taken on specific questions of policy. (A striking example of this is the way both Leuchtenburg and Cooper bracket Theodore Roosevelt and Albert J. Beveridge, though the two differed profoundly over the issues of neutrality and intervention in World War I.[7]) The second problem is the relationship between any or all of these outlooks on foreign policy and a progressive point of view on domestic issues. In respect to World War I in particular, Walter I. Trattner has suggested that there was no such relationship. Not only were progressives divided, but "their divisions merely reflected the divisions of the American people as a whole." Rather than discussing " 'the progressives' and World War I," he concludes, "should not one rather talk about America's or Americans' attitudes toward the World War?"[8] Responding to this challenge involves attempting to identify those elements in progressives' attitudes to foreign policy that were

---

[4] For a fuller critique of this approach to the history of American foreign policy attitudes, see J. A. Thompson, "William Appleman Williams and the 'American Empire,' " *Journal of American Studies*, 7 (Apr. 1973), pp. 91–104.

[5] For example, Eric F. Goldman, *Rendezvous with Destiny: A History of Modern American Reform* (New York, 1952), pp. 233–53.

[6] John Milton Cooper, Jr., "Progressivism and American Foreign Policy: A Reconsideration," *Mid-America*, 51 (Oct. 1969), pp. 260–77 at pp. 269, 274, 277.

[7] See J. A. Thompson, "An Imperialist and World War I: The Case of Albert J. Beveridge," *Journal of American Studies*, 5 (Aug. 1971), pp. 133–50.

[8] Walter I. Trattner, "Progressivism and World War I: A Re-appraisal," *Mid-America*, 44 (July 1962), pp. 131–45 at pp. 133, 145.

either exclusively or particularly associated with a commitment to domestic reform.

Approaching the foreign policy views of this group of progressive publicists with these questions in mind, we immediately encounter the further complication introduced by the element of time. Amos Pinchot enlisted to fight in the Spanish-American War and Steffens, too, according to his biographer, would have done so but for the urgings of his wife.[9] Although Pinchot frequently referred back to this experience to prove that he was not a pacifist, there is surely no reason to assume that the attitudes of 1898, when most of these men were not yet even committed to a progressive position on domestic policy, were of a piece with their later foreign policy views. Indeed, even in the comparatively short but momentous period between the outbreak of war in Europe in August 1914 and U.S. intervention in April 1917, there were to be significant changes in the thinking of many.

America's role in the world

In the pre-war years, as we have seen, few had devoted serious attention to any aspect of international affairs. Certainly, in U.S. foreign policy there had been little since the turn of the century to generate much interest or controversy. The issue of imperialism continued to provide a focus for most of the strong views that did exist. A few of these progressives remained favorable to American expansion. Rowell, who had vigorously supported the annexation of the Philippines, suggested in the autumn of 1914 that the Pacific island groups seized by Britain from Germany should be taken over by the United States as defensive outposts against Japan.[10] In *The Promise of American Life,* Croly, while expressing doubts about the wisdom of annexing the Philippines, strongly defended the principle of imperialism and stressed its connection with the cause of domestic reform. Indeed, he argued that it was Bryan's anti-imperialist campaign in 1900 that "has disqualified him for effective leadership of the party of reform."[11] The *Independent*'s commitment to American expansionism was neither so discriminating nor so sophisticated, but rather represented an uncomplicated view of Manifest Destiny. Not only did the paper advocate the absorption of Santo Domingo and oppose proposals to

[9] Kaplan, *Steffens*, p. 87.
[10] Everett, "Chester Rowell," p. 265; Rowell to James D. Phelan, 23 Nov. 1914, Rowell Papers.
[11] *Promise of American Life*, p. 157. See also pp. 169, 259–61, 308–9.

grant self-government to the Philippines, but it looked forward to the day "when, not by annexation, but by some future organic act in equal agreement, all of North America from Panama to the Pole shall embrace one united people, ruled by and for the people."[12] However, the predispositions of most progressives were anti-imperialist, with Single Taxers and Socialists constituting particularly fierce centers of opposition. The former upheld traditional Jeffersonian principles, deploring both the violation of the rights of the subjected peoples and what they saw as the related growth of government, militarism, and privilege in the United States.[13] Socialists, viewing imperialism as an inevitable and ugly consequence of capitalism, sought to arouse moral indignation against it. Thus, when the revolution in Mexico led to talk of U.S. intervention, Russell (who was well above military age) told a New York audience that, if drafted to fight in "such a war," he would refuse to serve. It was not that he did not love his country or honor the American flag, "but I want that flag to stand for liberty, justice, democracy, and the rights of the people."[14]

This sentiment would have commanded general assent from progressive publicists for, like most Americans, they adhered to an ideological form of nationalism.[15] Even that stern critic of an unthinking acceptance of traditional assumptions, Herbert Croly, insisted not only that the promise of American life was of more than national significance, but that U.S. foreign policy should reflect the country's commitment to certain ideals. While praising Hamilton for his realistic understanding of America's position in the world, he criticized him for "failing to foresee that the national interest of the United States was identified with the general security and prosperity of liberal political institutions – that the United States must by every practical means encourage the spread of democratic methods and ideas."[16] These propositions contained the essence of the idea of an American mission, which most of these progressives, in common with the vast majority of their fellow countrymen, had more or less unconsciously absorbed.

---

[12] *Independent*, 79 (31 Aug. 1914), p. 294; ibid., 80 (5 Oct. 1914), p. 6; ibid., 81 (22 Feb., 29 Mar. 1915), pp. 265, 445–6. On a later occasion, the editors implied that, with respect to Mexico at least, "our destiny and our duty" might demand armed conquest. "No Binding of Our Hands," *Independent*, 87 (3 July 1916), p. 4.

[13] For example, Stuart Portner, "Louis F. Post" (Ph.D. dissertation, University of Michigan, 1940), pp. 175–82; *Public*, 17 (2 Jan. 1914), pp. 2–3.

[14] *New Review*, 2 (June 1914), pp. 368–9.

[15] See "Progressive Values," Chapter 3.

[16] *Promise of American Life*, p. 293.

The outbreak of the European war seemed to many to provide further confirmation of the superiority of American ideals and institutions. Not only was the conflict seen as a characteristic product of the Old World but American noninvolvement was often attributed to more than the accident of geography. "It is the genius of our people to live in peace," boasted White. "We care little for glory and conquest. . . . The flag with the stars and stripes stands for the civilization that exalts the spirit of Jesus Christ."[17] "America today towers above the nations of the world like Saul among his brethren," declared the *Public,* but not on account of its armed strength, size, or wealth. "Our distinction is due wholly to the fact that we have an ideal, Democracy, and at the present time are led by a man who is trying to live up to that ideal."[18] "That we should have been kept out of the Great War was in the nature of the federal union," the *Independent* asserted at Thanksgiving, 1914.[19] There was little distinctively progressive about such national self-congratulation. As Creel observed in December 1914, "the racial mixture that is America may quiver with sympathy for those blood-brothers who go to death in European battlefields, yet the dominant thrill is one of national pride in the demonstrated superiority of American institutions and ideals."[20] Indeed, on reflection, several of these writers were inclined to puncture the moral complacency. "We sit untroubled in happy peace and thank God that we are not as other nations are," observed the *Independent* in November 1915. "Are we so much better than they? Is it that the lust of blood is not in our veins that we are not greedy to rob our neighbors of their possessions, or is it that the accident of our position and the dissevering ocean have made it easy for us to escape their fate?"[21] "We are a conceited nation – mistaking the possession of natural resources for the possession of ability," Baker noted. "So often we make a virtue of not doing what we have no need of doing. In the present crisis some Americans take credit to the nation because it is opposed to wars of conquest – but it has no need of more territory, it is still uncrowded, and the best opportunity for us lies still in developing our own resources – not in encroaching upon our neighbors."[22] "What we did need we could take from weak peoples," Weyl

17 *Emporia Gazette,* 29 Aug. 1914.
18 *Public,* 17 (18 Sept. 1914), pp. 890–1.
19 *Independent,* 80 (23 Nov. 1914), p. 267.
20 "Our 'Visionary' President," *Century,* 89 (Dec. 1914), pp. 192–200 at 195. "It was in no spirit of humility that we met the outbreak of the Great War," Weyl recalled in 1916. "It is not pleasant today to read the homilies which America, during those early months of the war, preached to unheeding Europe." *American World Policies,* pp. 32–3.
21 *Independent,* 84 (22 Nov. 1915), p. 292.
22 Notebook 5, June, May, 1915, pp. 115, 80–1, R. S. Baker Papers.

added after surveying American history, "and a nation which fights weak peoples need not be martial, just as a man who robs orphans need not be a thug."[23]

However, even those who stressed how much the absence of militarism in the United States was due to fortunate circumstances generally believed that the nation could and should help the world to find the way to peace. At the very least, it might serve as a beacon. "On us is the heavy responsibility of transmitting unimpaired this heritage of civilization which the rest of the world is now destroying," Rowell declared.[24] For progressives, this responsibility included what Devine called "the need for at least one strong nation in this troubled time to pursue the even path of social reform."[25] Yet the traditional interpretation of the American mission as essentially exemplary satisfied few of these publicists for long.[26] The grounds on which it was rejected varied somewhat. Croly was quick to argue that his earlier criticism of the isolationist shibboleth had been amply vindicated by the European war, "which the American people individually and collectively were powerless to prevent or mitigate, yet which may have consequences upon the future and policy of the country as profound and far-reaching as our self-made Civil War." In the very first issue of the *New Republic*, he claimed that the maintenance of American "independence" demanded "the adoption of the positive and necessary policy of making American influence in Europe count in favor of international peace."[27]

Although in calling for "a clearer understanding of the relation between our democratic national ideal and our international obligations"[28] Croly indicated that he was not advocating an amoral *Realpolitik*, his emphasis on the national interest remained exceptional among these progressives. But a broadly similar goal for American policy was widely recommended in the language of responsibility and duty. "There's no denying that we Americans have been too self-concerned, somewhat parochial in attitude, disposed to look on the Old World as an interesting

[23] *American World Policies*, pp. 32–5 at 35.
[24] *Fresno Republican*, 26 Nov. 1914. See also *Emporia Gazette*, 10 May 1915.
[25] "Civilization's Peril," *Survey*, 33 (6 Feb. 1915), p. 519.
[26] On the traditional idea of the American mission, see Frederick Merk, *Manifest Destiny and Mission in American History* (New York, 1963).
[27] "The End of American Isolation," *New Republic*, 1 (7 Nov. 1914), pp. 9–10. This unsigned editorial is attributed to Croly in Lippmann, "Notes for a Biography," *New Republic*, 63 (16 July 1930), p. 251.
[28] "The End of American Isolation," p. 10.

place to visit for the ruins and all that, but otherwise hardly worth consideration," the *Independent* confessed. "But we must now realize that the United States is, whether we wish it or not, a world power and has a responsibility that it cannot evade in the settlement of the questions that lie at the bottom of the present conflict."[29] Whether or not they accepted the implication of necessity, many progressives instinctively felt that, as the *Public* put it, "much has been given us; much will be required in return."[30] "What should be the purpose of a nation like America?" Baker asked himself. "We begin to perceive dimly that an individual has duties to others beside himself. . . . Is there no social gospel for nations? . . . America: servant of humanity. America: world-leader."[31] For those social work leaders and reformers who composed the "Henry Street group," which through the autumn and winter of 1914–15 worked on developing a peace program, the combination of the objective situation and human-itarian sentiment provided, as in domestic affairs, sufficient reason for action. "So much is at stake in both war and reconstruction," they de-clared, that "Americans should, as freemen and democrats and peace-lovers, express themselves in some affirmative way."[32] "Every people of Europe is looking to us," wrote Kellogg who was active in this movement from the beginning.[33] Under criticism for devoting so much space to it in the *Survey,* he encouraged Jane Addams to write a piece explaining the connection, which seemed to both of them so clear, "between social service and the will to peace through justice."[34]

The conviction that America had a responsibility to take an active part in establishing peace was reinforced by its possession of several apparent qualifications for the task. Many were impressed by the fact that the United States contained peoples from all the belligerent countries. "By assembling these races, by the gradual creation of a common type which is tinged with the traditions of these constituent races," the *New Republic* argued, "we are developing a nation which may to a degree act as an

[29] *Independent,* 80 (16 Nov. 1914), pp. 223–4.

[30] *Public,* 17 (18 Sept. 1914), p. 891. The biblical phrase – "much is required of them to whom much is given" – had been directly evoked by Bryan the previous year when defending his "missionary diplomacy" in the Caribbean. See Arthur S. Link, *Wilson: The New Freedom* (Prince-ton, N.J., 1956), p. 335.

[31] Notebook 5, Mar. 1915, pp. 1–3, 14–15, R. S. Baker Papers.

[32] "Towards the Peace That Shall Last," *Survey,* 33 (6 Mar. 1915), pt. 2. The Henry Street group included Holt and Howe as well as Devine and Kellogg. For a fuller account, see Marchand, *American Peace Movement,* pp. 224–35, 238–41.

[33] PUK to Jane Addams, 24 Oct. 1914, Kellogg Papers.

[34] PUK to Jane Addams, 31 July 1916, ibid.

interpreter between the nations of Europe, a go-between for peace."[35] The *Survey*, too, suggested that the United States offered "such a forum for testing out the terms of settlement as is not open abroad."[36] Although there was no logical or historical connection between the ethnic diversity of the American population and the federal system of government, by conflating the two several saw the United States as a model for that international organization which was widely perceived as an essential element in the lasting peace.[37] As a long-standing proponent of the idea, Holt was naturally to the fore in arguing that the war showed the need for "a great Confederation or League of Peace." "It would seem to be the manifest destiny of the United States to lead in the establishment of such a league," he wrote as early as September 1914. "The United States is a demonstration to the world that all the races and peoples of the earth can live in peace under one form of government, and its chief value to civilization is a demonstration of what this form of government is."[38] It was with deliberate symbolism that Holt chose Independence Hall, Philadelphia, for the inaugural meeting of the League to Enforce Peace and described the League's manifesto as "a Declaration of Interdependence."[39] "The time has come to make the attempt once more to form a confederation of the world," concluded George W. Nasmyth in the *Survey*, "with the initiative coming from America which has already worked out the problem of voluntary federation of forty-eight states on the principle of 'government of the people, by the people, for the people.'"[40]

As such statements implied, it was generally assumed that not least among the qualifications of the United States as a peacemaker was that the liberal and democratic principles to which it was committed constituted the best basis for a durable settlement. It was, after all, a natural concomitant of the belief that the war had been launched by privileged elites that the extension of popular control over foreign policy would make for peace.

---

[35] *New Republic*, 3 (15 May 1915), pp. 29–30.

[36] *Survey*, 33 (6 Mar. 1915), p. 631.

[37] On the latter point, see, for example, Hapgood, "The Great Settlement," *Harper's Weekly*, 59 (12 Sept. 1914), p. 250; Notebook 3, 2 Aug. 1914, pp. 70–2, and Notebook 5, 12 June 1915, pp. 104–13, R. S. Baker Papers; *Survey*, 33 (6 Mar. 1915), pt. 2.

[38] "The Way to Disarm: A Practical Proposal," *Independent*, 79 (28 Sept. 1914), pp. 427–9 at 429. Bourne, too, observed that "America is already the world-federation in miniature, the continent where for the first time in history has been achieved that miracle of hope, the peaceful living side by side, with character substantially preserved, of the most heterogeneous peoples under the sun." "Trans-National America," *Atlantic Monthly*, 118 (July 1916), pp. 86–97 at p. 93. See also Weyl, *American World Policies*, p. 12.

[39] Kuehl, *Holt*, pp. 122–9; *Independent*, 82 (14 June 1915), pp. 447–8.

[40] "Constructive Mediation," *Survey*, 33 (6 Mar. 1915), pp. 616–20 at 617.

"Let us leave the occasions for fighting no longer for idle war boards to decide," urged the Henry Street group in their manifesto, "Towards the Peace that shall Last." "Let us put the ban upon intrigues and secret treaties."[41] Related to the idea of democracy, and even more venerable in the American tradition, was the principle of national self-determination. "Really representative government," Howe argued, was that "in which the people themselves are permitted to decide as to what country they will be identified with."[42] Most progressives were naturally sympathetic to this point of view, particularly those, like Bourne, who had a concern for the vitality of diverse cultural traditions.[43] "Boundaries should be set where not force, but justice and consanguinity direct," declared the Henry Street group, or at least "however boundaries fall, liberty and the flowering of native cultures should be secure."[44] The qualification may be seen as tacit recognition of the difficulties in this area, which increasingly came to be openly acknowledged. Thus Weyl pointed out that the principle of self-determination frequently conflicted with the need for defensible frontiers and economic viability, or even, as in the case of Ireland and Ulster, with itself. "Though we sympathize with the aspirations of Poles, Finns, Armenians and Bohemians, an unlimited independence cannot always be desired," he concluded. "Some lesser form of self-government," such as "a local autonomy under a federal government," might well be a more practicable way of protecting small nations from economic exploitation or cultural imperialism.[45] Asserting that "many states mean many wars," the *Independent* likewise suggested that large confederations would best balance the claims of freedom and security.[46] Moreover, few could envisage applying the principle of national self-determination directly to the underdeveloped world. Instead, the Henry Street manifesto called for "the framing of a common colonial policy which shall put down that predatory exploitation which has embroiled the West and oppressed the East and shall stand for an opportunity for each latent and backward race to build up according to its own genius."[47] The need to eliminate the

---

[41] *Survey*, 33 (6 Mar. 1915), pt. 2. For other expressions of similar sentiments, see Chapter 4, "Causes of War – and Cures."

[42] *Survey*, 33 (6 Mar. 1915), p. 615.

[43] Bourne, "Continental Cultures," *New Republic*, 1 (16 Jan. 1915), pp. 14–16. See also Hapgood, "In London," *Harper's Weekly*, 59 (22 Aug. 1914), p. 177.

[44] "Towards the Peace That Shall Last."

[45] *American World Policies*, pp. 276–8.

[46] *Independent*, 89 (5 Mar. 1917), pp. 388–9. See also Devine, "Home-Rule," *Survey*, 37 (2 Dec. 1916), pp. 217–18.

[47] *Survey*, 33 (6 Mar. 1915), pt. 2.

imperialistic rivalries that were so widely seen as the root cause of the war led Lippmann to propose an elaborate scheme for the international administration of the "backward countries,"[48] but most of the writers who addressed this problem rested their faith in the traditional American remedy of the Open Door principle.[49]

This sort of peace program – the extension of democratic control of foreign policy, open diplomacy, national self-determination, the liberalization and equalization of trade barriers, and the replacement of the alliance system and "balance of power" concept by some international organization – was not an American monopoly. However, the fact that its leading advocates abroad, notably in England, were radical liberals tends to confirm its natural affinity with progressivism.[50] Certainly, there soon emerged a consensus among these publicists that the chief object of American policy should be the establishment of a liberal and lasting peace. As we have seen, several strands merged in this concern – the forward-looking, self-consciously "realistic," cosmopolitan liberalism of the *New Republic,* the humanitarian activism of the *Survey* group, and the high-minded, self-denying idealism of a Baker. All these were distinctively progressive. They were powerfully supplemented by a confident nationalism, as uncalculating as it was unsophisticated. The establishment of a new world order was seen as the fulfillment of the American mission. Early in the war, *Harper's Weekly* recalled Madame de Stael's remark to some traveling Americans: "You are the advance guard of the human race. In your hands is the future of the world."[51] "From us and our institutions shall proceed the peace and happiness and hope of the future of the world," Rowell declared.[52] "American ideals are high enough and the American Constitution is wide enough to cover any race or clime," proclaimed the *Independent*.[53] "If ever the phrase 'manifest destiny' had any meaning," concluded Devine, "it applies here and now to the task of our own nation in its obligation to act as a mediator between the nations of the earth and the new order of which we are all the integral factors."[54] To

[48] *Stakes of Diplomacy,* chaps. 9–11.
[49] Howe, *Why War,* p. 337; *Survey,* 33 (6 Mar. 1915), pp. 631–2; Weyl, *American World Policies,* pp. 267–8.
[50] "The proposals of the British Quakers, the Social Democratic groups of southern Germany, and the Union of Democratic Control in England, will be suggestive to you," Kellogg wrote to Jane Addams, as they worked together on drafting the Henry Street manifesto. PUK to Jane Addams, 24 Oct. 1914, Kellogg Papers.
[51] *Harper's Weekly,* 59 (19 Dec. 1914), p. 578.
[52] *Fresno Republican,* 25 Nov. 1915.
[53] *Independent,* 87 (28 Aug. 1916), p. 288.
[54] *Survey,* 37 (2 Dec. 1916), p. 217.

Weyl, as observant about the attitudes of his fellow progressives to foreign as to domestic issues, "the generous, somewhat ineffectual, peace ideal, which has grown up in a democratic people with no hostile neighbors," itself qualified the United States to be a peacemaker. "One may ridicule this cornfed, tepid idealism," he admitted, "but it is none the less the raw material out of which great national purposes are formed," to be compared with the first stirrings of antislavery sentiment in the previous century. "Some nation must take the initiative" toward "the realization that after all the common interests of the nations which are endangered by a world war do in the main outweigh the divisive interests," he argued. "This natural leadership, I conceive, falls to America, not because we are better or wiser than others, but because we are the child of all the peoples with allegiance to all, a nation without deep inherited hatreds, economically self-poised, comparatively satisfied, and inspired by ideals of democracy and peace."[55]

The debate over preparedness

To some observers, the most important of America's qualifications as a peacemaker may well have seemed to be, simply, power. Producing in 1913 more steel than Germany, Britain, and Russia combined, the United States was the greatest reservoir of economic and potential military strength in the world. Alone among the neutrals, it possessed the capacity to break the military deadlock, rectify the European balance, and underwrite a settlement. Yet this was not an aspect of the situation to which these publicists generally gave much attention. Only the *New Republic* discussed in any detail ways in which American power might be deployed to influence the conduct of the belligerents or the outcome of the war.[56] Nevertheless, the issue of force was central to the divisions of opinion that arose over American foreign policy. The possibility of intervention in the war may have been always implicit in these debates, but until 1917 it was rarely raised explicitly. During the first two years of the war the question upon which attitudes generally focused and alignments developed was whether America should build up its armed forces – in the political vernacular of the time, its "preparedness."

The predispositions of most progressives were strongly against arma-

---

[55] *American World Policies*, p. 3; "American Policy and European Opinion," *Annals*, 66 (July 1916), pp. 140–6 at 146.

[56] For example, *New Republic*, 3 (31 July 1915), pp. 322–3; 4 (28 Aug. 1915), pp. 82–3; 6 (29 Apr. 1916), p. 330. See also the references in nn. 68–71 below.

ment. Indeed, one of the most widespread reactions to the outbreak of the war was that "the doctrine that military preparedness prevents war" had been further discredited.[57] The initiation of a campaign to strengthen American defenses led Holt to express amazement that "at the very moment when . . . the pretension that militarism is a preserver of peace has utterly collapsed and Europe is on the verge of moral and material bankruptcy, we are told that the United States must imitate the folly of Europe and proceed forthwith to build up a great and ever greater army and navy."[58] In December 1914, Holt was one of those who took the lead in founding the American League to Limit Armaments, "to combat militarism and the spead of the militaristic spirit in the United States." Howe, Baker, and Devine were also associated with this organization, while Kellogg, Howe, and Amos Pinchot were to become actively involved with the more formidable American Union Against Militarism (AUAM), which developed later out of the Henry Street group.[59] A small number of progressive journals and publicists, however, were early supporters of preparedness. *Harper's Weekly* ran a series of articles in the winter of 1914–15 calling for the strengthening of the nation's defenses.[60] This unusual divergence from the position of the Wilson administration seems to have been linked to the extremely anti-German view of the war propounded by Hapgood's journal in these early months. Certainly, Russell's pleas for increases in American armed forces, which were to forfeit his chances of the Socialist Party's presidential nomination, reflected his strong feelings about the European conflict and his fear of a German victory.[61] At the same time, the *New Republic*'s early support for moderate preparedness probably owed less to the editors' pro-Ally partisanship, which at this stage they had under fairly firm control, than to their anxiety to repudiate a Jeffersonian-type "pacifism which is mere laissez-faire."[62]

[57] Hapgood, "In London," *Harper's Weekly*, 59 (22 Aug. 1914), p. 176. See also "Armies Do Not Preserve Peace," *Public*, 17 (31 July 1914), p. 721; "An End to Rival Armaments," *Independent*, 79 (17 Aug. 1914), p. 228; Creel, "The Ghastly Swindle," p. 196; Notebook 3, 2 Aug. 1914, pp. 70–2, R. S. Baker Papers.

[58] *Independent*, 80 (14 Dec. 1914), pp. 392–3. This unsigned editorial is attributed to Holt in the Holt Papers.

[59] See John Patrick Finnegan, *Against the Specter of a Dragon: The Campaign for American Military Preparedness, 1914–1917* (Westport, Conn., 1974), pp. 130–5; Marchand, *American Peace Movement and Social Reform, 1898–1918*, pp. 223, 240–8; *Survey*, 33 (9 Jan. 1915), p. 394; L. Hollingsworth Wood to Amos Pinchot, 5 Apr. 1916, Amos Pinchot Papers, box 24.

[60] *Harper's Weekly*, 59 (5, 12, 19, 26 Dec. 1914), pp. 529–33, 556–9, 587, 609–10; and 60 (2 Jan. 1915), p. 18.

[61] See, for example, "In the Shadow of the Great War," *San Francisco Bulletin*, 30 Oct. 1915; Speech to Socialist Literary Society, Philadelphia, 28 Nov. 1915, Russell Papers.

[62] *New Republic*, 2 (20 Mar. 1915). See also "Pacifism vs. Passivism," *New Republic*, 1 (12 Dec.

During the course of 1915–16 several came to take a more sympathetic view of the call for increased preparedness, producing a more even division on the issue among this group of publicists. This shift of opinion paralleled sentiment both in Congress and the country at large, which was itself doubtless connected with the administration's change of stance in the summer of 1915.[63] It is natural to relate this to the crisis in German-American relations following the sinking of the *Lusitania,* but, at least as far as most of these men were concerned, the connection was not a simple one.

The crux of the *Lusitania* dispute was the issue of American neutral rights, and this whole question tended to generate ambivalent attitudes. Those who most valued such rights as a token of neutrality were generally the most anxious to avoid involvement in the conflict, while those most willing to contemplate a break with Germany were usually among those least ready to press American grievances against the Allies. These dilemmas were reflected in the progressive journals. The *Public,* strongly pacifist, suggested that the United States should neither concede nor forcibly resist the claims of the belligerents, but seek reparation after the war.[64] As a means of "preventing war," Kellogg in August 1916 recommended "the systematic pushing of our protests against British interference with trade and mails – with anything like the vigor with which we maintain the right of life at sea against the Germans – so as to remove the impending mistrust in our good faith and neutrality by the German people."[65] The notably varying degrees of militancy with which the *Independent* demanded the pressing of American claims against Germany may well have reflected the different attitudes of the pacifically inclined Holt and the fiercely pro-Allied Giddings.[66] Under Croly's guidance, the *New Republic* made a particularly thoughtful and thorough attempt to evolve "a national policy in relation to the Great War . . . under the pressure of

---

1914), pp. 6–7. For support of preparedness, see *New Republic,* 1 (5, 12, 19 Dec. 1914, 9, 30 Jan. 1915), pp. 3–4, 3–4, 3, 9–10, 3. On the *New Republic's* attitude to the belligerents in 1914–15, see Forcey, *Crossroads of Liberalism,* pp. 231–2.

[63] See Finnegan, *Against the Specter of a Dragon,* pp. 37–41, 80–8, 92–120.

[64] *Public,* 18 (23 Apr. 1915), pp. 344–5.

[65] "A Bill of Particulars: Items in an International Policy for America," *Nation,* 103 (3 Aug. 1916), sec. 2, p. 1. Bourne, too, felt that Wilson should have made American neutrality more "effective and robust, by insisting, in cooperation with the other neutrals, on the observance of international law. Could he not have spiked Germany's submarine reprisals by holding England to a legal blockade?" "Doubts about Enforcing Peace," TS. [1916?], Bourne Papers, reel. 3.

[66] For examples both before and after the *Lusitania* sinking, compare "Constructive Neutrality," *Independent,* 80 (23 Nov. 1914), p. 268, with "Warring on Non-Combatants," ibid., 82 (12 Apr. 1915), pp. 56–7; and "International Law and the Submarine," ibid., 82 (31 May 1915), pp. 340–1 with "No More Words," ibid., 83 (2 Aug. 1915), p. 136.

new events."[67] Nonetheless, through 1915 and into 1916 the journal pursued a somewhat vacillating course, which may partly have reflected differences among the editors.[68] On the one hand, there were calls for the impartial defense, in association with other neutral countries, of rights recognized by international law as "the only way we have of showing that we are not satisfied to live in a world where power is the sole arbiter."[69] On the other hand, there were pleas for the frank avowal of a policy of "benevolent neutrality" toward the Allies, to be justified, variously or in combination, by a moral judgment on the belligerents' conduct and purposes or an assessment of which outcome of the struggle would best serve America's own interests.[70] These positions were eventually reconciled in the recommendation that "while still asserting the legal rights of American citizens under the law of nations as the clearest existing evidence of that international order for which the Allies claimed to be fighting, the American government could use its own discretion in pushing its protests home."[71]

Although attitudes to the defense of American neutral rights were both varied and complicated, it is clear that very few of these writers felt that such rights should be upheld for their own sake or as a simple matter of national honor.[72] Anti-imperialist predispositions inclined many to the view that, as Creel put it when defending Wilson's Mexican policy in December 1914, "hurt to a nation's honor comes always from within,

---

[67] *New Republic,* 10 (10 Mar. 1917), pt. 2, p. 3.

[68] See Forcey, *Crossroads of Liberalism,* pp. 228–9. Forcey has provided the fullest account of the *New Republic*'s attitude to the war. See also Robert E. Osgood, *Ideals and Self-Interest in America's Foreign Relations: The Great Transformation of the Twentieth Century* (Chicago, 1953), pp. 121–5; Lasch, *The New Radicalism in America,* chap. 6; Noble, *The Paradox of Progressive Thought,* chap. 3; Michael Wreszin, *Oswald Garrison Villard: Pacifist at War* (Indianapolis, Ind., 1965), pp. 72–3.

[69] *New Republic,* 2 (10 Apr. 1915), pp. 247–8 at p. 248. See also ibid., 1 (2, 9 Jan. 1915), pp. 8, 8; 2 (20 Feb., 6 Mar. 1915), pp. 59–60, 113–14; 4 (7 Aug., 4 Sept., 9 Oct. 1915), pp. 4–5, 111, 244; 5 (22 Jan. 1916), pp. 290–2.

[70] *New Republic,* 3 (15 May, 3, 10 July 1915), pp. 24, 218–19, 241–2; 4 (14 Aug., 2 Oct. 1915), pp. 29, 217; 5 (20 Nov. 1915, 15, 29 Jan. 1916), pp. 56–8, 263–4, 334–5; 6 (12 Feb., 18 Mar., 29 Apr. 1916), pp. 30, 167–8, 327; 7 (13, 20, 27 May, 22 July 1916), pp. 25, 28–9, 53–5, 76–8, 288.

[71] Ibid., 6 (26 Feb. 1916), p. 102. A few weeks earlier, the editors had observed that "the threat of an embargo on exports might bring Great Britain to terms, but the threat will not and should not be made." Ibid., 5 (13 Nov. 1915), p. 27.

[72] The only possible exceptions to this generalization were those, like Giddings and Russell, whose pro-Ally partisanship was so strong as to make them essentially interventionists. See Giddings, "Which Do You Prefer?" *Independent,* 85 (10 Jan. 1916), p. 42; and for Giddings's eagerness for the United States to take "its stand by the side of the Allies," F. H. Hankins, "Franklin Henry Giddings, 1855–1931," *American Journal of Sociology,* 37 (Nov. 1931), p. 353n.; Russell, Diary no. 3, 9 May 1915, Russell Papers.

never from without."[73] The progressive ethos was unsympathetic to the basing of foreign policy upon narrow self-interest. In January 1915, Holt sarcastically contrasted the silence of the United States government as atrocities were committed in Belgium and elsewhere with its prompt protests against the infringement of American commercial rights.[74] "We ought never go to war for national honor alone," he declared after the *Lusitania* sinking, "any more than we should kill a man who insults us on the street."[75] A similar comparison was later made by Baker as he complained that Theodore Roosevelt's attitude to foreign policy represented "the morals of 1825, with the gentlemanly code of the duello!" It was "this code, on its way to eternal damnation that has caused all the trouble in Europe"; moreover, it would be "wrong" to "fight for our property."[76]

More than the loss of property was involved, of course, when the *Lusitania* was torpedoed, and progressive publicists joined in the chorus of denunciation that this deed evoked.[77] Even the pacifist-minded agreed that, as Holt put it on behalf of the American League to Limit Armaments, "it would seem to be the duty of the United States to demand from Germany reparation for the wanton destruction of our citizens and pledges that such violations of international law and morality will not be repeated."[78] However, there was also general agreement, which again reflected the mood of the country, that these demands should not be

[73] "Our 'Visionary' President," p. 195.
[74] *Independent*, 81 (11 Jan. 1915), p. 41.
[75] Ibid., 82 (24 May 1915), p. 308.
[76] Notebook 12, 17 Nov. 1916, pp. 34–43; Notebook 9, Jan. 1916, pp. 2,4, R. S. Baker Papers. See also Notebook 8, Nov. 1915, pp. 36–40; Notebook 9, 3 Mar., 27 Apr. 1916,, pp. 42–9, 118–19, ibid.
[77] See, for example, *Harper's Weekly*, 60 (22 May 1915), p. 481; *Independent*, 82 (17 May 1915), pp. 267–8; *New Republic*, 3 (22 May 1915), p. 55; Russell, Diary no. 3, 9 May 1915, Russell Papers. Alone of these writers and editors, Samuel Danziger, at this time managing editor of *Public*, appears to have had more sympathy with Germany than with the Allies. He, too, condemned the "murderous deliberation" which sank the *Lusitania* but observed that it seemed that "something was inexcusably wrong with the lifeboats and other life-saving appliances," and hoped that the names of those who manned the U-boat would not be made public since "though what they did was done from the same motive and in the same spirit as the acts of the soldiers in the trenches, an inconsistent world will nevertheless discriminate against them." *Public*, 18 (14 May 1915), pp. 465, 467. In an editorial that his political enemies in Kansas would later use against him, White, too, bracketed his denunciation of "the barbarities of Germany's warfare" with condemnation of "English commercialism that would prompt the ship owners of the Lusitania to shield the shipment of arms by women and children; English complacence that would let a great war go on threatening humanity leaving noncombatants under her flag without the protection of all her naval recourse." *Emporia Gazette*, 10 May 1915; W. A. White to Charles F. Scott, 17, 24 Apr. 1918, White Papers.
[78] *New York Times*, 12 May 1915, Scrapbook 1, Holt Papers.

pressed to the point of war.[79] Only Russell, who perhaps significantly was in France at the time, called for intervention.[80] Even those journals most favorable to preparedness and the Allied cause displayed a notable caution. Like the *Independent, Harper's Weekly* argued that American entry into the war would actually help Germany by cutting off supplies of munitions and food to the Allies.[81] It would "destroy what is left of Belgium" by ending the work of the Relief Commission under the irreplaceable Herbert Hoover.[82] Above all, "from a world point-of-view the greatest evil would be in our lessened ability to do constructive work after the war because of our being an ally of one group of powers instead of a philosophic outsider wielding immense influence on both sides."[83] The importance of this last consideration had earlier been stressed by the editors of the *New Republic* as they sought to explain why they differed from pro-Ally interventionists. Arguing that the Allies had developed aggressive war aims of their own, and assuming that even if she entered the war America would not be prepared to make the direct military contribution that alone would secure her a major influence on the settlement, they concluded that "it will be well for the world to keep one great Power disinterested. The United States ought to be that power."[84] In the Middle West, the case against intervention needed less justification. "The world's highways are filled with homicides," White observed. "Let all sane men go in and shut their doors. To go out means contagion and death."[85]

It would seem, in fact, that the increased public support for preparedness following the *Lusitania* crisis owed as much to fear as to anger.[86] Certainly, White was soon to view the threat posed by Germany in vivid terms. "We can see the [German] army landing at Galveston and coming right "cross country to the Missouri Valley," he wrote to Roosevelt in October 1915.[87] Suggestions that a victorious Germany was likely to

[79] "It is a very ticklish situation: the country wants Mr. Wilson to be firm and yet almost no one wants war." Notebook 7, 17 July 1915, pp. 11–12, R. S. Baker Papers.

[80] Statement to Newspaper Enterprise Association, 9 May 1915, Diary no. 3 Russell Papers.

[81] *Harper's Weekly*, 60 (5 June 1915), p. 529; *Independent*, 82 (24 May 1915), p. 309. Hapgood seems to have been confirmed in this view by conversations in Britain. "Sorrow in Queenstown," *Harper's Weekly*, 60 (12 June 1915), p. 557. See also Norman Angell, "A New Kind of War," *New Republic*, 3 (31 July 1915), p. 329.

[82] *Harper's Weekly*, 60 (12 June 1915), p. 553; 61 (9 Oct. 1915), p. 339.

[83] Ibid., 61 (31 July 1915), p. 97.

[84] "Not Our War," *New Republic*, 3 (5 June 1915), pp. 108–10.

[85] *Emporia Gazette*, 10 May 1915. Rowell calmly prophesied that "between Germany and America there will be no war – for the reason, if no other, that it is physically impossible for either nation to get at the other." *Fresno Republican*, 10 June 1915.

[86] See Finnegan, *Against the Specter of a Dragon*, pp. 37–9.

[87] WAW to Theodore Roosevelt, 28 Oct. 1915, White Papers. A few months later, White seems

challenge the Monroe Doctrine or even attack the United States were often made by advocates of preparedness.[88] As early as December 1914, *Harper's Weekly* had published, with the imprimatur of former Secretary of War Henry L. Stimson, a sensational "history" of "the Attack on New York" in which an unnamed enemy defeated the United States fleet and landed an army of 150,000 men at New London.[89] Generally, however, this sort of alarmism did not impress these progressives. For some this was because even self-defense seemed too egoistical a posture. Thus Baker, who by December 1914 had persuaded himself into complete pacifism, countered with a fantasy of his own, in which the American response to a German invasion was one of nonresistance and fraternization, until ultimately the absurdity of the situation became apparent to all. "In an instant the whole paraphernalia of war, the whole absorption of grown-up human beings in devising machinery to kill one another, seemed the utterly childish and unreasonable thing that it really was. The Americans had been the first nation to laugh dueling out of existence; and they now began the laugh that was to end war."[90] "Lest some should feel discouraged that the sinking of the Lusitania followed so closely the Women's Peace Conference at The Hague," observed the *Public*, "let it be remembered that the crucifixion followed closely the Sermon on the Mount."[91] In most cases, however, the lack of concern with national security was due less to the spirit of self-sacrifice than to skepticism about the reality of the threat. To many, it seemed that with the European nations currently preoccupied and prospectively exhausted, "the United States never was so safe from invasion as it is today."[92] "Germany can no more do this country material harm by armed attack than she could invade the planet Mars," declared the *Public*.[93] This apparently extravagant claim was nearer the truth than the fanciful scenarios of the General Staff,[94] as was recognized by some

to have recovered confidence in the at least relative security of the Middle West, for he called for the transfer of the country's gold reserves "to the interior" from the cities of New York, Washington, and Boston, where they were easy prey to attack and seizure. *Emporia Gazette*, 11 Jan. 1916.

88 See, for example, *Harper's Weekly*, 61 (2 Oct., 11 Dec. 1915), pp. 313, 533; Russell, "In the Shadow of the Great War."

89 *Harper's Weekly*, 59 (12 Dec. 1914), pp. 556-9.

90 "The Last Phase of the Great War: The German Invasion of America – A.D. 1915–16," *American Magazine*, 79 (Jan. 1915), pp. 49, 66–72, For the ruminations that led Baker to pacifism, see Notebook 4, Nov.–Dec. 1914, pp. 11–12, 14, 70–4, 56–7, R. S. Baker Papers.

91 *Public*, 18 (14 May 1915), p. 466.

92 *Independent*, 84 (25 Oct. 1915), p. 121. See also ibid., 84 (18 Oct. 1915), pp. 85–6; *Public*, 18 (21 May 1915), pp. 489–90; AP to Frederick M. Kerby, 30 Nov. 1914, to Judson C. Welliver, 13 Sept. 1915, Amos Pinchot Papers, boxes 18, 20.

93 *Public*, 18 (21 May 1915), p. 490.

94 See Finnegan, *Against the Specter of a Dragon*, pp. 49–51.

advocates of preparedness. The *New Republic* praised Wilson for eschewing "the bogey of invasion" in his "swing around the circle" in early 1916.[95] "Few informed people imagine for a moment that any nation of the world contemplates seizing or holding our territory," wrote Lippmann in his Olympian manner. "That would be an adventure so ridiculous that no statesman would think of it."[96]

Banishing "the bogey of invasion" highlighted the question that the *New Republic* itself repeatedly asked in the latter part of 1915: "preparedness for what?"[97] "For our part," the editors declared, "we should regard these super-dreadnoughts as a hideous waste if we did not believe and expect that they can be eventually used by the American government as the instrument of a better understanding among nations, and of the organization of an international system which will diminish the danger and the costs of war. In the immediate future the nation which wishes to count for peace must be prepared if necessary to count against its enemies."[98] This approach was consistent with Croly's point of view since *The Promise of American Life* but, as before, its specific implications remained opaque, particularly in view of the *New Republic*'s expressed reservations about joining the Allied cause. The existence of this policy vacuum makes it easy to understand why, despite misgivings about earlier British proposals of the kind, the journal adopted what Croly called "a fundamentally sympathetic attitude" toward the program of the League to Enforce Peace in June 1915.[99] Indeed, the League's proposal that the United States should join in establishing an international organization which would compel countries, if necessary by the use of economic and military sanctions, to submit disputes to arbitration or conciliation, had wide appeal to progressive publicists. The idea of a world federation or league of nations, long advocated by Holt, had already been endorsed in general terms by Hapgood, Spargo, Baker, and the Henry Street group.[100] Holt was one of those who took the lead in organizing the

[95] *New Republic*, 6 (12 Feb. 1916), p. 30.

[96] *Stakes of Diplomacy*, p. 128. See also *New Republic*, 4 (18 Sept. 1915), p. 165.

[97] *New Republic*, 3 (26 June 1915), pp. 188–90; 4 (9, 23, 30 Oct. 1915), pp. 245, 293–4, 323–4; 5 (13, 27 Nov. 1915), pp. 29–30, 79–80.

[98] Ibid., 4 (23 Oct. 1915), p. 294.

[99] "Of course, we can be critical as well as sympathetic and point out its limitations and dangers," Croly wrote to Lippmann on June 18, 1915, "but in spite of any such limitations it is, it seems to me, the most promising concrete proposal that has been made since the war began." Lippmann Papers, ser. 1, box 3, folder 303. *New Republic*, 3 (26 June 1915), pp. 190–1; cf. ibid., 1 (2 Jan. 1915), pp. 6–7.

[100] Hapgood, "The Great Settlement," *Harper's Weekly*, 59 (12 Sept. 1914), p. 250; Spargo, "Socialism as a Cure for Unemployment," *Annals*, 59 (May 1915), p. 160n.; Notebook 5, 12 June 1915, pp. 104–13, R. S. Baker Papers; "Towards the Peace That Shall Last." See also Mrs. Alice T. Post, "Causes of War," *Public*, 17 (16 Oct. 1914), pp. 993–4.

League to Enforce Peace, which was to number Spargo, White, and Rowell among its members. [101] The League's program not only seemed to provide a way to bring American influence to bear but represented what White called "a fairly good compromise on the peace question." [102] "It seems to me," he wrote, "the way to help peace is to prepare for it and join all other good people who are willing to prepare for peace by fighting for it." [103] Some who had previously opposed preparedness were reconciled to it on this basis. In October 1915, Holt argued that both "the pacifists and preparationists" should rally behind the program of the League to Enforce Peace for "their only difference seems to be this: The pacifists dwell more on the end than the means; the preparationists more on the means than the end." A month later, he decided with "deep regret" that Wilson's preparedness proposals must be supported, but insisted that they should be supplemented by "the League of Peace road." [104] Baker, too, abandoned pacifism for a more active idealism. As early as December 1914, he was criticizing the program of the League to Limit Armaments as too negative: "It is not enough to be against armament. We must work for the principle." [105] After the *Lusitania*, he was ready to "admit reluctantly that we shall have to strengthen our military forces," but only on the condition that "as soon as possible we are to unite with other nations to prevent the up-growth of a new militaristic policy in the world." [106] "The trouble with Wilson's policy of preparedness is that it does not tell us *what for*," he complained in November 1915. "No vision of internationalism. No constructive policy." [107]

By no means all progressives, of course, became reconciled in this way to preparedness. However, the responsibility of the United States to make its influence count for peace was generally accepted even by those who felt that building up armaments was no way to do this. "If we arm in panic now," Amos Pinchot argued in March 1916, "we will simply be meeting a non-existent danger, and we will be preventing the only decent thing

---

101 Kuehl, *Holt*, pp. 117–33; "Reminiscences of John Spargo," p. 244; White to Governor Arthur Capper, 6 Oct. 1916, White Papers; Rowell to Benjamin Ide Wheeler, 21 Mar. 1916, Rowell Papers. On the League to Enforce Peace, see Ruhl J. Bartlett, *The League to Enforce Peace* (Chapel Hill, N.C., 1944); Warren F. Kuehl, *Seeking World Order: The United States and International Organization to 1920* (Nashville, Tenn., 1969), pp. 184–92, 214–16; Marchand, *American Peace Movement*, pp. 151–61; Sondra R. Herman, *Eleven against War: Studies in American Internationalist Thought* (Stanford, Calif., 1969), pp. 55–78.

102 WAW to Dr. F. B. Lawrence, 30 June 1915, White Papers.

103 WAW to Ralph Stout, 31 Dec. 1915, White Papers.

104 "Pacifists and Preparationists," "Three Roads and One," *Independent*, 84 (4 Oct., 22 Nov. 1915), pp. 4, 292–3. Both these unsigned editorials are attributed to Holt in the Holt Papers.

105 Notebook 4, Dec. 1914, p. 59, R. S. Baker Papers.

106 Notebook 5, 12 June 1915, pp. 104–13, R. S. Baker Papers.

107 Notebook 8, Nov. 1915, p. 36, R. S. Baker Papers.

that can come out of this war, to wit, disarmament."[108] Some opponents
of preparedness were among the keenest advocates of American initiatives
to end the war and establish a lasting peace. During the summer and
autumn of 1915, the Henry Street group and the *Survey* actively promoted
the idea of mediation either by a conference of neutral nations or by an
unofficial international gathering.[109] (The former proposal was also endorsed by pro-preparedness journals, enthusiastically by the *Independent,*
cautiously by the *New Republic.*)[110] The American Union against Militarism included among the planks it sought to press upon the Republican
convention in 1916 a declaration of "belief in the practical possibility of
World Federation" and a pledge of "America's service to that end."[111]
Shortly afterward, Kellogg called for "the formulation of an American
public policy along such constructive lines" as "unlike either a do-nothing
neutrality or a blind national defence, would be affirmative and fired with
a vision for mankind."[112]

As the controversy developed, however, some opponents of preparedness were to be found celebrating what Howe called "the policy of isolation and detachment that has served us so well for a century."[113] Howe
had earlier enthusiastically endorsed the Henry Street manifesto and the
call for a conference of neutral nations.[114] But in 1916 he was warning
that "it is not possible for America to lay down the rules of the game in
international affairs." Moreover, "those who are most actively urging that
America take a more positive place in international affairs" did not even
wish to change the rules of the game. "They would have us assume the
paraphernalia of imperialism, of a great navy; they would have the United
States be in a position to use the mailed fist to back financial interests,

---

[108] AP to Schuyler Schieffelin, 24 Mar. 1916. See also AP to Frederick M. Kerby, 30 Nov. 1914,
Amos Pinchot Papers, boxes 24, 18; Devine, "America and Peace: 1915," *Survey,* 33 (2 Jan.
1915), p. 387.

[109] PUK to George W. Nasmyth, 14 July 1915, to Louis P. Lochner, 21 July 1915, to Jane
Addams, 21, 29 Sept. 1915, and memorandum on Henry Street meeting, 27 Sept. 1915,
Kellogg Papers; *Survey,* 35 (2 Oct. 1915, 22 Jan. 1916), pp. 24–5, 495; Marchand, *American
Peace Movement,* pp. 238–9.

[110] *Independent,* 81 (29 Mar. 1915), pp. 443–4; 83 (26 July 1915), p. 104; 84 (6 Dec. 1915), p.
372; 87 (31 July 1916), pp. 143–4; *New Republic,* 4 (23 Oct. 1915), pp. 296–7.

[111] Minutes of meeting of executive committee of American Union against Militarism, 29 May
1916, Amos Pinchot Papers, file 15.

[112] Kellogg, "A Bill of Particulars," p. 1.

[113] "Democracy or Imperialism – The Alternative That Confronts Us," *Annals,* 66 (July 1916), pp.
250–8 at 258.

[114] Howe to Kellogg, 23 Oct. 1914, 16 Feb. 1915, 18 July 1915, Kellogg Papers, folders 308,
309.

enforce their demands, and otherwise adopt the accessories of imperialism such as those of Germany, Russia, England and the great powers of Europe."[115] Amos Pinchot's hostility to preparedness, too, was intimately connected with his distrust of its chief advocates. He had been quick to note sardonically that the concern in the rhetoric of Roosevelt and others with the deleterious effects of soft living betrayed the movement's upper-class character, since "the great mass of the citizens of all countries do not lack struggle in their lives."[116] Before long, he was seeing more sinister implications in the fact that the Navy League was "composed of the strongest business interests in the country."[117] Imbibing from Howe and others the doctrine of surplus production, he concluded that "we have a situation where a great navy is quite indispensable to a great scheme of aggressive, commercial aggrandizement, whose scene has been moved to distant climes, because the opportunities for enormous profit are exhausted here and limited here by the very completeness of the process of extortion."[118]

Such an interpretation of the preparedness movement implied that its triumph would be reactionary in its domestic effects. According to Howe, not only would the "colossal expense" involved be borne by labor through indirect taxes, but social legislation would be checked.[119] "Already, the democratic gains of recent years have been submerged," he observed in 1916.[120] "The shouters for exorbitant armament are using preparedness as an argument with which to intrench more firmly the doctrine of the sacredness of monopoly and extortion," Amos Pinchot warned President Wilson.[121] "During the Civil War banking interests, financial interests, tariff interests, railroad interests, land grabbing interests, made their way into the government," Howe recalled. "Imperialism, a great budget, a

---

[115] "Democracy or Imperialism," pp. 251, 250.

[116] "American Militarism," *Public,* 18 (22 Jan. 1915), p. 88. See also AP to Roy Howard, 25 May 1916, Amos Pinchot Papers, box 24. For a similar contemporary interpretation of the preparedness movement, see Simeon Strunsky, "Armaments and Caste," *Annals,* 66 (July 1916), pp. 237–46.

[117] AP to Dr. W. S. Rainsford, 20 July 1916. Some months after this assertion, Pinchot proposed to the AUAM executive committee that it employ an investigator "who should get reliable statistics showing the relation between the military training and preparedness movement and the manufacture of munitions." Minutes of AUAM executive committee meeting, 2 Jan. 1917. Amos Pinchot Papers, box 25, subject file 15. The *Public,* too, was convinced "that special interests are back of the preparationist movement." *Public,* 18 (5 Nov. 1915), pp. 1065–6.

[118] AP to Rev. Stephen S. Wise, 26 Apr. 1916, Amos Pinchot Papers, box 24.

[119] "Democracy or Imperialism," pp. 251–2.

[120] *Why War,* pp. 314–15.

[121] AP to Woodrow Wilson, 27 Jan. 1916, Amos Pinchot Papers, box 25.

great navy, and the possible wars which may come from imperialism mean that the financial interests will continue to be powerful. In case of great emergency they will be called in to rule, much as they have been in Europe."[122]

This case against military preparedness rested on the assumption that it was not required for the sake of national defense. Some of its advocates evidently believed it was and thus, like *Harper's Weekly,* were ready to acknowledge "the pity of it." "It is not the amount of preparedness we shall arrange that does the harm, it is the killing of the spiritual note we should wish to strike," the editors wrote. "We give up the privilege of insisting on hope and faith, not because we will but because we fear we must."[123] As we have seen, however, others viewed preparedness not so much as a necessity imposed on the United States but as the concomitant of a national decision to play a more active role in world affairs. Lippmann upbraided its critics for their faintheartedness. "To be sure, contact is dangerous," he admitted. "The danger of war will be increased, and the danger of what is known as militarism. Now, our virtue may be so poor a thing that it will vanish with temptation. We may be like one of those teetotalers who does not dare to pass a saloon. Having tasted world power, we may go drunk with it. But if that is the kind of people we are, how impudent of us to utter one word in criticism of the military empires. If experience of democracy, if a century of comparative order and prosperity and human equality have made no difference, if we are bound to act like all the rest as soon as we touch the world's affairs, then we might as well humbly retire and cultivate our private gardens."[124] "To have refused to prepare would under the circumstances have been an indication of inertia and weakness," wrote Croly a year later. "To have begun to prepare is on the whole a symptom of self-confidence. It indicated that the country is not afraid to plunge forward even though somewhat blindly and to risk the assumption of a perilous and costly responsibility which before it is redeemed may diminish many prescriptive rights, damage many vested interests and perhaps change the whole outlook of the American democracy."[125]

As he hinted here, Croly hoped that preparedness would have beneficial

---

[122] "Democracy or Imperialism," p. 252.
[123] *Harper's Weekly,* 61 (4 Dec. 1915), p. 531. See also ibid., 11 Dec. 1915, p. 553.
[124] *Stakes of Diplomacy,* pp. 223–4.
[125] "The Effect on American Institutions of a Powerful Military and Naval Establishment," *Annals,* 66 (July 1916), pp. 157–72 at 162.

effects at home. The preparedness movement as a whole seems to have derived much of its appeal from a sense that it would help to cure a national malaise.[126] To conservatives, this was a matter of instilling discipline and a sense of national loyalty into the youth of all classes and ethnic groups. Croly, unlike Giddings and Creel, did not accept the argument of some preparedness zealots that universal military training would promote "democratic solidarity". "An army is one thing and a democracy is another," he insisted.[127] However, in common with a great many of these progressive publicists, he did argue that true preparedness required the adoption of many of the reforms they had long been advocating. In the first place, the efficient mobilization of the nation's resources would necessitate a greater degree of central planning and control of the economy. Russell called for the government ownership of the railroads, *Harper's Weekly* for an executive budget; the *New Republic* demanded both.[128] Moreover, as we have seen, the war also seemed to have shown that a country's morale and fighting spirit depended upon social justice. "Unless we as a nation take some thought of the men who must fill the trenches, must man the guns, must do the actual fighting and dying for this country," White wrote to Roosevelt, "by giving them decent social environment, decent wages, decent treatment as American citizens . . . with all our guns and machinery we may lose any great contest that is forced upon us through a lack of genuine loyalty, of real patriotism, of intelligent conviction that this is after all the fairest country to fight for in the world."[129] "In no sense is patriotism an instinct," warned Creel. "Oppression and injustice check its development or crush it utterly. It cannot live side by side with a stark individualism that preaches the doctrine of every man for himself and devil take the hindmost."[130] To regain the allegiance of those immigrants whose "hyphenism" was causing so much anxiety, Creel recommended a wide-ranging program of

---

126 Finnegan, *Against the Specter of a Dragon*, pp. 106–14.
127 Giddings, "The Democracy of Universal Military Service," *Annals*, 66 (July 1916), pp. 173–80; Creel, "Military Training for Our Youth," *Century*, 92 (May 1916), pp. 20–26; Croly, "Effect on American Institutions," p. 168. See also *New Republic*, 4 (9 Oct. 1915), pp. 248–50; Lippmann, "Integrated America," *New Republic*, 6 (19 Feb. 1916), p. 63.
128 Russell, "Some Obscured Lessons of the War," *Pearson's*, 33 (Feb. 1915), p. 171; *Harper's Weekly*, 59 (26 Dec. 1914), p. 610; *New Republic*, 6 (19 Feb. 1916), p. 66; 5 (6 Nov. 1915), p. 4; 7 (29 July 1916), pp. 326–8. For similar arguments, see *Independent*, 83 (12 July 1915), p. 41; *New Republic*, 5 (20 Nov. 1915), p. 55, and 9 (9 Dec. 1916), pp. 140–1; *Emporia Gazette*, 5 Dec. 1915; Creel, "Sound Methods of Preparedness," *Hearst's*, 29 (Apr. 1916), pp. 261, 311–13; *Harper's Weekly*, 62 (6 May 1916), p. 485.
129 WAW to Theodore Roosevelt, 27 Aug. 1915, White Papers.
130 "The Preparedness with a Punch," *Hearst's*, 29 (Mar. 1916), pp. 190, 228–30.

federal action, including long-term loans to prospective farmers, a national system of employment bureaus, funds for education, and a variety of measures in the health field.[131]

The case for such "real" preparedness was often endorsed by progressives who opposed the military version. Sometimes, this seems to have been little more than an attempt to make use of prevailing currents of opinion to reach a desirable destination. In such a spirit, Kellogg called for "a programme of social and industrial upbuilding, without which, as the events in Europe have shown, military preparedness is a thatch of straw."[132] A conference on "real preparedness" in June 1916, attended by such opponents of increased armament as Amos Pinchot, Howe, and Steffens as well as by Weyl, called for a child labor bill, progressive taxation on large incomes and inheritances, federal acquisition of natural monopolies, and social insurance against sickness and accident.[133] Two much-touted proposals were that the government should take over and operate all plants manufacturing munitions and that the new defense expenditure should be financed through increases in direct taxation rather than by indirect taxes or bonds. Although both these ideas were supported by several of those who accepted the case for military preparedness but nevertheless favored progressive taxation on principle, and, like White, did "not believe that our peace should be at the mercy of a lot of agitators who profit by our warlike activities,"[134] they each had a particular appeal to those who continued to believe that "the gravest danger to the country is from within."[135] Howe played an active part in the Association for an Equitable Federal Income Tax, which apparently helped to secure the substantial increases in direct taxation eventually included in the 1916

[131] "The Hopes of the Hyphenated," *Century*, 91 (Jan. 1916), pp. 350–63. See also *New Republic*, 4 (9 Oct. 1915), p. 249; 5 (29 Jan. 1916), pp. 319–21; 7 (27 May, 10 June, 8 July 1916), pp. 75–6, 137–9, 236. Also *Harper's Weekly*, 61 (17 July 1915), p. 56; Russell, "Why England Falls Down," p. 219; Lippmann, "Integrated America," *New Republic*, 6 (19 Feb. 1916), pp. 62–7.

[132] Kellogg, "A Bill of Particulars," p. 1. See also Amos Pinchot, "Preparedness," *Public*, 19 (4 Feb. 1916), pp. 110–13; Address at Washington Irving Labor Forum, 5 Mar. 1916; AP to Roy Howard, 25 May 1916, Amos Pinchot Papers, box 24.

[133] "A Prescription for 'Real' Preparedness," *Survey*, 36 (15 July 1916), pp. 420–1; *Public*, 19 (8 Sept. 1916), p. 851. For Steffens's opposition to military preparedness, see LS to Mrs. J. James Hollister, 1 July 1916, *Letters*, 1, pp. 374–5. See also Marchand, *American Peace Movement*, p. 247.

[134] WAW to Frank Dale, 13 Mar. 1916, White Papers. See also *Harper's Weekly*, 60 (13 March 1915), pp. 244–7, and 61 (27 Nov., 11 Dec. 1915), pp. 505, 553; *New Republic*, 4 (9, 30 Oct. 1915), pp. 244–5, 319–20, and 5 (4 Dec. 1915), p. 107.

[135] Howe, *Why War*, pp. xi–xii. See also *Public*, 17 (18 Dec. 1914), p. 1201.

Revenue Act.[136] Other opponents of military preparedness, notably Baker, Bourne, and Spargo, sought something akin to William James's "moral equivalent of war" in the notion that young Americans of both sexes might be conscripted into "a work-army," which, Bourne suggested, "could perform all those services of neatness and mercy and intelligence which our communities now know how to perform and mean to perform, but have not the weapons to wield."[137]

For some at least, the presumed domestic implications of preparedness seem to have added significantly to their enthusiasm for it. This was particularly the case with the editors of the *New Republic*. As early as November 1915, they suggested that preparedness might serve as "a Trojan Horse" for the infiltration of radical reforms.[138] "The agitation for preparedness, military and naval, may help public opinion to understand that an inefficient, wasteful, and socially callous nation cannot be prepared for fighting," the editors wrote six months later. "An intentionally conservative movement has developed into a most useful social ferment which in the end is likely to make American national consciousness more intense, more sensitive, and more alert."[139] The frustration from which such thoughts sprang was revealed by Croly's lament that "the most conspicuous aspect of the progressive movement during the past fifteen years has been the contrast between the enormous effort and the meagre results."[140] The confidence that, whatever the social forces involved, they possessed special insight into the logic of the situation was best expressed by Lippmann. "I wonder," he wrote in June 1916, "whether the defense societies have any notion of the consequences of their propaganda."[141]

---

[136] Link, *Wilson: Campaigns for Progressivism and Peace* (Princeton, N.J., 1965), pp. 60–5.
[137] Bourne, "A Moral Equivalent for Universal Military Service," *New Republic*, 7 (1 July 1916), pp. 217–19. See also Baker, "The Great American Conscription," *American*, 81 (Jan. 1916), pp. 42–4, 60–4; Spargo, "Socialists and the Problems of War," *Intercollegiate Socialist*, 5 (Apr.–May 1917), p. 24. For Spargo's opposition to preparedness, see Friedberg, "Marxism in the United States," pp. 185–8.
[138] *New Republic*, 5 (6 Nov. 1915), pp. 6–7.
[139] Ibid., 7 (20 May, 22 July 1916), pp. 52, 290–1.
[140] "Effect on American Institutions," p. 164.
[141] "The Issues of 1916," *New Republic*, 7 (3 June 1916), pp. 107–9. Russell remarked on "the naive inconsistency of the gentlemen that are now calling attention to our undefended condition. There is not one of them who would not shiver at the proposal that the government should take over the railroads and the telegraphs, and yet . . . without governmental ownership of the means of communication, all our defense schemes would be merely ludicrous failures." "Some Obscured Lessons of the War," *Pearson's*, 33 (Feb. 1915), p. 171.

The progressive consensus on foreign policy

It will be seen that while the question of preparedness produced serious differences of opinion among these progressive publicists, as far as the great majority were concerned such differences were limited both in depth and scope. This was partly because, aside from a few individuals such as Russell and Giddings, even those who advocated military preparedness did so in a moderate fashion, often reluctantly, sometimes belatedly. It also resulted from the common interest of both supporters and opponents of armament in using the issue of preparedness as a way of promoting social and economic reform. Not least, however, it reflected a wide measure of agreement about the purposes that should animate U.S. foreign policy. Both the extent and the nature of this agreement were to become clearer in the period after the quietening of the preparedness controversy with the passage of legislation in the summer of 1916 and before the German announcement of unrestricted submarine warfare on January 31, 1917.

In policy terms, the nature of this consensus is perhaps best indicated by the response to President Wilson's note to the belligerent powers of December 18, 1916, and particularly to his address to the Senate on January 22, 1917. In this address, Wilson reiterated the affirmation he had first made in a speech the previous May before the League to Enforce Peace of American readiness to participate in "some definite concert of power which will make it virtually impossible that any such catastrophe should ever overwhelm us again." However, by setting forth "the conditions upon which" the government "would feel justified in asking our people to approve its formal and solemn adherence to a League for Peace," he sought to make the promise of this American contribution to European security into a means of influencing the terms of peace. "No covenant of cooperative peace that does not include the peoples of the New World can suffice to keep the future safe against war," he warned, "and yet there is only one sort of peace that the peoples of America could join in guaranteeing." Such a peace would have to "recognize and accept the principle that governments derive all their just powers from the consent of the governed, and that no right anywhere exists to hand peoples about from sovereignty to sovereignty as if they were property"; otherwise "the ferment of spirit of whole populations will fight subtly and constantly against it and all the world will sympathize." Moreover, "the paths of the sea must alike in law and in fact be free." There needed to be limitation of both naval and military armaments. Above all, "it must be a peace without victory" since "only a peace between equals can last." "Victory would mean peace forced upon the loser, a victor's terms imposed upon the vanquished. It would be accepted in humiliation, under duress, at an intolerable sacrifice, and would leave a sting, a resentment, a bitter memory upon which terms of peace would rest, not permanently, but only as upon quicksand."[142]

This speech of Wilson's received almost unanimous approval from these progressive journals and commentators. To Baker, it seemed "the very quintessence of the American ideal applied to world affairs and . . . the greatest and most daring act of statemanship I have known in my time."[143] "In that address," Croly wrote to the president, "you have marshalled with great lucidity and eloquence every important fact which has been brought by the two and a half years of world warfare, and every important principle which the experience of that two and a half years has made authoritative and real."[144] "On the 22nd January President Wilson rose into the international realm," declared Holt, with "an address to the world that penetrates to the very heart of the peace problem."[145] To Holt, naturally, the core of Wilson's message was the willingness to lead the United States into a postwar league to enforce peace, but this aspect in no way diminished the enthusiasm of antimilitarists. The *Public* judged Wilson's address as "all things considered, the greatest pronouncement of a generation," while Amos Pinchot undertook the difficult task of defending it to a nephew serving with the British Expeditionary Force in France.[146]

The fury aroused in the Allied countries by the phrase "peace without victory" found no echo even with the most pro-Allied of these progressive editors. It is true that some sought to gloss it somewhat. Thus, the *Independent* interpreted it as "a warning to Germany to yield before overwhelming defeat had become her portion," while Lippmann in the *New Republic* warned that "if the Germans think they are offering peace now because their armies are victorious, then the war will have to go on till the military situation changes."[147] Long before Wilson voiced the idea, how-

---

142 Arthur S. Link et al., eds., *The Papers of Woodrow Wilson*, 40 (Princeton, N.J., 1982), pp. 533–9.

143 Notebook 12, 23 Jan. 1917, pp. 131–3, R. S. Baker Papers.

144 Croly to Woodrow Wilson, 23 Jan. 1917, quoted in Forcey, *Crossroads of Liberalism*, p. 267.

145 "The Declaration of Interdependence," *Independent*, 89 (5 Feb. 1917), p. 202. This issue of the *Independent* also reprinted Wilson's speech in full (pp. 224–7). The unsigned editorial is attributed to Holt in the Holt Papers.

146 *Public*, 20 (26 Jan. 1917), p. 75; AP to Harcourt Johnstone, 30 Jan. 1917, Amos Pinchot Papers, box 29. Pinchot's sister, Antoinette, had married a British diplomat, Sir Alan Johnstone.

147 "Peace without Victory," *Independent*, 89 (5 Feb. 1917), p. 203; "America Speaks," *New Republic*,

ever, many of these men had come to the conclusion that a stalemate would be the best result since it would show, in Baker's words, "the utter and final impotence and uselessness of war." "Much as I think Germany wrong, I do not wish for her humiliation and utter defeat," he had written in May 1915.[148] The widespread sympathy for the western Allies at the beginning of the war had owed much to the belief that, as democracies, they were fighting a defensive battle. "I am perfectly sure England would never consent to having Germany maimed in the manner that Germany herself wishes to maim France and England," declared Hapgood in September 1914.[149] During the course of 1915, such assumptions came to seem increasingly questionable. The *New Republic,* true to its injunction that the war should be considered "not in relation to its 'moral' causes, but in relation to its realistic results," insisted in April that "magnanimity has become an absolute practical necessity," since a crushed Germany would become "in the heart of Europe a festering sore."[150] "The original allies may have come together to curb German aggression," the editors observed in May, but "the late accessions to the alliance, such as Japan and probably Italy, are themselves intentional aggressors."[151] By the end of the year their skepticism had extended to the leading western powers. "Influential Frenchmen and Englishmen are now in serious danger of repeating Germany's error, of playing Germany's game, not for her but after her," they commented in December. "They are wrapping up an ambition almost as inimical as that of the Germans to the peace of Europe, in pretentious and meaningless phrases about the future of civilization."[152] This criticism reflected the judgment that "an inconclusive ending to the war and a treaty of compromise and adjustment has a much better chance of contributing to the ultimate peace of Europe than has the ruthless subjugation of Germany." It would even be the best way of undermining autocratic militarism since "the revolutions are most likely to take place in case both Germany and Russia do not emerge from the war either decisively victorious or badly beaten."[153] By this time, Hap-

---

9 (27 Jan. 1917), pp. 340–2. Lippmann also observed that Wilson "seems to us not altogether sound" on the freedom of the seas. This unsigned editorial is attributed to Lippmann in Schlesinger, ed., *Walter Lippmann: Early Writings,* pp. 63–8.

[148] Notebook 5, 23 May 1915, pp. 75–6, R. S. Baker Papers. See also *Fresno Republican,* 11 Sept. 1914; Devine, "America and Peace: 1915," *Survey,* 33 (2 Jan. 1915), pp. 387–8.

[149] "The Prussian Menace," *Harper's Weekly,* 59 (19 Sept. 1914), p. 274.

[150] *New Republic,* 1 (23 Jan. 1915), p. 8; 2 (24 Apr. 1915), p. 292.

[151] Ibid., 3 (22 May 1915), p. 56.

[152] Ibid., 5 (4 Dec. 1915), pp. 108–10 at 109.

[153] Ibid., (27 Nov. 1915), pp. 84–5.

good's *Harper's Weekly,* too, had decided that "Germany has suffered so much that if peace were made today on the basis of the 'status quo ante' the people of Germany would soon land a blow on the solar plexus to the regime that made them pay such a price for nothing."[154] An immediate, compromise settlement, it argued repeatedly, "would mean democracy, acceptance of peace, the end of shining armor, conceit and predatory plotting; and that is the very object of the war."[155] The *Independent,* also, became increasingly aware that the "peace without vengeance" it had recommended from the start could best be achieved, as the war aims of both sides escalated, through a "peace without victory," and both in 1915 and in 1916 it advocated that the United States take the initiative in calling for negotiation on the basis of "the restoration of the status quo of August 1, 1914."[156]

Not only did the objects of Wilson's diplomacy in the winter of 1916–17 accord with the established convictions of most progressive publicists,[157] but the means by which he sought to achieve them had also been more or less anticipated on occasion. Thus in November 1915, the *Independent* had suggested that the United States ask the belligerent powers, as Wilson was to do in his notes of December 1916, to state their peace terms. "If we could learn what of these vaguely defined aims and ambitions are to be seriously regarded as expressions of the present intentions of the respective governments," they might prove reconcilable, an editorial argued, "for, after all, what every nation is now fighting for is primarily peace."[158] The direct appeal over the heads of governments and diplomats to the peoples of the belligerent countries that Wilson sought to make in his address to the Senate was not only an adaptation of a tactic he had successfully used in domestic politics, but something that those many progressives who had advocated some form of uninvited mediation by representatives from the neutral nations had put their faith in.[159] Even Wilson's basic strategy, of attempting to use a conditional American offer

---

[154] *Harper's Weekly,* 61 (20 Nov. 1915), p. 482.
[155] Ibid., 61 (25 Dec. 1915), p. 601. See also ibid., 61 (4, 11, 18 Dec. 1915), pp. 529, 553, 579.
[156] *Independent,* 79 (21 Sept. 1914), pp. 396; 84 (29 Nov. 1915), pp. 332–4; 88 (11, 25 Dec. 1916), pp. 438, 512–14.
[157] Even the phrase "peace without victory" had been used in *New Republic* editorials. See *New Republic,* 9 (23, 30 Dec. 1916), pp. 201–2, 230. Lippmann's later claim that Wilson employed the phrase "in a sense we had never intended" was misleading. See "Notes for a Biography," *New Republic,* 63 (16 July 1930), pp. 251–2.
[158] *Independent,* 84 (29 Nov. 1915), pp. 332–4.
[159] See above, nn. 109–10.

to abandon isolation as a way of influencing the nature of the peace settlement, had been recommended for some time by the *New Republic*. "The amount of responsibility America can be made to assume will depend on America's judgment of the good faith, the liberalism and the ambitions of the major belligerents," Lippmann wrote in July 1916.[160] The *New Republic* editors tended to envisage this policy in terms of providing assistance to the Allies, during as well as after the war, in return for their adherence to liberal war aims, and this perspective (together, perhaps, with misleading briefings from House) led them to interpret Wilson's "peace offensive" of December 1916–January 1917 as designed to lay the basis for such cooperation[161] However, this only served to highlight the fact that their most fundamental commitment was not to particular nations but to a particular point of view. "Everywhere the division of liberal and tory has begun," they observed. Wilson's note to the belligerents "is a declaration of our alliance with the liberals of Europe. . . . The offer of our aid plus the request for definition is a fatal blow at the ascendancy of the European reactionaries."[162]

A similar set of priorities was manifested in the comments of many progressives on the kind of postwar international organization that was to be desired. Leading members of the League to Enforce Peace tended, as C. Roland Marchand has pointed out, "to conceive of the Allied nations as a league to enforce peace already called into existence to 'discipline the lawbreaker.'"[163] This view was shared by Giddings and Walling,[164] but not by the great majority of these writers. Those who opposed preparedness were naturally hesitant about the whole idea of using force to keep the peace. "Care must be taken to prevent the league for the enforcement

---

[160] *New Republic*, 7 (29 July 1916), p. 321. This unsigned editorial is attributed to Lippmann in Schlesinger, ed., *Walter Lippmann: Early Writings*, pp. 42–5. Earlier the *New Republic* had argued that "neutrals . . . are justified in insisting that they shall not abandon the advantages of neutrality until the plans of the new community of nations, against which all belligerency will constitute rebellion, are sketched and approved." "Our Relations with Great Britain," *New Republic*, 5 (29 Jan. 1916), p. 292.

[161] This interpretation of Wilson's policy is explicitly set out in Lippmann to C. P. Scott, 24 Dec. 1916, C. P. Scott Papers. (For this reference, I am indebted to Dr. Peter Clarke.) It is implicit in *New Republic*, 9 (30 Dec. 1916, 20, 27 Jan. 1917) pp. 228–31, 311–15, 390–2. For the editors' contacts with House, see Forcey, *Crossroads of Liberalism*, pp. 265–7.

[162] "Beneath the Outcry," *New Republic*, 9 (30 Dec. 1916), pp. 231–2. Charles P. Trevelyan of the Union for Democratic Control in Britain had made a plea for just such an alliance a few weeks earlier. See "Hands across the Sea: An Open Letter to Americans," *Survey*, 37 (2 Dec. 1916), pp. 261–2.

[163] *American Peace Movement*, p. 160.

[164] Giddings, "Introduction" to Bourne, ed., *Towards an Enduring Peace*, p. xi; Walling in *New York World*, 20 Oct. 1916, p. 2.

of international peace from falling into the hands of the militarists," warned the *Public,* which thought "the essence" of the scheme was "passive resistance toward an aggressor, and a greater reliance upon the force of public opinion."[165] Kellogg was prepared to endorse "united action" against any nation that refused to submit a dispute to arbitration or conciliation and even to envisage "an international naval force as a step towards these ends." He insisted, however, that "no amount of international governmental machinery may be presupposed to keep the world at peace, or to make that peace tolerable, unless it be shot through with such principles of democracy as will call for the protection of the weaker peoples, no less than of the weaker nations, in their culture, language, religion, and the like."[166] From the beginning Kellogg had deprecated "the strict adherence to legal formulae" in the League to Enforce Peace's program,[167] and this criticism was also made by some who were less troubled about the issue of force. Rowell, for example, argued that the court and council proposed by the League needed to be supplemented by some form of international legislature to deal with "the unsettled problems involved in the unfinished growth of the world," which might require the redrawing of boundary lines or the creation of new nations. "To submit these things to a court would be to compel the fixation of the status quo forever."[168]

The *New Republic* had expressed similar misgivings as early as January 1915 after the idea of a league had been put forward by the British liberal, G. Lowes Dickinson. "Has Mr. Dickinson faced the fact that a League of Europe would be based on the *status quo,* would be a sort of legalization of every existing injustice?" asked the editors, who remarked a few months later that such schemes "come quite naturally from citizens of satisfied powers, weary of the burden of defending what they have got."[169] As we have seen, these reservations did not prevent the *New Republic* (though not Bourne) from becoming an enthusiastic advocate of American participation in a postwar international organization, but they did lead naturally to the insistence that it should be liberal, flexible, and inclusive. Not only was the participation of Germany "indispensable to the league of peace,"

---

[165] *Public,* 20 (2 Feb. 1917), pp. 100–1. See also, ibid., 19 (4 Aug. 1916), p. 722; Steffens, "Catching the Kaiser, Killing the Kaiser, Where the Kaiser Is" [1915?], TS., Steffens Papers, reel 9; AP to Mrs. Henry Hulst, 26 Mar. 1917, Amos Pinchot Papers, box 30.

[166] "A Bill of Particulars," p. 1.

[167] *Survey,* 34 (26 June 1915), p. 293.

[168] *Fresno Republican,* 5 May 1916.

[169] *New Republic,* 1 (2 Jan. 1915), p. 7; 3 (26 June 1915), pp. 190–1.

but "some kind of legislature" would have to be established that would enable the league to "deal with causes . . . provide some means alternative to war by which large grievances can be redressed and legitimate ambitions satisfied." As a specific example, the editors suggested such a body would have granted Morocco to Germany rather than France.[170]

This concern that the league of nations should not come to constitute a new "Holy Alliance," maintaining order at the expense of liberty, was of a piece with a general outlook on world affairs which may be best characterized as anti-imperialist. Certainly, this was the appropriate description for the attitudes of the great majority of these progressives to the only foreign policy issue that vied with the European war for the attention of Americans in these years. This was Mexico, at this time experiencing revolutionary turmoil and civil war. In the United States, there were vociferous demands for intervention to protect the lives and property of Americans, to prevent the despoliation of the Church, or simply to end the fighting and restore order. With the exception of the *Independent* and on occasion the *New Republic*,[171] these progressives evinced scant sympathy with such demands. Many, including Steffens for whom Mexico in these years was a major preoccupation, assumed that the agitation for intervention derived most of its impetus from capitalist interests seeking to check the revolution.[172] President Wilson's acceptance of this interpretation and – notwithstanding the dispatch of the Punitive expedition in March 1916– his general reluctance to intervene with force in Mexico won him much support from these writers, particularly at the expense of Theodore Roosevelt.[173] "His latest performance in regard to Mexico" showed that "T.R. will not do," Lippmann declared to Felix Frankfurter in January 1916.[174] By contrast, he wrote to C. P. Scott in December, Wilson's "attitude towards Mexico is proof of his radical benevolence towards the weak and his hatred of conquest and aggression."[175] Baker, too, decided that "in no way does he [Wilson] show his

---

[170] Ibid., 9 (18 Nov. 1916), pp. 60–2; 3 (26 June 1915), pp. 190–1.

[171] See *Independent*, 81 (22 Mar. 1915), p. 407; 85 (24 Jan. 1916), pp. 107–8; 87 (17 July 1916), pp. 79–80; *New Republic*, 1 (21 Nov. 1914), pp. 3–4; 5 (22 Jan. 1916), p. 288.

[172] See Steffens, "Making Friends with Mexico," *Collier's*, 58 (25 Nov. 1916), pp. 5–6, 22–3; "President Wilson's Mexican Policy," TS, [1916]; speech in Pittsburgh, Pa., 16 Oct. 1916, Steffens Papers, reel 9, scrapbook 3, p. 8. See also *Public*, 17 (20 Nov. 1914), pp. 1108–9; AP to Editor, *New York World*, 30 March 1916; Open Letter, *New York Times*, 30 June 1916, Amos Pinchot Papers, box 26; Howe, "The New Imperialism," *Public*, 20 (23 Feb. 1917), p. 178.

[173] See Link, *Wilson: Confusions and Crises, 1915–16* (Princeton, N.J., 1964), especially pp. 220–1, 316–17.

[174] WL to Felix Frankfurter, 17 Jan. 1916, Lippmann Papers, box 10.

[175] Lippmann to C. P. Scott, 24 Dec. 1916. See above, n. 161.

fundamental progressiveness and democracy [more] than in this attitude towards Mexico," while Roosevelt was "urging us with might and main to think only of ourselves; of our honor, our commerce, our integrity."[176] The implication that some national as well as special interests ought to be sacrificed had been earlier endorsed by Lippmann's gratified observation that "when America refused to protect Americans in Mexico, it struck a great blow against nationalism."[177] Steffens, ever the iconoclast, even took a shot at the idea of the American mission: "Why have another United States? . . . Isn't one enough?"[178] A more thoroughgoing attack on Americans' "militant benevolence" was mounted a little later in the *Public* by John Willis Slaughter, a writer and educationalist recently returned after many years working in England, who was to join the magazine as an editor in June 1917.[179]

The unity of views and strength of feeling that the Mexican issue revealed among the great majority of these progressive publicists demonstrated the connections that existed between views on domestic and on foreign policy. Forceful action to defend the rights of Americans and to restrain the course of the revolution was likely to appeal more to conservatives. To a lesser extent, the stance toward the European war adopted by President Wilson in 1916–17 created a similar division of opinion. In both cases, progressives who differed over the issue of preparedness found themselves in broad agreement over the principles that should shape American foreign policy. "It suddenly appears," Weyl wrote in late 1916, "as though the true cleavage in American thought and feeling runs perpendicular to the division between those who favor and those who oppose armament. The real issue is the purpose to which the arms are to be put. We may use our armed strength to secure concessions in China or Mexico, to 'punish' small nations, to enter the balance of power in Europe or to aid in the promotion of international peace."[180] To most progressives, the last was the proper goal of American policy.

---

[176] Notebook 10, pp. 55–62, 12 May 1916; Baker to Theodore Roosevelt, 14 Jan. 1916. See also Baker to Woodrow Wilson, 8 June 1914, R. S. Baker Papers, ser. 2, boxes 94, 95. For similar reactions, see *Public*, 17 (18 Dec. 1914), pp. 1202–3; Hapgood to Woodrow Wilson, 18 Jan. 1916, Wilson Papers, ser. 4, case file 510.

[177] Diary, 20 May 1915, p. 33, Lippmann Papers.

[178] "The Sunny Side of Mexico," in *The World of Lincoln Steffens*, ed. Winter and Shapiro, pp. 4–20 at p. 7.

[179] *Public*, 20 (26 Jan. 1917), pp. 82–4.

[180] Weyl, *American World Policies*, p. 10.

The debate over intervention

When the German resort to unrestricted submarine warfare at the beginning of February raised the question of American intervention in the war more urgently and explicitly than ever before, differences of view among these progressive publicists reappeared, also in an accentuated form. The lines of division, particularly initially, showed much continuity with the later stages of the controversy over preparedness. Before seeking to probe the reasons why individuals took the positions they did, we need to review the arguments that were employed on each side in the final weeks during which the United States moved slowly and reluctantly toward its declaration of war with Germany.

The German action put those who continued to oppose intervention at a tactical disadvantage since they had to devise an alternative response to this flagrant disregard for American rights and contemptuous defiance of American ultimata. In the *Survey* in early February, Carlton J. H. Hayes, a professor of history at Columbia University, suggested that the United States should adopt a policy of "armed neutrality," using force to protect those rights directly threatened by the submarine campaign but not entering the war as a full-scale belligerent on the side of the Allies.[181] This proposal was urged on the president by the leaders of the AUAM and publicly endorsed by the newly formed Committee for Democratic Control, whose four active members included Amos Pinchot and Bourne.[182] But after Wilson seemed to be adopting this course in his request to Congress for permission to arm American ships and protect American commerce on the high seas (February 26), Amos Pinchot, for one, developed cold feet. "The armed neutrality business at one time seemed to me to make for delay," he explained to Senator La Follette, who was filibustering the armed ship bill Wilson had requested. "But now, it looks as if armed neutrality, unless carefully circumscribed and defined, as the country is perhaps unwilling to circumscribe and define it, will mean war."[183] After this, Pinchot, like most other opponents of intervention,

---

181 Carlton J. H. Hayes, "Which? War without a Purpose? Or Armed Neutrality with a Purpose?" *Survey*, 37 (10 Feb. 1917), pp. 535–8.

182 Minutes of the executive committee of the American Union against Militarism, 9 Feb. 1917, Amos Pinchot Papers, subject file 15; advertisement in *New Republic*, 10 (17 Feb. 1917), p. 82. See also Amos Pinchot, "Armed Neutrality," *Public*, 20 (16 Feb. 1917), p. 154; Kellogg, "The Fighting Issues," *Survey*, 37 (17 Feb. 1917), pp. 575–7. On the Committee for Democratic Control, see Marchand, *American Peace Movement*, p. 249.

    Hayes's article reached Wilson and may have influenced his thinking. See Link, *Wilson: Campaigns for Progressivism and Peace*, pp. 306–7, 340.

183 AP to Senator Robert La Follette, 5 Mar. 1917, Amos Pinchot Papers, box 27.

concentrated on emphasizing the undesirability of war without suggesting any specific alternative.

Opponents of intervention emphasized the horrors of modern warfare and the comparative triviality of the issue between Germany and the United States. Citing estimates that up to January 1, 1917, almost five million men had been killed and more than twice that many wounded in the fighting, Amos Pinchot asserted that the war was "the most gigantic, unparalleled catastrophe to humanity that the world has ever known or imagined in the cold sweat of a nightmare."[184] "If we are to have democracy, brotherhood, Christianity, or any civilization worth living in," he wrote to La Follette, "some nation, for the sake of these things and in the name of a stricken world, must be human enough, great enough, brave enough and humble enough to say 'This thing shall spread no farther, whatever may be the cost to us.' No personal considerations, no prating about international rights and law and national honour, no talk about commercial losses or gains is tolerable at this time of the world's necessity."[185] In a more temperate and extended statement in the *Survey*, Kellogg claimed that he would "want the United States to go into the war if, as some of the advocates of the League to Enforce Peace seem to believe, that were the way to lay the ghost of war," or if he were convinced that the existing contest was "a clear case of struggle between democracy and Prussianism." "But the issue as it practically confronts the American people is different from either of these questions," he reminded his readers. "It has to do with the defence of American rights – of American lives and American ships – on the high seas."[186] This, as we have seen, was not a cause that aroused much enthusiasm among these progressives. "There may be worse things than war," the *Public* observed, "but one of them is not a temporary stoppage of ocean commerce or travel."[187]

The reply to such arguments most commonly advanced by advocates of intervention was that by its declaration of unrestricted submarine warfare, the Imperial German government had finally shown itself to be a regime whose overthrow was an essential prerequisite of a new world order. "Our country belongs to a family of nations, and must assume its share of

---

[184] "Keep Out of War," *Public*, 20 (16 Mar. 1917), p. 251.
[185] AP to Senator La Follette, 5 Mar. 1917.
[186] "The Fighting Issues," pp. 573–4.
[187] *Public*, 20 (2 Mar. 1917), p. 195. Two weeks earlier, the *Public* had noted that the death of a Negro seaman on a torpedoed British ship was thought by some to provide a *casus belli* until he was found to be a British subject, and had asked sardonically "What sort of figure would the United States have presented in going to war over the illegal killing of a citizen whom a mob in many parts of this country could have lynched with impunity?" *Public*, 20 (16 Feb. 1917), p. 148.

responsibility for the maintenance of just international relations," Russell, Walling, and other pro-war Socialists argued in a statement. "If a nation runs amuck, it must be overcome by the superior force of united action."[188] "While this spirit of lawlessness and frightfulness is abroad in the world, the United States should oppose it with all the force at its command," declared the *Independent*. "The battle we wage is for a far greater cause than the vindication of national honor or the defense of our national rights. We shall fight to overthrow an implacable enemy of humanity, an unrelenting menace to democracy and the rights of man."[189]

Those who opposed intervention did not attempt to excuse the policy or defend the character of the German government. But they maintained, firstly, that the evil of "Prussianism," although most developed in Germany, was not a German monopoly, and, secondly, that U.S. intervention would not be the most effective way to combat it. Reverting to the analysis that underlay the call for a "peace without victory," Kellogg argued that "the struggle has built up, in each of the Allied countries, a new Prussianism, so that even England, the home of civil liberties and the refuge of idealists of all Europe, has slipped back and back." As for "the overthrow of Prussian militarism itself," was not that the "particular job" of the German people? Would not "the bitterness and insecurity of defeat" drive them "into permanent bondage to their junker caste" and "into an alliance towards the East that will split Europe for a century, and create only a newer, greater threat against the democratic West?"[190] On the basis of a brief survey of German history, Amos Pinchot explained German militarism and aggression as a form of psychological overcompensation for a sense of inferiority arising from repeated defeats. "A crushing victory for the Allies" would "set the stage upon which the old progressions from inferiority to compensation, from compensation to over-compensation, and from over-compensation to aggression and world mastery, will be re-enacted in another tragedy, terrible for both Germany and the rest of the world."[191]

---

188 Advertisement in *New York Call*, 24 Mar. 1917.

189 *Independent*, 89 (12 Mar. 1917), p. 434.

190 "The Fighting Issues," p. 573. It will be apparent that this argument, like the opposing one of the *New Republic* (see n. 192 below), was developed before the Russian Revolution, which occurred in the second week of March 1917. Just as this revolution apparently had no influence on Wilson's decision to ask for a declaration of war, so it does not seem to have perceptibly altered the views of any of these progressives on the question. On Wilson, see Link, *Wilson: Campaigns for Progressivism and Peace*, p. 396.

191 "War and the King Trust," pp. 8–9, Amos Pinchot Papers, subject file 14. This essay, originally an address to the Anglo-German Club, was in large part published under the title, "The Courage of the Cripple" in the *Masses*, 9, March 1917.

On the other side of the argument, Lippmann offered a different reading of the internal dynamics of Germany diplomacy. The success of the submarine campaign, he asserted in an editorial that his subsequent writings were to make famous, "would be a triumph of that class which aims to make Germany the leader of the East against the West, the leader ultimately of a German-Russian-Japanese coalition against the Atlantic world." "Our aim," he wrote, "must be not to conquer Germany as Rome conquered Carthage, but to win Germany as Lincoln strove to win the South, to win her for union with our civilization by the discrediting of those classes who alone are our enemies."[192] In less elaborate form, an emphasis on the distinction between the German people and their rulers was, of course, a standard feature of the interventionist case. "There is no nation, considered as a nation, which Americans of every descent love more than Germany," claimed the *Independent*. "Down with the Kaiser! Long live the German people!"[193]

The desirability or otherwise of a German defeat received much more attention than the dangers of a German victory. It is true that the *New Republic* did argue that "if the submarine succeeds," it "would be calamitous to the American national interest."[194] This was in line with the thesis, which Lippmann and the other editors had intermittently propounded over the previous two years, that the United States was dependent "on British maritime supremacy for its prosperity and even its safety."[195] Yet if such invocations of the demands of national security were prophetic, as some later writers of the "realist" school have suggested,[196] it might also be noted that these demands were already often being seen in an extended sense, going well beyond the strict requirements of military defense. Thus at various times the *New Republic* observed that "security in the United States and in America must be primarily a reflection of security in Europe," "only in a world where Belgium is safe can the United States be safe," and "we must act to help make the world

[192] "The Defense of the Atlantic World," *New Republic*, 10 (17 Feb. 1917), pp. 59–61. Lippmann quoted from this article at length both in "The Atlantic and America: The Why and When of Intervention," *Life*, 10 (7 Apr. 1941), pp. 84–8, 90–2, and in *U.S. Foreign Policy: Shield of the Republic* (Boston, 1943), pp. 33–5. See Osgood, *Ideals and Self-Interest*, pp. 115–21.

[193] *Independent*, 89 (19 Feb. 1917), p. 292. See also ibid., pp. 291–2; *Emporia Gazette*, 21 Mar. 1917; Spargo in *Spokane Daily Chronicle*, 22 March 1917, Spargo Papers, box 1; *Fresno Republican*, 3 Apr. 1917; Wallings statement, 30 Apr. 1917, J. G. Phelps Stokes Papers, box 26; *New Republic*, 10 (28 Apr. 1917), pp. 359–61.

[194] *New Republic*, 10 (24 Feb. 1917), pp. 89–90.

[195] Ibid., 3 (15 May 1915), p. 24. See also ibid., 5 (20 Nov. 1915), pp. 56–8; 6 (26 Feb. 1916), p. 102; Lippmann, "What Program Shall the United States Stand for in International Relations?" *Annals*, 66 (July 1916), pp. 67–9.

[196] See Osgood, *Ideals and Self-Interest*, pp. 121–5.

secure because our own security depends upon it."[197] Moreover, delineation of the dire consequences of a German victory should not be mistaken for expectation of it. The *New Republic* seemed less anxious that the U-boat campaign might ultimately succeed than that it would quickly fail before fulfilling its appointed mission of bringing the United States into the war. "The time to strike is now," the editors wrote in mid-February. "In another fortnight the whole campaign may collapse because the British navy has defeated it. . . . Germany should not be allowed to experiment with frightfulness and then quit if it doesn't pay."[198] This confidence was widely shared, doubtless because Americans received their news about the war ultimately from Allied public sources, but opponents of intervention naturally drew a different moral. "A month will probably decide the submarine issue," Slaughter observed in the *Public* in mid-March. "Is it not worth a little patience?"[199]

If there was little chance of a German victory and if the American interests directly at stake in the submarine dispute itself were not deemed vital, intervention was an option rather than an inescapable necessity. As such, the effects at home might well seem a relevant consideration, particularly to those like Amos Pinchot who had already concluded that "our own fights to be made here in the United States . . . should take precedence over all foreign questions, except those that are so vital as to force themselves upon us in a way that cannot be denied."[200] The implications of war for freedom in America were portrayed by some opponents of intervention in apocalyptic terms. "Already a bill is before Congress for establishment of a censorship," the *Public* noted in February. "That sacrifice is alone too much to pay for whatever may be at stake in a war arising out of the submarine question."[201] Worse still was the threat of compulsory military service, seen by both the *Public* and Amos Pinchot as a form of slavery.[202] "I am more afraid of conscription than I am of war itself," Pinchot wrote in a letter to a number of labor leaders. "For, while war means the suffering and misery of millions, and the degradation of a nation's ethical standards, conscription means the degradation of our only

197 *New Republic*, 5 (20 Nov. 1915), p. 57; 6 (22 Apr. 1916), pp. 304–5; 3 (3 July 1915), p. 218. See also *New Republic*, 4 (14 Aug. 1915), pp. 33–4; 7 (13 May 1916), p. 25; 9 (30 Dec. 1916), p. 229.
198 Ibid., 10 (17 Feb. 1917), p. 57.
199 "Peace Still Possible," *Public*, 20 (16 Mar. 1917), pp. 251–2.
200 AP to Elmer T. Reid, 6 July 1916, Amos Pinchot Papers, box 24.
201 *Public*, 20 (16 Feb. 1917), p. 147. See also ibid. (2 Mar. 1917), p. 198; Amos Pinchot letter, "In Defense of Armed Neutrality," *New Republic*, 10 (10 March 1917), p. 164.
202 *Public*, 20 (16 Feb. 1917), p. 149; AP to Samuel Gompers, 10 Mar. 1917, Amos Pinchot Papers, box 32. See also *Public*, 20 (30 Mar.; 6, 13 Apr. 1917), pp. 295, 320, 344–5.

great weapon against tyranny – the human mind."[203] The downfall of the Czar was greeted by the *Public* with the comment that "Russia overthrows despotism while American tories are working hard to fasten the discredited Russian system upon the United States."[204] Those of an antimonopoly or single tax outlook were particularly sensitive about individual freedom, but progressives of all kinds anticipated that belligerency would pose a threat to civil liberties. "The day war is declared, that day we are invaded – our liberties, our reason, our power to choose for ourselves," Kellogg wrote.[205] The issue concerned some supporters of intervention. Thus, the *New Republic* "reluctantly" suggested compulsory military training "for certain age classes" but insisted not only that "sincere exemption be provided for the conscientious objector" but also, interestingly, that "the men trained would not be compelled to fight in Europe."[206] Later, it acknowledged that "war always brings with it a tendency to intolerance" and advocated the establishment of a national organization for the protection of free speech.[207]

Nevertheless, to the *New Republic* these dangers were of less significance than the opportunities that war would provide to extend collectivism and promote economic equality. "Our pacifist fellow-citizens," the editors complained, "are making democracy depend more upon the observance of scruples than upon the successful use of the new conditions, brought into existence by American participation in the war, in order to penetrate the national organization and policy with a democratic impulse."[208] Before war was even declared, they urged that liberals should work for "government regulation of output, prices, profits, and labor conditions," "immediate conscription of income" to pay for the war, official encouragement of unionization and the protection and improvement of working standards, and "a vast expansion of educational opportunity and means for scientific research."[209] Socialists, whether or not they favored intervention, naturally were also alert to the likelihood that it would produce an extension of collectivism.[210]

[203] AP to James Wilson and ten other trade unionists, 22 Mar. 1917, Amos Pinchot Papers, box 32.
[204] *Public*, 20 (23 Mar. 1917), pp. 268–9 See also ibid., pp. 269–70. For earlier warnings that the United States was in danger of betraying its heritage, see ibid., 20 (23 Feb; 9, 16 Mar. 1917), pp. 176, 219, 245–7.
[205] "The Fighting Issues," p. 577.
[206] "America's Part in the War," *New Republic*, 10 (10 Feb. 1917), pp. 33–4.
[207] *New Republic*, 10 (14 Apr. 1917), p. 307.
[208] "Public Opinion and the War," *New Republic*, 10 (21 Apr. 1917), p. 335.
[209] "A War Program for Liberals," *New Republic*, 10 (31 Mar. 1917), pp. 249–50.
[210] See "Socialists and the Problems of War," *Intercollegiate Socialist*, April–May 1917, pp. 7–27, particularly the comments of Bourne and Walling on pp. 10, 27.

However, the thesis that war was bound to be socially progressive was more seriously challenged in 1917 than it had been earlier. The *Public* published two full-length articles taking issue with the proposition. In the first of these, Victor Yarros argued that "the 'good' effects of the world war are as dust in the balance beside the evil effects," which included not only the treatment of conscientious objectors and the suppression of free speech, but also an increase in juvenile crime in every belligerent country, profiteering and disregard of the law, not to mention "the vulgar and flippant vaudeville and music-hall 'shows' that correspondents from London, Berlin and Vienna tell of."[211] A few weeks later, George P. West (who, like Slaughter, was to join the *Public*'s team of editors in June) pointed out that "just as Mr. A. M. Simons, writing as a Socialist in *The New Republic,* sees the war as an opportunity for revolutionists, so Mr. Frank A. Vanderlip, in the monthly letter of the National City Bank, sees it and the universal service that is so big a part of it, as an inculcator of a correct attitude on the part of the masses toward discipline and authority." That the latter was the more realistic prophet, West had no doubt. "Today the mere breath of war has checked every militant movement for a better social order in the United States." The requirements of mobilization would be made an excuse for reversing some of the advances, particularly in terms of minimum labor standards, that had already been made.[212] "War will check the forward movement of labor," Amos Pinchot warned Samuel Gompers, "suppress the radical impulses of the nation and put the average citizen in his place – the place that the industrial absolutist and bureaucrat wants him to occupy."[213] Supporters of intervention were not entirely free of such forebodings. "I fear some of our cherished plans may find their place in the wreckage of war," Rowell wrote to a fellow Progressive.[214] "I think the war will bring either a large forward jump or a large backward jump – I am not sure which," White wrote. "The great Civil War in America, it seems to me, was vastly more reactionary in its later influence than could have been imagined. . . . This war in Europe may have a similar effect. One can't say."[215] Even the *New Republic* concluded that "the possible benefits are incalculably great but no less incalculable and considerable are the possible disasters."[216]

211 "War and Its Social Effects," *Public,* 20 (23 Feb. 1917), pp. 179–80.
212 "The Price of War," *Public,* 20 (6 Apr. 1917), pp. 324–5.
213 AP to Samuel Gompers, 10 Mar. 1917, Amos Pinchot Papers, box 32.
214 Rowell to G. W. Stone, 21 Apr. 1917, Rowell Papers.
215 WAW to Effie June Franklin, 13 Mar. 1917, White Papers. A similar observation on the political effects of the Civil War was made by West, "The Price of War," p. 324.
216 "Public Opinion and the War," *New Republic,* 10 (21 Apr. 1917), p. 334.

The crux of the debate, however, remained the effects of intervention upon the international situation and particularly upon the prospects for peace. The course of the argument tended to weaken the connection Wilson had made in his address to the Senate between the desirability of "a peace without victory" and the vision of a new world order embodying liberal and democratic principles. A distinction, which was to become important during the next year and a half, between an early, negotiated peace and a liberal "Wilsonian" settlement began to emerge.

In the spring of 1917, those who opposed war said comparatively little about the liberal principles that a peace should embody. Slaughter in the *Public* did warn that American entry into the war would mean that the league "to enforce or insure peace will be an Anglo-American alliance" rather than "a concert of nations."[217] Mostly, however, they claimed that if the United States remained aloof the European belligerents would be bound to come to terms before long. "It would be nothing less than calamitous for this country to engage in war, and even as the light of peace begins to illumine the sky," the *Public* observed in February.[218] "Our entrance into the war will prolong the war," Amos Pinchot insisted, "but if we stay out of the war . . . it is more than probable that we can bring about a conference between the Central Powers and the Allies before the time set for the great spring hostilities."[219] In any case, "unless some great power not a party to the strife can remain beyond the reach of this madness, there is little hope for peace, except the peace of exhaustion and death."[220] Kellogg, too, felt that the United States should "not forfeit our supreme vantage ground as the one strong neutral from whom conceivably great mediatory steps can be looked for in bringing in peace without victory." "Are we sure," he asked, "that we can count most for democracy, as an unwilling ally in the empire parcellings of a military settlement in which the civil forces of France and England might be submerged, than we can count as friend to those hopeful forces in a negotiated peace, devoted not to the gains of conquest but to the framing of an enduring structure of internationalism?"[221]

However, it was not only opponents of intervention who recognized that the enemies of a liberal peace were to be found on both sides of the battle lines. "It may become the duty of the United States to enter the war

[217] "Entanglements," *Public*, 20 (9 Mar. 1917), pp. 224–5.
[218] *Public*, 20 (9 Feb. 1917), p. 128. See also ibid., 20 (16, 30 Mar. 1917), pp. 252, 300.
[219] Letter in *New York Evening Post*, 27 Mar. 1917, p. 9.
[220] AP to Senator Robert La Follette, 5 Mar. 1917, Amos Pinchot Papers, box 27.
[221] "The Fighting Issues," pp. 577, 573.

on the side of the Allies, but before that we hope that they will define their aims more concretely and completely than they have yet done," remarked the *Independent,* which insisted that "the war must end, not merely in the cessation of conflict, but in a durable and guaranteed peace."[222] The *New Republic* urged in February that the possibility of an American expeditionary force be used as a bargaining counter. "If the Allies wish us to put an army in the field we can do so only when they have defined their terms so specifically that we are assured of a just settlement," the editors wrote. "Now while things are still in the balance is the time to negotiate with them not only about actual aid but about political purposes."[223] A week later, however, Lippmann was more reassuring. "The real danger to a decent peace has always been that the western nations would become so dependent on Russia and Japan that they would pay any price for their loyalty. That danger is almost certainly obviated by our participation."[224] Once "the great decision" had been made, and after the revolution in Russia, the *New Republic* asserted that "it is now as certain as anything human can be that the war which started as a clash of empires in the Balkans will dissolve into democratic revolution the world over."[225] "Now we know that the blood we shed shall be shed in a holy cause," White declared confidently after Wilson's War Message. "We are going in to fight a war for a democratic peace in the earth."[226]

Such faith that American participation would transform the nature and outcome of the war presented an easy target for critics of intervention. In the summer of 1917, Bourne was to trace "the collapse of American strategy" from "the highwater level" of Wilson's address to the Senate to the point where the United States had become "a rudderless nation, to be exploited as the Allies wish, politically and materially, and towed, to their aggrandizement, in any direction which they may desire."[227] In their turn, however, supporters of intervention could plausibly point to the costs of inaction. The *New Republic* reminded its readers that the hope of achieving a liberal peace was based upon the willingness of European

---

[222] *Independent,* 89 (19, 26 Feb. 1917), pp. 289, 371.

[223] "America's Part in the War," p. 34.

[224] "In Defense of the Atlantic World," *New Republic,* 10 (17 Feb. 1917), p. 61.

[225] "The Great Decision," *New Republic,* 10 (7 Apr. 1917), p. 280.

[226] *Emporia Gazette,* 3, 6 Apr. 1917.

[227] "The Collapse of American Strategy," *Seven Arts,* 2 (Aug. 1917), pp. 409–24, reprinted in Bourne, *War and the Intellectuals: Collected Essays, 1915–1919,* ed. Carl Resek (New York, 1964), pp. 22–35.

countries to accept the idea that an international organization could provide the security that they had hitherto sought in alliances and armaments. Their confidence in such a project would depend a great deal upon their assessment of the reliability of the American guarantee. Failure to act now in response to a direct attack upon American rights and interests would undermine the credibility of any such guarantee. "What is now hanging in the balance," the editors concluded, "is the present and future ability of the American nation to serve, as it undoubtedly aspires to serve, the cause of international order and justice."[228]

The division over intervention

It will be apparent from this review of the way in which the cases for and against intervention were argued in 1917 that there remained much common ground among progressives on both sides. The debate was conducted in terms which assumed that the objectives to be sought were a lasting peace based on liberal principles abroad and the extension of equality together with the protection of liberty at home. It was generally accepted that the maintenance of U.S. rights and economic interests was not in itself sufficient justification for war and that, although the preservation of American security would be, this was not directly at stake. Moreover, at a more specific level, the overthrow of German autocracy was seen as desirable even by opponents of intervention, while most supporters of intervention retained their suspicions of Allied war aims. On the domestic consequences of war, those on both sides feared that it would present threats to civil liberties but also hoped that it would provide an opportunity for the extension of government control over the economy.

The extent of this common ground raises the questions of why progressives differed so fiercely over the decision to enter the war and what led individuals to adopt the particular positions they did. It is important to recognize that, although the situation in the spring of 1917 did compel some sort of decision, attitudes were often ambivalent and sometimes tentative. By no means all of these publicists played an active part in the debate over intervention. Furthermore, a survey of American opinion toward the war over the whole period from 1914 until after American

---

[228] "Where the Threads Converge," *New Republic*, 10 (10 Mar. 1917), pt. 2, pp. 26–9 at pp. 28–9. For a more recent statement of this argument, see Patrick Devlin, *Too Proud to Fight: Woodrow Wilson's Neutrality* (London, 1974), p. 680.

entry reveals not a single division between pro-interventionists and anti-interventionists but a whole spectrum of positions. There were a few who openly advocated American participation in the war before 1917 and a somewhat larger number who seem implicitly to have favored it. The German declaration of unrestricted submarine warfare, and subsequent events including the Zimmermann telegram, led many who had not previously favored intervention to see no real alternative in the spring of 1917. Even among those who continued to oppose war before it was declared, a distinction can be made between those who thereafter supported the war effort and those "bitter-enders" who maintained a critical and hostile posture.

It is an indication of the fissiparous effect of this foreign policy issue upon this group of progressive publicists that some can be found who adopted each of these positions. Russell and Giddings seem to have been the only ones openly to urge American intervention before 1917, but there is some evidence that Walling, Spargo, Post, and maybe Lippmann, would also have welcomed it.[229] Hapgood and Croly had been drawn in this direction by some of their emotions but had been restrained by apparently genuine reservations. In 1917, however, they clearly wanted the United States to enter the war.[230] Baker, Holt, and White had earlier been anxious that the United States keep out of the war but they each accepted the case for intervention in the spring of 1917.[231] So, it would seem, did Creel, who before war had been declared was pressing his claim to head a "Bureau of Publicity" that would issue "big, ringing statements" to rally support for the cause.[232] Weyl was in the Far East during the crucial period, but he was later to write that the United States had been "forced into the war" and that "there was no way out."[233] Rowell also came to feel that there was no alternative in the circumstances,

---

229 Walling, ed., *Walling: A Symposium*, p. 17; Walling to his mother, [May 1917?], Walling Papers; Spargo in *Spokane Daily Chronicle*, 22 Mar. 1917, Spargo Papers, box 1; Post to W. J. Bryan, 11 June 1915, Post Papers; Lippmann to Graham Wallas, 21 Apr. 1916, Lippmann Papers, box 33, folder 1245; Hutchins Hapgood, *A Victorian in the Modern World* (New York, 1939), pp. 402–3. For Russell and Giddings, see n. 72 above.

230 Hapgood to Colonel E. M. House, 7 Feb., 4 Mar. 1917, House Papers; Forcey, *Crossroads of Liberalism*, pp. 273–6.

231 Baker, Notebook 12, 4 Feb. 1917, pp. 150–3, and Notebook 13, 10, 28 Mar., 3 Apr. 1917, pp. 78–81, 97–103, 103–4, R. S. Baker Papers; *Independent*, 89 (12 Mar. 1917), p. 434; *Emporia Gazette*, 21 Mar. 1917.

232 Creel to Josephus Daniels, 19, 28 Mar. 1917, quoted in Stephen Vaughn, *Holding Fast the Inner Lines: Democracy, Nationalism, and the Committee on Public Information* (Chapel Hill, N.C., 1980), p. 17.

233 *The End of the War* (New York, 1918), p. 33; Forcey, *Crossroads of Liberalism*, p. 278.

though he argued that the regrettable eventuality could have been avoided "if our neutrality had been from the beginning as positive and resolute as our belligerency must be now."[234] Neither Howe nor Steffens went on record with their views during the weeks of decision. In the light of their previous attitudes, it is unlikely that either was enthusiastic about the prospect of war, but they both seem to have been prepared to follow Wilson's lead. Howe, after all, held an official position (as Commissioner of Immigration at New York), and Steffens at this time greatly valued his good standing with the administration. As we have seen, Howe's colleagues in the American Union against Militarism, Kellogg and Amos Pinchot, had no such inhibitions about publicly arguing the case against intervention. However, Kellogg, whose anti-war editorial had greatly disturbed some members of the Survey Associates' board of directors, abandoned his opposition as soon as America entered the conflict.[235] The *Public* also abruptly ceased its opposition with the declaration of war, thus avoiding the danger of a conflict between the editors and Mrs. Mary Fels, who had taken over the ownership of the magazine from the Posts in January 1917 and was strongly in favor of intervention. Although Amos Pinchot was to claim in November 1917 that he had "said nothing against the war since we entered it,"[236] he continued to agitate for an early peace and in the elections of 1917 supported the campaign of Morris Hillquit, an anti-war Socialist, for mayor of New York City. Bourne's hostility to the war remained unequivocal and undisguised.

This diversity of attitudes forms no simple pattern. On the basis of a study of politicians as well as publicists, John Milton Cooper, Jr. concluded that the "matter of basic attitudes toward political power . . . offers the most fruitful line of interpretation of the three different positions that progressives took toward the relation between domestic reform and foreign policy." He implies that Rooseveltian nationalists, Wilsonian internationalists, and anti-war isolationists occupied different positions on a spectrum running from "affirmation of power" to "fundamental distrust of power."[237] Certainly, the division of opinion among progressive journals and publicists does suggest some such connection between attitudes to the prospect of war and types of progressive outlook. Single Taxers and antimonopolyists were prominent in the opposition to intervention

---

[234] *Fresno Republican*, 19 Mar. 1917. See also ibid., 3 Feb, 1 Mar., 3 Apr. 1917.
[235] See Chambers, *Kellogg*, pp. 59–64.
[236] AP to George Creel, 14 Nov. 1917, Amos Pinchot Papers, box 37.
[237] "Progressivism and American Foreign Policy," pp. 276–7.

whereas the most eager advocates of war were collectivists, if not socialists. It is surely plausible to link this, at least in part, to different predispositions toward the enhancement of the power of the state. However, this connection can offer only a partial explanation of the alignment over intervention. In the first place, there were some important segments of progressive opinion to which it does not apply. The clearest instance is the humanitarian—pacifist viewpoint represented by Kellogg, Jane Addams, and others in the *Survey* group, which combined opposition to intervention with strong commitment to the extension of government's role at home. On the other side of the divide, the readiness of such men as Baker, White, and Creel to support the war seems to have owed less to a particularly vivid sense of the potentialities of organized public power than to a susceptibility to appeals to idealism and the spirit of sacrifice on behalf of a noble cause which evoked hallowed memories of the Civil War. Moreover, even with respect to those varieties of progressivism to which it seems most applicable, the connection between attitudes to state power and views about intervention does not always hold. Thus, while the *Public* was antiwar, Post was a keen interventionist. Bourne, however, thought of himself as a socialist. It might fairly be said that he was a socialist with an exceptional sensitivity to the claims of individuality, but it must be remembered that on the war issue he was more representative of the American Socialist Party than were Russell, Walling, and Spargo.

The most obvious reason for the difficulty in finding a pattern in the divisions over intervention is that in many cases differences in political philosophy were less significant than differences in attitudes toward the conflict in Europe. The earliest and most fervent supporters of intervention were to be found among those with the strongest sympathy for the Allied cause. The nature of this partisanship varied. Thus Russell, though hostile to Germany, had no particular affection for Britain, which he saw as imperialistic and caste-ridden.[238] He had, however, developed a deep commitment to France. This was apparently less the product of any feeling for French culture than of a sentimental attachment to a sister republic and the home of the Revolution. "France was the mother of European democracy, its fervent champion and may now be its martyr," he wrote in November 1915.[239] As this indicates, Russell's strong feelings about the war contained a large element of anxiety about its outcome.

---

[238] See Chapter 4, "War and reform." Also, "France and the Common Good," *Pearson's*, 34 (Nov. 1915), p. 485; *Why I Am a Socialist*, pp. 123–31.
[239] "France and the Common Good," p. 489.

He had, as we have seen, feared for the fate of France from the moment he heard of the war's outbreak, and the months he spent in Europe during 1914 and 1915 left him with a much less complacent view than most Americans had about the likelihood of a German victory. By the fall of 1915, he was warning American audiences that "Germany . . . will win the gigantic contest in Europe and will establish the greatest empire the world has ever seen."[240] The partisanship of Russell's fellow Socialist, Walling, was barely less intense but the reasons are a little more obscure. Characteristically, it seems to have been based on ideological passion rather than cultural or ethnic sympathies. Early in the war he made clear his wish for a German defeat, and in justification of this position he was to maintain that Socialists should "favor the victory of the democratic as against the autocratic government, on the ground that bourgeois political democracy represents a great step in economic progress and a great step towards internationalism when compared with aristocratic or even plutocratic monarchism, where existing forms of parliamentary government are a farce."[241] The essence of this argument was, of course, common currency among pro-Allied Americans of all political persuasions. Thus Post, who had long admired the English tradition of liberty, wrote to Bryan in June 1915 that "at this juncture I fear the Hohenzollern policy of despotic world government more than I fear war."[242] No one outdid Giddings in denunciation of "the Prussian military machine and the Hohenzollern family." "I do not want to see the war end," he explained to Kellogg in declining to sign the Henry Street manifesto, "until the greatest menace to civilization which has arisen in generations is not merely whipped and restrained, but is destroyed. . . . For the people of South and West Germany, I have both respect and affection. The Prussian is a mongrel, a wretched cur, produced by the mixing of Lapp, Finn, Hun and German. The milk of human kindness has been bred out of him; he is a savage and a brute. To Hell with him and his Kaiser!"[243]

---

[240] *Rochester (N.Y.) Herald*, 29 Nov. 1915; Russell Papers. See also "In the Shadow of the Great War."

[241] *Intercollegiate Socialist*, 5 (Oct.–Nov. 1916), pp. 15–16. See also "British and American Socialists on the War," *New Review*, 2 (Sept. 1914), p. 512; "Kautsky's New Doctrine," *New Review*, 3 (Jan. 1915), pp. 44–5; "The New Trend of Bourgeois Pacifism," *New Review*, 3 (1 June 1915), pp. 64–5; *Socialists and the War: A Documentary Statement of the Position of the Socialists of All Countries; with Special Reference to Their Peace Policy* (New York, 1915), p. 383.

[242] Post to W. J. Bryan, 11 June 1915. See also Portner, "Louis F. Post," pp. 250–2.

[243] Franklin Giddings to Paul Kellogg, 13 Feb. 1915, Kellogg Papers, folder 308. For slightly more moderate but still emphatic public statements of Giddings's views, see "Leadership vs. Lordship," *Independent*, 79 (14 Sept. 1914), p. 363 (which is attributed to Giddings in the Holt

As this outburst abundantly demonstrates, Giddings's partisanship in the European conflict was unconcealed. The same was true of Russell, and to a lesser extent Walling, but others were probably more emotionally involved than they admitted in public. Thus Spargo not only campaigned vigorously against preparedness but claimed as late as February 9, 1917, that "there is no member of the Party more anxious than I am to have America keep out of the war."[244] However, he had confessed to Morris Hillquit in November 1914 that "it is impossible for me to feel other than that the defeat of Germany is essential to our movement,"[245] and his actions after America's entry into the war certainly suggested that he welcomed it. Spargo's opposition to preparedness, which led to a public debate with Russell in December 1915, could be justified by the unwavering confidence in an Allied victory that he claimed in later recollections, but it perhaps also reflected a reluctance to defy the overwhelming sentiment of a party which, as he was to admit, had formed the whole context as well as purpose of his life.[246] Prudential considerations of a somewhat different kind may have moderated the *New Republic*'s expression of its editors' feelings about the European conflict. "My guess is that you have missed in The New Republic the emotional warmth toward the cause of the Allies our real feelings would justify," Lippmann wrote to Graham Wallas in April 1916. The reason for this was that, in working for an Anglo-American understanding, "we felt . . . that the traditional hostility to England in this country could not be overcome by a paper that didn't take what might be called a strongly American view of the situation. . . . But . . . our hearts have been with you every minute."[247] Lippmann may not have spoken for his colleagues,[248] but of his own passionate involvement in the Allied cause his reactions to such events as Mons and the *Lusitania* left little doubt.[249] However, Lippmann's partisanship, like Hapgood's, seems to have owed much to his personal

---

Papers); "The Larger Meanings of the War," *Survey*, 33 (7 Nov. 1914), pp. 143–4; "Which Do You Prefer?" *Independent*, 85 (10 Jan. 1916), p. 42.

244 To Comrade [Adolph] Germer, 9 Feb. 1917. Spargo Papers, box 1. See also Friedberg, "Marxism in the United States," pp. 185–6.

245 Spargo to Morris Hillquit, 12 Nov. 1914. Quoted in Friedberg, "Marxism in the United States," p. 172.

246 Friedberg, "Marxism in the United States," pp. 187–8, 177–8; "My association with Woodrow Wilson to 1917," [c. 1960], unpublished TS., Spargo Papers, box 1; Spargo to J. G. Phelps Stokes, 25 Apr. 1917, Phelps Stokes Papers, box 26; Spargo to "my friends," 31 May 1917, Spargo Papers, box 1.

247 Lippmann to Graham Wallas, 21 Apr. 1916, Lippmann Papers, box 33, folder 1245.

248 Croly and Weyl were also pro-Allied, but a little less intensely. See Forcey, *Crossroads of Liberalism*, pp. 228–9.

249 Diary, 30 Aug. 1914, p. 23, Lippmann Papers; Hutchins Hapgood, *A Victorian in the Modern*

contacts with British liberals, and to have been qualified by this shared ideological perspective.[250] "If America is to participate in the settlement," he warned one of his English correspondents in July 1916, "it will have to be with a Britain governed by liberals and not by your Carsons et al."[251]

It was the depth of their feelings rather than the nature of their views that distinguished such men from the majority of progressive publicists. Baker, for example, had noted in his diary even before war in Europe broke out that "without knowing just why, . . . I should be with Russia, France and England against Austria, Germany and Italy – in spite of the autocracy of Russia."[252] A year later, struck by the alarming thought that "the Germans may win," he assured himself that "the Allies *must* win: they have right on their side."[253] White seems to have been slower to make up his mind, but by the autumn of 1915 he had concluded that "it is a war between the democratic ideas of the earth and the autocratic military ideas of the earth, . . . and there should be no peace until that [German military] party is thoroughly vanquished."[254] Even among opponents of American intervention there was some pro-Allied sentiment. Indeed, of this group of editors and publicists, only Samuel Danziger of the *Public* showed any real sign of pro-German inclinations.[255] Steffens and Howe appear to have been genuinely neutral in their feelings of hostility to both German and British imperialism, though Steffens did express some sympathy with the plight of France.[256] Kellogg, too, was not strongly partisan but he did assure correspondents objecting to his anti-war editorial that he was "absolutely for the destruction of Prussian autocracy," and in September 1915 he had been ready to delay any peace initiative until "a new balance is struck by a big victory for the Allies."[257] Initially, at least, Amos Pinchot, whose sister had married a British

World, pp. 402–3. See also "What Program Shall the U.S. Stand for in International Relations?" *Annals*, 66 (July 1916), pp. 63–4, 70.

[250] For Hapgood, see *Harper's Weekly*, 60 (29 May 1915), p. 505; Norman Hapgood to E. M. House, 7 Feb., 4 Mar. 1917, House Papers.

[251] Lippmann to Prof. N. S. Amos, 24 July 1916, Lippmann Papers, box 2, folder 58.

[252] Notebook 3, 2 Aug. 1914, pp. 67–70, R. S. Baker Papers. See also Notebook 3, Nov. 1914, pp. 101–4; Notebook 4, Dec. 1914, pp. 59–62; Notebook 5, 15 June 1915, pp. 120–1; Notebook 13, 28 Mar. 1917, pp. 100–3, ibid.

[253] Notebook 7, Aug. 1915, pp. 65–6, ibid.

[254] *Emporia Gazette*, 26 Nov. 1915. See also ibid., 12 Jan. 1916.

[255] See above, n. 77.

[256] Steffens to Allen and Lou Suggett, 25 Dec. 1915, to Laura Steffens, 1 Aug. 1916, *Letters*, 1, ed. Winter and Hicks, pp. 366, 382; Steffens to Laura Steffens, 4 Nov. 1914, quoted in Cheslaw, "Intellectual Biography," p. 210; Howe, *Why War*, pp. x–xi.

[257] Chambers, *Kellogg*, p. 56; PUK to Kimball C. Easton, 3 Apr. 1917, PUK to Jane Addams, 21 Sept. 1915, Kellogg Papers.

diplomat, was much more wholeheartedly pro-Allied. In February, 1915, he proffered advice to the Foreign Office on how to appeal to American public opinion, and later that year he declared that the war would end only "when the German people wake up and realize how an ambitious military caste has fooled and fuddled them into unspeakable disaster."[258] Nor were Bourne's predispositions any more pro-German. It is true that during his trip to Europe in the year before the war he had left England "just about ready to renounce Anglo-Saxon civilization," but he had also found "the whole German atmosphere . . . unsympathetic," and it was to France that he gave his heart.[259]

However, Bourne, Amos Pinchot, and other opponents of intervention seem to have cared less about the conflict in Europe than about that in America. Increasingly, as time went on, their view of the struggle was refracted through the lens of American opinion, and the Allied cause suffered from the character of its most evident adherents within the United States. "It must never be forgotten that in every community it was the least liberal and least democratic elements among whom the preparedness and later the war sentiment was found," Bourne wrote. "The nerve of the war-feeling centred, of course, in the richer and older classes of the Atlantic seaboard, and was keenest where there were French or English business and particularly social connections. The sentiment then spread over the country as a class-phenomenon, touching everywhere those upper-class elements in each section who identified themselves with this Eastern ruling group."[260] Bourne, with his "cosmopolitan vision" of a "trans-national America" liberated from "the Anglo-Saxon predominance," was particularly sensitive to the ethnocultural dimension. "The unpopular and dreaded German-American of the present day," he had written in 1916, "is a beginning amateur in comparison with those foolish Anglophiles of Boston and New York and Philadelphia whose reversion to cultural type sees uncritically in England's cause the cause of Civilization."[261] Amos Pinchot was more inclined to see the issue in economic terms and attributed the pressure for intervention to "the old

---

[258] AP to Sir William Tyrell, 4 Feb. 1915; to Newspaper Enterprise Association, 15 July 1915, Amos Pinchot Papers, boxes 19, 24.

[259] Bourne to Carl Zigrosser, 13 Dec. 1913; to his mother, 28 July 1914, Bourne Papers. See also Bourne to Edward Murray, 26 Dec. 1913; to Mary Messer, 28 Dec. 1913; to Alyse Gregory, 18 Mar., 10 Apr., 30 July 1914, ibid.

[260] "The War and the Intellectuals," *Seven Arts*, 2 (June 1917), pp. 133–46, reprinted in *War and the Intellectuals*, ed. Resek, pp. 4–5.

[261] "Trans-National America," *Atlantic Monthly*, 118, July 1916, pp. 86–97, reprinted in *War and the Intellectuals*, ed. Resek, pp. 121, 111, 110.

war horses of Wall Street."[262] He was later to claim that he "opposed the war, though my sympathies were all with the Allies, because I knew . . . that it was a minority war, into which the majority were dragged against their will."[263] Certainly, it seems that the passion with which he fought against intervention owed much to his alienation from members of his own class. "The editors and ex-Presidents will not do the fighting," he wrote sardonically, "nor will our bellicose lawyers, bankers, stock brokers and other prominent citizens, who mess at Delmonico's, bivouac in club windows, and are at all times willing to give to their country's service the last full measure of conversation. No, the people themselves will do the fighting, and they will pay the bill."[264]

Hostility to the attitudes of the American upper class was, of course, not confined to those progressives who opposed intervention. Thus, the *New Republic* in July 1916 had written scornfully of those "Americans who had always looked upon the British Tory as the apex of the social pyramid," who were "as full of futile hate against Germany as the *Morning Post* or the *National Review*."[265] That this distaste was not sufficient to discredit the interventionist case in their eyes may have been partly due to a somewhat greater concern with events abroad rather than their domestic implications. But it more clearly reflected a greater reluctance to assume an essentially negative, critical position. Much of this reluctance derived from the activist, confident outlook expressed in John Dewey's remark that "politics means getting certain things done".[266] "I am so much in agreement with your premises," Dewey wrote in reply to one of Amos Pinchot's anti-war manifestos, "that I feel moved to write you as to why I am not in full accord with your conclusions. . . . I agree with you as to the ultimate results in view of which we should determine our course. But . . . I am of the judgment that these ultimate results are much more likely of accomplishment if we go in than if we do not. My reasons for thinking so concern matters of fact with respect to which proof is impossible, and with respect to which therefore an honest difference of opinion is possible. I do not think that Germany is ready to accept, by means of any conference or mediation, any reasonable terms – reasonable in the sense of contributing to the kind of future world which I think we agree in

262 AP to James Wilson and other labor leaders, 22 Mar. 1917, Amos Pinchot Papers, box 32.
263 AP to Rev. W. S. Rainsford, 29 Sept. 1917, Amos Pinchot Papers, box 30.
264 Advertisement, "Do the People Want War?" 28 Feb. 1917, Amos Pinchot Papers, box 15.
265 *New Republic*, 7 (29 July 1916), p. 321.
266 "What America Will Fight For," *New Republic*, 12 (18 Aug. 1917), p. 69.

desiring . . . I think it is extremely doubtful if Germany will not win, unless her foes receive additional help."[267] However, Pinchot does not seem to have felt that such "matters of fact" were the crucial issue. Like Bourne, he was implicitly both more pessimistic about the prospects for achieving progressive goals and more skeptical of the ability of liberal intellectuals to control events. Bourne's famous controversy with Dewey and the *New Republic* was not so much about different means to the same end as it was about the relative importance of means and ends.[268]

Readiness to adopt the role of critic or dissenter seems to have been less a matter of philosophy than of temperament. While some rejected it as frustratingly and irresponsibly ineffective, others condemned it as arrogant. Thus Baker, despite his earlier endorsement of a Tolstoyan doctrine of nonresistance, did not oppose the drift to war in 1917. "Oh God, in this whirling time, let me not think of my opinion," he instructed himself in February. "Let me base my action . . . not upon pride of opinion, nor upon dogma; and let me not be fearful of changing my whole course of action if the realities of today overturn the opinions of yesterday."[269] Later, he expressed in revealing terms his irritation with his old friend and hero, La Follette, when the latter led the filibuster of the Armed Ships bill. "It is true as Socrates said that if a man would take issue with his time he must have a private place and not a public one. It seems to be a moment when it is more important for us all to work together for one great purpose than it is for men to stand off because of variant opinion or dogma."[270]

Easing the way to war

Baker's reaction is a reminder that the situation in the spring of 1917 was quite different from that at any earlier stage of American neutrality. Following the German resort to unrestricted submarine warfare, American intervention became, as Wilson himself testified, hard to avoid. Yet

---

[267] John Dewey to Amos Pinchot, 30 Mar. 1917, Amos Pinchot Papers, box 30.

[268] The chief contributions to this controversy were Dewey, "Conscience and Compulsion," *New Republic*, 11 (14 July 1917), p. 298; "The Future of Pacifism," *New Republic*, 11 (28 July 1917), p. 358; "What America Will Fight For"; Bourne, "The War and the Intellectuals"; "The Collapse of American Strategy"; "A War Diary," *Seven Arts*, 2 (Sept. 1917), 535–47; "Twilight of Idols," *Seven Arts*, 2 (Oct. 1917), pp. 688–702, reprinted in *War and the Intellectuals*, ed. Resek, pp. 3–14, 22–35, 36–47, 53–64.

[269] Notebook 13, 14 Feb. 1917, pp. 18–20, R. S. Baker Papers.

[270] Notebook 13, 6 Mar. 1917, pp. 68–70, ibid.

the issue immediately at stake remained neutral rights and national honor, and for many Americans this still did not seem sufficient justification for embroiling their country in the conflict. In view of their earlier attitudes, it remains remarkable that not only did the great majority of these progressive publicists accept the decision for war, but that several seem to have positively welcomed American belligerency.

One important element easing the acceptance of war was undoubtedly the widespread confidence in Wilson's leadership and in his devotion to progressive goals at home and abroad. "In time of crisis the instinct to choose a leader and then *trust* him is sound," noted Baker in March.[271] As Arthur Link has observed, "virtually the entire leadership of the advanced wing of the progressive movement" had supported Wilson in the 1916 presidential election,[272] and this included a large number of these publicists. Some, such as Hapgood and Howe, had been in the Wilson camp since 1912, but in the course of the campaign the president also received endorsements from former Bull Moosers as diverse as Amos Pinchot, Lippmann, Croly, and Kellogg, as well as from the unpredictable Walling.[273] White, watchful of his position in Kansas politics, dutifully named the entire Republican ticket on the editorial page of the *Emporia Gazette,* but later interpreted Wilson's reelection as a victory for progressivism.[274] As we have seen, Wilson's peace initiative following the election was enthusiastically received by these and other progressive commentators.[275] Significantly, it did much to restore his standing with the peace groups, which had been damaged by his *bouleversement* over preparedness. At an executive committee meeting of the AUAM in late February, "the general opinion seemed to be that the President would handle the international situation at least as wisely as Congress."[276]

For many of these publicists, confidence in a political leader led naturally to an active commitment. By the spring of 1917, a remarkable

[271] Baker's italics. Notebook 13, 10 Mar. 1917, pp. 78–81, ibid.

[272] Link, *Wilson: Campaigns for Progressivism and Peace,* pp. 124–6.

[273] AP to Fenton Lawson, 6 July 1916, to John D. McSparrin, 13 Oct. 1916, Amos Pinchot Papers, boxes 25, 24; *New Republic,* 8 (14, 21 Oct. 1916), pp. 263–5, 286–91; Forcey, *Crossroads of Liberalism,* pp. 256–63; *Survey,* 37 (28 Oct. 1916), p. 98; Chambers, *Kellogg,* pp. 54–5; *New York World,* 20 Oct. 1916.

[274] WAW to Rodney Elward, 16 Oct. 1916, White Papers; "Who Killed Cock Robin?" *Collier's,* 58 (16 Dec. 1916), pp. 5–6, 26–7. See also Link, *Wilson: Campaigns for Progressivism and Peace, 1916–17,* p. 126.

[275] See "The Progressive Consensus on Foreign Policy."

[276] Minutes of meeting of executive committee of AUAM, 27 Feb. 1917, Amos Pinchot Papers, subject file 15. See also *Public,* 20 (2, 23 Feb., 9 Mar. 1917), pp. 104, 176, 223.

number of them had developed connections of some kind with the administration. Following the demise of *Harper's Weekly* in the spring of 1916, Hapgood had devoted most of his energies to aiding Wilson's reelection, and in particular to building up his support among progressives.[277] To this end he organized the Woodrow Wilson Independent League, on the executive committee of which Baker also served. In May 1916, Baker had a lengthy, private interview with the president, which served to deepen his admiration and allegiance. During the campaign, he published laudatory articles on Wilson and his achievements in *Collier's* and the *Kansas City Star*.[278] Creel apparently had a more official role in the publicity department of the Democratic Party.[279] In this capacity, he not only produced a little book entitled *Wilson and the Issues* but also composed an open letter to the Republican candidate, Charles Evans Hughes, asking ten belligerent and loaded questions in the name of thirty-seven "professional writers who . . . have small interest in parties but a very deep interest in democracy." Among those who signed both this letter and a later Wilson manifesto couched in Creel's characteristically hyperbolic terms were Baker, Howe, and Steffens.[280] Steffens, who believed that by talking to Wilson he had played a crucial role in averting war with Mexico in the summer of 1916, drafted a chapter defending the administration's Mexican policy for the Democratic campaign handbook.[281] On a nationwide speaking tour sponsored by the Single Tax Joseph Fels Fund in the fall, he combined a sympathetic account of the Mexican revolution with extravagant praise of Wilson.[282] Meanwhile, another antimonopolist, Amos Pinchot, had widened the political rift with his brother Gifford by serving as chairman of "the Wilson volunteers" in New York State. The roster of this organization included Howe, Hapgood, Baker, and Lippmann.[283] Lippmann had for some time been sending campaign advice

---

[277] This involved urging Wilson to make progressive appointments and adopt progressive policies. See N. Hapgood to Woodrow Wilson, 18 June, 5, 6 July 1916, Woodrow Wilson Papers, ser. 2, box 147; ser. 4, case file 510.

[278] Semonche, *Ray Stannard Baker*, pp. 299–304.

[279] Mark Sullivan, "Creel-Censor," *Collier's Weekly*, 60 (10 Nov. 1917), p. 36.

[280] *Wilson and the Issues* (New York, 1916); Scrapbook, Creel Papers; Creel to Ray S. Baker, 7 July 1916, R. S. Baker Papers, ser. 2, box 95.

[281] Steffens's chapter was not published exactly as he wrote it, but he maintained that Wilson himself was not responsible for this. See Steffens to Lou and Allen Suggett, 16 July 1916; to Laura Steffens, 28 July, 6 Sept. 1916, Hicks and Winter, eds., *Steffens Letters*, 1, pp. 376–7, 381, 383; *Autobiography*, pp. 735–40.

[282] "President Wilson's Mexican Policy," Scrapbook 3, Steffens Papers; Cheslaw, "Intellectual Biography," pp. 200–3.

[283] AP to John D. McSparrin, 13 Oct. 1916, Amos Pinchot Papers, box 24. Gifford Pinchot was

through Hapgood, and in September had an apparently successful meeting with the president.[284] A week later, Weyl, too, visited Wilson's summer home. The *New Republic*'s contacts with the administration developed further after the election. By January 1917, Croly and Lippmann were going each week to House's apartment in New York for conferences.[285]

"Both Mr. Lippmann and I are more interested in doing what little we can to back the President up in his work than in anything else we have ever tried to do through the New Republic," Croly wrote to House in December 1916.[286] Although Lippmann was later to suggest that the *New Republic*'s links with the administration were never as strong as had been widely supposed,[287] there seems little doubt that at the time the editors valued both the additional weight its reputation as a semi-official organ gave the journal and the opportunity for influence apparently provided by private communication with House and Wilson. In March 1917, Lippmann submitted to Wilson an extensive memorandum urging the public justification of the administration's discriminatory enforcement of neutral rights in terms of "America's vital interest in a just and lasting peace."[288] Proximity to those in power provided other satisfactions that might add to the stake in its maintenance. One was simply the sense of being "in the know." Soon after his interview with Wilson, Baker read newspaper speculation on the president's intentions regarding peace proposals. "Had strongly that feeling of knowledge, certainty, which comes to one who knows," he noted. "It is certainly the most satisfying feature in the work of a publicist that he has been taken *into* the event, and knows not by hearsay or speculation, but by actual contact."[289] There was also an excitement in being associated with the glamour of power. Watching the president address Congress, Baker was "struck of a sudden that I was looking upon the man, who in the world at that moment was potentially the most powerful. What he said would carry to every part of the earth,

driven by his hatred of Wilson into a rather unenthusiastic endorsement of Hughes. See Gifford Pinchot to Amos Pinchot, 4 Sept. 1916, and press statement, 7 Sept. 1916, Gifford Pinchot Papers.

[284] Lippmann to N. Hapgood, 22 Sept. 1916; Hapgood to Lippmann, 25 Sept. 1916; Hapgood to W. Wilson, 25 Sept. 1916; Wilson to Hapgood, 27 Sept. 1916, Woodrow Wilson Papers.

[285] Forcey, *Crossroads of Liberalism*, pp. 257–65.

[286] H. Croly to House, 26 Dec. 1916, E. M. House Papers.

[287] "Notes for a Biography," *New Republic*, 63 (16 July 1930), pt. 2, pp. 251–2.

[288] See Edward H. Buehrig, "Wilson's Neutrality Re-examined," *World Politics*, 3 (Oct. 1950), pp. 16–18.

[289] Notebook 10, 17 May 1916, p. 72, R. S. Baker Papers.

and might change the course of world-events."[290] The feeling of being involved in the historical process could prove intoxicating. "It seems," Steffens reported to his brother-in-law in March 1917, "that just before the German U-boat order was published private arrangements for the beginning of peace negotiations had proceeded so far with Germany that I was about to be sent for."[291]

This desire to play a part in momentous events has sometimes been seen as in itself an explanation of the eagerness with which some of these progressives welcomed American intervention. In his study of the *New Republic* and the war, Christopher Lasch concluded that "the thirst for action, the craving for involvement, the longing to commit themselves to the onward march of events – these things dictated war. The realists feared isolation not only for America but for themselves."[292] This is to go too far. It is true that from the beginning the very scale of the European conflict had exercised a certain fascination. "I feel now," Lippmann confessed to Graham Wallas, "as if I had never before risen above the problems of a district nurse, a middle western political reformer, and an amiable civic enthusiast."[293] But some of those who felt this pull, such as Amos Pinchot, were to be among the strongest opponents of intervention.[294]

There is, however, no doubt that from 1915 several of these writers had expressed attitudes toward American noninvolvement more complex and ambivalent than the initial thankfulness that their country was escaping the horror. In an essay on "uneasy America" in December 1915, Lippmann wrote that "we cannot think with any pride of the part we have played in the supreme event of our lives."[295] Naturally, it was those most drawn to the Allied cause who felt this most keenly. "It is not a joyous thing to see other countries bleeding for our benefit, while we pay nothing, but instead prosper," observed *Harper's Weekly*.[296] Infuriated by American "optimism," Russell denounced the "compound of greed and bullheadedness which only sees that more money must be had, more

[290] Notebook 13, 28 Feb. 1916, p. 60, ibid.
[291] Steffens to Allen H. Suggett, 18 March 1917, Hicks and Winter eds., *Steffens Letters*, 1, pp. 391–2.
[292] Lasch, *The New Radicalism in America*, p. 223.
[293] Lippmann to Graham Wallas, 5 Aug. 1915, Lippmann Papers, box 33, folder 1244.
[294] AP to James W. Gerard, 1 Sept. 1914, Amos Pinchot Papers, box 18.
[295] *New Republic*, 5 (25 Dec. 1915), pp. 195–6.
[296] *Harper's Weekly*, 61 (6 Nov. 1915), p. 433.

money for pleasures, to buy more automobiles, more money for women to move in society."[297] By contrast, Giddings noted, "frivolity and efferves-cent foolishness have nearly disappeared in France and England" while "thruout Europe the liquor traffic and the consumption of spirits have been brought under control."[298] This comparison also came to distress some progressives less pro-Allied in their sympathies. "We are in a state of drunken prosperity, fat with the spoils of the world," Rowell warned his readers in November 1916. "We are the only great people with character untested, with hidden heroisms unrevealed. We are the only ones who have not stripped life naked of fictions; we alone have not discovered how much better altruism is than selfishness; how much more patriotism is worth than life, or even than money."[299]

Such collective self-castigation had been an element in progressivism since the early days of muckraking, but it did not easily overcome the aversion to war. When the progressive novelist, Robert Herrick, published his "recantation of a pacifist" in the *New Republic* in October 1915 – "the youths whose graves now dot the pleasant fields of France have drunk deeper than we can dream of the mystery of life" – the editors were quick to insist that "no more mischievous idea could have come to us than this of the contrast between the 'reality' of Europe's war, and the 'unreality' of America's peace. It is mischievous because it assumes that we can save our souls by joining the war, and forgets that the best way for us to save our souls is by resolutely continuing social reconstruction at home."[300] Yet when this course was not followed, it was difficult to resist the idea that some external challenge might have a salutary effect upon public opinion. "The American nation needs the tonic of a serious moral adventure," Croly observed in the summer of 1916 as he advocated preparedness. "It has been too safe, too comfortable, too complacent and too relaxed. Its besetting weakness is the prevalence of individual and collective irresponsibility,

---

[297] *San Francisco Bulletin*, 30 Oct. 1915. In this respect, too, perceptions of the domestic scene varied with attitudes to foreign affairs. "I think making money out of the war is little short of criminal," Amos Pinchot wrote. "But the fact is most Americans are not engaged in money-making at all, either out of the war or otherwise, but in making a bare and meagre living; which is a very different thing." AP to Judson C. Welliver, 13 Sept. 1915, Amos Pinchot Papers, box 22.

[298] "Moral Reactions of the War," *Independent*, 84 (4 Oct. 1915), p. 6. This unsigned editorial is attributed to Giddings in the Giddings Papers.

[299] *Fresno Republican*, 30 Nov. 1916. See also *Independent*, 87 (17 July 1916), pp. 81–2; *Emporia Gazette*, 1 Jan. 1917.

[300] *New Republic*, 4 (30 Oct. 1915), pp. 328–30, 322–3.

based on the expectation of accomplishing without effort."[301] Even in the *Survey*, Devine was showing signs by the end of 1916 of envying the European belligerents. "The fellowship of the armies, of the hospitals, of the prison camps prophesies a new and better social order," he wrote. "We who hate war and who labor and hope, and it may be pray, for peace have to discover whether it is true, as we believe, that there are moral substitutes for war, whether by gentler means the good Lord will deliver us from the evils of selfishness, sordidness, slothfulness, pettiness of soul, sectarianism, sectionalism, provincialism, and above all the conceit of ignorance."[302]

Nowhere does this impression that the period of American neutrality presented progressives with what might be called a disagreeable foretaste of the 1920s emerge more clearly than in the private journal of Ray Stannard Baker. "Of all the nations of the world at war, there is none in greater danger than our own," he wrote in August 1915. "England, Germany, Russia give promise of being disciplined and improved by this war, but we are only likely to grow richer out of it – richer through the blood and suffering of other men, richer not by wealth hardly wrung from nature, but by wealth, profit, interest, derived from furnishing weapons for other men to use in slaughtering their brothers, and while they are thus slaughtering we steal their trade."[303] This ill-begotten prosperity was producing a thoughtless, selfish materialism – "we are thinking only of ourselves, our trade, our society and not at all of our duty in the world."[304] By the autumn of 1916 he was shocked by the "insane speculation" he had noticed in every part of the country while covering the election.[305] It was not, however, until after the United States had entered the war that Baker carried this line of thinking to its logical conclusion. On a visit to Minneapolis in June 1917, he was appalled by the spectacle of "a whole common people rolling carelessly and extravagantly up and down these streets in automobiles, crowding insipid 'movie' shows by the tens of thousands – there are seventy-six such houses in this one city – or else drinking unutterable hogsheads of sickly sweet drinks or eating decorated icecream at candy shows and drug stores! . . . Too much money, too easily had, too much pleasure, not earned." "If this war had not come, we should all have been rotten," he concluded. "The whirlwind had to

[301] "The Effect on American Institutions of a Powerful Military and Naval Establishment," *Annals*, 66 (July 1916), p. 162.
[302] "Ourselves and Europe, I," *Survey*, 37 (4 Nov. 1916), p. 100.
[303] Notebook 7, Aug. 1915, pp. 55–7, R. S. Baker papers.
[304] Notebook 9, 16 Feb. 1916, pp. 28–31, ibid.
[305] Notebook 12, 14 Sept. 1916, pp. 4–5, ibid.

come! I *hate* war, I love peace, and yet at moments I fear lest this war be over too soon – before the people are scourged into an awakening."[306]

Although significant connections existed between these publicists' views on domestic and on foreign affairs, they were not sufficient to determine attitudes to specific questions of policy, even on such an important issue as intervention. It is true that in some respects their responses were characteristic of Americans as a whole – for example, the initial relief and pride that the United States was not involved, and the later movement toward acceptance of preparedness and eventually war. These latter questions, of course, created divisions, which can be explained only to a limited extent by the sort of ideological differences apparent in the domestic field. Variations in the degree of involvement and partisanship in the European conflict seem to have been more salient, and these in turn corresponded remarkably little with differences of political philosophy.

Nonetheless, progressives generally shared convictions about the desirable nature of international relationships and the proper purposes of American policy that were less widely held in other political circles. If belief in an American mission was pervasive, progressives were more likely than most to interpret it in an anti-imperialist spirit. From 1914, they were particularly inclined to see the paramount responsibility of the United States as being to lead the world to a liberal and lasting peace. The extent to which these assumptions united progressives, and distinguished them from other schools of opinion, became apparent in 1916–17 in their support for Wilson's foreign policy.

Furthermore, progressives inevitably had a special interest in the relationship between war and the preparation for war on the one hand, and social reform and liberal values on the other. The nature of this relationship was recognized as both contentious and ambiguous. It seems clear, however, that the readiness of the majority of these publicists to support intervention in 1917 owed something to the weakness of progressivism at home. The increasingly unqualified allegiance of many to Wilson, together with the eagerness to cultivate personal relationships with those in power, may be seen as reflecting a loss of confidence in their importance as spokesmen for a substantial section of public opinion. The self-indulgent materialism denounced as the product of a tainted prosperity was doubtless associated with disregard of progressive appeals to

[306] Notebook 13, June 1917, pp. 147–9, ibid.

conscience and idealism. Certainly, frustration with the conservative temper of public opinion was implicit in the *New Republic*'s hope, after war
had been declared, that "liberals who can gain public attention will have a
chance to put to good use the forced draught of patriotism. . . . They can
bring home to their fellow-countrymen that a war on behalf of organized
international security and the rights of all peoples would be the basest
hyprocrisy in case it supplied to foreigners a quality of security and
opportunity to the national industrial organization denied to Americans."
In this way, it would "serve the cause of compulsory popular education"
in "the implications of democracy."[307]

[307] "Public Opinion and the War," *New Republic*, 10 (21 Apr. 1917), pp. 334–6.

CHAPTER 6

The wartime experience

The atmosphere of war

American entry into the war had a profound and cumulative effect on the mood of the country and the temper of public debate. As the nation, with widespread reluctance, faced the as yet unfamiliar prospect of sending hundreds of thousands of its young men to risk their lives on foreign battlefields, the strain showed. The divisions revealed during the years of neutrality were exacerbated, and tolerance was at a premium. Progressive publicists were affected by this change of atmosphere, both as participants and as victims. Even during the preceding debate, the emotional gulf dividing advocates and opponents of intervention had generally been greater than the intellectual distance between them, and this became even more the case after the declaration of war on April 6, 1917.

In part, this was because the scope of disagreement narrowed as the issue receded into history. Once the decision had been made, most of those who had opposed intervention abandoned, or at least suspended, overt criticism of it. The spirit in which they did so varied. Kellogg seems to have been moved by a mixture of patriotism and prudence. "I am not for blocking the prosecution of the war, now that the decision has gone against me," he wrote to the secretary of the American Union against Militarism, the more unyielding Crystal Eastman.[1] His most immediate concern, as he explained to Jane Addams when returning to her an article on "Patriotism and Pacifists," was "to conserve the Survey," at a time when "the cleavages are so real."[2] He apparently gave some assurance to the board of directors that he would not "re-open the question of justification of the war, once the country was committed to it."[3] The *Public*, which had maintained its opposition up to the very eve of American intervention, was brought into line by its owner in a more direct fashion.

---

[1] Crystal Eastman memo, 14 June 1917, Kellogg Papers.
[2] PUK to Jane Addams, 5 May 1917, and to Robert W. de Forest, 26 May 1917, Kellogg Papers.
[3] Chambers, *Kellogg,* p. 72.

As Newton D. Baker later explained to the postmaster-general, "Mrs. Fels, as the head of the single tax group of radicals in this country, set the pace when we went into war and practically put out of the movement everybody who was not thoroughly loyal and heartily for the war."[4] Having long financed the *Public*'s deficits, she joined its Board of Editors herself and was doubtless primarily responsible for its sturdy support both of the war and of the administration.[5] Amos Pinchot also formally accepted intervention as a fait accompli, frequently insisting that he had "said nothing against the war since we entered it."[6] However, some of his public activities, such as becoming chairman of the AUAM and supporting Morris Hillquit's Socialist candidacy in the New York mayoralty election, maintained his association with the pacifist cause.[7] Bourne, uniquely among these publicists, persisted in open opposition to American participation in the war.

Bourne's essays in the *Seven Arts* during the summer and fall of 1917 contributed much to his posthumous fame, but at the time he was very conscious of his isolation. "I seem to disagree on the war with every rational and benevolent person I meet," he wrote sadly. "I feel . . . very much out of touch with my times."[8] Amos Pinchot, who also found it "not much fun bucking the majority,"[9] was subjected to more palpable harassments and indignities. An attempt, which he strenuously resisted, was made to force him to resign from the exclusive Boone and Crockett club, false and discreditable stories were circulated about him, while a

[4] N. D. Baker to A. S. Burleson, 19 Aug. 1918, N. D. Baker Papers, box 5.
[5] The Board of Editors was augmented during the summer of 1917 by John Willis Slaughter and George P. West as well as by Mrs. Fels. Of the existing editors, Danziger, who cannot have been happy with the *Public*'s new line, left the board in March 1918. Stoughton Cooley, however, may have been quite easily reconciled to the war. Even while participating in the antipreparedness agitation of 1916, he had written privately that "terrible as this war is, and much as I wish peace, I do not wish a Kaiser's peace. . . . For the Kaiser to dictate terms, even though they were reasonable, would, in my judgement, be a vindication for autocracy, and be an almost certain cause of another war at an early day, with all the burden of armament rivalry in the meantime." Cooley to George F. Peabody, 26 May 1916, George F. Peabody Papers, box 75.
[6] AP to George Creel, 14 Nov. 1917, Amos Pinchot Papers, box 37. See also AP to Louis F. Post, 2 Oct. 1917; to Ogden Reid, editor of the *New York Tribune*, 22 Nov. 1917, ibid., boxes 34, 30.
[7] AP to John A. McSparran, 11 Oct. 1917, and to Marco Aurelio Herradora, 15 Nov. 1917, Amos Pinchot Papers, box 30; Pinchot's *History*, ed. Hooker, p. 71.
[8] Bourne to Alyse Gregory, [September 1917?]; to Everett [Benjamin], 28 Nov. 1917, Bourne Papers, reel 1.
   "The pacifist in war time," Jane Addams observed, "finds it possible to travel from the mire of self pity straight to the barren hills of self-righteousness and to hate himself equally in both places." *Peace and Bread in Time of War* (New York, 1922), p. 139.
[9] AP to Mrs. G. C. La Farge, 15 June 1917, Amos Pinchot Papers, box 29.

film starring Douglas Fairbanks featured "a pro-German spy masquerad-
ing as a pacifist" under the name of "Pinchit."[10]

Such intolerance of dissent had been, as we have seen, generally anticipated by progressives as one of the likely costs of war, but in the event
some of these publicists themselves contributed to it. Of none was this
more true than the pro-war Socialists, who showed little patience with
anything less than a wholehearted commitment to total military victory.
Thus in June 1917, Walling complained to Theodore Roosevelt that even
the *New York Tribune* was allowing "some of its leading writers" to carry
on a "pacifist agitation." "I am confident you can and will put an end to
it," he wrote to the Colonel.[11] It might be thought natural for socialists
to be less concerned than liberals with individual rights, but in fact, like
most American Socialists, Walling, Russell, and Spargo had previously
cherished them, not least when defending the cause of free speech for
dissenters.[12] Not philosophy but passion seems to have accounted for
their wartime attitudes. Walling had a particularly intolerant temperament, as even his friends acknowledged,[13] but in this instance his attitude
differed only in degree from that of Russell and Spargo, and indeed of
several other Socialist supporters of the war.[14] The fervor of their bellig-
erence must be linked to the emotions engendered by breaking with their
party, which in Walling's case (as later in that of J. G. Phelps Stokes) also
involved a breach with his wife.[15] A move regarded by their former
colleagues as backsliding if not betrayal demanded unequivocal justification, which provided an opportunity to articulate previously suppressed
resentments and antagonisms. Spargo, whose analysis of "the German
domination of American Socialism" was comparatively restrained,[16] insisted that in his case the break was not solely due to the war. "My revolt

---

[10] AP to William A. Wadsworth, 5 Dec. 1917; to executive committee, Boone and Crockett Club,
26 Apr. 1921; to Rev. W. S. Rainsford, 29 Sept. 1917; to A. J. McKelway, 18 May 1917,
Amos Pinchot Papers, boxes 29, 42, 30, 29.

[11] Walling to Colonel Roosevelt, 12 July 1917, Walling Papers.

[12] See Chapter 3, "Goals and Policies."

[13] J. G. Phelps Stokes to Upton Sinclair, 19 May 1919, Stokes papers, box 31A.

[14] For example, W. J. Ghent, J. G. Phelps Stokes, and A. M. Simons. See Ghent to Stokes, 22
June [1918], and Stokes to Mrs. Anna M. Sloan, 29 Oct. 1918, Stokes Papers, boxes 30, 31;
Kent and Gretchen Kreuter, *An American Dissenter: The Life of Algie Martin Simons, 1870–1950*
(Lexington, Ky. 1969), chap. 8.

[15] "Of course, I think your proposal to attack in the back those who are giving up their lives for
democracy, peace and antimilitarism is criminal to the last degree . . . neither I nor mankind,
nor the genuine idealists and revolutionaries of the world will ever forget or forgive what your
kind has said and done in this great hour." Walling to Anna Strunsky Walling, 1917, Walling
Papers.

[16] "The German Domination of American Socialism," *Metropolitan*, 46 (Oct. 1917), pp. 15, 64–5.

was against the whole syndicalist trend," he explained. "The time has come for a very vigorous restatement of Socialism in terms which will not repel the American people."[17] For Russell, however, as for Walling, it was the influence of "Germans, pro-Germans and wild-eyed Kaiserists" that made the party impossible.[18] (Privately, Russell also attributed the party's behavior to "the bitter, malignant, covert but insatiable hatred that many Jews in America feel for the United States."[19] Spargo, more charitably, perceived a broader "contempt for nationality" on the part of "the Jewish proletariat," a consequence of their being "without a country" and hence an argument for "the restoration of Israel."[20] Walling, however, made no reference to Jewishness, asserting merely that Hillquit "was born in the German part of Russia, in the town of Riga, and only represents a certain foreign born portion of the working people of this country."[21])

In these different ways, the persistent opponents of intervention and the pro-war Socialists were particularly caught up in the emotions of war, but all of these publicists were affected by them to some extent. The most widespread feeling was a desire to participate in, and contribute to, the nation's effort. As early as April 5, 1917, a group of writers, including Baker, Lippmann, and Creel, dined at the Players in New York to discuss, according to Baker, "what *we* could do to help in this war-crisis – to do our 'bit.'"[22] By this time, Creel was already promoting his claims to take charge of censorship and official publicity, and he was shortly to be appointed chairman of the Committee on Public Information (CPI).[23] Immediately following the declaration of war, Hapgood and Spargo sent telegrams to the president, volunteering "every service."[24] Lippmann, the only one of these men of military age and fit, was a little more cautious. "I am convinced that I can serve my bit much more effectively than as a private in the new armies," he wrote to the secretary of war. "I have made it my business to understand the administration's foreign

[17] Spargo to "my friends," 31 May 1917, Spargo Papers, box 1; to W. S. Greeley King, 17 July 1917, and to J. G. Phelps Stokes, 18 Apr. 1917, Stokes Papers, boxes 27, 26.
[18] Telegram to Ralph Blumenfeld, 14 June 1917, Russell Papers.
[19] Diary no. 6, 25 June 1917, Russell Papers.
[20] "Russia and the World Problem of the Jew," *Harper's Monthly Magazine*, 137 (June 1918), pp. 73–5.
[21] *New York Sun*, 4 May 1917.
[22] Notebook 13, 5 Apr. 1917, pp. 105–6, R. S. Baker Papers.
[23] Vaughn, *Holding Fast the Inner Lines*, pp. 16–19.
[24] Norman Hapgood to Woodrow Wilson, 8 Apr. 1917, Woodrow Wilson Papers, ser. 4, case file 510; "Reminiscences of John Spargo," pp. 242, 262.

policy, and to realize the problems it was up against."[25] In the event, Lippmann became an assistant to Newton Baker in the War Department, dealing chiefly with labor matters, until in October 1917 he moved back to New York to help Colonel House set up "the Inquiry."[26] Ray Stannard Baker also received an assignment from the administration in February 1918, when he was sent to Europe to report confidentially on the state of liberal opinion in the Allied countries. After having been depressed by a sense of the worthlessness and self-indulgence of his activities, Baker was happy to have been given a role in which, as he wrote more than once, "I feel as much under orders as a soldier."[27] Even Kellogg seems to have felt something similar when he made a five months' trip to Europe on behalf of the American Red Cross. "Of course I did no actual fighting at all," he remarked on his return. "But I am glad to feel that I did help in a small way in building up forces of resistance against the great German drive now on."[28]

Appointments such as those of Creel and Lippmann showed, Crystal Eastman argued in June 1917, that "the President is . . . obviously bidding for liberal support."[29] No doubt, the administration did see some advantage in associating well-known reformers and radicals with a war effort to which significant opposition came only from the left. Pro-war socialists were evidently seen as particularly valuable in this respect.[30] In selecting the members of the Root Mission to Russia, one of whose chief objectives was to counter peace agitation in revolutionary circles, Wilson and Secretary of State Lansing lighted first upon Walling, who made it clear he did not think himself suitable, and then upon Russell, who accepted the invitation with alacrity.[31] The American Alliance for Labor and Democracy, an organization formed in July 1917 by Samuel Gompers and the AFL and clandestinely financed by the administration through the

[25] Lippmann to Newton D. Baker, 7 May 1917, Newton D. Baker Papers, box 2.
[26] Lippmann to Graham Wallas, 18 Oct. 1917, Lippmann Papers, box 33, folder 1245; Steel, *Lippmann*, pp. 116–17, 123–30.
[27] Notebook 15, 1 Feb. 1918, p. 71; Notebook 21, 20 Oct. [1918], pp. 26–7; Baker to Frank Polk, 24 Aug. 1918, R. S. Baker Papers.
[28] PUK to Louis Kellogg, 1 May 1918, Kellogg Papers, folder 4.
[29] Crystal Eastman memo, 14 June 1917, Kellogg Papers.
[30] See Ronald Radosh, *American Labor and United States Foreign Policy* (New York, 1969), especially chaps. 1 and 7.
[31] William B. Wilson to Woodrow Wilson, 30 Apr. 1917; Robert Lansing to Woodrow Wilson, 3, 7 May 1917; William B. Wilson to Woodrow Wilson, 9 May 1917; Charles Edward Russell to Woodrow Wilson, 11 May 1917, *Wilson Papers*, 42 (Princeton, N.J., 1983), pp. 165–6, 203–4, 239–40, 252, 280.

CPI, had Spargo as its vice-president and Russell and Walling on its Advisory Council.[32]

On the whole, however, the desire of the administration to enlist progressive publicists was exceeded by their own eagerness to play an active part at this momentous time. "I think I know more about the conflict that has been going on in Europe for the last thirty years over what is commonly known as the 'Drang nach Osten' than anybody in this country with one or two exceptions," Howe claimed to his old friend, Newton Baker, as he sent his thoughts about the likely direction of the next German offensive.[33] "I have been trying to connect up some way with the war," White wrote rather plaintively from Emporia. "I want to get to Europe again, preferably Russia, for of all the places in the world it seems to me Russia is the most interesting. But Heaven knows I would do "most anything to serve."[34] White had already made a trip to the western front on behalf of the American Red Cross, in the company of his Kansan friend and fellow editor, Henry J. Allen, but he was not to fulfill his ambition of visiting Russia until 1933.[35] Steffens, by contrast, had been on his way to Russia at the time that Congress declared war, and he was quick to assume the role of interpreter of the revolution to Americans. On his return to the United States in June 1917, he managed through Creel's good offices to secure an interview with Wilson at which he pressed, in Kerensky's name, for a restatement of war aims that explicitly repudiated the secret treaties.[36] Like many of these publicists, Steffens continued throughout the war to pass on to the administration opinions, requests, and advice, as well as offers of service, by means of letters to the president and Colonel House.[37]

In doing so, they generally manifested their continuing commitment to pre-war progressive objectives. At the initial meeting of writers at the

[32] Frank L. Grubbs, Jr., *The Struggle for Labor Loyalty: Gompers, the A.F. of L., and the Pacifists, 1917–1920* (Durham, N.C., 1968), pp. 40–6, 67–8; Simeon Larson, *Labor and Foreign Policy: Gompers, the AFL and the First World War, 1914–1918* (London, 1975), pp. 41–2, 142–4.

[33] Howe to Newton D. Baker, 26 June 1917, Newton D. Baker Papers, box 2.

[34] White to O. G. Villard, 30 Sept. 1918, White Papers.

[35] Johnson, *White's America*, pp. 277–83.

[36] Kaplan, *Lincoln Steffens*, pp. 216–25; Stein, "Lincoln Steffens," pp. 208–11.

[37] For example, *Steffens Letters*, 1, pp. 402–3, 419–20, 427, 430–1; Croly to Woodrow Wilson, 19 Oct. 1917, *Wilson Papers*, 44 (Princeton, N.J., 1983), pp. 408–10; Howe to Wilson, 15 Dec. 1917, *Wilson Papers* 45 (Princeton, N.J., 1984), pp. 309–11; Amos Pinchot to Wilson, 12, 25 July 1917, to Colonel House, 28 Jan. 1918, Woodrow Wilson Papers, ser. 4, case file 4122, and Amos Pinchot papers, boxes 27, 37. Also Croly to House, 17 Apr., 9 May, 7, 28 Sept. 1917, 6 Mar. 1918; Norman Hapgood to House, 23 Aug. 1917, 5 Apr., 27 May, 17 June, 7 Oct., 1918, E. M. House Papers.

Players, Baker reported, "As a group we resolved to stand firmly against profiteering in this war, to arouse sentiment that will prevent large business enterprises from making extravagant profits: to fight hatred and excessive emotion, and to keep the struggle on a high plane."[38] Such a program could be supported by those who had opposed intervention. The most energetic lobby for heavier taxation on large incomes and profits was, indeed, the American Committee on War Finance, which had been formed by Amos Pinchot and others at the end of March 1917 in the hope that such a movement would "tend to prevent war with Germany."[39] Once war had been declared, however, Pinchot insisted that "there is absolutely no pacifist side to our propaganda."[40] On the contrary, "we are trying to have the war paid for in a way that will not 'queer' the war with the public": "I feel that any rich man who stands out against a practically confiscatory income tax is playing the Kaiser's game. . . . He ought to have the Kaiser's iron cross pinned on him."[41] Most pro-war progressives rallied to the committee's campaign.[42] Norman Hapgood praised Pinchot's congressional testimony and numerous press releases: "You are certainly doing your share to keep our course straight."[43] The National Party, a stillborn attempt to realize Spargo's dream of a pro-war, truly American, Socialist party, invited Pinchot to join its executive committee. In declining, Pinchot raised no objection to the party's program: "You are doing a fine piece of constructive work."[44]

[38] Notebook 13, 5 Apr. 1917, pp. 105–6, R. S. Baker Papers.

[39] *New York American*, 31 Mar. 1917; AP to W. C. Durant, 1 Apr. 1917, Amos Pinchot Papers, file 15, box 34.

[40] Telegram to E. W. Scripps, 12 Apr. 1917, Amos Pinchot Papers, box 27.

[41] AP to Z. B. Cutler, 29 May 1917; to William M. Reedy, 7 May 1917, Amos Pinchot Papers, boxes 32, 29.

[42] *Independent*, 90 (28 Apr. 1917), p. 193; 93 (16 Feb. 1918), p. 259. See also *New Republic*, 11 (5 May 1917), pp. 5–6; 12 (15, 29 Sept. 1917), pp. 174–5, 232–3; 13 (15 Dec. 1917), pp. 168–9; *Public*, 20 (6, 27 Apr., 18 May, 28 Sept., 19 Oct. 1917), pp. 320–1, 367, 473–4, 931–4, 1003–4; *Survey*, 38 (7 Apr. 1917), pp. 20–1, and 39 (Dec. 1, 1917), p. 251; *Emporia Gazette*, 31 May 1917.

Russell, on the other hand, refused to sign the declaration of the American Committee on War Finance, although "I agree entirely with the program outlined," because the committee was composed of "persons that have actively opposed the war." C. E. Russell to AP, 15 Apr. 1917, Amos Pinchot Papers, box 34.

[43] Norman Hapgood to AP, 24 Sept. [1918], Amos Pinchot Papers, box 35. Also 17 June 1917, 28 Aug. 1918, ibid., box 29, Pinchot's contributions to the campaign included a statement before the Senate Finance Committee, 15 May 1917; an open letter to a conference committee of the Senate and the House of Representatives, 18 Sept. 1917; "Why People Freeze," a press release, 21 Jan. 1918; and an open letter to the chairman of the House Ways and Means Committee, 10 Aug. 1918, Amos Pinchot Papers, subject files 55, 50, 81.

[44] J. A. H. Hopkins to AP, 23 Oct. 1917; AP to J. A. H. Hopkins, 24 Oct. 1917, Amos Pinchot

Yet as the psychology of war took hold, cooperation even for the promotion of genuinely shared objectives became more difficult. The publication of an AUAM plea for the discussion of peace terms, signed by Amos Pinchot, brought an indignant protest from A. J. McKelway of the National Child Labor Committee who had been retained by the American Committee on War Finance as its Washington lobbyist. "Our understanding at the beginning was that you were going to 'can the pacifist stuff' and identify yourself particularly with the war finance proposition. . . . You know I have as big a stake in the war as any other father can have, and I do not suppose you can appreciate the cold fury which the millions of American parents feel with anything which looks like giving aid and comfort to the enemy."[45] That McKelway correctly judged the public mood was suggested by the tone of some editorials even in the progressive journals. "There must be no compounding of the Teutonic felonies," declared the *Independent*. "The American copperheads, whatever mask they may wear, from the white disguise of pacifism to the red disguise of anarchy, will henceforth be known to all men as haters of free government and the willing tools of Nero."[46] In their efforts to arouse patriotic feeling, some pro-war progressives were not too fastidious. Among the "distinguished Americans" who contributed interpretative comment to a volume of rather crude anti-German cartoons by the Dutchman, Louis Raemaekers, published in 1918 were Holt and White as well as Russell, Walling, and Spargo.[47]

However, most of these men deplored such simplistic propaganda and its effects upon the popular mind. In early 1918, Ray Stannard Baker distanced himself from the group of writers and artists in New York, now calling itself "the Vigilantes" because "it is beginning to scream and sing the hymn of hate!" To Baker, this was a negation of the purpose of war. "What we are most in danger of doing is, while seeking to kill Prussianism in Europe, not to kill the spirit of Prussianism in our own souls." It was also the antithesis of progressivism, as was demonstrated by the sort of people now to be found at "the Vigilantes." "There were around me last night a number of rich manufacturers who spent the time abusing Wilson and Baker. The organization is being supported by contributions

Papers, box 31. On the National Party, see Spargo, *Americanism and Social Democracy* (New York, 1918); Friedberg, "Marxism in the United States," pp. 222–51.

[45] A. J. McKelway to Amos Pinchot, 30 July 1917, Amos Pinchot Papers, box 29.

[46] *Independent*, 93 (23 Mar. 1918), p. 478; 91 (8 Sept. 1917), p. 377.

[47] Louis Raemaekers, *America in the War* (New York, 1918).

from these rich men."[48] A few months later, Weyl found himself welcoming the prospect that the *New York Tribune* "will make a drive against the N.R. like it made against Hearst" for "it is better to die fighting than to die of mere inanition and senility." Urging upon Croly "a definite program of fighting," he stressed three points – a "diplomatic offensive and preparation for a democratic peace," the "maintenance of liberalism in America during war," and the struggle for "an industrial and social democracy after the war."[49]

Weyl's program represented, of course, a concise summary of the objectives in terms of which the liberal debate over intervention had been conducted. It remained the essence of a progressive consensus, to which even the most militant warriors and the most intransigent pacifists were theoretically committed. In reality, the former tended to subordinate these goals to the crushing of Germany, while the latter were reluctant to conceive that any good could come from the evil of war. Such differences, as we shall see, somewhat confused and presumably weakened the presentation of the progressive viewpoint. Nevertheless, the substantial body of these publicists remained committed to the war for liberal purposes that they endeavored in every way to promote as American power was mobilized to intervene in a Europe torn by war and revolution.

War aims, 1917: negotiated peace or total victory?

The chief of these purposes was the achievement of a "democratic peace." This commonly used phrase, with its echo of pre-war reform slogans, provided a banner to which both supporters and opponents of intervention could rally. In July 1917, Kellogg, who was particularly keen to reunite the divided forces of liberalism, helped to draft an open letter to Wilson calling for a "fresh statement of peace terms by the allies," which was signed by more than five hundred delegates to the annual social workers' conference, among them Walling.[50] Shortly afterward, Kellogg began arranging meetings of "journalists and university men" to provide a forum "for an intensive study of the concrete problems of international adjustment upon which public opinion in the United States must become

---

[48] Notebook 15, Feb. 1918, pp. 72–5, 90, R. S. Baker Papers.
[49] Weyl Diary, 25 July, 3 Aug. 1918. Also 26, 28 July 1918.
[50] Statement signed by 500 delegates to the National Conference of Social Work, Pittsburgh, 8 July 1917, Kellogg Papers. Chambers, *Kellogg*, pp. 62–3.

crystalized either before or during the time of settlement of the war."[51] It was to this group that Croly turned for advice when he was asked by Gilbert Murray to "recommend us one or two speakers who would address meetings of working men and others in England in support and explanation of Mr. Wilson's policy: i.e. vigorous and unflinching war, but war for the sake of future peace, the self-determination of peoples, making the world safe for democracy and so on."[52] In October 1917, soon after Amos Pinchot had taken over as chairman, the AUAM was reorganized "on a more conservative basis" under a new name.[53] "I have taken the Chairmanship of the American Union for a Democratic Peace, with the one object of using whatever strength it has (which is small) to get public opinion behind Wilson's war-for-democracy policy and backfire the annexationists," Pinchot explained to Creel. "We have got to fight it out along effective lines, which will accomplish the objects which all liberals share – a world more democratic and a peace with a fair chance of permanence."[54]

"We see these things as you see them," Creel assured Pinchot in reply.[55] Nonetheless, during the course of 1917 progressives of all persuasions urged upon the administration a more explicit commitment to liberal war aims. In private communications they tended to stress its potential for strengthening the war effort, particularly on the eastern front. Thus, returning visitors as divergent in their attitudes as Steffens and Russell assured Wilson that the Russians could be kept in the war if it was made clear that they were being asked to fight for "idealistic ends" and "democracy" rather than "certain secret treaties" and the czar's "pledge to the Allies."[56] Many thought this argument had a wider application. "Men will not die and starve and freeze for the things which orthodox diplomacy holds most precious," Lippmann declared in a preliminary memorandum for the Inquiry.[57] In the early weeks of the war, Croly had recommended to House "that the Allies under Mr. Wilson's

[51] Kellogg to Professor Henry R. Mussey, 27 July 1917, Kellogg Papers.
[52] Herbert Croly to Paul Kellogg, 20 July 1917, enclosing Gilbert Murray to H. Croly, 27 June 1917, Kellogg Papers, folder 319.
[53] AP to John A. McSparran, 11 Oct. 1917, Amos Pinchot Papers, box 30; Charles Chatfield, *For Peace and Justice: Pacifism in America, 1914–1941* (Boston, 1971), p. 29.
[54] AP to George Creel, 14 Nov. 1917, Amos Pinchot Papers, box 37.
[55] Creel to Amos Pinchot, 20 Nov. 1917, Amos Pinchot Papers, box 37.
[56] Steffens to Colonel House, 20 June 1917, *Steffens Letters*, 1, pp. 399–400; Russell to Woodrow Wilson, 7 Nov. 1917, Creel Papers.
[57] "Preliminary Memorandum on Great Powers," Lippman Papers, box 38, folder 1360. See also *New Republic*, 11 (9 June 1917), pp. 149–50.

leadership make some declaration of their peace terms based upon the President's Senate address which would deprive Germany of the advantage which she might derive from herself initiating a possible liberal basis for peace."[58] Editorials in progressive journals made similar appeals. Although the *Public* loyally remarked in August 1917 that if Wilson felt "that Europe must see American steel on the battlefront before American idealism can function effectually, we are not prepared to challenge his judgement," the lack of response to its frequent calls for a "clarification of war aims" led it by November to perceive a "crisis in war policy."[59] The *New Republic* persistently demanded the restatement of American purposes, emphasizing the extent to which the Russian Provisional Government's difficulties and eventual downfall were due to the failure of the Allies to purify their war aims.[60] As well as the Russian collapse, the Italian reverses in the latter part of 1917 were attributed to the uninspiring character of Allied war aims.[61] "We cannot blame the Allies, in the excitement and suffering of the war, for wanting to get all they can," Amos Pinchot remarked in December. "But we must point out to them that their published policy of annexations has already been a terrible boomerang."[62]

Yet, despite such arguments, the campaign for a clarification of war aims met a hostile reception from much of American press and congressional opinion. "When we try to draw attention to the pacific and constructive purposes which underlie American participation in the war," Croly complained to Wilson, "we are accused of being half-hearted, and even of being pro-German."[63] This was partly because, to many, demands for a revision of war aims were inevitably associated with the search for an early, negotiated peace. Thus, in an extended denunciation of the *New Republic*'s "high-brow Hearstism," Walling accused it of assisting the "intrigue to secure peace now — that is a peace favorable to German

[58] Herbert Croly to E. M. House, 9 May 1917, House Papers.

[59] *Public*, 20 (17 Aug., 9, 16 Nov. 1917), pp. 783, 1073–4, 1095. See also ibid. (15, 29 June, 13 July 1917), pp. 567–8, 615, 663.

[60] *New Republic*, 11 (9 June, 28 July 1917), pp. 146–8, 342–3; 12 (18 Aug., 8, 22 Sept., 6, 27 Oct. 1917), pp. 57, 146–7, 202–4, 258–60, 339–41; 13 (10, 17 Nov., 8, 15 Dec. 1917), pp. 32–4, 60–2, 138–9, 162–4.

[61] Lippmann to Judge M. S. Amos, 5 Nov. 1917, Lippmann Papers, box 2, folder 58; AP to George Creel, 14 Nov. 1917, Amos Pinchot Papers, box 37; *New Republic*, 13 (10 Nov. 1917), pp. 32–4; *Public*, 20 (16 Nov. 1917), p. 1096; Hapgood, "The New Republic and the War," *New Republic*, 13 (26 Jan. 1918), p. 379; Weyl, *End of the War*, pp. 2–3.

[62] "War Aims," *Forward*, no. 6 (Dec. 1917).

[63] Croly to Woodrow Wilson, 19 Oct. 1917, *Wilson Papers*, 44, pp. 408–10 at 410.

militarism."[64] Walling's particular targets, which he tirelessly attacked, were the movement for an international Socialist conference at Stockholm and the call by the Petrograd Soviet in May 1917 for "peace without annexations or indemnities on the basis of the self-determination of peoples."[65] This appealing formula swiftly became the rallying cry for antiwar groups such as "the People's Council of America for Democracy and Terms of Peace."[66]

None of these publicists directly participated in such agitation but sympathy for the idea of a negotiated settlement in 1917 was not confined to those, like Bourne and Amos Pinchot, who had openly opposed intervention.[67] Among others who remained favorably disposed toward a "peace without victory" were Steffens, Howe, Hapgood, and Weyl.[68] In a book published in 1918, Weyl claimed that "during the six months from April 1 until October 1, 1917, and even afterwards, the war might have been concluded on the basis of internationalism and democracy." The Petrograd formula, the projected Stockholm conference, and the July Resolution of the German Reichstag were all seen by Weyl as opportunities neglected by American diplomacy out of misguided deference to the Allies.[69] Although Weyl took leave from the *New Republic* while writing his book, his viewpoint found expression in the journal. In May 1917, an editorial urged Wilson to "seek for a peace by means of diplomacy irrespective of a military decision. . . . The American people did not enter this war to add to the sum of human goods and beings which were being calamitously annihilated; they entered it chiefly in order to make a promising and indispensible contribution to a scientific and just settlement. Such a settlement cannot be obtained merely by working for

---

[64] *New York Globe and Commercial Advertiser*, 24 Nov. 1917, Amos Pinchot Papers, subject file 33.
[65] For example, *New York Sun*, 4 May 1917; "No Annexations, No Indemnities," *Independent*, 90 (19 May 1917), pp. 327–8; Russell Diary 5A, 18 May 1917, Russell Papers; Walling to Woodrow Wilson, 21 May 1917, Wilson Papers, National Archives [NA] RG 59.763.72119/612; Walling to Theodore Roosevelt, 12 July 1917, Walling Papers.
   On the projected Stockholm Conference and the Petrograd Formula, see Arno J. Mayer, *Political Origins of the New Diplomacy* (New Haven, 1959).
[66] Grubbs, *Struggle for Labor Loyalty*, chap. 2; Marchand, *American Peace Movement and Social Reform*, pp. 266–7.
[67] See Bourne, "The Collapse of American Strategy," *Seven Arts*, 2 (Aug. 1917), pp. 409–24; telegram, AP to John D. Works, 10 July 1917, Amos Pinchot Papers, box 27.
[68] Steffens to Laura Steffens, 1 Nov. 1917, *Steffens Letters*, 1, pp. 411–12; Howe, "New Ideals for Peace," *Century*, 96 (May 1918), pp. 98, 103; Hapgood, "The New Republic and the War," *New Republic*, 13 (26 Jan. 1918), pp. 379–80; Hapgood, *The Advancing Hour* (New York, 1920), p. 9; Weyl, *The End of the War* (New York, 1918), pp. 2–6; Weyl Diary, 10 Aug. 1918.
[69] Weyl, *End of the War*, pp. 2, 5–6, 180–1.

victory. Victory itself can best be obtained by working for the settlement."[70]

It was articles like this, presumably, that led Lippmann in "a dingy talk with Herbert Croly" to complain that "the paper sounded as if it were bored with the war, and was ready to snatch at any straw no matter how thin pointed towards peace."[71] The divergence of such close associates as Lippmann and Croly was an indication of the uneasiness felt by many pro-war progressives toward the end of 1917. "The whole question is bitterly full of complexity," Baker lamented after dining at the Players "with those two Radicals, Steffens and Fred Howe," who had assured him "that victory – a real victory – for either side is impossible and that the only outcome must be an arranged peace." Baker was not convinced. "I would go forward with the war until there is some reasonable chance of getting a peace which will prove to the Germans (and to the world) that war is not a profitable business."[72] The same argument was advanced in a more bellicose tone by the *Independent*. "Deeper than any other reason . . . for pushing the war against the Central Powers until they surrender and acknowledge that they have been in the wrong, is the necessity . . . of insuring the world against a repetition of a king-made war of aggression. . . . The practical substance of unconditional surrender is an imperative requirement in the issue as it now stands."[73]

The *Independent*'s editorial had been provoked by Pope Benedict XV's appeal for peace in August 1917, but when in his reply to the pope Wilson stressed the distinction between the German people and their government, the *Independent* applauded this as "both right and politic."[74] This distinction, which accorded so well with progressive predispositions, made it possible to combine promises of generous treatment of Germany with a refusal to negotiate with the Imperial government. In drawing it, Wilson was following advice from Lippmann, who had earlier declared publicly that the war must end either in the conclusive defeat of the Central Powers or in revolution within them.[75] To many progressives, the

[70] *New Republic*, 11 (19 May 1917), pp. 66–7.
[71] Lippmann Diary, 5 Oct. 1917, p. 89, Lippmann Papers.
[72] Notebook 14, 27 Dec. 1917, pp. 102–3, 105–6, R. S. Baker Papers.
[73] *Independent*, 91 (25 Aug. 1917), pp. 272–3. See also ibid., (8 Sept. 1917), p. 376; 92 (29 Dec. 1917), p. 577.
[74] *Independent*, 91 (15 Sept. 1917), pp. 410–11. See also *New Republic* 12 (27 Oct. 1917), pp. 340–1.
[75] Lippmann memorandum, "Reply to the Pope's Proposal," enclosed in Newton D. Baker to WW, 20 Aug. 1917, *Wilson Papers*, 43, pp. 532–4; "The World Conflict in Its Relation to

latter was the more fundamental objective. "A revolution in Germany would be more advantageous than a dozen Jenas," argued Weyl.[76] "With the Hohenzollerns, not with the German people, is our war," White declared. "And it should be pushed to an everlasting defeat for that proud house."[77] Among these publicists, it was, ironically, the Socialists who were least ready to confine their hostility to the German ruling class, insisting on the shared responsibility for German policy of the German Socialists, who were in a sense their special enemy. Spargo and Russell respectfully exempted Karl Liebknecht and his followers from their censures,[78] but Walling maintained that even "the Liebknecht conception of peace is precisely the same as that of the Kaiser in the essential point, namely that there is no reason why peace should not be based on German military victories." "Doubtless a German Social Democracy defeated in war will be more amenable to a genuinely democratic peace program than would be a Junker caste defeated in war," he concluded. "Hence, a German revolution is invaluable – provided it is preceded or accompanied by a German defeat."[79]

The insistence that, as Spargo put it, "the Allies are fighting for socialist internationalism"[80] was, of course, a direct and deliberate repudiation of the Leninist doctrine that the working class had no interest in the military outcome of this capitalist conflict. So it is not surprising that American pro-war Socialists became early and bitter opponents of the Russian Bolsheviks. The latter were Russell's chief antagonists when, as a member of the Root Mission, he exhorted the workers of Petrograd to continue the fight against Germany. He found Lenin a "strange figure" but Trotsky seemed more familiar: "I have talked to whole audiences like him in New York."[81] In October 1917, Spargo deplored "the spread among American Socialists of doctrines similar to those which the fanatical Nikolai Lenin and his followers have promulgated in Russia with such

American Democracy," *Annals*, 72 (July 1917), pp. 9–10. For Lippmann's influence on Wilson, see Steel, *Walter Lippmann*, pp. 126–7. The account of Lippmann's memorandum in Christopher Lasch, *The American Liberals and the Russian Revolution* (New York, 1962), pp. 51–2, 230, is seriously misleading.

76 *End of the War*, p. 222.
77 *Emporia Gazette*, 4 May 1917.
78 Spargo, *Americanism and Social Democracy* (New York, 1918), pp. 144–8; Russell, "The New Socialist Alignment," *Harper's Monthly Magazine* 136 (March 1918), pp. 563–70.
79 "The German Socialists, IV, Herr Scheidemann, President Wilson and German Socialists," syndicated newspaper articles, March 1918, Walling Papers.
80 "Why Socialism Is Pro-Ally," *Independent*, 95 (20 July 1918), p. 90.
81 Diary no. 6, 25, 27 June 1917, Russell Papers.

disastrous consequences to the new Social Democratic Republic."[82] Barely two months after the November revolution, Walling was writing that "the Bolsheviki regime has been a reign of violence, not to say a reign of terror."[83] In a February 1918 memorandum that evidently impressed President Wilson, Walling argued that "the continuing success of Bolshevism in Russia and the growing strength of pacifist strikes in Germany and Austria immensely aid the already dangerous pacifist movements among the workingmen of France, England and Italy – movements united in the demand for a Stockholm conference to bring about 'an immediate democratic peace'." "The danger," Walling emphasized, "is that these widespread strikes will begin before the power of America has been fully developed, that is before Germany has lost anything whatever of her conquests." It followed that recognition of the Bolshevik regime, or "any friendly steps" toward it, would be a serious mistake.[84]

In general, reactions to the Bolshevik revolution were largely conditioned by attitudes to the war, as Christopher Lasch has pointed out.[85] It was, as the *Independent* made clear, "the amazing conduct of the Petrograd group" in entering upon "separate peace parlays with the Potsdam highwayman" that aroused most hostility.[86] Initially, there was a tendency to portray the Bolsheviks as more unworldly than sinister. Thus the *Public* could not imagine those "professional talkers and critics" holding on to power for long. "The danger to which Russia is exposed is not domination by the Bolsheviki, but the opening made by their uprising for the entrance of reactionary forces." A few weeks later, the journal was still maintaining that "compromise or overthrow is the approaching fate" of "these fantastic rulers."[87] "The Bolsheviks are doomed," Russell insisted in December 1917. They "are poor old dreamers, that's all."[88] However,

---

[82] "The German Domination of American Socialism," *Metropolitan*, 46 (Oct. 1917), p. 64.

[83] *New York Times*, 14 Jan. 1918.

[84] In forwarding Walling's memorandum to Lansing, Wilson observed, "It seems to me to speak an unusual amount of truth and to furnish a very proper basis of the utmost caution in the conduct of the many troublesome affairs that we are from time to time discussing." Woodrow Wilson to Robert Lansing, 13 Feb. 1918, *Wilson Papers*, 46 (Princeton, N.J., 1984), pp. 310–13, 334.

[85] Christopher Lasch, *American Liberals and the Russian Revolution*, p. xi. George F. Kennan has stressed the extent to which the whole Western response to the Bolshevik revolution was shaped by the preoccupation with the World War. See *Russia and the West under Lenin and Stalin* (New York, 1960), especially pp. 9–17.

[86] *Independent*, 93 (19 Jan. 1918), p. 92.

[87] *Public*, 20 (5 Oct., 16 Nov. 1917), pp. 954, 1095; 21 (18 Jan. 1918), p. 67.

[88] Russell to Cyrus McCormick, 2 Dec. 1917 (cited in Radosh, *American Labor*, p. 101); *Milwaukee Sentinel*, 1 Jan. 1918.

following the dissolution of the Constituent Assembly and the Ukrainian treaty, a sterner tone became apparent in the comments of some pro-war editorialists. "Russia is paying dearly for the uncritical idealism that has tolerated these doctrinaire impossibilists," the *Public* declared in February 1918. "It is the hope of those who desire the good of that country, that she be quickly freed from this unmitigated curse."[89]

Less wholehearted supporters of the war were generally more sympathetic to the Bolshevik regime. Its publication of the secret treaties was widely welcomed as strengthening the campaign for a liberalization of war aims. The *New Republic* recognized that the speeches of Lloyd George and Wilson in January 1918 were to a large extent a response to this challenge.[90] "The Russians have been the only people that have dared to tell the truth about the war," Amos Pinchot maintained.[91] Steffens, uniquely, seems to have cared more about the revolution than the war. While in Russia, far from countering Bolshevik propaganda, he had, as Russell indignantly noted, endorsed the charge that the United States was not a real democracy.[92] On his return, he suggested to the CPI "that what would help us most with the Russians would be a confession of the facts and a very humble admission that we had democracy and liberty still to achieve."[93] Steffens greeted the Bolshevik seizure of power as "good news for Russia," and, from his understanding of "the science, the technique of revolution," he confidently explained "the inevitability in such crises of autocracy; minority government; the abolition of liberty, etc. etc."[94] He stressed, however, that the Bolsheviks were not "trying to make a separate peace": "They want a general democratic peace by and in the interests of peoples, not of the grafting governments, which are all (but ours) out for conquest and increase of empire."[95]

---

[89] *Public*, 21 (16 Feb. 1918), pp. 195–6. See also *Independent*, 93 (26 Jan. 1918), pp. 133–4. For the dissolution of the Constituent Assembly in January 1918 and the German-Ukrainian treaty at Brest-Litovsk in February, see George F. Kennan, *Russia Leaves the War* (Princeton, N.J., 1956), pp. 343–53, 184–6.

[90] *New Republic*, 13 (12 Jan. 1918), pp. 295–7.

[91] Speech, 17 Feb. 1918, Amos Pinchot Papers, box 36.

[92] Diary no. 6, 1 July 1917, Russell Papers.

[93] "No use. The demand is for liars and lying," he concluded. Steffens to Allen H. Suggett, 6 Nov. 1917, *Steffens Letters*, 1, p. 412.

[94] Steffens to Laura Steffens, 17 Nov. 1917; to Allen H. Suggett, 30 Dec. 1917, *Steffens Letters*, 1, pp. 414, 415.

[95] Steffens to Mrs. J. James Hollister, 5 Jan. 1918, *Steffens Letters*, 1, p. 416. Steffens's propensity to take Bolshevik propoganda at face value was further demonstrated when he sought through John Reed to convince Trotsky and Lenin of the "literal sincerity" of Wilson's commitment to anti-imperialist war aims. See Steffens to Colonel House, 1 Feb. 1918, and telegram to John Reed, [February 1918], *Steffens Letters*, 1, pp. 419–20, 422. Cf. Kennan, *Russia and the West*, pp. 39–40.

Steffens's anxiety to acquit the Bolsheviks of the charge that they were seeking a separate peace, like the widespread demand for a clarification of war aims, may be seen as indicating the breadth and coherence of the consensus that the war was worth fighting provided it resulted in a liberal and lasting peace. This was further demonstrated by the response to the Marquis of Lansdowne's appeal in the London *Daily Telegraph* against the prolongation of the war in pursuit of total victory. "The strength of Lord Lansdowne's letter is his demand for a definition of war aims," the *Public* observed. "The weakness . . . is that it is in effect a bid for a premature peace." The *Public* attributed Lansdowne's war-weariness to "the notable social transformation that England is undergoing": "The moment arrives when the reactionary and tory elements of every nation want peace, because the continuance of war leads to their destruction."[96] This interpretation was developed by Baker in his reports from Britain during 1918. "The Lansdowne movement," he explained to the State Department, "is a movement mostly of old rich aristocrats and captains of industry who see their wealth and power dribbling away in income taxes." It was aiming at "an arranged and inconclusive peace" in which "both sides would get something valuable in territory or in trade concessions."[97] Even Weyl made it clear that in lamenting the lost opportunities for ending the war in 1917 he did not imply that *any* settlement was to be welcomed. "The war might have ended in a compromise which would have been a victory had the compromise been based on a new international order," he maintained. "If, however, the compromise ending the war is nothing but a dividing up of Russia, China and a few other countries by nations too tired to fight, by nations reconciled solely by the privilege of spoiling enemy and ally, then we have an ignoble peace, and the war for democracy is a failure and our high pretensions are a mockery."[98]

The substance of a democratic peace

This insistence that it was the nature, rather than the timing, of the peace that was crucial raised the question of what precisely was meant by "a democratic peace" and a "new international order." As these phrases themselves implied, progressive thinking about the peace was woven from two main strands – the long-standing assumption that war resulted from

---

[96] *Public*, 20 (7 Dec. 1917), pp. 1167–8. See also ibid., 21 (28 Sept. 1917), pp. 1232–4.
[97] Baker to Frank L. Polk, 10 Aug., 25, 10 Mar. 1918, R. S. Baker Papers.
[98] *End of the War*, pp. 12–13.

the undemocratic character of traditional diplomacy and the denial of popular aspirations, and the more recently acquired faith in the potentialities of an international organization for collective security. The two were seen as being integrally linked. Thus Lippmann pointed out that only if an alternative system of international security existed would states be prepared to abandon economic discrimination and claims for strategic frontiers that violated the principle of national self-determination.[99] Similarly, Baker argued that truly democratic control of foreign policy could never be established without a League of Nations, since "in case of necessity a committee of the House of Commons, or indeed the whole House, would probably be as willing to make a secret treaty as the foreign office."[100] He also believed, however, that "strong self-determined nationalities" were "the only basis upon which a League of Nations can rest securely."[101]

Baker, indeed, provided a fairly comprehensive summary of a typical progressive point of view when in March 1918 he set down in his notebook "a statement as nearly as possible of my own beliefs upon coming to England":

> I am against imperialism wherever it may raise its ugly head, whether in Germany, in England or in America . . .
> I believe in a league of nations:
> a. Reduction of armaments
> b. Freedom of the seas under international control
> c. National self-determination with international federalism.
> d. Real international control and encouragement of half-developed peoples, Africa chiefly.
> e. International control of waterways. Suez and Panama. Dardenelles. . . .
> Trade after the war should be as free as possible. . . . Vast social changes are necessary within each nation including America to make them really democratic. Democracy must be made safe for the world.[102]

Such sentiments underlay most progressive discussions of the ingredients of a desirable settlement.[103] There were, naturally, individual

99 Lippmann to Colonel House, 2 Sept. 1918, E. M. House Papers.
100 Notebook 16, 19 Mar. 1918, pp. 62–3, R. S. Baker Papers.
101 Baker to Frank L. Polk, 28 May 1918, R. S. Baker Papers.
102 Notebook 16, 10 Mar. 1918, pp. 27, 23–5, R. S. Baker Papers.
103 See, for instance, Weyl, *End of the War*, especially pp. 226–30, 276, 305–11; Spargo, *Americanism and Social Democracy*, pp. 214–40; *Independent*, 92 (15 Dec. 1917), pp. 497–8, and 96 (12 Oct., 9 Nov. 1918), pp. 39–40, 149; Howe, "New Ideals for Peace," *Century*, 96 (May 1918), pp. 97–104; Social Democratic League of America, *A Program of Social Reconstruction* (New York, [1918]), "III – International Program," pp. 16–19.

differences of interpretation and emphasis. Thus, to Holt all that really mattered was the League of Nations, which seemed to promise the realization of his pre-war dream of a world federation.[104] For Lippmann, who remained convinced of the importance of maritime supremacy for the defense of the liberal Atlantic community, "freedom of the seas" implied not the recognition of neutral rights but making "Anglo-American sea power the nucleus of world organization, to guarantee its uses before the whole world, to bind ourselves in honor to employ it only for the security of all nations."[105] Single Taxers like Steffens and Howe (whose view of international relations was avowedly Cobdenite) attached primary importance to freedom of trade, the "open door," and the ending of "financial imperialism."[106] Howe, persuaded that the war had originated in the German drive to dominate the Near East, energetically propounded an ambitious plan for the "neutralization" and disarmament of the whole Mediterranean region, as well as for the "internationalization" of all trade routes.[107] Such proposals were anathema to Walling who, while favoring the neutralization of the Dardanelles, maintained that "the neutralization of the Suez and Panama Canals, which are in no way involved in the war . . . would be to further cripple the pacific sea powers as compared with the militaristic land powers and to rob the coming league of nations of its most effective means of preserving world peace." Naturally, Walling also deplored "the obsolete pacifist demand for the 'inviolability of private property at sea,' which would . . . deprive civilization of the most civilized weapon against autocracies."[108]

As Walling's dissent made clear, the treatment of Germany and her allies remained the most emotionally charged aspect of the peace, and it had an inescapable bearing upon other central questions, notably the character and composition of the projected league of nations, and the meaning and scope of the principle of national self-determination.

On the league of nations, the pro-war Socialists once again represented

[104] Kuehl, *Hamilton Holt,* chaps. 5–6, 9–10.

[105] Lippmann, *The Political Scene: An Essay on the Victory of 1918* (New York, 1919), pp. 51–2.

[106] See Steffens speeches in the Middle West, Sept. 1917, especially that at Grand Rapids, Michigan, 23 Sept. 1917, Scrapbook 3, Steffens Papers; Howe, "Financial Imperialism," *Atlantic Monthly,* 120 (Oct. 1917), pp. 477–84. For Howe's debt to Cobden, see "New Ideals for Peace," pp. 103–4; *The Only Possible Peace* (London, 1919), pp. v–vi.

[107] Howe to Woodrow Wilson, 31 Dec. 1917, Woodrow Wilson Papers, ser. 4, case file 324A; "The Heart of the War," *Harper's Monthly Magazine,* 136 (Apr. 1918), pp. 728–34; "New Ideals for Peace," pp. 97–104; *The Only Possible Peace,* chaps. 3–21.

[108] "The German Socialists . . . V, The Anti-Democratic Peace Terms of the German Minority Socialists," Walling Papers.

an extreme position. "We must insist," Spargo wrote, "that the United States enter no league of nations . . . unless all the nations in the league are democratized and their governments chosen by and responsible to popularly elected parliaments."[109] The manifesto of the Social Democratic League of America envisaged the development of organized economic cooperation until it led to the political federation of "the United Democracies of the World."[110] Such statements implied, as did Walling more directly, that the league of nations would be essentially a continuation of the wartime alliance, maintaining the power to keep Germany in line through the use of economic and other sanctions.[111] This point of view was easily compatible with the proposal, mooted in Allied circles and secretly endorsed by the League to Enforce Peace in August 1918, that the league be established immediately by the countries fighting the Central Powers.[112]

Such a proposal had some appeal to many progressives. The requirements of coalition warfare did seem to provide a rare opportunity for creating international agencies of real authority. "Without previous design, through experiment in meeting the needs of the moment, the Allies are shaping an instrument of confederated action which, extended and perfected, will bring the world commonwealth within measurable distance," the *Public* observed. The aim should be "to further, while war provides the temporary unity, a machinery of permanent international cooperation. What is the product of the moment's exigency should be studied with the conscious intention of making it a block in the building which it is the peculiar duty of this country to erect."[113] In a letter to President Wilson in November 1917, Lippmann argued that Allied "unity of administrative control over the scarce and essential supplies which German industry needs" was "not only essential to victory, but to that general purification of aims which must precede a fine peace. Merely selfish purposes cannot survive a movement towards unity. . . . It would, I believe, . . . give enormous vitality to the idea of a League of Na-

[109] Spargo, *Americanism and Social Democracy*, p. 234.

[110] Social Democratic League of America, *Program of Social Reconstruction*, pp. 16–19.

[111] "The German Socialists . . . V, The Anti-Democratic Peace Terms of the German Minority Socialists," Walling Papers.

[112] That is, a resolution was passed that the chairman of the executive committee of the League should urge the American government "to consider the establishment of a League of Nations now" but "it was ordered that this resolution be not published." Holt to Sir Willoughby H. Dickinson, 3 Aug. 1918; also Holt to W. H. Short, 27 Apr., 8 May 1918, Holt papers, box 2, folder 1.

[113] *Public*, 20 (18 May, 16 Nov. 1917), pp. 472, 1096.

tions."[114] Weyl, too, hoped that "we may find in the present alliance opposed to Germany and in the economic and political concert which that alliance has been forced to adopt, an embryonic form, which in the years after the war may develop a relatively permanent and more or less complete unity."[115] In a "statement of principles" published in November 1918, the newly formed League of Free Nations Association claimed that "the administrative machinery of a workable internationalism already exists in rudimentary form" in "the international bodies that have already been established by the Allied belligerents . . . to deal with their combined military resources, shipping and transport, food, raw materials, and finance."[116]

However, the statement went on, this "international machinery will need democratization." It was, indeed, to emphasize this point that the new organization had been launched. It grew out of another initiative by Kellogg, who on his return from England in the spring of 1918 had lamented the fact "that the only consistent work in preparing for the time of settlement by a lay body is that of the League to Enforce Peace, which is mostly absorbed in the machinery of international control rather than the democratic principles which must shoot through all such arrangements to make them tolerable, and whose leaders seem of the type which, for example, were lined up against the Brandeis appointment to the supreme court."[117] To remedy this situation, Kellogg organized a series of informal meetings of liberal publicists, including the members of the editorial staffs of the *Independent,* the *Nation,* the *New Republic,* and the *Public,* as well as the *Survey* itself.[118] (Holt, who remained one of the vice-chairmen of the League to Enforce Peace, had already warned its secretary against the danger of creating a "league of nations based more on military power than on justice" and a "tendency to make the League aristocratic and not subject to the popular will."[119]) In its public manifesto, endorsed by Holt as well as Kellogg, Hapgood, Croly, and Stoughton Cooley of the *Public,*

---

114 W. Lippmann to Woodrow Wilson, 21 Nov. 1917, N. D. Baker Papers, box 2. See also undated memorandum in Lippmann papers, box 38, folder 1361.
115 Weyl, *End of the War,* chap. 13 at p. 232.
116 "League of Free Nations Association: A Statement of Principles," *Independent,* 96 (14 Dec. 1918), pp. 364, 376–8 at 376.
117 "Memorandum by Paul U. Kellogg," [April 1918], Kellogg Papers.
118 The group was known originally as the "Committee on Nothing at All" and later as the "Committee on American Policy." In the spring of 1921, the League of Free Nations Association itself became the Foreign Policy Association. See Chambers, *Kellogg,* pp. 63, 165, and the material in the Kellogg Papers.
119 Holt to W. H. Short, 2 Jan. 1918, Holt Papers, box 2, folder 1.

the League of Free Nations Association insisted that there ought to be "some representation of the peoples in a body with legislative powers over international affairs – which must include minority elements – as distinct from the governments of the constituent states of the League."[120]

Together with flexibility and responsiveness to popular control, inclusiveness remained, for most progressives, an essential characteristic of a desirable league of nations.[121] "All the great nations, including Germany, to be represented," the Kellogg group resolved, "so that it may be a world organization rather than a belligerent league."[122] The *New Republic* attempted to persuade "American conservatives" that this was the course recommended by enlightened self-interest. "The inclusion of the enemy peoples within the League of Nations will be called for and justified, not by the fact that we can trust them or their governments – we know that we cannot – but by the fact that it is to our advantage to bring their peoples ultimately to look to the League instead of to the military strength of their own governments for the enforcement of *our* settlements. If we can persuade them that our League stands for the real guaranty of our own treaties, even against our own Allies, sooner or later the enemy peoples will cease to oppose its power, for they will see in it protection of their right. If they see that its guaranty is one-sided, they will turn to their own military force as their sole protection."[123]

On the whole, then, conceptions of the proper shape and character of a liberal league of nations were not essentially altered by the emotions of belligerency. To a lesser but still notable extent, the same was true of the issue of national self-determination. Certainly, earlier differences in attitude persisted, with Single Tax antimonopolyists, for example, evincing much more unqualified sympathy with the principle than those who had looked with favor upon America's own imperial expansion.[124] Thus Howe, a particularly strong proponent of the virtues of small states, claimed that Germany had been "a greater cultural force when Bavaria, Baden, Saxony, and a dozen states and free cities produced their philosophers, poets and artists."[125] On the other hand, the *Independent* remained more skeptical, remarking that Hungary and Rumania, once oppressed

[120] *Independent*, 96 (14 Dec. 1918), p. 376.
[121] See Chapter 5, "The Progressive Consensus on Foreign Policy."
[122] "Committee on American Policy. Minute on League of Nations proposed by sub-committee for adoption," [Sept. 1918?], Kellogg Papers.
[123] *New Republic*, 16 (21 Sept. 1918), pp. 213–16. See also Weyl, *End of the War*, pp. 245–6.
[124] See Chapter 5, "America's Role in the World."
[125] *The Only Possible Peace*, pp. 218–19. See also "New Ideals for Peace," pp. 99–101.

nationalities, were now themselves oppressive, and arguing that "the United States at the present time is an efficient political unit, notwith-standing the amazing diversity of ethnic elements composing the popula-tion."[126] So, too, Steffens's appeal for "big countries to withdraw from the countries of weaker peoples" (including the Philippines and Puerto Rico)[127] could only have confirmed Rowell's misgivings about the ab-stractions of Wilsonian rhetoric. "The right of self-determination, which ought to apply to Belgium, may have to be thrust rather arbitrarily on the Balkan states," he explained, "with orders to do their determining peace-fully and intelligently or have it done for them, while to apply it to the cannibals of the Solomon Islands and New Guinea, recently wrested from German exploitation, would be worse than imbecile."[128]

It is true that previous differences of view were complicated by the evident relationship between the claims of small nations and the fate of the enemy powers. Thus, the bellicose Walling insisted that the right of self-determination must apply not only to existing nations (such as Belgium) but also to peoples or nationalities such as "the Czechs, Serbs, Roumanians and Croats."[129] "The triumph of the Allies will give free-dom to Jews, Jugoslavs, Armenians, Poles and other oppressed na-tionalities," declared Spargo.[130] This impeccably democratic case for the dismemberment of the Central Empires might have been more compel-ling if it had been less obviously partial. "If you are going to free all the oppressed peoples that are held in bondage, or against their will under a sovereignty which they do not prefer, follow that policy out logically," Amos Pinchot demanded. "If you are going to free Poland, why not free Ireland? If you are going to give self-determination to the people in the German East African and the German West African colonies, why not give self-determination to the people of India? And why not give self-determination to the people of Porto Rico and the Philippines."[131]

Generally speaking, these progressives were notably cautious about

126 *Independent*, 96 (21 Dec. 1918), p. 385; 95 (3 Aug. 1918), pp. 139–40.
127 Address in Milwaukee, 21 Sept. 1917, scrapbook 3, Steffens Papers.
128 Rowell to Mark Sullivan, 9 July 1918, Rowell Papers.
129 "High-Brow Hearstism," New York *Globe and Commercial Advertiser*, 24 Nov. 1917. See also Walling to Woodrow Wilson with enclosure, 21 May 1917, *Wilson Papers*, 42, pp. 364–5.
130 "Why Socialism is Pro-Ally," *Independent*, 95 (20 July 1918), p. 90.
131 Address at mass meeting, 17 Feb. 1918, Amos Pinchot Papers, box 36. By the spring of 1918, Walling had convinced himself that "the demand for the independence of an 'Irish Republic' was invented by the German propagandists and launched by German money from Berlin." "The German Socialists . . . V, The Anti-Democratic Peace Terms of the German Minority So-cialists," Walling Papers.

underwriting the principle of self-determination, even with respect to Europe. "Clearly there can be no universal rule," the *Public* observed, as it contrasted "the Scandinavian states, the Netherlands and Switzerland" with the Balkans. "In so far as the Balkan state is independent, it is an imitation of one of the Great Powers with a little autocracy or oligarchy, armed to the teeth and clamoring for its rights to be respected with a background of valorous blood-letting and a future dominated by calculated rivalry. . . . The right of people to choose their own allegiance might easily create in the Balkans something comparable to a bag full of cats."[132] The Balkans, indeed, seemed a particularly dramatic illustration of the complexity of the Old World's problems. At a meeting (presided over by Weyl) of "the old X-club," Baker heard "a talk on Jugo-Slavism" given by a former member of the Serbian government. "It was a little difficult to understand the speaker," he noted, "but of one thing I was convinced and that was the enormous difficulties in the way of any just or decent settlement of the Balkan problem."[133] Meanwhile, behind the scenes, the Inquiry, according to Lippmann's later recollection, "tried to slow the President down on self-determination."[134]

However, as Lippmann was also to observe, "American diplomacy was turned during 1918 from the policy of compromise with Austria to that of dismemberment,"[135] and this change had some effect upon the attitudes of these publicists. In August 1918, Lippmann himself, now involved with the propaganda effort in Europe, urged a further presidential commitment to the "liberation of the Slavs and other subject peoples of Eastern Europe under international protection."[136] As the *New Europe*, according to Lippmann, became "the one most indispensable periodical in the English-speaking world," the claims of oppressed nationalities came to receive more sympathetic attention in the liberal journals.[137] Nev-

---

[132] *Public*, 20 (6 July 1917), pp. 644–5.

[133] Notebook 15, 9 Jan. 1918, pp. 18–19, R. S. Baker Papers. The Serbian minister may well have been Milenko R. Vesnić, who earlier the same day had seen Colonel House: "Vesnitch gave me a history of the Balkans, particularly that of Serbia, and I had to check him, saying I had an engagement with the President." House Diary, 9 Jan. 1918, *Wilson Papers*, 45, p. 554.

[134] See Mayer, *Political Origins of the New Diplomacy*, pp. 364–5.

[135] Lippmann, *The Political Scene*, p. 21. For accounts of this change of policy, see Victor S. Mamatey, *The United States and East Central Europe: A Study in Wilsonian Diplomacy and Propaganda* (Princeton, N.J., 1957), pp. 252–72, 307–9; and Sterling J. Kernek, *Distractions of Peace during War* (Philadelphia, 1975), pp. 38–41, 69, 80–1, 85, 101.

[136] Lippmann to Colonel House, 21 Aug. 1918, E. M. House Papers. For Lippmann's propaganda work, see Steel, *Lippmann*, chap. 12.

[137] *The Political Scene*, p. 21. See, for example, *Independent*, 93 (2 Mar. 1918), pp. 335–6; *New Republic*, 15 (15 June 1918), pp. 188–90; White, *The Martial Adventures of Henry and Me* (New York, 1918), p. 214.

ertheless, there remained reservations. "The establishment in their independence of Serbia and Rumania; the safeguarding of Greece; the establishment of the Jugo-Slav and the Czecho-Slovak nations, and the creation
of an independent Poland, are all conditions to which liberals will sub-
scribe," the *Public* conceded in commenting on a speech by Senator Lodge.
But Lodge's argument that "we must have these independent states created so that they will stand across the pathway of Germany to the East"
was condemned as belonging to a "world of territorial arrangements and
Realpolitik, where new states are legislated into existence for the conve-
nience of great powers."[138] In September 1918, Hapgood took issue with
the *New Republic*'s apparent eagerness to break up Austria-Hungary. "I
think we liberals should look with great suspicion on any drift in ourselves
toward increasing sweep in our forcible rearrangements – increasing with
the habit of combat and the glow of victory. After defeating the German
armies and disillusioning the German people, we should seek a minimum
by force and a maximum by consent."[139]

Hapgood was appealing, of course, to the spirit of Wilson's "peace
without victory" address, to which most of these publicists remained
essentially loyal despite the pressure of wartime emotions. Thus the *Public*
never really abandoned its commitment of June 1917 to "a peace that
means the checking of Germany and the discrediting of her political
philosophy – not her humiliation and embitterment."[140] It is true that
the editors came to the conclusion that the discrediting of militarism
demanded the loss of Alsace-Lorraine and that by the time of the armistice
they were writing of the "punishment" to be "inflicted upon Germany."
But they still insisted that this "should be designed with a view to her
restoration to the full fellowship of nations at the earliest possible moment," warning that "it is possible, unless great foresight is exercised, for
this war to become to the world what the Civil War was to this country,
where the great questions of reconstruction were conceived in passion and
decided by men who persisted in re-fighting the war."[141] Weyl, too,
stressed that generosity would be the course of prudence: "To place a
revengeful, even though a weakened Germany in the middle of Europe is
to lay a train which will blow up the peace of the world."[142]

[138] *Public,* 21 (7 Sept. 1918), pp. 1134–6.
[139] *New Republic,* 16 (21 Sept. 1918), pp. 231–2.
[140] *Public* 20 (15 June 1917), pp. 567–8.
[141] Ibid., (12 Oct. 1917), p. 976; ibid., 21 (14 Dec. 1918), pp. 1495–6.
[142] *End of the War,* p. 212.

Friends and foes of a democratic peace

On January 8, 1918, President Wilson not only satisfied the demand for a clarification of America's war aims but also provided progressives with a shorthand description of the nature of a desirable peace. The Fourteen Points speech was greeted by progressive publicists with almost as much enthusiasm as the Peace without Victory address had been a year earlier. There were, it is true, a few who had some reservations. Walling regretted the "somewhat vague" character of the commitment to the "subject nationalities of Austria-Hungary."[143] More surprisingly, Baker's initial reaction upon reading Wilson's speech was that he did "not like it as well as some of the former ones." "I wonder sometimes if he has grasped firmly the new economic and social implications of democracy," he noted. Baker was particularly concerned with the economic consequences of applying the principle of self-determination to such places as Lorraine and Trieste.[144] In respect to Trieste, and also more generally, Wilson would have been less vulnerable to this criticism had he followed more closely the Inquiry memorandum on which the Fourteen Points were based.[145] Nevertheless, Lippmann, one of the three authors of that memorandum, "was exultant over Wilson's speech."[146] So, too, were the liberal weeklies, which paid less attention to the specific points than to the general character and tone of Wilson's pronouncement. "Gratitude is due to President Wilson for his unflinching insistence upon principles even more than for their enunciation, with unexampled clarity and power," declared the *Public*. "For the first time since the beginning of the war, its issues are clear and unmistakable."[147] "This purges the Allied cause of whatever selfish aims still clung to it," Holt maintained in the *Independent*. "Woodrow Wilson is today the acknowledged leader of the forces of democracy engaged in the overthrow of absolutism, and the great champion of liberalism on earth."[148]

[143] "The German Socialists . . . V, The Anti-Democratic Peace terms of the German Minority Socialists," Walling Papers.
[144] Notebook 15, 8 Jan. 1918, pp. 16–17, R. S. Baker Papers.
[145] For the Inquiry memorandum and its relation to the Fourteen Points, see *Wilson Papers*, 45, pp. 459–85, 506–39, 550–9, and the analyses in Mamatey, *The United States and East Central Europe*, pp. 177–85, and Lawrence E. Gelfand, *The Inquiry: American Preparations for Peace, 1917–1919* (New Haven, 1963), pp. 136–51.
[146] Steel, *Walter Lippmann*, p. 134. Later, however, Lippmann was to recall that the Inquiry had rather unsuccessfully "tried to slow the President down on self-determination." Mayer, *Political Origins of the New Diplomacy*, pp. 364–5.
[147] *Public*, 21 (18 Jan. 1918), p. 67.
[148] *Independent*, 93 (19 Jan. 1918), p. 89. (This unsigned editorial is attributed to Holt in the Holt papers.) See also *New Republic*, 13 (12 Jan. 1918), p. 292.

Once again, Wilson had demonstrated an ability to appeal to a broad segment of progressive opinion. Men whose feelings about the war differed as widely as Spargo's and Steffens's were among those who sent their congratulations to the White House.[149] Steffens, indeed, seems to have helped persuade Amos Pinchot that the president was proceeding on the basis of radical anti-imperialist premises. "As long as there is imperialism, that is to say, while nations go on scheming to get hold of land, especially in undeveloped nations, there will be militarism," Pinchot explained to his wife. "Wilson's idea is to call a halt to land-grabbing and all its modifications running through the categories of protectorates, suzerainties, spheres of influence, etc. Give everybody or as many people as possible self-determination. Build up a public opinion to the effect that war, or rather conquest is simply larceny. Establish free trade."[150] The treaty of Brest-Litovsk in March 1918, generally seen as demonstrating the irredeemable ruthlessness of the German government, further consolidated progressive support for Wilson and the war.[151] By May 1918, Steffens, on a new tour, was giving a lecture under the title, "The Menace of Peace." "It's a warning against a negotiated imperialist peace," he explained to Colonel House, and "urges the continuation of the war until we achieve a democratic peace."[152]

If the German government was conclusively discredited by the Brest-Litovsk treaty, the Allies were not thereby placed in a better light. Indeed, some continued to argue that they bore indirect responsibility for Russia's fate. "Rather than revise their imperialistic war aims, they permitted Russia to go down, almost forced her to make a separate peace, and allowed Germany to break her up into a number of smaller states," Weyl concluded.[153] On the eve of the treaty's signature, Hapgood had pleaded for the offer of "a fair trade" to the Germans, in the sense of a moderate peace on both fronts, arguing that "the sweeping demands now made on Russia by the German imperialists" would only be supported by the

---

[149] *Wilson Papers,* 45, pp. 542, 593.

[150] AP to Gertrude [Pinchot], 4 Mar. 1918. For other favorable comments by Pinchot on Wilson at this time, see AP to Frank Harris, 31 Jan. 1918, and to George F. Peabody, 19 Feb. 1918, Amos Pinchot Papers, box 35. For Steffens's views, see Cheslaw, "Lincoln Steffens," p. 219.

[151] "Personally, the German-Russian peace and the German career in Finland, etcetera, have greatly modified my own attitude, if not toward the war, at least toward an immediate peace. An immediate peace leaving the Eastern situation untouched would be full of combustibles for another explosion." Charles T. Hallinan, secretary of the AUAM to the members of the executive committee, 15 Apr. 1918, Amos Pinchot Papers, subject file 15.

[152] Steffens to Colonel House, 8 May 1918, *Steffens Letters,* 1, p. 427. For condemnations of Brest-Litovsk, see *New Republic,* 14 (16, 23 Mar. 1918), pp. 185–6, 220–1; *Independent,* 93 (16, 23 Mar. 1918), pp. 437–9, 478.

[153] *End of the War,* pp. 2–3. See also Hapgood, *The Advancing Hour,* p. 104.

German people and Reichstag as long as "they conceived themselves fighting against Entente territorial demands."[154]

Such arguments reflected the persistent distrust of Allied ambitions among American progressives. This, as we have seen, had been widespread during the debate over intervention,[155] and, even after American entry into the war, it was generally recognized by progressive publicists that, as the *Public* delicately put it, "the war aims of France and England, while primarily intending to secure the future of democratic civilization, were also regardful of some inconsistent elements of imperialistic policy."[156] Such suspicions received confirmation with the publication of the "secret treaties" by the Bolsheviks in November 1917. Of course, the existence of the treaties had not been previously unknown (Hapgood had written of them to House in December 1916),[157] but the revelation of their terms nevertheless deepened progressives' anxieties. "I see nothing to do but to concentrate our efforts upon trying to get the war straightened out so that at least we shall not have made the sacrifices for unworthy aims and prolonged the war unnecessarily," Amos Pinchot wrote to La Follette. "But how England can be brought to repudiate her secret agreements with other countries, I do not now see."[158] "What is most highly objectionable in all these treaties," Weyl explained, "is that they constitute a program not dictated by a sense of international justice, nor by a desire to produce a better international order, but by self-interest."[159] Both Wilson's Fourteen Points speech and Lloyd George's address a few days earlier to the British Trades Union Congress (TUC) had been designed specifically to counter this impression.[160] Despite these declarations, however, the conviction remained that, as Baker reported in May

---

[154] Letter, "What to Do for Russia," *New Republic*, 14 (2 Mar. 1918), p. 145.

[155] See Chapter 5, "The Debate over Intervention."

[156] *Public*, 20 (18 May 1917), p. 471. See also, for example, Amos Pinchot to George Creel, 14 Nov. 1917, and to F. E. Walker, 15 Nov. 1917, Amos Pinchot Papers, box 27.

[157] Hapgood to Colonel House, 30 Dec. 1916, E. M. House papers. See also *Public*, 20 (29 June 1917), p. 615; Steffens in *Kansas City Post*, 21 Sept. 1917, scrapbook 3, Steffens Papers.

[158] AP to Senator Robert La Follette, 11 Dec. 1917, Amos Pinchot Papers, box 27.

[159] *End of the War*, p. 119. See also Howe to Woodrow Wilson, 31 Dec. 1917, Woodrow Wilson Papers, ser. 4, case file 324A.

[160] See Mayer, *Political Origins of the New Diplomacy*, chaps. 8–9. The Inquiry memorandum on which Wilson based the Fourteen Points was itself, according to Lippmann (its principal author), "keyed upon the secret treaties." In 1919, Lippmann claimed that the Fourteen Points themselves "were phrased with a special reference to the secret treaties and memoranda, and were consciously designed as a substitute for them." Steel, *Walter Lippmann*, pp. 133–6, 609; "The Fourteen Points and the League of Nations," address before the League of Free Nations Association, 5 Apr. 1919, Walter Lippmann Papers, Robert O. Anthony collection, box 46, folder 94. For the relationship of the Inquiry memorandum to the Fourteen Points, see n. 145 above.

1918, the governments of Britain and France "are not sympathetic with our highest purposes, and [they] are more or less bound by secret understandings and special interests with which we have nothing to do, and which would embarrass, if not defeat, the whole great constructive plan we have in mind for a democratic settlement at the close of the war."[161]

It was significant that Baker wrote from London since it would seem that direct acquaintance with the European scene tended to intensify doubts about Allied intentions in the minds even of the most committed supporters of the war. White came back from his trip to Europe in the winter of 1917–18 disturbed by "the talk that Great Britain was preparing to put both feet into the trough at the end of the war."[162] On his return to London in the summer of 1918, Russell saw no evidence of a transformation in Britain's war aims. "She's in the war to save the Empire and nothing else," he concluded. "There's just as much idea of democracy in the British support of this war as you could take on the point of a knife." "I wonder," he added, "if President Wilson is well-informed about the real attitude here."[163] If he was not, it was through no fault of Baker, who in his weekly letters to the State Department constantly warned that the governments of Britain and France "want our powerful armies and our vast money resources but they really think our war-aims, as expressed by Mr. Wilson, a kind of moonshine."[164]

Just as such distrust of the governments of the Old World had been a basic feature in American progressives' view of the European war from the beginning, so it continued to run parallel with a belief that the liberal peace program represented "the hopes of the plain people of every nation."[165] Even Lippmann in an Inquiry memorandum stressed that it was "in official circles" that there was a lack of interest in "what may be called the program of an enduring peace, the program for which the workers, the farmers, the small capitalists and the liberal intellectuals of Western Europe and America accepted the war."[166] In reporting that "Great Britain opposed the interallied conference because England wanted to conduct England's war for England's gain," White explained that "by England I

---

161 Baker to Frank L. Polk, 28 May 1918, R. S. Baker Papers.
162 White to George H. Lorimer, 20 Feb. 1918, White Papers.
163 Diary no. 8, 11, 24 June 1918, Russell Papers; Holt to Theodore Marburg, 15 Oct. 1918, Holt Papers, box 2, folder 1.
164 Baker to Frank L. Polk, 27 July 1918. See also Baker to Polk, 11 Apr., 28 May, 10, 24 Aug., 1918, R. S. Baker Papers.
165 *Public*, 20 (17 Aug. 1917), p. 783. See Chapter 4, "Causes of War – and Cures."
166 "Memorandum," [1917], Lippmann Papers, box 38, folder 1360.

mean the military caste in England – the imperial aristocracy," which was "also closely related to the diplomatic caste."[167] To Amos Pinchot, the very secrecy of the "secret treaties" proved that they expressed the aims of "not the people of the allies but the governments of the allies."[168] Of the peace conference, he prophesied, "the people will be altruistic, but not the governments."[169] Faith in this simple dichotomy, however, was not always easily sustained, particularly after prolonged exposure to the European scene. There was surely a perceptible difference in tone between Baker's confident assertion on his arrival in England that "the only hope is in common people who trust one another: and not in the old, evil governments of the earth," and his somewhat defiant insistence to Brand Whitlock four months later that "I can see no refuge but the old refuge of an abiding faith in common people."[170]

By this time, however, Baker had located European support for Wilson's peace program rather more precisely. He told Whitlock that he could "see no light or hope in this situation in any direction, except in the direction of organized labor, especially in England."[171] Since March, indeed, the British Labour Party had bulked large in Baker's letters to the State Department. His interest and sympathy were initially engaged by the "Memorandum on War Aims" officially adopted by the party in February 1918. This, Baker reported, advocated "essentially the Wilson program, indeed quoting Wilson's four proposals as bedrock principles."[172] Further acquaintance, including interviews with Arthur Henderson and other leaders and observation of its performance in by-elections, left Baker impressed by the party's "democratic" character and organizational strength.[173] After providing "a somewhat lengthy account" of the Labour Party Conference in June, he wrote, "The more I see of the labor party the more I feel that it is the most precious and vital force in British life to-day."[174] He thought it "certain" that "in the days after the war the labour group [would come] into greater political power in

[167] W. A. White to George H. Lorimer, 20 Feb. 1918, White Papers.
[168] Address to mass meeting, 17 Feb. 1918, Amos Pinchot Papers, box 37.
[169] AP to J. H. McKeever, 2 Dec. 1918, Amos Pinchot Papers, box 37.
[170] Notebook 16, p. 139, 25 Mar. 1918; Notebook 19, 4 Aug. 1918, pp. 10–11, R. S. Baker Papers.
[171] Notebook 19, 6 Aug. 1918, p. 35, R. S. Baker Papers.
[172] Baker to Frank L. Polk, 18 Mar. 1918, R. S. Baker Papers. The four proposals Baker refers to are presumably the "principles" Wilson set out in his address to Congress, 11 Feb. 1918. See *Wilson Papers*, 46, pp. 322–3.
[173] R. S. Baker to Frank L. Polk, 25 Mar., 30 Apr., 7 June, 1918, R. S. Baker Papers.
[174] R. S. Baker to Frank L. Polk, 30 June, 6 July 1918, R. S. Baker Papers.

England," and conceived of himself "as one of the diplomats of the New Order – making my symbolic bow to the Coming Monarch": "Why should anyone want to be Ambassador to St James', when he can be Ambassador to the South Wales miners and the cotton spinners of Lancashire?"[175]

In pinning such hopes on the British Labour Party, Baker was by no means alone. Indeed, in the course of 1918 the party received from American progressives a quite remarkable amount of enthusiastic attention. Hailing them as "probably the most enlightened documents of the kind ever brought forth by a political party," the *New Republic* published both the Memorandum on War Aims and the report on domestic reconstruction, "Labor and the New Social Order," as special supplements.[176] Kellogg, who was present at the Nottingham conference of the British Labour Party in February 1918, not only produced an extensive and sympathetic account of it for the *Survey* but also gave addresses on the subject to the National Civic Federation and other carefully selected audiences.[177] "My feeling is that that movement has tremendous potentialities and I want to help in any way I can in getting it before people who will count," he explained.[178] Later Kellogg was to recall how lonely he had felt in Belgium, France, and Italy, until at Nottingham he "saw this great belt of Britishers, and the thousands they spoke for, striking out for things I believed in."[179] Among the eager readers of Kellogg's report was White, who confessed to being "more interested in that phase of the war than in anything else."[180] White himself had returned from England convinced that "the first political cabinet to arise after the coalition cabinet goes will be a labour cabinet," an expectation apparently shared by Steffens and the *Independent* as well as the *Survey*.[181] Already, the *New Republic* observed in February 1918, "the Labor party can be characterized

[175] R. S. Baker to Kenyon L. Butterfield, 8 June 1918; to Frank L. Polk (drafted but unsent), 3 Sept. 1918, R. S. Baker Papers.

[176] *New Republic*, 14 (16 Feb. 1918), p. 70; ibid., pt. 2; (23 March 1918), pt. 2.

[177] "The British Labor Offensive: The London and Nottingham Meetings," *Survey*, 39 (2 Mar. 1918), pp. 585–8; "British Labor and the War," address to National Civic Federation, New York, 16 Mar. 1918, Kellogg Papers.

[178] PUK to Miss Grace Abbott, 23 Mar. 1918, Paul Kellogg Papers, folder 131.

[179] Address to Women's International League for Peace and Freedom, 20 Feb. 1940. See Chambers, *Kellogg*, p. 67.

[180] White to P. U. Kellogg, 16 Mar. 1918, White Papers.

[181] *Martial Adventures of Henry and Me*, pp. 316–17; Steffens to Allen H. Suggett, [January 1918?], *Steffens Letters*, 1, p. 418; *Independent*, 96 (23 Nov. 1918), pp. 242–3; *Survey*, 39 (24 Nov. 1917), p. 204.

without exaggeration as the most powerful organized political force in the United Kingdom excepting only the state."[182]

The rise of the Labour Party was generally seen as having implications reaching beyond Great Britain. "What is now going forward among the wage-earning population of the island commonwealth may be the shadow of coming events which will affect and condition western civilization in the time to come," the *Survey* declared.[183] In particular, as Baker stressed, it had "lessons for us in America."[184] "The time is ripe," Amos Pinchot assured American union leaders in late 1917, "for labor to go into politics and become a great political power, just as it is doing in England."[185] The *New Republic,* the *Public,* and the *Independent* also urged the AFL to enter politics as the TUC had done, while the *Survey* optimistically reported every stirring of support for the idea of an American Labor Party within state Federations of Labor.[186] Naturally enough, such agitation for a change in the AFL's long-established policy was not well received by the federation's national leadership. Gompers devoted much of his speech at the 1918 annual convention of the AFL to denouncing "intellectualist" meddlers in the affairs of labor,[187] and later in the year Gompers's lieutenant, Matthew Woll, stressed the differences between British and American conditions in a paper to a conference of the Academy of Political Science. "Among advanced thinkers and so-called 'intellectuals,'" he observed, "the idea prevails that these difficulties can easily be swept aside, and reconstruction can be effected by a labor party which is to be led by these intellectuals who hope to get the offices."[188]

Ironically, the only defenders of the AFL's leadership among these publicists were the pro-war Socialists of the Social Democratic League. It is true that Walling had long been opposed to the idea of an American Labor Party but the grounds of his objection were now strikingly different. Whereas before the war he had feared that socialism would be contaminated by the attitudes of organized labor, now it seemed to be the other way round. "The miserable collapse of international Socialism and the

[182] *New Republic,* 14 (16 Feb. 1918), p. 70.

[183] *Survey,* 41 (2 Nov. 1918), pt. 2, p. x.

[184] R. S. Baker to Frank L. Polk, 12 Sept. 1918, R. S. Baker Papers.

[185] AP to Joseph D. Cannon, 30 Nov. 1917; to John F. McNamee, 13 Dec. 1917, Amos Pinchot Papers, boxes 30, 34.

[186] *New Republic,* 15 (13 July 1918), pp. 307–8; *Public,* 21 (10 Aug. 1918), pp. 1009–11; *Independent,* 95 (14 Sept. 1918), pp. 342–3; *Survey,* 40 (8 June 1918), p. 288, and 41 (2 Nov. 1918), pp. 132–3.

[187] George P. West, "The Progress of American Labor," *Nation,* 106 (29 June 1918), pp. 753–5.

[188] *Survey,* 41 (14 Dec. 1918), p. 338.

utter failure of the European labor movement to resist Kaiserism as soon as it cloaks itself under the name of Socialism" showed, he argued, that "what is needed is an extension to Europe of our old fashioned Jeffersonian democracy – with the very important amendment that organized labor of the A.F. of L. type is taken into partnership with the government."[189]

Evidently for Walling the issues and emotions directly related to the war overrode all else. No doubt he was particularly obsessed by them, but it was generally true that in 1918 political alignments and antagonisms were largely determined by the question of war aims. It was this that drew the vast majority of these publicists, including men as different as Amos Pinchot and Hamilton Holt, to the British Labour Party and set them against Gompers and his allies among the pro-war Socialists.[190] The leaders of the American labor movement, complained the *Public,* were "men whose international creed just now is not far from a demand that all Germans be shot, all Socialists hung, and the Bolsheviks treated with the contempt so richly merited by a body that has departed so far from recognised trade union principles."[191] "Gompers has laid down on British Labor, and we intellectuals must act in his stead," Steffens observed.[192] However, when Kellogg gave his sympathetic reports on British labor's attitude to the war, he was accused by Walling of peddling "insidious pro-German pacifist propaganda."[193] The particular object of Walling's ire was the renewed proposal for an international socialist conference to which German representatives would be invited. When the Interallied Labor Conference of February 1918 appointed a delegation to press this idea on American labor, Russell confidentially informed the State Department that its leader, the Belgian Camille Huysmans, "has become a pro-German."[194] On the other hand, Croly warned House that "it would be very discouraging for the British Labor Party in case this delegation were met with a wholly unsympathetic reception here" and hoped "that pressure will be brought to bear upon Mr. Gompers not to throw up an impassable barrier against it."[195] That pressure would be needed was

[189] Walling to A. M. Simons, 29 Apr. 1918, A. M. Simons Papers; cf. Walling to Eugene Debs, 14 Dec. 1909, and to H. M. Hyndman, 19 Feb. 1910, Walling Papers.
[190] AP to Colonel House, 28 Jan. 1918, Amos Pinchot Papers, box 37; Holt, "A League of Nations Now?" *Survey,* 40 (31 Aug. 1918), p. 607.
[191] *Public,* 21 (11 Jan. 1918), pp. 40–1.
[192] Steffens to Allen H. Suggett, [January 1918?], *Steffens Letters,* 1, p. 418.
[193] *Survey,* 39 (23 Mar. 1918), p. 688.
[194] Russell to Robert Lansing, (24 Mar. 1918), NA RG 59, 763.72119/1531 1/2.
[195] Croly to Colonel House, 6 Mar. 1918, E. M. House Papers. See also *New Republic,* 14, (23 Mar. 1918), pp. 218–20; *Public,* 21 (23 Mar. 1918), pp. 357–60.

suggested by the belligerent and "cocksure" attitude displayed by an AFL mission to Europe.[196] When Gompers himself set out in August 1918, avowedly to "oppose the radicals under Arthur Henderson and the Socialists desiring an immediate peace," he did not receive a good press in the liberal weeklies.[197] Baker, who had strongly urged the administration to prevent the trip, characteristically found Gompers's private behavior as deplorable as his public pronouncements.[198] Even Spargo, the chairman of a parallel mission from the Social Democratic League designed to counter the spread of "pacifism and Bolshevism" in the Allied countries, soon concluded that "the situation in England and in France differs as radically as possible from Walling's theories."[199] When Spargo, to Walling's fury, publicly declared that he had found only a negligible amount of defeatism among the labor and socialist groups of France and Britain, the *New Republic* felt vindicated. "This is true, and it always has been true. The impression to the contrary is the work of people who differ from the labor representatives as to the test of victory."[200]

To many progressive commentators, then, it seemed that, as Steffens put it, "the world is fighting on perpendicular lines, but the real division is along a horizontal line."[201] "The issue of internationalism versus militarism uncovers . . . a new cleavage, cutting athwart the alignment between the hostile nations," Weyl explained. "Upon this issue British Liberals and German Liberals stand closer together than do British Liberals and Conservatives or German Liberals and Conservatives."[202] Moreover, the fight for a democratic peace would be waged by those who sought democracy at home. "When we look about the world for the allies

---

[196] *New Republic*, 15, (25 May 1918), pp. 96–7. On the AFL mission, see Radosh, *American Labor*, chap. 5.

[197] *Public*, 21 (31 Aug. 1918), pp. 1102–3. For similar views, see *New Republic*, 15 (15 June 1918), pp. 190–3; *Nation*, 107 (7 Sept. 1918), p. 240; AP to Louis D. Budenz, 14 June 1918, Amos Pinchot Papers, box 36.

[198] "He is an old reprobate, and scandalized even Rome by his actions during two of the nights he was here! It makes one angry to see such a man sent as a representative of American Labor!" Notebook 20, 13 Oct. [1918], pp. 84–5, R. S. Baker Papers. See also Baker to Frank L. Polk, 30 June, 19, 24 Aug., 1 Sept. 1918, ibid.

[199] Spargo to Robert Lansing, with enclosure, 9 June 1918, NA RG 59, 763.72/10310; Spargo to J. G. Phelps Stokes, 22 Sept. 1918, Stokes Papers, box 30–31. On the SDL mission, see Radosh, *American Labor*, chap. 7; Friedberg, "Marxism in the United States," pp. 254–5; Kreuter and Kreuter, *An American Dissenter*, pp. 178–91.

[200] *New Republic*, 16 (10 Aug. 1918), p. 31. On the conflict between Spargo and Walling, see Spargo to J. G. Phelps Stokes, 18, 22 Sept. 1918, Stokes Papers, box 30–31; "Reminiscences of John Spargo," p. 291; Radosh, *American Labor*, pp. 204–6.

[201] Steffens to Mrs. J. James Hollister, 10 Oct. 1918, *Steffens Letters*, 1, p. 430.

[202] Weyl, *End of the War*, pp. 161–2.

of internationalism," Weyl noted, "we find them in the democratic, liberal and socialistic groups of all nations."[203] "One is strongly impressed here as in England," reported Baker from Paris, "that the sincerest support of American war-aims, as voiced by President Wilson, is found among the radical and labour groups."[204] Indeed, it seemed that, in Weyl's words, "the centre and core of the democratic international movement in each country lies in the labour group."[205] On the other side, Amos Pinchot stressed, it was "the bankers and business interests who are in all countries fighting for annexations."[206] "It's a class war, or it will be at the peace conference," Steffens concluded.[207]

Nor was the United States exempt from this internal conflict, even though its government was committed to a liberal peace. The *Public* attributed the storm of criticism directed at the administration's conduct of the war in early 1918 to the fact that "the masters of business enterprise have awakened to the direction and intent of President Wilson's international policy" and the threat it presented to their "vision of America as the financial and industrial center and master of the world."[208] When Senator Lodge in August 1918 publicly expressed his dissent from Wilson's peace program, the *New Republic* linked his views, as the *Public* had done, with the Republican Party's commitment to protection: "Economic nationalism; therefore no League of Nations; therefore not merely the decisive defeat but the destruction of Germany."[209] Although the *Public* believed that Lodge's demands "must cause astonishment wherever Americanism has meant a liberalizing and unselfish spirit,"[210] Amos Pinchot warned that they had powerful support. "Millions are being spent to force an imperialist policy on the United States," he averred. "The international profiteers want to fight on at whatever cost to humanity until an

[203] *End of the War*, pp. 167–8.

[204] Baker to Frank L. Polk, 27 July 1918, R. S. Baker Papers.

[205] *End of the War*, p. 170.

[206] AP to George L. Record, 28 Jan. 1918, Amos Pinchot papers, box 36. See also Pinchot's address to mass meeting, 17 Feb. [1918], ibid.

[207] Steffens to Mrs. J. James Hollister, 10 Oct. 1918, *Steffens Letters*, 1, p. 430. See also F. C. Howe to Woodrow Wilson, 31 Dec. 1917, Woodrow Wilson Papers, ser. 4, case file 324A.

[208] *Public*, 21 (25 Jan. 1918), pp. 100–4.

[209] *New Republic*, 16 (31 Aug. 1918), pp. 122–3. Ironically in view of later radical historiography, the *Public* had attributed business hostility to the anti-imperialist implications of Wilson's call for "the removal of all economic barriers and the establishment of an equality of trade conditions among all the nations consenting to the peace." *Public*, 21 (25 Jan. 1918), p. 103.

[210] *Public*, 21 (7 Sept. 1918), p. 1134. On Lodge's speech and the thinking behind it, see William C. Widenor, *Henry Cabot Lodge and the Search for an American Foreign Policy* (Berkeley and Los Angeles, 1980), pp. 283–7 and passim.

imperialism has been established which will result in an Anglo-American banking and business supremacy. That is the big plot, the haut politique of the day. . . . This is much more important than any revenue bill."[211]

The war at home: collectivism and labor

Nevertheless, Pinchot did write a long open letter to Claude Kitchen, chairman of the House Ways and Means Committee, urging that the 1918 Revenue bill should include an excess profits tax levied, as in Britain, at a rate of 80 percent.[212] Substantially increased direct taxation was, of course, one of the chief domestic advances that progressives had hoped American belligerency would produce. Others had been an extension of government control over the economy, an enhancement of the position of labor, and a more cooperative social spirit.[213] These expectations doubtless shaped perceptions, particularly those of pro-war progressives who generally maintained that such hopes had been sufficiently fulfilled to vindicate their arguments and to provide encouragement for the future. On the other hand, the misgivings that had been widely expressed about the oppressive and reactionary tendencies of war also received more than enough confirmation to make America's domestic wartime experience an ambiguous one for progressives.

Recent studies of America's mobilization for war have stressed the comparative lack of central direction and legal coercion[214] but these features were rarely remarked by progressive publicists, whose observations tended to accord with their predictions. Indeed, prophecy merged almost indistinguishably into commentary. Thus in May 1917, Lippmann assured a correspondent that "we stand at the threshold of a collectivism which is greater than any as yet planned by a socialist party."[215] In June, even before the Lever bill had been enacted, White claimed that "food, fuel, iron, steel, lumber and transportation are now under a government control as strong as government ownership." "The back of the profit

[211] AP to William Kent, 28 Aug. 1918; to R. F. Paine, 28 Aug. 1918, Amos Pinchot Papers, boxes 36, 35.

[212] "New Patriotism for Old: An Apology for our Profiteers," an open letter to Hon. Claude Kitchen, 10 Aug. 1918, Amos Pinchot Papers, subject file 81.

[213] See Chapter 5, "The Debate over Intervention."

[214] Robert D. Cuff, *The War Industries Board: Business–Government Relations during World War I* (Baltimore, Md., 1973); David M. Kennedy, *Over Here: The First World War and American Society* (New York, 1980), chap. 2.

[215] W. Lippmann to J. G. Phelps Stokes, 1 May 1917, Phelps Stokes Papers, box 26.

system is broken," he asserted. "The world wherein the right of the individual to profits was paramount to the right of society to fair prices was blown up with the Austrian grand duke."[216] More temperately, Devine in the *Survey* remarked that "the food administration bill is of extraordinary interest to social workers because of the bold policy of social control which it embodies."[217] "The United States is quietly absorbing the sounder elements of the Social Democratic theory," the *Independent* concluded in July, and by January 1918 a writer in the *Survey* had followed Howe in announcing "the demise of a highly respected doctrine" – "the *laissez-faire* philosophy that the government should do as little as possible."[218] This was after the administration's takeover of the railroads, which was interpreted as a further major step toward collectivism. "Another stronghold of privilege has been stormed," Baker noted with satisfaction.[219]

Equally gratifying were the gains made by labor. In the early months of the war, writers in the liberal weeklies were concerned to counter moves in some states to suspend existing labor legislation and the established rights of trade unions.[220] Not only was this resistance largely successful but, according to the *Survey*, which devoted particular attention to the subject, "labor standards in war time continued to advance."[221] Full employment helped to keep wages high and create opportunities for unionization, while further social legislation was passed at the state level. Above all, the federal government recognized the legitimacy and importance of the organized labor movement in an unprecedented manner. Trade union representatives were included on many of the wartime boards and commissions and the president himself addressed the AFL's annual convention in November 1917. The *New Republic* appraised the administration's motives coolly: "If the loyal co-operation of the workers was to be secured during the present war, something decisive had to be done to indicate the definite adoption of a new attitude and policy."[222] It was

---

216 *Emporia Gazette*, 30 June 1917.
217 "Regulation of Food," *Survey*, 38 (30 June 1917), p. 291.
218 *Independent*, 91 (21 July 1917), p. 87; Neva R. Deardorff, "The Demise of a Highly Respected Doctrine," *Survey*, 39 (5 Jan. 1918), pp. 390–7; Howe, *High Cost of Living*, p. 259.
219 Notebook 14, 28 Dec. 1917, pp. 112–13, R. S. Baker Papers. See also *Public*, 21 (4 Jan. 1918), pp. 7–8; *Independent*, 93 (5 Jan. 1918), p. 8; Howe, "The Railroads and the New Democracy," *Public*, 21 (4 Jan. 1918), p. 14.
220 *New Republic*, 10 (28 Apr. 1917), pp. 365–6; *Public*, 20 (4, 11 May 1917), pp. 415, 453; *Survey*, 38 (28 Apr., 26 May, 2, 9 June 1917), pp. 46, 194, 225, 241; 39 (29 Dec. 1917), p. 372.
221 *Survey*, 40 (7 Sept. 1918), p. 642. See also *New Republic*, 15 (22 June 1918), pp. 220–1.
222 *New Republic*, 13 (24 Nov. 1917), p. 84.

nonetheless the case, the *Public* observed, that "President Wilson and Secretaries Baker and Daniels are carrying out a policy more enlightened and democratic than any previously conceived by federal executives."[223] Progressive publicists reported with satisfaction the government's role in protecting and promoting collective bargaining, organizing a rudimentary national employment service, and building houses for munitions and shipbuilding workers.[224] The most dramatic single assertion of federal authority on behalf of labor was probably the commandeering of the Smith and Wesson plant in Springfield, Massachusetts, when the company refused to abide by a ruling of the National War Labor Board (NWLB) forbidding discrimination against union employees.[225] At least equally impressive, however, was the NWLB's successful fight, fully reported in the *Survey*, to compel the steel industry to accept the principle of the eight-hour day.[226] "The wage-earners have gained an enormous strategic advantage," the *Independent* noted. "A real social revolution is already under way."[227] To Howe, "the consideration . . . shown for the workers in the midst of a war that commanded all of our energies, exceeds anything the most optimistic reformer felt could be achieved in a quarter of a century."[228]

Such conclusions nourished a sense of vindication, particularly on the part of those whose support for American intervention had exposed them to attack. Of none was this more true than the pro-war Socialists. Even Walling insisted that "the war is leading rapidly to a radical form of collectivism," and the program published by the Social Democratic League in the summer of 1918 stressed that "the war has brought about a socially conscious and intelligent organization of society" in which "Labor has gained a rapidly growing and direct control not merely over labor conditions but over industry itself and over the entire economic structure of the nation."[229] With the bitter divisions the question of intervention

223 *Public*, 20 (21 Dec. 1917), p. 1239.
224 *Survey*, 39 (12 Jan., 2, 23 Feb. 1918), pp. 411–13, 494–5, 545–6, 561–2, 575–6; 40 (8 June 1918), p. 288. Also Howe, *The Land and the Soldier* (London, 1919), pp. 10–11; *New Republic*, 13 (24 Nov. 1917), pp. 84–6, and 15 (22 June 1918), pp. 220–1. For an analysis of the Wilson administration's war labor policies, see Kennedy, *Over Here*, pp. 258–70.
225 *Survey*, 40 (21 Sept. 1918), p. 696; *New Republic*, 16 (14 Sept. 1918), pp. 185–6; *Independent*, 95 (28 Sept. 1918), pp. 409–10.
226 *Survey* 40 (28 Sept. 1918), p. 722; 41 (5 Oct., 2 Nov. 1918), pp. 19, and pt. 2, p. vi. This achievement was genuine and important, if short-lived. See David Brody, *Labor in Crisis: The Steel Strike of 1919* (Philadelphia and New York, 1965), pp. 59–60.
227 *Independent*, 95 (7 Sept. 1918), pp. 306–7. See also *Public*, 20 (2 Nov. 1917), pp. 1052–3.
228 *The Land and the Soldier*, p. 3.
229 Walling to J. G. Phelps Stokes, 27 Dec. 1917; "A Program of Social Reconstruction," pp. 8, 5, Phelps Stokes Papers.

had created among its writers as well as its readers, the *New Republic*'s situation was not entirely dissimilar from that of the pro-war Socialists, and it, too, stressed the scale and significance of the advances the war had brought. "These stupendous increases in the functions of the national government are threatening to the interests and even to the survival of many powerful classes in the community," an editorial bearing the marks of Croly's style observed in January 1918. "They involve a radical change in the balance of economic power." Therefore, "these economic innovations should be watched as a deeply significant experiment which, although rendered practicable by the accident of the war, is far from being a violent and irrelevant episode in American economic development. Their final adoption had been emphatically foreshadowed by the economic agitation and fermentation of recent years. Those who shared in that agitation have been vindicated by the policy which the government has been obliged to pursue under the pressure of a manifest public necessity."[230]

Such "agitation" had not ceased, of course, with the war. Progressive publicists continued to work for the sort of measures they favored. When the Lever Food Control Bill ran into trouble in Congress, several of them rallied to its support.[231] The idea of public housing for war workers in shipbuilding centers was put forward in the *New Republic*, which also argued steadily for government ownership of the railroads.[232] Howe was another persistent advocate of this cause, both in published articles and in private communications to Secretary Baker and President Wilson.[233] Post and Lippmann were in a position to affect administration policy more directly – Post, as assistant secretary of labor, being responsible for the reorganization of the Employment Service in 1917, while Lippmann helped to shape the War Department's liberal labor policy.[234] The American Committee on War Finance, to which Amos Pinchot contributed

---

[230] *New Republic*, 13 (19 Jan. 1918), pp. 331–3.

[231] *Independent*, 90 (23 June 1917), pp. 527–9; *Survey*, 38 (30 June 1917), p. 291; *Emporia Gazette*, 21 June 1917; Rowell to Hiram Johnson, 20 June 1917, Rowell papers. The *Public*, however, criticized the bill for relying "more on arbitrary bureaucratic management than on economic law." *Public*, 20 (15 June 1917), pp. 573–4.

[232] *New Republic*, 13 (22 Dec. 1917), pp. 201–2; 11 (7, 21 July 1917), pp. 262–3, 322–3; 13 (10 Nov., 1 Dec. 1917), pp. 37–8, 107.

[233] "Shall the Government Mobilize Transporation"; "The Railroads, the Mine Owners and the Government," *Public*, 20 (1 June, 6 July 1917), pp. 526–8, 646; "The Necessity for Public Ownership of the Railways," *Annals*, 93 (March 1918), pp. 157–66; Howe to Newton D. Baker, 6 Dec. 1917, Newton D. Baker Papers; Howe to Woodrow Wilson, 15 Dec. 1917, *Wilson Papers*, 45, pp. 309–11, 283–5, 334.

[234] Post, "Living a Long Life Over Again," pp. 387–8 (revised numbering), L. F. Post Papers; Lippmann to Newton D. Baker, 19 Sept. 1917, 16 Dec. [1917], Newton D. Baker Papers; Steel, *Walter Lippmann*, p. 123.

about half the funds and at least as high a proportion of the energy, sought to influence Congress as well as the administration.[235] Its call for "the conscription of income" met only moderate success in 1917, but the ever-mounting costs of war proved a powerful ally and the Revenue bill of 1918 was hailed by the *New Republic* as "an equalitarian measure" which "cuts deep."[236] However, the atmosphere of war was not always conducive to progressive reform, as Chester Rowell found in California where he was one of the leaders in a movement for state health insurance. Although Rowell felt that the campaign, to which he committed most of his attention and remaining political influence, was "real war work," opponents of the measure branded it as "made in Germany."[237] Such "demagogy" infuriated Rowell – "Would you abolish printing because it was invented in Germany?" he asked one correspondent – but it doubtless contributed to the heavy defeat of the proposed constitutional amendment in the 1918 elections.[238]

Such contests demonstrated that the battle over progressive reform was no more "adjourned" for the duration of the war than was party politics. Indeed, in the eyes of some observers, the two had become intimately related. The storm of criticism that broke over the administration's conduct of the war in the winter of 1917–18, was, Ray Stannard Baker thought, "traceable to the great business interests of the country which resent being forced to do this and not do that by the Administration when they have for so many years practically dictated governmental policies. They dread governmental control of the railroads and the mines: they chafe under taxation: they fear the growing power of labor in the councils of the nation. They recognize in Wilson, clearly, a truly progressive if not radical leadership and they fear and despise him."[239] Some months later,

---

[235] AP to Chester B. Goolrick, 19 June 1918, Amos Pinchot Papers, box 37. For Pinchot's major statements on behalf of the war finance campaign, see above, n. 43.

[236] *New Republic*, 16 (14 Sept. 1918), pp. 183–5. Many of the progressive features of the 1918 Revenue Bill were dropped after the Armistice before the bill became law. See Kennedy, *Over Here*, p. 112; for an excellent review of the whole topic of war finance, see pp. 98–113.

[237] Rowell to Hiram W. Johnson, 27 Aug. 1918; to the editor, *Stockton Record*, 29 Oct. 1918, Rowell Papers. See also Rowell to Alexander McCabe, 10 Sept. 1917, and to Hiram W. Johnson, 3 June 1918, ibid.; Edward T. Devine, "Will California Lead?" *Survey*, 41 (26 Oct. 1918), pp. 91–2.

[238] Rowell to Mrs. Frances N. Noel, 7 June 1918; to A. Scott Ballagh, 20 June 1918, Rowell Papers. See also Rowell to John A. Lapp, 18 Nov. 1918, ibid.

[239] Notebook 15, 21 Jan. 1918, pp. 60–1, R. S. Baker Papers. Also 30 Jan. 1918, p. 67, ibid. For the "winter crisis," see Seward W. Livermore, *Politics Is Adjourned: Woodrow Wilson and the War Congress, 1916–1918* (Middletown, Conn., 1966), chaps. 5–7; and Cuff, *War Industries Board*, pp. 135–41.

Weyl felt the *New Republic* "should begin already in the defense of the Administration policy of taking over the railroads, telegraphs, etc. and against the attacks, for the most part partisan, on government owner-ship."[240] In this political and ideological fight, it was evident that pro-gressives were not alone in seeking to take advantage of the war. "The crooks and the tories know what they want," Steffens warned. "They are using the emergency to get even with their enemies and fight for their Cause."[241]

In this context, it was by no means to be taken for granted that the extended scope of government action would necessarily serve progressive purposes. From the beginning, some were suspicious of the heavy reliance on "dollar-a-year men" to staff the new wartime agencies. "American business is in the saddle at Washington," George P. West reported in the *Public* after six weeks of war. "In no other field could the Government find expert knowledge and executive efficiency. Our radicals are nowhere." "With Germany before us," he observed, "we need no reminder that nationalization of industry and consequent reduction of waste can be achieved without gain in the direction of democracy and the well being of the individual. All that is saved may be appropriated to the sinister and anti-social purposes of a ruling class, and the power for evil of that class merely strengthened thereby. . . . The war may nationalize our business. Will it help to socialize it?"[242]

Answers to this question revealed both divisions of opinion and uncer-tainty. Single Taxers and antimonopolyists were instinctively suspicious. Post commented sardonically on "the rush to Washington of 'what-price-patriots' eager to 'do their bit' as they themselves put it, and no less eager to 'get their bite',"[243] Amos Pinchot, long convinced that pecuniary motives had inspired much of the demand for American entry into the war, sought to substantiate Post's charge. In an open letter on war fi-nance, he traced, in what some felt was an "ungentlemanly" way, the involvement of individual members of the Council of National Defense in corporations making vast excess profits from the war.[244] Even the *Public,* while endorsing Pinchot's call for heavier taxation of war profits, deplored

---

[240] Weyl Diary, 6 Sept. 1918.
[241] Steffens to John Reed, 17 June 1918, *Steffens Letters*, 1, p. 428.
[242] George P. West, "Business Takes Charge," *Public*, 20 (11 May 1917), pp. 456–8.
[243] "Living a Long Life Over Again," p. 383 (renumbered), L. F. Post Papers.
[244] AP to Conference Committee of Senate and House of Representatives, 18 Sept. 1917; to Rev. W. S. Rainsford, 29 Sept. 1917, Amos Pinchot Papers, boxes 34, 30.

this attack, insisting that "the Administration has acted with vigor to prevent exorbitant prices and to protect the government from extortion."[245] Not even the strong inflationary pressures of a free market in wartime, however, shook Amos Pinchot's long-standing distrust of business-government collusion.[246] "I am myself very fearful of government price-fixing," he insisted. "Certainly, uniform prices should not be fixed for high and low cost concerns; that is what the Steel Corporation has been longing for since 1908."[247] The *Public,* too, remained sufficiently uneasy about "the endowment with governmental powers of our captains of industry"[248] to be happy to deflect upon them the accusations of incompetence directed at the administration in early 1918. "Every day that passes," it reported, "now sees power and responsibility passing to Government officials, enlisted to correct the mistakes of the supermen of business."[249]

Not even the *Public,* however, viewed the business community as consisting exclusively of reactionary incompetents. "None of us," it admitted rather grudgingly in June 1918, "has failed to note the emergence during the past year of a number of commercial and industrial leaders as prophets of a new economic order and preachers among their own people of a policy of lessened resistance to change." To some progressive observers, as we have seen, this was not such a new phenomenon.[250] Noting that "the big business man . . . has become in places the servant of the public," Weyl related this to "the change in the character of our industrial leaders during the last twenty years. . . . Bringing science, foresight to bear. . . . Bringing in the journalist and the college professor; the technical expert."[251] "Business men have become trustees," the *Survey* concluded.[252] In characteristically sentimental fashion, White lauded the "purely altruistic" activities of those American businessmen and financiers involved with the war effort in Europe. "They are sacrificing comforts at home, money-making opportunities at home," he reported. "But they are get-

[245] "Patriots and Profits," *Public,* 20 (28 Sept. 1917), pp. 931–4.

[246] See Pinchot's *History,* ed. Hooker, pp. 39–42; Graham, *Encore for Reform,* pp. 74–7.

[247] AP to Alfred Bishop Mason, 28 Aug. 1918, Amos Pinchot Papers, box 36. The assumption, general at the time, that the U.S. Steel Corporation's rate of return was higher than that of smaller companies was not well founded. For this and the story of price fixing in steel, see Melvin I. Urofsky, *Big Steel and the Wilson Administration: A Study in Business–Government Relations* (Columbus, Ohio, 1969), chap. 6.

[248] *Public,* 20 (18 May 1917), p. 472.

[249] Ibid., 21 (4 Jan. 1918), pp. 6–7. See also ibid. (1, 16 Feb. 1918), pp. 137–8, 198–9.

[250] Ibid. (1 June 1918), p. 691.

[251] Diary, 19 May 1918. See also Diary, 20 June 1918.

[252] *Survey,* 41 (16 Nov. 1918), p. 185.

ting something real out of it all. The renewal of youth in their faces through unstinted giving is beautiful to see." Their Herculean achievements were "the marvel of the French."[253]

Nevertheless, there remained much skepticism about the attitudes and motives of businessmen among progressives of all schools of thought. His problems in the War Department led Lippmann to complain that "business men on the whole are still worrying about ancient problems such as whether trade unions are seditious or not."[254] In the same article in which it recognized the existence of some more enlightened business voices, the *Public* observed that spokesmen for the National Association of Manufacturers continued to interpret such terms as "industrial co-operation" and "industrial freedom" as "meaning the enforced co-operation of individual workmen, unorganized, inarticulate and helpless, and the freedom of the employer to drive the workman to the limit of his physical endurance for as little pay as will keep body and soul together."[255] Reflecting upon the wartime experience a month before the Armistice, Baker noted "it has made one understand how deep the business passion was in America."[256] To Bourne, the sort of satisfactions perceived by White were but another example of the psychic gratifications war provided for the upper classes. "The man who moves from the direction of a large business in New York to a post in the war management industrial service in Washington does not apparently alter very much his power or his administrative technique. But psychically, what a transfiguration has occurred! His is now not only the power but the glory! And his sense of satisfaction is directly proportional not to the genuine amount of personal sacrifice that may be involved in the change but to the extent to which he retains his industrial prerogatives and sense of command."[257]

Suspicion of the motives of those in charge of the wartime collectivism was paralleled by misgivings about its methods. Bourne, in his bitterness, referred to "the riveting of a semi-military State-socialism on the country."[258] But even supporters of the war did not forget their fears of bureaucratic authoritarianism.[259] The *Independent* admitted that "the vast

253 *Martial Adventures of Henry and Me*, pp. 169–70.
254 WL to Judge M. S. Amos, 5 Nov. 1917, Lippmann Papers, box 2, folder 58.
255 "The Old Order Dies Hard," *Public*, 21 (1 June 1918), p. 691.
256 Notebook 20, 16 Oct. 1918, p. 104, R. S. Baker Papers.
257 "The State," [1918], in Bourne, *The War and the Intellectuals*, ed. Resek, pp. 74–5.
258 "A War Diary," *Seven Arts*, 2 (Sept. 1917), reprinted in Bourne, *The War and the Intellectuals*, ed. Resek, p. 38.
259 See Chapter 3, "Goals and Policies."

extensions of governmental control and dictation already achieved and in prospect" had their "bureaucratic" aspects, while remaining confident that "this control need not be so rigorous in days of peace."[260] The *New Republic* took the matter more seriously. From the beginning, the journal's emphasis on the experiment's fruitful potential was accompanied by warnings that it "would be likely to degenerate into a hideous instrument of tyranny if continued unchanged after the war."[261] By January 1918, the editors were insisting that the dangers inherent in "the recently adopted measures of state socialism" could only be averted if "equally effective measures are taken to build up within the state independent centers of economic and social allegiance which will be capable of balancing and, if necessary, of resisting the political leviathan."[262] This editorial clearly reflected a significant shift of emphasis in Croly's political thinking. In a signed article a few months earlier, he had observed that "in spite of all that the secular state has accomplished for civilization during its period of supremacy, it is proving to be an unnecessarily powerful and dangerous servant and an unnecessarily jealous master," and had looked forward to the strengthening of "class, trade and professional associations which will compete with the state for the loyalty of its citizens."[263]

The war at home: civil liberties and public opinion

This reevaluation of the virtues of pluralism by the prophet of "national organization" was not prompted solely by the largely mythical powers of such agencies as the War Industries Board. Apart from the obvious connection between the authority of national states and war itself, the chief impetus came from the American government's role in the restriction of civil liberties. In October 1917, Lippmann found Croly "in the depth of gloom chiefly about Wilson and the suppression of free speech."[264] Croly's distress may have been particularly acute, but for most progressive publicists its effects upon individual freedom within America was certainly a negative aspect of the wartime experience.

---

[260] *Independent*, 95 (21 Sept. 1918), pp. 374–5; 91 (11 Aug. 1917), pp. 209–11.
[261] *New Republic*, 11 (12 May 1917), pp. 37–8. See also ibid. (2, 30 June, 28 July 1917), pp. 129–31, 230–1, 349.
[262] *New Republic*, 13 (19 Jan. 1918), pp. 332–3.
[263] "The Future of the State," *New Republic*, 12 (15 Sept. 1917), pp. 179–83. On the shift in Croly's thinking, see Forcey, *Crossroads of Liberalism*, pp. 281–2.
[264] Diary, 12 Oct. [1917], Lippmann Papers.

There remained, however, significant differences in both the nature and the intensity of concern about this issue. As we have seen, some viewed compulsory military service as a fundamental violation of the principles of a free society,[265] but opposition to it was largely confined to opponents of intervention and the first weeks of the war. Kellogg wrote to Newton D. Baker urging that the United States should follow the examples of Canada and Australia and rely on volunteers.[266] The *Public* campaigned vigorously against conscription in April 1917 but ignored the issue thereafter.[267] The most persistent critic of the draft was Amos Pinchot. "The people were against it, and still are," he claimed in September 1917.[268] By this time, however, the focus of attention had shifted to the treatment of conscientious objectors. This was the issue that led the American Union against Militarism, at the instigation of the radical Roger Baldwin, to establish a Civil Liberties Bureau.[269] However, Kellogg objected to what he perceived to be the encouragement of conscientious objection,[270] and even Amos Pinchot, though more sympathetic, severed his formal connection with the bureau in order not to prejudice his "work . . . along the war profits line."[271]

Sympathy for the position of conscientious objectors was not entirely confined to opponents of the war. Croly had participated in an attempt to secure more liberal rules for conscientious objection, and the *New Republic* urged the government not to turn conscription into "an instrument of tyranny."[272] Kellogg's misgivings about the Civil Liberties Bureau did not prevent him publishing an eloquent plea by Norman Thomas on behalf of "War Heretics."[273] Weyl in his diary cited "the C.O's" as part of the evidence for "the decline of Liberalism in America."[274] Nev-

[265] See Chapter 5, "The Debate over Intervention."

[266] See Chambers, *Kellogg*, p. 63.

[267] *Public*, 20 (6, 13, 27 Apr. 1917), p. 320, 344–5, 399–400.

[268] AP to Rev. W. S. Rainsford, 29 Sept. 1917, Amos Pinchot Papers. See also AP to Elsa Hallor, 11 May 1917, and to George Edward Hall, 17 May 1917, ibid., boxes 30, 34.

[269] See Marchand, *American Peace Movement*, pp. 253–5; Donald Johnson, *The Challenge to American Freedoms: World War I and the Rise of the American Civil Liberties Union* (Lexington, Ky., 1963), pp. 18–25.

[270] Marchand, *American Peace Movement*, p. 255. On the split in the AUAM, see also Kennedy, *Over Here*, pp. 34–6.

[271] AP to Roger N. Baldwin, 15 Nov. 1917, and to John Haynes Holmes, 11 Dec. 1917, Amos Pinchot Papers, box 27.

[272] AP to J. Howard Whitehouse, 7 May 1917, Amos Pinchot Papers, box 29; *New Republic*, 11 (9 June 1917), pp. 148–50.

[273] Norman Thomas, "War's Heretics: A Plea for the Conscientious Objector," *Survey*, 38 (4 Aug. 1917), pp. 391–4.

[274] Weyl Diary, 28 July 1918.

ertheless, most progressive commentators approved of conscription, which was generally seen as embodying the principles of democracy. "Historically," Devine explained in the *Survey*, "universal service has been associated with democratic ideals and institutions, as hireling armies have been associated with monarchy, and as a pseudo-universal system which countenances paid substitutes has been associated with aristocracy – or, more accurately, with plutocracy."[275] Unequivocally welcoming conscription as "a plan . . . to sink the individual into the social unit," White later hailed the repression of antidraft law agitators as "a splendid precedent": "When this nation passes a law cracking down on the big food gamblers, or taking over the railroads, or adding a 40 per cent inheritance tax to all fortunes over 10 millions, the same drastic methods should be taken against those who agitate against those laws."[276] Such an inference, however, ran counter to the justification for conscription that in the spring had been advanced by Lippmann privately and publicly by the *New Republic* – that it would enable dissent to be more easily tolerated than would reliance on "the hate-mongering of a recruiting campaign."[277]

Attractive in its logic, this argument was hardly vindicated by the course of events. Indeed, in the chorus soon calling for the repression of dissent, a few progressive voices were to be heard. "Break the IWW Now," the *Independent* demanded in July 1917.[278] For the most part, however, even supporters of the war deplored the persecution of the IWW, which, it was suspected, arose from hostility to its domestic radicalism rather than simple concern about its loyalty. While not defending the movement's philosophy and methods, the *New Republic* and the *Survey* argued that repression would be counterproductive and that the only real remedy would be to remove "the economic causes of the unrest in the industries affected."[279] When the federal government arrested over

275 *Survey*, 38 (21 July 1917), p. 352. See also *Independent*, 90 (14, 21, 28 Apr. 1917), pp. 98, 151–2, 191–3; Rowell to Hiram W. Johnson, 20 June 1917, Chester Rowell Papers.
276 *Emporia Gazette*, 1, 31 May 1917.
277 Walter Lippmann to Woodrow Wilson, 6 Feb. 1917, quoted in Daniel R. Beaver, *Newton D. Baker and the American War Effort, 1917–1919* (Lincoln, Nebr., 1966), pp. 26–7; *New Republic*, 10 (14 Apr. 1917), pp. 311–12; and 11 (9 June 1917), p. 149. Stoughton Cooley also hoped that "one of the compensations that should accompany the passage of the conscription law should be a relaxation of the zeal of the petty officials who have taken it upon themselves to censor the utterances of citizens." *Public*, 20 (18 May 1917), p. 473.
278 *Independent*, 91 (21 July 1917), p. 87. See also ibid., 90 (23 June 1917), p. 529; 91 (28 July 1917), p. 118.
279 *Survey*, 38 (25 Aug. 1917), p. 457. See also *New Republic*, 11 (21 July 1917), pp. 320–2.

a hundred IWW officials in September 1917, both Creel, within the administration, and Steffens, in a memorandum to House, urged that the prosecution be dropped. "The war," Steffens warned, "is dividing men along the class line."[280] As the trial approached, Weyl was among those who signed an appeal to "American liberals to make it financially possible for the defense to present fully the industrial evils underlying the IWW revolt."[281] Even the *Public*, while loyally defending the administration's actions, struck an apologetic note: "The IWW cannot expect to stay out of jail in war time. But the moral tone of our prisons will not deteriorate because these rebel souls must languish there."[282] This last sentiment would have been endorsed by Baker, who in his notebook compared the IWW to primitive Christianity: "In its methods it may often be wrong, but in the great democratic ideals it is striving for it is sound and true, as I firmly believe."[283]

Not surprisingly, however, the civil liberties issue that most exercised these writers and journalists was the government's direct interference with the free expression and dissemination of opinion. As we have seen, the danger had been anticipated,[284] and attempts were made to forestall it. It had been as an alternative to censorship that Lippmann had recommended the establishment of a federal "publicity bureau," and, indeed, as chairman of the Committee on Public Information, Creel always maintained that "expression, not suppression, was the real need."[285] Only ten days after the U.S. declaration of war, Croly, Kellogg, and Amos Pinchot were among the signatories of a plea to President Wilson that he publicly remind all officials of the obligation "to uphold in every way our constitutional rights and liberties."[286] Wilson sent a sympathetic, if noncommittal reply, but at the same time sought legislative authority to censor the

---

[280] Steffens to Colonel House, 18 Oct. 1917, *Steffens Letters*, 2, pp. 1031–4; Johnson, *Challenge to American Freedoms*, pp. 92–3.

[281] *New Republic*, 15 (22 June 1918), p. iii.

[282] *Public*, 20 (5 Oct. 1917), pp. 957–8. See also ibid., 20 (14 Sept., 12 Oct. 1917), pp. 884–5, 975. The *Public* struck a somewhat similar note a year later when it lauded Eugene Debs for having "the nobility to accept his punishment like a man," when he was imprisoned under the Espionage Act. Ibid., 21 (21 Sept. 1918), pp. 1198–9.

[283] Notebook 20, 15 Sept. 1918, pp. 22–3; Notebook 15, 20 Jan. 1918, pp. 49–59, R. S. Baker Papers.

[284] See Chapter 5, "The Debate over Intervention."

[285] Vaughn, *Holding Fast the Inner Lines*, pp. 5–6, 240; Creel, *Rebel at Large*, pp. 157–8. On Creel's behind-the-scenes involvement in censorship, see Vaughn, *Holding Fast the Inner Lines*, pp. 222–32.

[286] Lillian Wald and others to Woodrow Wilson, 16 Apr. 1917, *Wilson Papers*, 42, pp. 118–19; for Wilson's reply, see p. 153.

press. Progressive journals contributed only slightly to the Republican-led opposition that secured the defeat of this proposal,[287] but when the postmaster-general used his powers under the Espionage Act to deny mailing privileges to Socialist and other radical papers, it was progressives who were most disturbed. Those, such as Amos Pinchot, who had some sympathy with the anti-war sentiments that were being suppressed, were naturally the most prompt and unequivocal in their protests.[288] But, as Spargo wrote to Wilson, there were also many "who desire above all things to give you their solid support, but whose resentment at the unwarranted and unnecessary suppression of criticism by the press compels them to be in spite of themselves constant critics of your Administration."[289] Howe, Stoughton Cooley, Spargo, and Steffens associated themselves with public protests, while regretful editorials appeared in the *Public* and the *New Republic*.[290] In addition to Spargo, Croly, Lippmann, Steffens, and Hapgood pleaded privately, either directly to Wilson or through House, for a change in the administration's policy.[291]

Not all progressive publicists shared even this concern. Walling, characteristically, claimed that demands "for a degree of personal freedom impossible in war time" were part of "the Kaiser's program for Socialists (outside of Germany)," and cited its stand upon this issue as one of his reasons for deploring Spargo's National Party.[292] Without going so far, the *Public* evinced little sympathy for the "few score" who demanded "the right to make a noise when the hundred million have no taste for it," and observed that "free speech never prevails when popular passion rises to war

[287] For their moderately stated opposition to the censorship proposal, see *Public*, 20 (11, 18 May 1917), pp. 447, 473; *Independent*, 90 (2 June 1917), pp. 395–7. For its acquiescence, see *New Republic*, 10 (21 Apr. 1917), pp. 335–6. On the defeat of Wilson's request, see Kennedy, *Over Here*, pp. 25–6.

[288] Amos Pinchot and others to Wilson, 12 July 1917, and AP to Wilson, 25 July 1917, *Wilson Papers*, 43, pp. 165, 276–8; address at mass meeting, 17 Feb. 1918, Amos Pinchot Papers, box 36. Pinchot was to become treasurer of the *Masses* defense fund. See Pinchot's *History*, ed. Hooker, p. 67.

[289] John Spargo to Woodrow Wilson, 1 Nov. 1917, *Wilson Papers*, 44, pp. 491–2.

[290] Amos Pinchot to J. P. Tumulty, 14 July 1917, *Wilson Papers*, 43, pp. 175–6; *New York Times*, 3 Sept. 1917, pp. 1, 3; Spargo address, "America's Democratic Opportunities," 6 Oct. 1917, Amos Pinchot Papers, subject file 33; Stein, "Lincoln Steffens," p. 213; *Public*, 20 (31 Aug., 12 Oct. 1917), pp. 831, 976–7; *New Republic*, 12 (22 Sept. 1917), pp. 204–7.

[291] Croly to Woodrow Wilson, 19 Oct. 1917, *Wilson Papers*, 44, pp. 408–10; Lippmann to House, 17 Oct. 1917, Newton Baker Papers, box 2. (It was at House's own suggestion that Lippmann wrote this letter to be forwarded to Wilson. See Diary, 17 Oct., [1917], p. 102, Lippmann Papers.) See also Hapgood to House, 27 May 1918, E. M. House Papers; Steffens to House, 18 Oct. 1917, *Steffens Letters*, 2, pp. 1031–4.

[292] "The German Socialists . . . VI, The Kaiser and the Socialists." March 1918, Walling Papers; Walling to J. G. Phelps Stokes, 27 Dec. 1917, Phelps Stokes Papers, box 29.

pitch. When the war is over we shall have free speech again without even the necessity of asking for it."[293] The *Independent* was also confident that "the liberty-loving instincts and practical good sense of the American people" would reassert themselves in peace, and, like White and Rowell, thought it right as well as inevitable that ordinary freedoms should be curtailed in wartime.[294] In its broadest terms, indeed, this point was not contested. Even Amos Pinchot rather grudgingly conceded that "reasonable censorship is, no doubt, necessary,"[295] and all the private representations and protesting editorials proposed not the abandonment of control but a modification of its methods. Croly suggested direct negotiations with the Socialist press on the model of those conducted by the War Industries Board with business corporations.[296] It was generally accepted that responsibility for overseeing the press should be removed from Postmaster General Albert S. Burleson — "that elderly village-idiot," as Amos Pinchot privately called him.[297] Several suggested the establishment of a special commission including "well known and trusted liberals" to "pass upon questionable publications" — by September 1918, after the prestigious *Nation* had run into trouble with the Post Office, even White told its editor, Oswald Garrison Villard, that he would be happy to serve on such a board.[298]

Similarly, despite occasional appeals such as Spargo's to "the fundamental principles of democracy" or Amos Pinchot's to "the Anglo-Saxon tradition of intellectual freedom,"[299] the case for a more tolerant policy was generally couched in strikingly pragmatic terms. The *New Republic*, in true New Nationalist fashion, was explicitly dismissive of "the 'right' to free speech": "If it were true that respect for freedom of speech could invoke no greater reason than the right of certain individuals to enjoy intellectual exercise unhampered by the needs of the community for com-

293 *Public*, 20 (12 Oct. 1917), p. 975; 21 (21 Sept. 1918), p. 1199. At other times, the *Public* did take a more critical line. See, for example, *Public*, 21 (12 Oct. 1918), pp. 1283–4.
294 *Independent*, 95 (21 Sept. 1918), pp. 374–5; White to W. W. Ligott, 13 Apr. 1918, W. A. White Papers; Rowell to Hiram W. Johnson, 27 Aug. 1918, Rowell Papers.
295 AP to the Editor, *Los Angeles Times*, 5 Mar. 1917, Amos Pinchot Papers, box 30.
296 Croly to Woodrow Wilson, 19 Oct. 1917, *Wilson Papers*, 44, pp. 408–10.
297 AP to George P. West, 15 Oct. 1917, Amos Pinchot Papers, box 29. See also *Public*, 20 (12 Oct. 1917), pp. 976–7, 985–7; Walter Lippmann to Colonel House, 17 Oct. 1917, Newton Baker Papers, box 2; Spargo to Woodrow Wilson, 1 Nov. 1917, *Wilson Papers*, 44, pp. 491–2.
298 Spargo to Woodrow Wilson, 1 Nov. 1917, *Wilson Papers*, 44, pp. 491–2; *Public*, 20 (12 Oct. 1917), pp. 976–7; White to O. G. Villard, 30 Sept. 1918, White Papers.
299 Spargo to Wilson, 1 Nov. 1917, *Wilson Papers*, 44, pp. 491–2; Amos Pinchot and others to Wilson, 12 July 1917, ibid., 43, p. 165.

mon action, such a 'right' should not survive a state of war for a single day."[300] The argument most often advanced against the suppression of dissenting opinion was simply that it was counterproductive. Noting that Burleson had announced he would deny mailing privileges to any paper stating that "American participation in the war is part of a capitalist conspiracy for the exploitation of the working classes," Croly commented that "there is only one course of action which could be taken by the government which would give it [this statement] any plausibility and that . . . is precisely the action which is now being taken by the Post Office Department."[301] "Suppression of course gives these papers an importance that intrinsically they would never have," Lippmann remarked, as he assured House that "the overwhelming number of radicals can be won to the support of the war simply by conserving the spirit of the President's own utterances, and by imaginative administration of the censorship."[302] Even Amos Pinchot argued that "if our administration would take a little more liberal view, I think the war would be more popular."[303]

The hardening of the opposition to the war was, in progressive eyes, by no means the only damaging consequence of the suppression of dissenting opinion. "The real reason for preserving minority criticism," the *New Republic* stressed, "is the need for it on the part of the community, of the majority. For without it the majority is bound, sooner or later, to go wrong, to show defective judgement, to adopt and execute disastrous policies."[304] "The policy pursued by the government in relation to public opinion," Croly complained to Wilson, "tends to create on the one hand irreconcilable pacifists and socialists who oppose the war and all its works, and a group of equally irreconcilable pro-war enthusiasts who allow themselves to be possessed by a fighting spirit and who tend to lose all sight of the objects for which America actually went into the war."[305] The former, it was recognized by supporters as well as critics of American intervention, were alienated from Wilson's peace program by the administration's repressive actions.[306] The latter, such as "the propagandists connected

[300] *New Republic*, 12 (22 Sept. 1917), p. 205.
[301] Croly to Wilson, 19 Oct. 1917, *Wilson Papers*, 44, pp. 408–10.
[302] Lippmann to Colonel House, 17 Oct. 1917, Newton Baker Papers, box 2. See above, n. 291.
[303] AP to C. H. Myers, 11 Dec. 1917, Amos Pinchot Papers, box 27. See also, AP to Louis D. Budenz, 14 June 1918, ibid., box 36.
[304] *New Republic*, 12 (22 Sept. 1917), p. 205.
[305] Croly to Wilson, 19 Oct. 1917, *Wilson Papers*, 44, pp. 408–10.
[306] *Public*, 20 (21 Dec. 1917), pp. 1239–40; AP to Louis D. Budenz, 14 June 1918, and to George F. Peabody, 19 Dec. 1918, Amos Pinchot Papers, boxes 36, 37.

with the American Security League and the American Defense Society,"
were, Croly warned, "the very people who will subsequently make the
task of realizing the constructive purposes which lie behind American
fighting excessively and unnecessarily difficult."[307] Forwarding his letter
on free speech to Newton Baker's secretary, Ralph Hayes, Lippmann
wrote, "What I am afraid of is that if things go on much longer as they are
going at this moment our Tory friends will take the bit in their teeth and
there will be no managing them after that."[308] By the autumn of 1918,
such fears seemed to many to have been amply confirmed. "It is a bad
time to see America," Hapgood warned Ray Stannard Baker. "Canning
the Kaiser is about as far as the American mind goes at present."[309]
"Americans," the *Public* concluded, "are showing a capacity for cheap
malice and vindictiveness that threaens to ruin the plans of liberals
everywhere for a new world order."[310]

If several progressives believed that the curtailment of civil liberties
engendered public intolerance, others were more impressed by the reverse
process. "The only lack of liberty I felt was the war-time intolerance of
private sentiment," Rowell recalled. "But that was the intolerance of
democracy, not autocracy."[311] Certainly, the most energetic repression of
dissent took place below the federal level, particularly in western states.
The actions of state and local governments were stimulated and supplemented by those of state and municipal Councils of Defense and numerous
unofficial patriotic organizations.[312] In addition to the IWW, the Non-
Partisan League, an agrarian protest movement centered in North Dakota
and Minnesota, became a major target. The league's neo-Populist economic program and talk of a farmer–labor alliance appealed to a wide
spectrum of progressive opinion,[313] and most of these publicists (including such belligerent warriors as Russell and Creel) sought to defend it
against accusations of disloyalty.[314] However, White, who made many

[307] Croly to Wilson, 19 Oct. 1917, *Wilson Papers*, 44, pp. 408–10.

[308] Lippmann to Ralph Hayes, 23 Oct. 1917, Lippmann Papers, box 13, folder 521.

[309] Norman Hapgood to Baker, 7 Oct. 1918, Ray Stannard Baker Papers, box 96.

[310] *Public*, 21 (23 Nov. 1918), p. 1419. See also, Weyl Diary, 9 June, 28 July 1918; Notebook 19,
6 Aug. 1918, pp. 33–4, R. S. Baker Papers.

[311] Rowell to Hiram W. Johnson, 6 July 1919 (not sent), Rowell Papers.

[312] H. C. Peterson and Gilbert C. Fite, *Opponents of War 1917–1918* (Madison, Wisc., 1957), pp.
17–20; Kennedy, *Over Here*, p. 83.

[313] For example, Howe, "The Problem of the American Farmer," *Century*, 94 (Aug. 1917), pp.
628–9; *High Cost of Living*, pp. 30–1; *Survey*, 38 (29 Sept. 1917), pp. 564–5; *New Republic*, 13
(3, 10, 17 Nov., 1 Dec. 1917), pp. 15–17, 44–6, 71–3, 121–3; Russell, *The Story of the
Nonpartisan League: A Chapter in AMERICAN Evolution* (New York, 1920).

[314] *New Republic*, 13 (3 Nov. 1917), pp. 8–9; Russell, *Story of the Nonpartisan League*, pp. 233, 237–

public speeches attempting to arouse greater enthusiasm for the war among Kansas farmers, denounced the league as a "nasty pacifist movement" despite his support for its economic program.[315]

Such verbal assaults were the least that dissenters, or supposed dissenters, had to fear in wartime America. The more violent manifestations of public intolerance, such as the whipping of the pacifist minister, the Reverend Herbert S. Bigelow, in October 1917, and the lynching of the German-born baker, Robert Prager, in April 1918, were unequivocally condemned by the progressive weeklies.[316] Even Creel, whose propaganda was blamed by some critics for stimulating the hysteria, never sought, as some did, to minimize or excuse such incidents. In public, he advanced the ingenious argument that while some German agents were busy agitating among the IWW and pacifist groups, "other German agents are leading mobs to tar and feather the victims of this German propaganda of social unrest."[317] Privately, he pointed out to Wilson the folly of the drive against the speaking of foreign languages, and prepared the way for the president's condemnation of mob violence on July 26, 1918 – a step that was welcomed as a salutary, if belated, gesture by liberal journals.[318] But the lynchings that Wilson denounced seemed to many to be merely the most shocking symptom of the diseased state of the public mind. Steffens was quick to diagnose the spread to the United States of "the war rage" – "as dangerous as madness and as unapproachable to reason" – and in May 1918 he suffered personally from it when he was prevented from lecturing on peace terms in San Diego.[319] Howe, as Commissioner of Immigration at New York, found himself "branded as pro-German" as a

48; Creel to Woodrow Wilson, 7, 29 Jan., 19 Feb., 2 Apr., 18 Sept. 1918; Wilson to Creel, 18 Feb., 1 Apr. 1918, Creel papers. Some of these letters – Creel to Wilson 29 Jan. and 19 Feb. 1918; Wilson to Creel, 18 Feb. 1918; and Creel to Wilson, 2 Apr. 1918 – have also been printed in *Wilson Papers*, 46, pp. 160, 386–7, 369; and 47, p. 226. On the embarrassment that Creel's involvement with the Nonpartisan League caused the administration, see Livermore, *Politics Is Adjourned*, pp. 153–8.

[315] White to Walter Lippmann, 20 Nov. 1917; to Arthur D. Hill, 27 Nov. 1917; to Senator Charles Curtis, 5 Dec. 1917; to R. M. McClintock, 23 Feb. 1918; to Elmer Peterson, 17 May 1918; and to H. S. Gilbertson, 23 May 1918, White Papers.

[316] *Public*, 20 (2 Nov. 1917), pp. 1047–8; *Independent*, 92 (10 Nov. 1917), p. 275; *New Republic*, 13 (10 Nov. 1917), pp. 35–7, and 14 (13 Apr. 1918), pp. 311–12; *Survey*, 40 (27 Apr. 1918), pp. 101–2.

[317] *Independent*, 94 (6 Apr. 1918), p. 5.

[318] Creel to Woodrow Wilson, 6 Aug. 1918, Creel papers; Peterson and Fite, *Opponents of War*, pp. 206–7; *New Republic*, 16 (3 Aug. 1918), pp. 5–6; *Independent*, 95 (10 Aug. 1918), p. 176.

[319] Steffens to Robert M. La Follette, 17 Aug. 1917; to Colonel House, 29 Apr., 8 May 1918, *Steffens Letters*, 1, pp. 401–2, 426–7. In the same month, Amos Pinchot wrote of "the wave of popular insanity that is surging through the country now." See AP to Horace B. Liveright, 3 May 1918, Amos Pinchot Papers, box 35.

result of his attempts to secure decent treatment for the thousands of enemy aliens interned on Ellis Island.[320] Baker, who had been disgusted by the talk he heard in New York clubs of "skewering Germans on bayonets and then twisting the bayonets," stressed in his reports to the State Department the anxieties felt by European liberal and labor groups about the temper of American opinion.[321] "No other people – not even the Germans – have had as little spiritual independence in this war as we Americans," he concluded in November 1918. "A man who dared to disagree with the mass opinion in America was in danger of having his head knocked off!"[322]

It was not therefore surprising that when Weyl took stock of the wartime experience, he concluded that public opinion was "the weakest link of the chain." He planned to write an article for the *New Republic* showing "how the government efficiency was rapidly increasing, how the machine, military and administrative, was improving, how Public Opinion was falling down. Too much Hun talk . . . a craven fear of being considered disloyal if you have independent thoughts."[323] A conversation with Steffens and Howe strengthened Weyl's belief that the *New Republic* had work of "very great importance" to do in educating the American people in the anti-imperialist point of view. However, Steffens's advice was not entirely encouraging. The man who had to be reached, he explained, was "the *Dub,* the Club bore" for "when you listen to him you are listening to the million." "If you want to be a journalist you must possess something of the commonness of mind," Weyl noted piously.[324] Reconsidering his advocacy of intervention, Croly was later to confess sadly that "the miscalculation in my own case consisted chiefly in false anticipation of what the psychology of the American people would be under the strain of fighting in a world war."[325]

Yet such was the ambivalence of the wartime experience that some aspects of the social atmosphere appealed to many progressives. The subordination of selfish ambitions to a common purpose seemed a realization of pre-war hopes for a "new social spirit" that would express the real meaning of democracy.[326] To the more puritanically minded, the purging

[320] Howe, *Confessions,* pp. 272–3.
[321] Notebook 14, 13 Dec. 1917, pp. 79–80; to Frank Polk, 8 July 1918, R. S. Baker Papers.
[322] Notebook 21, pp. 49–50, ibid.
[323] Weyl Diary, 9 June 1918.
[324] Ibid., 22 Oct. 1918.
[325] "Liberalism vs. the War," *New Republic,* 25 (20 Dec. 1920), p. 37.
[326] See Chapter 3, "Progressive Values."

of materialism and self-indulgence was the mark of a healthier society. "We have revised our scale of values," the *Independent* noted with satisfaction. "In our enjoyment of day by day pleasures and in the struggle for social recognition and preferment, we had fallen into a cynical indifference to the essentials of life."[327] "God knows in America we needed something to destroy our security, comfort, conventionality, respectability and set us adventuring again," Baker reflected in his diary. "This war, terrible as it seems, may do us much good. . . . It caught us just soon enough: before swelling luxury ruined us: while the spirit of sacrifice was still strong upon us."[328] "It has overthrown the altars of Mammon," Rowell declared.[329] Others stressed the psychological and intellectual implications of collectivism. "The war has called into service thousands of men, who found in social activities greater enjoyment than they ever had before in private employment," Howe observed. "Quite as important, it has shown us that life is the important thing; that man is of more consequence than inanimate wealth, and that the great agencies of banking and credit, of transportation, of fuel, of iron, and of steel, can be made to provide a higher standard of living, and promote a wider distribution of comforts than was believed possible during three centuries of competitive struggle."[330] "Every industry in America, every commercial institution, indeed all of commerce and all the various expressions of organized labor are feeling the impulse of this war, and are changing their methods by reason of their changed ideals," White maintained.[331] Devine in the *Survey* argued that "unity in sentiment, harmony in planning, co-ordination in action" were as essential to "social welfare" as they were to "effective warfare," and sought ways to "capitalize for the programs appropriate to peace the social enthusiasms which it [the war] has generated."[332]

The ambiguous nature of America's wartime experience for progressives might be seen as an indication of the tensions within their own values and the contradictory nature of their aspirations. However, to most of those publicists, it seemed simply that the war had brought both positive and negative developments. Views of the comparative importance of these

[327] *Independent*, 94 (29 June 1918), p. 491.
[328] Notebook 14, Dec. 1917, p. 150; Notebook 20, 16 Oct. 1918, p. 104, R. S. Baker Papers.
[329] *Fresno Republican*, 28 July 1918.
[330] *The Land and the Soldier*, pp. 3–4.
[331] To George Lorimer, 7 May 1918, White Papers.
[332] *Survey*, 38 (30 June 1917), p. 290; 41 (16 Nov. 1918), p. 185. This was a common theme in social work circles. See also ibid., 40 (15 June, 6 July 1918), pp. 316, 395–9.

varied widely, of course. While the pro-war Socialists of the Social Democratic League hailed the "socially conscious and intelligent organization of
society . . . in the spirit of service to the common good," Bourne insisted
that "the effect of the war will be to impoverish American promise."[333] A
similar if less extreme contrast can be drawn between White, Rowell, and
the *Independent* on the one hand, and Amos Pinchot, Steffens, and Howe
on the other. The former group might be seen as nationalist collectivists
and the latter as more libertarian radicals. But in reality divergent attitudes to intervention and differences of temperament were probably
more important than ideological or programmatic disagreement. In their
domestic as in their international aspirations, these publicists continued
to share much common ground.

Indeed, some felt that progressive unity had never been greater. "A very
remarkable thing is happening in America," the *Public* observed in May
1918. "Liberals and radicals of all shades and degrees of opinion are finding
a common ground, and see before them a common road leading to that new
social order of which we have dreamed and toward which we have striven so
long without hope of arriving at our destination in this generation or the
next. That common ground is the program of the British Labor Party. It has
electrified liberal America as the speeches of President Wilson have electrified liberal Europe. And if liberal England looks to Wilson today as a
Moses, we in turn look to the British Labor Party's program as the Ten
Commandments."[334] If extravagantly phrased, this editorial was right to
emphasize the widespread enthusiasm in American progressive circles for
the manifesto, drafted by Sidney Webb, which was issued by the British
Labour party in early 1918.[335] As well as the *New Republic*, the *Survey*
published it in full, while the *Independent*, describing it as the "best
expression" of "the new ideals of industry," urged its readers to buy the
pamphlet.[336] At the annual conference of social workers in 1918, according
to the *Survey*, "speaker after speaker . . . referred to the far-reaching
program of the British Labor Party" and "it became evident that many

---

[333] Social Democratic League of America, *A Program of Social Reconstruction* (New York, 1918), p. 8;
Bourne, "A War Diary," *Seven Arts*, 2 (Sept. 1917), reprinted in Bourne, *War and the Intellectuals*, ed. Resek, p. 46.
[334] *Public*, 21 (4 May 1918), p. 556.
[335] See A. M. McBriar, *Fabian Socialism and English Politics, 1884–1918* (Cambridge, England,
1962), pp. 343–4.
[336] *New Republic*, 14 (16 Feb. 1918), pt. 2; Arthur Gleason and Paul U. Kellogg, "The England
They've Been Fighting For," *Survey*, 41 (30 Nov. 1918), pp. 243–9; *Independent*, 97 (8 March
1919), p. 319. See also the discussion earlier in the chapter.

social workers here, as well as in England, are responding with enthusiasm to this vision of radical changes in the economic and industrial order."[337] "I am pretty well satisfied that the British Labor Party is going to lead the way in economic reform," White assured his friend, Henry Allen, as he advised him on his presidential prospects. "If I were you, I would spend my time in studying its program."[338] Rowell defended the British Labour program to the Republican Party chairman, Will H. Hays, as did his Californian colleague, Meyer Lissner, to Theodore Roosevelt.[339] "In the next few years the world will take some steps toward economic democracy," Hapgood declared as the war ended. "It will take them with knowledge, after the manner of the British Labor party, or with doctrinaire and destructive violence, after the manner of Lenin."[340]

The hortatory prophetic mode adopted by Hapgood had long been favored by progressive publicists, but in the autumn of 1918 their concern with the immediate future was particularly intense. For if the war had, as Baker put it, "brought out both good and bad" qualities in American life,[341] it was an important question which would prove the more long lasting. The stakes were high, particularly for those who had advocated intervention on the grounds that it would lead to progress at home as well as a new world order. For the most part, wartime anticipations of the postwar period had been optimistic. The extension of government control over the economy was widely assumed to be permanent. "They will never be returned to private control and management," Baker had noted confidently when the railroads were taken over.[342] "What war impels us to now we will learn to value too much to throw away," the *Independent* had agreed.[343] The combination of the trend toward collectivism with the growing power of labor persuaded even the skeptical Amos Pinchot that "the war is evidently tending to break down industrial autocracy."[344] Moreover, as we have seen, those who were disturbed by the more au-

337 *Survey*, 40 (1 June 1918), p. 252.
338 White to Henry J. Allen, 27 Apr. 1918, White Papers. See also *Martial Adventures of Henry and Me*, pp. 317–18.
339 Rowell to Will H. Hays, 18 July 1918, Rowell Papers; Mowry, *The California Progressives*, p. 293.
340 "A Programme of Reconstruction," *New Republic*, 25 (16 Nov. 1918), p. 70. See also Amos Pinchot to Rev. Herbert S. Bigelow, 20 Dec. 1918, Amos Pinchot Papers, box 37, and the discussion earlier in the chapter.
341 Notebook 20, 16 Oct. 1918, p. 104, R. S. Baker Papers.
342 Notebook 14, 28 Dec. 1917, p. 113, ibid.
343 *Independent*, 93 (5 Jan. 1918), p. 8.
344 Article published in *Issues and Events*, 19 Jan. 1918, Amos Pinchot Papers, box 224.

thoritarian aspects of wartime collectivism hoped that these, like the
official and unofficial suppression of dissenting opinion, would not survive the freer atmosphere of peacetime.[345]

There were few illusions that such hopes would be realized without
difficulty. "The great trial and contest in America is coming *after this
war,*" Baker prophesied in February 1918.[346] Internationally, likewise, it
was expected that what Baker called "the final death grapple between the
old order and the new" would take place after Germany had been defeated.[347] But in the course of 1918, as the weakness of liberal sentiment in
America became more evident, some anticipated this struggle with a
notable lack of confidence. In August, Weyl, in conversation with Croly,
"talked strongly on the difficulty of America carrying out any of her
policies effectively at the Peace Conference, owing (1) to the opposition of
other Powers; and (2) to our own ignorance of what we want."[348] In
October, Steffens lamented that "the country shows no preparation for
peace."[349] Baker expressed their apprehension most concisely. On hearing
of the Armistice negotiations, he wrote in his diary that *"the real trouble is
now about to begin."*[350]

---

345 See the discussion earlier in the chapter.
346 Notebook 15, 8 Feb. 1918, pp. 90–1, R. S. Baker Papers. Italics in original.
347 RSB to Frank L. Polk, 24 Aug. 1918; Notebook 21, pp. 12–15, R. S. Baker Papers.
348 Weyl Diary, 10 Aug. 1918.
349 Steffens to Allen H. Suggett, 20 Oct. 1918, *Steffens Letters,* 1, pp. 435–6.
350 Notebook 20, 14 Oct. [1918], pp. 91–2, R. S. Baker Papers. Italics in original.

CHAPTER 7

Reaction

Versailles – and after

As the war drew to an end, progressive publicists evinced both excitement and nervousness. There was a general sense of momentous events occurring and impending. To Baker, at the beginning of November it seemed as if "the very world" was "on fire" with "dynasties crumbling, great battles in progress, new nations being born, the statesmen of the world sitting at Versailles to decide the fate of the world."[1] With the downfall of the Austrian and German empires, some of the hopes and prophecies of American liberals were already being fulfilled, as pro-war editorialists stressed. "In all Europe east of the Rhine," the *New Republic* declared confidently, "the spell that made the common man humble himself before the hereditary landowner . . . has been broken."[2] "We have done what the French Revolution in its first ardor tried to do," boasted Devine in the *Survey*.[3] However, the liberal journals also warned against over-optimism. "Far be it from us to play the part of a kill-joy in these days of rejoicing over the destruction of monarchic absolutism and militarism, its instrument," the *Independent* observed, but "those of us who are impatient for the realization of our dreams of a world made securely democratic, peace-abiding and enlightened, may as well prepare ourselves for many disappointments and much tedious waiting."[4] There was, nevertheless, a widespread feeling that both abroad and at home the forces of reform were on the verge of a unique opportunity. "Never I think," Baker wrote, "was the world in such plastic state."[5]

The immediate focus of attention, of course, was the forthcoming peace

---

[1] Notebook 21, 1 Nov. [1918], p. 35, R. S. Baker Papers.

[2] "The Lords of the Earth," *New Republic*, 16 (30 Nov. 1918), pp. 118–20.

[3] "Between War and Peace," *Survey*, 41 (16 Nov. 1918), pp. 179–85 at p. 179. See also *New Republic*, 16 (19 Oct. 1918), p. 332; *Independent*, 96 (23 Nov. 1918), pp. 239, 240–2.

[4] *Independent*, 96 (30 Nov. 1918), p. 275.

[5] Notebook 22, 27 Dec. 1918, p. 25, R. S. Baker Papers.

conference, and it was in respect of this that nervousness was most apparent. As it approached, it became clear that the central question would be
the treatment of the defeated foe. "Peace vs. punishment (of Germany):
This is the issue," Steffens concluded briskly. "We cannot have both our
vengeance and permanent peace."[6] Related to this was concern over the
nature and role of the league of nations, establishment of which in some
form was by this time taken for granted. The fear was that it would be, as
Devine put it, "a police league" rather than "a league of development."[7]
To avert these dangers, progressive publicists continued to look to
Wilson, though with less than total confidence. Skepticism from those
who had always opposed intervention was perhaps only to be expected.
Predicting that "if the President is going to try for a democratic peace,
based on self-determination, if he is out to curb the land-grabbing program of the secret treaties, he is in for the fight of his life," Amos Pinchot
declared that "I haven't much faith in Woodrow's hay maker any more
and I think he has something of a glass jaw."[8] But eve the president's
staunchest supporters expressed anxiety. "I have curiously this feeling of
doom in the coming to Europe of Wilson," Baker confessed.[9] Baker, in
fact, oscillated between fear and hope, noting at one moment the "great
up-surging of this spirit of revenge and of blasting punishment" in the
victor nations, and then, following Wilson's enthusiastic reception in
London, persuading himself that "a great wind of moral enthusiasm is
sweeping through the world."[10] Liberal editors back home seemed more
pessimistic, particularly after the election results in America and Britain.
"If President Wilson is able to overcome Allied opposition and realize his
program at the Peace Conference, he will have won the most glorious and
the most amazing moral victory in history," the *Public* concluded in
December. "The cards are against him, and his complete success is no
longer expected."[11] By January, Croly, too, had decided that "the pros-

6 To Laura Suggett, 28 Oct., 30 Dec. 1918, *Steffens Letters*, 1, pp. 437, 451. See also Weyl Diary,
  23 Nov. 1918.
7 *Survey*, 41 (16 Nov. 1918), p. 180. See also, "League of Free Nations Association: A Statement
  of Principles," *Independent*, 96 (14 Dec. 1918), pp. 364, 376–8; and Holt, "The Birth of the
  League of Nations," *Independent*, 97 (15 Feb. 1919), p. 217. On the origins and composition of
  the League of Free Nations Association, see Chapter 6, "The Substance of a Democratic Peace."
8 To Frank H. Kent, 6 Dec. 1918; to James G. Blauvelt, 5 Dec. 1918, Amos Pinchot Papers, box
  37.
9 Notebook 21, [December 1918], p. 160, R. S. Baker Papers.
10 Notebook 21, pp. 94–6; Notebook 22, p. 27, ibid. See also, Notebook 21, p. 73, cf. p. 77.
11 *Public*, 21 (14 Dec. 1918), pp. 1496–7.

pects of a magnanimous and durable peace" were "poor" and was seeking consolation in the long view: "The retaliationists may beat the President now, but they will win a Pyrrhic victory."[12]

Such pessimism was to become the prevailing mood among that substantial number of progressive publicists who gathered in Paris for the conference. The auspices under which many were there reflected the tendency for them to become directly involved in affairs. Creel, Howe, and Steffens as well as Baker and Lippmann owed their presence to their connections with the administration, though only Baker, as its press secretary, was a full member of the American Commission to Negotiate Peace. But Creel, Howe, and Steffens did undertake official missions of varying degrees of significance, as did White who was there in a journalistic capacity.[13] Holt served as liaison between the Peace Commission and the League to Enforce Peace, while Russell and Walling constituted half of a delegation from the Social Democratic League of America to the International Socialist and Labor Congress.[14] Having failed to secure a place on the peace commission, Weyl journeyed to Europe at his own expense, "not as a reporter . . . but because he needed to be in the heart of the world during its days of great decisions."[15]

Such eagerness seems ironical in retrospect for, of course, the experience of being in Paris in 1919 was a disheartening one for American liberals, and one often recalled as the epitome of disillusionment.[16] The speed varied with which hopes were abandoned. Lippmann, having been squeezed out of the Inquiry, left Paris in a very depressed state of mind soon after the conference began.[17] On the other hand, observers as different in their outlooks as Steffens and Russell felt that the reports being cabled back to America in these early days were overly pessimistic, attributing this to the fact that most of the journalists were "in a strange

[12] "Victory without Peace," *New Republic*, 17 (11 Jan. 1919), pp. 301–3.

[13] See Creel, *Rebel at Large*, pp. 205–15, 219–22; Howe, *Confessions*, pp. 290–301; Steel, *Walter Lippmann*, pp. 149–53; Baker, *American Chronicle*, pp. 373–4; Steffens, *Autobiography*, pp. 777, 790–802; White, *Autobiography*, pp. 559–64. On the tendency to become directly involved in public affairs, see Chapter 5, "Easing the Way to War."

[14] *Independent*, 98 (5 Apr. 1919), p. 3; Russell to Emile Vandervelde, 7 Jan. 1919, Russell Papers. On the SDL delegation's rather confused role and activities, see Radosh, *American Labor*, pp. 286–9.

[15] Forcey, *Crossroads of Liberalism*, p. 288; Weyl Diary, 4 Dec. 1918; [Brubaker], *Walter Weyl*, p. 129.

[16] For example, Howe, *Confessions*, pp. 287–320.

[17] Steel, *Lippmann*, p. 153.

environment" and "out of their element."[18] One very ready to admit this was White, who was quick to condemn the failure to observe the first[19] of the Fourteen Points more literally, arguing that the secret nature of the negotiations would be fatal to the chances of a liberal peace.[20] But all found hope hard to sustain in a climate of opinion in which even Frenchmen who admired Wilson assumed that his wartime addresses had been clever propaganda, designed to weaken enemy morale.[21] "Disillusion," White recalled, "came at Paris, slowly in an excruciating anticlimax, but inexorably and without extenuation or relief."[22] Despair became contagious, almost evangelical. "Ray Baker," Weyl noted with satisfaction in April, "is at last pessimistic and angry."[23]

Baker's depression has acquired a special significance, for his close contact with Wilson has made his diary an important source for historians of the peace conference. Some have cited the notes he made at this crucial time as evidence that American policymakers were preoccupied with the danger of Bolshevism spreading through Europe.[24] In assessing the significance of this evidence, it is necessary not only to weigh the importance of this particular consideration in comparison with others in Baker's account,[25] but also to recognize that it had long figured in progressive

---

[18] Steffens to Allen H. Suggett, 14 Jan. 1919, *Steffens Letters*, 1, pp. 453–4; Diary no. 10, 1 Feb. 1919, Russell Papers.

[19] "Open covenants of peace, openly arrived at. . . ."

[20] Oswald Garrison Villard, *Fighting Years: Memoirs of a Liberal Editor* (New York, 1939), p. 388; White, "Tale That is Told," *Saturday Evening Post*, 192 (4 Oct. 1919), pp. 19, 158, 161–2, 165; "Will They Fool Us Twice?" *Collier's*, 68 (15 Oct. 1921), pp. 5–6, 24–5.

[21] Norman Hapgood recalled that before Wilson arrived in Paris, "there was printed in La Victoire a little essay by one of the most distinguished of French publicists. It was a shock to me, for I knew the man and what he stood for in Paris opinion. The article proposed two statues to celebrate the victory. One was to be Foch, with a bludgeon as emblem. The other was to be Wilson, and the emblem was to be a fishing-rod, because of the wily treatment of Germany that finally induced her to sign the armistice. The worst of it was that the man who wrote the article intended his interpretaion of the President to be genuine praise." *The Advancing Hour*, pp. 246–7.

[22] "Will They Fool Us Twice?" p. 5.

[23] Weyl Diary, 7 Apr. 1919.

[24] See Arno J. Mayer, *Politics and Diplomacy of Peacemaking: Containment and Counterrevolution at Versailles, 1918–1919* (New York, 1967), especially pp. 10, 29, 515, 570–5. On Mayer's debt to Baker, see also Inga Floto, *Colonel House in Paris: A Study of American Policy at the Paris Peace Conference 1919* (Princeton, N.J., 1980), pp. 254–6. The first historian to use Baker's diary as an important source was Baker himself. See his *Woodrow Wilson and the World Settlement* (New York, 1923), and *American Chronicle* (New York, 1945), pp. 375–443.

[25] As Floto points out, Baker's diary makes it clear that his pessimism in late March was due to the general political situation in Europe and the United States and, in particular, the difficult state of the negotiations following Wilson's return to Paris. See Floto, *Colonel House in Paris*, p. 254.

analyses of the situation facing the peacemakers. In such analyses, however, Europe's revolutionary potential was presented not as a reason for
conceding Allied demands but as a compelling argument for a liberal
peace. "If during the next two years the spread of Leninism is to be
checked," the *New Republic* had maintained in November 1918, "the
western democracies must depend upon Wilsonism to do the job."[26]
"Shrewd observers," the *Survey*'s correspondent reported from Paris in
January 1919, "see only two possible solutions, Wilson's or Lenine's [sic].
Reaction would mean revolution."[27] Such an assumption obviously provided no rationale for compromise on Wilson's part, but, doubtless for
this very reason, it was invoked by progressives ranging from Amos
Pinchot to Hamilton Holt.[28] The argument, of course, was one that had
often been used in advocating domestic reform. Bolshevism became the
incarnation of the long-postulated revolutionary alternative to progressivism.[29] "Lenin," Lippmann warned, "has no doubts that if ever the
choice is narrowed so that the masses must choose between him and the
reaction, his own victory is assured. He is quite right. Men will prefer a
violent hope to a terrible despair."[30]

Such prophecies, however, were to prove no more efficacious than had
their domestic counterparts. "If not Wilson, then Lenin, was a current
phrase not long ago," the *New Republic* recalled rather ruefully when the
treaty of Versailles was published. "There was a third possibility, Clemenceau, and that was what we got."[31] The treaty was from the first
regarded as the negation of "a democratic peace." In Paris, during the
interval before the Germans signed the treaty, a delegation to Baker
which included Hapgood and Steffens sought to persuade Wilson to rally
liberal opinion behind a further effort to modify its terms.[32] Unlike much
of the later opposition in the United States, they focused on the treatment
of Germany. "Made up as it was in sections, the cumulative effect of the

---

26 *New Republic*, 17 (30 Nov. 1918), pp. 113–14.
27 Lewis S. Gannett, "A League of Nations without Russia?" *Survey*, 41 (25 Jan. 1919), p. 552.
28 Amos Pinchot, "A Liberal Peace," *Nation*, 108 (25 Jan. 1919), p. 124; Holt, "The League or
    Bolshevism?" *Independent*, 98 (5 Apr. 1919), pp. 3–4.
29 See Chapter 3, "The Way Forward."
30 *The Political Scene: An Essay on the Victory of 1919* (New York, 1919), p. xi. See also Lippmann,
    "The Fourteen Points and the League of Nations," address before the League of Free Nations
    Association, New York City, 5 Apr. 1919, pp. 5–6, Lippmann Papers, Robert O. Anthony
    collection, box 46, folder 94; Croly, "The Obstacle to Peace," *New Republic*, 18 (26 Apr. 1919),
    p. 406.
31 *New Republic*, 19 (24 May 1919), p. 103.
32 Notebook 24, 23 May [1919], pp. 11–12, R. S. Baker Papers.

whole of it is tremendous," Steffens reported in a letter home. "It reads as if each section has been intended to do full justice to the Germans, so that they get all that was coming to them time and time again."[33] To Lippmann, who had adopted an almost proprietorial commitment to the Fourteen Points, the treaty represented a dishonorable breach of trust. "How in our consciences are we to square the results with the promises?" he asked his former "chief," Newton Baker, as he detailed the injustices done to the Germans.[34] Together with Croly and Weyl, Lippmann was responsible for the *New Republic*'s dramatic decision to oppose ratification of the treaty.[35] "The Treaty of Versailles subjects all liberalism and particularly that kind of liberalism which breathes the Christian spirit to a decisive test," the journal maintained. "If a war which was supposed to put an end to war culminates without strenuous protest by humane men and women in a treaty of peace which renders peace impossible, the liberalism which preached this meaning for the war will have committed suicide."[36]

This argument was explicitly directed to those pro-war liberals "whose sense of justice and fair dealing is outraged by the treaty, but who cannot quite decide to place themselves in open and uncompromising opposition to it."[37] One such whom the editors seem to have had in mind was William Allen White. On the eve of his departure for America, White had confessed to Baker that he was "torn about my duty in the matter." On the one hand, he fully shared the sense of betrayal. "We had such high hopes of this adventure; we believed God called us, and now at the end we are put to doing hell's dirtiest work, starving people, grabbing territory — or helping to grab it for our friends; standing by while the grand gesture of revenge and humiliation links this war up with the interminable chain of wars that runs back to Cain!" Yet to reject the treaty would be to reject the League of Nations. "Unless I see things differently between now and my landing I am going to stand for the League and the treaty," he concluded, "but I shall say that the only hope of the world is in . . . the common people turning out their governments and putting in new gov-

---

[33] To G., 25 May 1919, *Steffens Letters*, 1, pp. 468–9.
[34] WL to NDB, 9 June 1919, Newton D. Baker Papers, box 10. For Lippmann's commitment to the Fourteen Points, see also WL to B. Berenson, 6 May [1919], Lippmann Papers, box 3, folder 138; "The Fourteen Points and the League of Nations," 5 Apr. 1919, ibid., Anthony collection, box 46, folder 94.
[35] See Forcey, *Crossroads of Liberalism*, pp. 289–91.
[36] "Peace at Any Price," *New Republic*, 19 (24 May 1919), pp. 100–2.
[37] Ibid., p. 100.

ernments which will void that treaty and make over the League of Nations." Baker stuck White's letter into his diary with the comment that it
expressed "what so many of us feel."[38] A few weeks earlier, Baker himself
had written: "Never was I more in doubt as to my own course. This treaty
is abominable: unjust: based upon wrong principles. How can I go home
and support it, support the League of Nations founded upon it, support
Wilson? Yet . . . would the world be better off if the treaty were defeated
and the League rejected?"[39]

   To Baker, anxious to avoid "the folly of mere empty criticism," the
force of this last question was inescapable. By July, he, too, could "see
only one course ahead for true liberals: get the treaty ratified, get the L. of
N. and the mandatory systems into operation and then work harder than
ever to get the various governmental machines, which will control the
League into the hands of liberals who really believe in the League."[40]
Baker, like White, was to throw himself energetically into the campaign
for ratification.[41] As the battle lines formed in the summer of 1919, this
was the side on which the majority of these publicists, together with the
journals and organizations with which they were associated, were to be
found.[42] Nevertheless, with the *New Republic* – "that erratic and unprin-
cipled sheet," as Spargo took the opportunity to call it[43] – as well as

38 White to Baker, 3 June 1919; Notebook 24, p. 107, R. S. Baker Papers.
39 Notebook 23, 9 May 1919, pp. 58–9, R. S. Baker Papers.
40 Notebook 23, 9 May 1919, p. 58; Notebook 25, July 1919, pp. 152–3, R. S. Baker Papers. See
    also, Notebook 24, 27 May 1919, p. 33; to Mrs. Elizabeth G. Evans, 7 Aug. 1919; Notebook
    26, [Oct. 1919], p. 17, 4 Feb. 1920, pp. 110–11, ibid.
41 As well as writing the newspaper articles later published as *What Wilson Did at Paris* (New York,
    1919), Baker made some speeches. See text of speech, 19 July 1919, R. S. Baker Papers. White
    made a speaking tour in support of the League of Nations. See WAW to Horace Plunkett, 2 Oct.
    1919, White Papers.
42 Kellogg and Howe endorsed the League of Free Nations Association's call for Senate ratification
    of the treaty with Germany, 17 Sept. 1919, Kellogg Papers. The Social Democratic League of
    America's appeal to the AFL to support ratification, 30 Sept. 1919, was signed by Russell and
    Walling, Stokes Papers. Holt devoted himself more or less full time in 1919–20 to the campaign
    for the league. See Kuehl, *Holt*, pp. 142–3. See also, the *Independent*, 99 (2, 9 Aug. 1919), pp.
    151–2, 183–4; 100 (8 Nov. 1919), p. 61; 101 (31 Jan. 1920), p. 172; 102 (3 Apr. 1920), pp.
    11–12. Also *Public*, 22 (26 July, 23 Aug., 29 Nov. 1919), pp. 787, 893, 1103; *Survey*, 42 (21
    June, 5 July 1919), pp. 451, 513–14; Creel, *The War, the World and Wilson* (New York, 1920);
    address to St. Louis Advertising Club, 28 Apr. 1919, Scrapbook, George Creel Papers;
    Hapgood, *The Advancing Hour*, pp. 41–58; "Concerning the League," *Independent*, 103 (25 Sept.
    1920), p. 371; Post, "The League of Nations Covenant as Revised," *Public*, 22 (10 May 1919),
    pp. 482–3, and "The President's Fourteen Points," *Public*, 22 (23 Aug. 1919), pp. 898–9;
    Rowell to H. L. Ickes, 9 June 1919, and to D. S. Jordan, 22 Oct. 1919, Rowell Papers; Spargo,
    "'Farmer–Labor' Reactionaries," *Independent*, 103 (24 and 31 July 1920), pp. 110–12; "A
    Socialist View of the Landslide," *Independent*, 104 (20 Nov. 1920), pp. 264–5.
43 Spargo to Walling, 15 July 1919, Stokes Papers.

unreconciled anti-interventionists such as Amos Pinchot among the treaty's opponents, the liberal case against ratification did not lack effective spokesmen.

Among liberals, the debate revolved around the relationship between the treaty and the league. As we have seen, advocates of ratification maintained that the league represented the most promising way forward, not least because, in the *Independent*'s words, it provided "the only chance of rectifying" the "inequities" in the treaty.[44] Even Kellogg, whose unhappiness with the treaty led him to formulate and promote specifically liberal reservations, accepted that "to reject the treaty would be to scrap the hope of the world that inheres in the covenant."[45] However, the *New Republic* insisted that "the League is not powerful enough to redeem the treaty. But the treaty is vicious enough to incriminate the League."[46] The argument was that the league, excluding as it did Germany and Russia, would be no more than, in Amos Pinchot's words, "the executive machinery with which this shameful business is to be clamped upon civilization."[47] This perspective cast a sinister light on Article 10's guarantee of "the territorial integrity and existing political independence of all Members of the League," and seemed to justify earlier fears that such an international organization would merely be an instrument by which satisfied powers could maintain the status quo.[48] The danger that the league might become "a league of conservation and imperialism like the Holy Alliance" was admitted by Hapgood, an advocate of ratification, to be the "one objection of first-class importance." It could be averted "only by the election of advanced liberal legislatures."[49]

The familiar reiteration of such hopes for the future should not disguise the reality of the discouragement suffered even by those who rallied to the

---

[44] *Independent*, 98 (31 May 1919), p. 307. See also *Public*, 22 (14 June, 5 July, 30 Aug., 1919), pp. 621–2, 703, 926–7.

[45] "To the Unfinished Work," *Survey*, 42 (5 July 1919), pp. 513–14. For Kellogg's campaign, which involved the League of Free Nations Association, see Kellogg to N. D. Baker, 3 July 1919, Newton D. Baker Papers, box 10; "A Cablegram to the President," *Survey*, 42 (21 June 1919), p. 451; League of Free Nations Association statement, 17 Sept. 1919, Kellogg Papers; Chambers, *Kellogg*, pp. 74–6.

[46] *New Republic*, 19 (29 May 1919), p. 102. See also Walter Weyl, *Tired Radicals and Other Papers* (New York, 1921), p. 99.

[47] AP to Peter Golden, 9 June 1919, Amos Pinchot Papers, box 38. See also Pinchot's article, "League of Nations Covenant Analyzed by One Who Regards It as a Great Peril," *Reconstruction: A Herald of the New Time*, 1 (June 1919), pp. 172–5; and Howe, *Confessions*, pp. 313–14.

[48] See Chapter 5, "The Progressive Consensus on Foreign Policy"; Chapter 6 "The Substance of a Democratic Peace."

[49] Hapgood, *The Advancing Hour*, p. 58.

support of the league in 1919–20. Already by July 1919, Baker was referring to himself in his diary as "a Bruised Idealist," as he contrasted his hopes during the war with "the savage greed of Paris."[50] Nor is there any reason to believe that Hapgood modified his initial hostility to the treaty.[51] As we have seen, much of the argument among liberals over the league was premised on the injustice of the peace settlement. With the exception of Walling – who astonished even his close associate, Phelps Stokes, by claiming that it conformed to "every one of Wilson's fourteen points"[52] – none of these publicists defended the Treaty of Versailles without qualification and most saw it as the antithesis of their idea of "a democratic peace."[53]

Such a debacle required explanation, and much attention was devoted to this task. The most obvious recourse was to blame President Wilson himself for his failure to secure – or, as some thought, even to try to secure – the objectives he had proclaimed. The attack was led, with apparent relish, by those who had felt betrayed earlier when he had reversed his position on intervention and before that on preparedness. Not only had Wilson "failed to fight for what he said he believed in," Amos Pinchot charged, but his ignorance and "utterly sloppy" preparation for the conference had rendered him "a booby in the hands of the foreigners."[54] Some of those whose investment of hope in the president had been both larger and more recent were no less critical. Lippmann attributed Wilson's defeat to his "apathy about administration" and "shrinking from intellectual effort." "Liberalism was triumphant on the day of the armistice," he maintained, "and could, I believe, have consummated that triumph at Paris had the official liberals grasped the mechanics of the peace."[55] This view, that Wilson had held a strong hand which he had misplayed through his own ineptitude, was common in

---

50 Notebook 25, July 1919, pp. 143–53, R. S. Baker Papers.
51 See the discussion earlier in the chapter, and N. Hapgood to E. M. House, 1 June 1919, House Papers.
52 Stokes to Upton Sinclair, 19 May 1919, Phelps Stokes Papers, box 31A.
53 For examples of criticism of the treaty from some of the stoutest advocates of ratification, see Creel, *The War, the World and Wilson*, pp. 242–271; Spargo, "The Plain Truth about Germany," *Independent*, 105 (15 Jan. 1921), pp. 62–3, 78–9.
54 AP to John S. Codman, 9 Sept. 1919; to Robert La Follette, 22 Sept. 1919, Amos Pinchot Papers, box 38. See also AP to George L. Record, 6 May 1919; to George S. Viereck, 10 June 1919; to Medill McCormick, 25 Aug. 1919, ibid.
   Before the conference met, Pinchot prophesied that Wilson would not "make a real fight for open diplomacy and a liberal peace . . . but he is going to make believe make it and make himself think he is making it, and he is going to come home claiming that he has made it, and more than that, that he has won it." AP to Roy W. Howard, 23 Jan. 1919, Amos Pinchot Papers, box 38. See also, AP to Mrs. Arthur M. Scott, 3 Jan. 1919, ibid., box 39.
55 "Liberalism in America," *New Republic*, 21 (31 Dec. 1919), pp. 150–1.

American liberal circles even before it was given wider currency by John Maynard Keynes.[56] "He was no match for the crowd he faced at that table," White reported. "It was as if a man sat down at a card-table with players he scarcely knew, with cards he could not comprehend, playing a game whose rules were beyond him and who was playing for different stakes from the others."[57] To Howe, the conflict Wilson faced in Paris "disclosed his loneliness, his fearfulness, his hatred of men who challenged his power," while Weyl attributed the downfall of "the prophet" to overconfidence, vanity, and "the invincible abstractness of his mind."[58] "We must learn what we can from our mistakes," the *New Republic* observed. "And the first lesson is that it is a mistake to isolate a man's virtues from his defects. It leads to disappointment and joy among the Philistines."[59] For many, Wilson's weaknesses were highlighted by his refusal to acknowledge that the final treaty diverged from the Fourteen Points. Even the loyal Baker found this "extraordinary," while to the unforgiving Lippmann it signaled a collapse of "inner integrity" that led logically to the president's dishonest denial of any knowledge of the secret treaties prior to his arrival in Paris.[60]

To Steffens, the most regrettable aspect of Wilson's refusal to admit the extent of his failure was that he would "not help, as he could and should, to direct the attention of the public mind to the cause of the failure."[61] However, Steffens soon concluded that this was because the president himself "does not see fundamentals at all; not at all; he sees things only politically and morally. He is the most perfect example we have produced of the culture which has failed and is dying out."[62] Steffens was convinced that "other, newer men, with a fresher culture, – the men I have seen lately, – they will have their turn now."[63] "Lenin predicted all along, way there off in Moscow, all the big turns in Paris, and gave reasons," he reported. "My impression is that it is only the so-called lower-class or radical social culture which comprehends practically economic forces and

---

[56] John Maynard Keynes, *The Economic Consequences of the Peace* (London, 1919). Keynes's account first reached an American audience through the columns of the *New Republic*. See "When the Big Four Met," *New Republic*, 21 (24 Dec. 1919), pp. 103–9.

[57] "A Tale That is Told," *Saturday Evening Post*, 192 (4 Oct. 1919), p. 162. See also Baker, Notebook 13, 9 May 1919, p. 57, R. S. Baker Papers.

[58] Howe, *Confessions*, pp. 307–16 at 312; Weyl, "Prophet and Politician," *Tired Radicals*, pp. 83–101. See also Hapgood, *The Advancing Hour*, p. 236.

[59] *New Republic*, 19 (7 June 1919), pp. 169–70.

[60] Notebook 24, 30 May 1919, p. 49–50, R. S. Baker Papers; WL to Bernard Berenson, 16 July, 15 Sept. 1919, Lippmann papers, box 3, folder 138.

[61] To Laura Suggett, 18 June 1919, *Letters*, 1, pp. 471–2.

[62] To Allen H. Suggett, 28 June 1919, ibid., pp. 473–4.

[63] To Allen H. Suggett, 13 Apr. 1919, ibid., pp. 465–6.

movements."[64] This perspective, as Steffens recognized, implied that the president's failure had been inevitable: "There are natural laws at work . . . They knocked Wilson into a cocked hat."[65]

Without necessarily adopting such a deterministic view, several of these publicists attributed the nature of the peace to economic forces. In April, Croly, emphasizing the importance of economic considerations in the negotiations, had argued that "it is chiefly capitalism which is on trial at the Peace Conference."[66] He had little doubt that it was failing the test, nor why this was so. "The characteristic virtue of capitalism," he wrote, "has always been its ability to get special objects, whether personal or national, effectively and unscrupulously accomplished. Its characteristic failings have always been blindness, egotism, want of public spirit and the hypocritical identification of the interests of its beneficiaries with those of the community. Enlightenment is not born of selfish preoccupation. When capitalism needed for its own perpetuity the ability to see and to tell the truth, social aspiration and moral faith, its representatives and creatures could not recruit these qualities." Few found it necessary to specify the connection so elaborately. To Amos Pinchot, it was axiomatic that "the shameful peace of Versailles" was the product of "the secret diplomacy of imperialists and international profiteers."[67] From this he drew the conclusion that "the only way to prevent war was to take the economic power out of the hands of the privileged class, which could only be done by the government taking over the railroads and the great natural resources which are the main raw materials and sources of energy in industry."[68] By this time Pinchot's thought had largely hardened into dogma but others, too, took for granted "the capitalistic nature of the peace" (Hapgood) or that "the treaty of peace was the last word of capitalism; of a capitalism that had become a system of world imperialism" (Howe).[69] Even White was to write that "the treaty binds mankind to autocracy; not kings and hereditary despots; not the old medieval order, but a new order just as wicked. For the treaty is . . . sown with avarice and with intrigue and with commercial and political and imperial greed."[70]

[64] To Allen H. Suggett, 14 May 1919, ibid., pp. 467–8.
[65] To Allen H. and Laura Suggett, 26 July 1919, ibid., pp. 477–8.
[66] "The Obstacle to Peace," *New Republic*, 17 (26 Apr. 1919), pp. 403–7 at 403, 405.
[67] "The Economic Blockade – an Enormous Crime," *Bulletin of the People's Council of America*, June 1919, pp. 5–6, Amos Pinchot Papers, box 39.
[68] To Miss Grace Scribner, 24 Dec. 1919, ibid.
[69] Hapgood, *The Advancing Hour*, p. 161; Howe, *Revolution and Democracy* (New York, 1921), p. xii.
[70] "Will They Fool Us Twice?" p. 6.

Adherence to this sort of economic interpretation opened the way for a continued faith in the enlightened character of public opinion. In this respect, too, White was strikingly unreconstructed. "The common people of Europe and of America desired no hate nor greed nor revenge," he wrote in 1921. "It was a ruler's treaty, and a ruler's peace."[71] Likewise, Howe continued to maintain that "the peace was not made by peoples."[72] However, many of those who had been in Paris felt that this generalization required some qualification. "I do not think that we in America can understand in any degree what the situation in Europe is," Baker wrote to one correspondent, "a condition in France bordering on national shell-shock, dominated by fear and frantic desire for security."[73] Baker was arguing that Wilson had done as well as he could in the circumstances, but the more critical Lippmann also recognized that by the time of the conference the president's "only fervent supporters" in Europe "were a section of the working class somewhere about the left centre."[74] At the time, Weyl had noted that the pathological aftermath of the war was making it impossible to make a true peace.[75] And in his *Autobiography*, White, too, was to suggest that the realities in Paris had been rather more complicated than his preconceptions. "After all, I was just Republican precinct committeeman in the Fourth Ward of Emporia, Kansas, who had been on the state committee and had been on the National Committee, and so walked with what I thought was a heroic tread. But the vast complexity of European politics, built on centuries of tradition, usage, prejudice and conflicting desires, was not even remotely in any corner of my consciousness."[76]

Such perceptions could be a rationale for isolationism and certainly implied some questioning of the simpler assumptions associated with the idea of an American Mission. Indeed, more than one of these publicists had already reacted against the view of their country's role in the world manifested in much wartime propaganda. Thus, Baker had deplored the attempt "to make more or less faded Americans out of perfectly good and interesting Italians," while Amos Pinchot had pleaded for "an internationalism that is based upon mutual respect for the rights of other nations,

---

[71] Ibid., pp. 5–6.
[72] *Revolution and Democracy*, p. xii.
[73] To Elizabeth G. Evans, 7 Aug. 1919, R. S. Baker Papers. See also Rowell to Harold L. Ickes, 9 June 1919, Rowell Papers.
[74] "The Peace Conference," *Yale Review*, n.s., 8 (July 1919), pp. 717–20. Lippmann attributed this unfortunate situation to the president's misguided trust in his (Lippmann's) old enemy, Creel.
[75] Weyl Diary, 22 Mar. 1919.
[76] White, *Autobiography*, p. 558.

and not on a moralistic impulse to save them by making them conform to our stone-age standards."[77] Nevertheless, the League of Free Nations Association manifesto of November 1918, signed by Hapgood, Kellogg, Croly, Cooley, and Holt among others, had continued to maintain that the liberal peace program was "merely an extension of the principles that have been woven into the fabric of our national life." "In search of freedom, our forefathers turned their faces to the West," the authors declared. "It has remained for our generation . . . to turn our faces toward the East and set out overseas across the Atlantic to aid the peoples from whom we sprang to achieve those things ["independence, unity, and democracy"] in the midst of the more rigid social fabric of the Old World, and against the forces of despotism, autocracy, imperialism, privilege, and militarism."[78]

By the summer of 1919, it was less easy to assume that the United States was the champion of liberalism. "Why is it that the worst, the meanest, the most revengeful, the most German public opinion in the world is the American?" Steffens asked. "It is worse than that of England, where there are protests against this treaty; where the ideals of Wilson exist and are expressed."[79] The Republican victory in the elections of 1918 had been a disappointment, even though some recognized that it reflected "local" considerations and that, as Hapgood put it, "Americans did not go to the polls to vote against the Golden Rule or the Sermon on the Mount."[80] The debate over the league in 1919–20 was a better indication of American sentiment on foreign affairs, and it was not encouraging. For, as Rowell pointed out, "the strongest criticism in the United States Senate is based on the charge not that Wilson failed to live up to his ostensible idealism, but that he failed to live down to the purely selfish nationalism of Clemenceau and Orlando."[81] Many, including the loyal Creel, were inclined to lay the blame for this state of affairs on the administration's suppression of radical and liberal opinion during the war.[82] Rowell, depressed by the low and personal tone of the debate over

---

[77] Notebook 21, Nov. 1918, pp. 48–9, R. S. Baker Papers; AP to Francis Nielson, 27 Nov. 1918, Amos Pinchot Papers, box 37.

[78] *Independent*, 96 (14 Dec. 1918), p. 377.

[79] To Dan Kiefer, 5 June 1919, Steffens Papers, reel 5; to G., 25 May 1919, *Steffens Letters*, 1, p. 469.

[80] Hapgood, *The Advancing Hour*, p. 245. See also Notebook 21, 8 Nov. 1918, p. 73, R. S. Baker Papers; Creel, *The War, the World and Wilson*, chap. 8.

[81] To H. L. Ickes, 9 June 1919, Rowell Papers.

[82] Creel to Wilson, 18 Nov. 1918, Creel Papers. See also *New Republic*, 17 (30 Nov. 1918), pp. 113–14; Lippmann to Newton D. Baker, 9 June 1919, Newton Baker Papers, box 10.

the league, clung to the hope that politicians and newspaper editors underestimated "the intellectual powers of the American democracy." If this were not so, he observed mordantly, "democracy needs the dictatorship of whoever is the champion demagogue and for my part, I vote to send for Willie Hohenzollern and establish an intelligent Kaiserism at once, as the lesser evil."[83] But it became hard to resist Hapgood's conclusion that the "political conservatism of our people is a dominant cause of the President's failure to obtain all that he might have obtained in Paris."[84] "Wilson could have got everything he wanted at Paris if he had had sufficient support," Baker stressed. "The fundamental difficulty, after all, is that only a very small minority of people in the world – small also in America – *really* believe in the principles laid down in the Fourteen Points."[85]

"Reconstruction" and the persistence of progressivism

If Paris and its aftermath represented an intense and concentrated form of disillusionment for most progressive publicists, events at home in the postwar period constituted a more diffuse but even greater source of discouragement. In both cases, significant differences of view existed, but these were overshadowed by the common experiences of disappointment and defeat.

To all appearances, hopes for domestic advance were at the time of the Armistice at least as great as those for a new world order. They were built on the long-standing expectation that the social implications of the war would prove to be both profound and progressive.[86] Several sounded as confident of this in 1918 as they had been three or four years earlier. "The guns battering down the forts of Liège were battering no less at the foundations of the established social order, and it went down with the forts," Russell insisted. "The crowning grandeur of this war . . . is the promise that the industrial system that has cursed mankind and blighted so many millions of lives is passing with the other anomalies of the dead old Night."[87] The same image was employed by White as he described

[83] To Mrs. Katherine Edson, 10 June 1919, Rowell papers. See also Rowell to David Starr Jordan, 22 Oct. 1919, ibid.

[84] Hapgood, *The Advancing Hour*, pp. 244–5.

[85] Notebook 25, July 1919, pp. 127–8; to Elizabeth G. Evans, 7 Aug. 1919, R. S. Baker Papers.

[86] See Chapter 4.

[87] Russell, *After the Whirlwind: A Book of Reconstruction and Profitable Thanksgiving* (New York, 1919), pp. 297, 313.

"the new heaven and the new earth that is forming during this war."[88] The rise of British labor occupied a central place in White's vision, and the *Independent*, too, prophesied that "in its essential features the program of the Labor party will be put into enactment" as it assured its readers at the end of the war that in England and France "the old order is gone . . . as surely as it is gone in Russia."[89]

With regard to their own society, American progressives were not perhaps quite so confident as such declarations might imply. As several historians have noted, they attached great hopes to the process of "reconstruction."[90] In so doing, they were again following the example of Britain and the Labour Party.[91] But it was presumably their own experiences that led them to emphasize the rarity as well as the scale of the opportunity. In the *Survey*, which devoted particular attention to "Reconstruction," the veteran social reformer, Felix Adler, stressed that "now is 'the day', now is our time, now the hour has come when we have an opportunity, such as never existed before in this country, to do great things."[92] "The people of the country – the most conservative of modern peoples – are in a mental condition so fluid that they would accept a radical programme of improvement," Hapgood argued. "After a little while they are likely to settle back into the mood that makes it a desperate struggle to get the simplest pieces of democratic progress through the legislatures, thence to run the gauntlet of our singular courts. . . . If we do not strike before the public hardens into its customary inertia, no economic and social gains will be captured. The opportunity will pass."[93] "Our society today is as fluid as molten iron; it can be run into any mold,"

88 White, *Martial Adventures of Henry and Me,* chaps. 7–8, quotations at pp. 318, 285. "It was for those two chapters that the book was written," White explained to Hiram Johnson, 30 Apr. 1918, White Papers.

89 *Independent,* 96 (23 Nov. 1918), pp. 242–3.

90 Chambers, *Seedtime of Reform,* pp. 21–3; Allen F. Davis, "Welfare, Reform and World War I," *American Quarterly,* 19 (Fall 1967), pp. 531–2; Stanley Shapiro, "The Twilight of Reform: Advanced Progressives after the Armistice," *Historian,* 33 (May 1971), pp. 352–3; Burl Noggle, *Into the Twenties: The United States from Armistice to Normalcy* (Urbana, Ill., 1974), chap. 3; Kennedy, *Over Here,* pp. 245–7; John F. McClymer, *War and Welfare: Social Engineering in America, 1880–1925* (Westport, Conn., 1980), chap. 6.

91 See Paul Barton Johnson, *Land Fit For Heroes: The Planning of British Reconstruction, 1916–1919* (Chicago, 1968).

92 "A New Purpose," *Survey,* 41 (7 Dec. 1918), p. 289. Adler was president of the National Child Labor Committee. In September 1918, Kellogg, seeking to "stake our claim to the term," had set up a special department on reconstruction, and a regular monthly section on the subject was launched in the *Survey,* 41 (2 Nov. 1918). See Chambers, *Kellogg,* pp. 68–9.

93 "A Programme of Reconstruction," *New Republic,* 17 (16 Nov. 1918), pp. 70–3.

the *New Republic* agreed. "Let it once harden, however, and any change, however slight, will be obstinately resisted."[94]

The perceived opportunity had several elements. One was simply the existence of wartime agencies and programs that might be continued or adapted. In the *Survey,* Felix Frankfurter expressed the hope that the minimum labor standards established by the War Labor Board might be sustained by the force of public opinion.[95] There was general support for the retention of the railroads in public ownership, and several calls for the extension of the principle of government insurance beyond the ranks of war veterans. "Peace cripples," Devine prophesied, "will surely derive some benefit from the widespread concern for war cripples."[96] Secondly, there were the immediate problems of demobilization and transition to a peacetime economy. Amos Pinchot was not alone in anticipating that these would lead to an "unemployment crisis" if left to market forces.[97] This seemed to many to justify the continuance of wartime price controls and the federal employment service,[98] while the scheme sponsored by the Secretary of the Interior, Franklin K. Lane, to settle returning soldiers on the land was energetically advocated by Howe and endorsed by White, Rowell, Russell, the *Public,* the *New Republic,* and the Social Democratic League.[99] More broadly, there were demands for a program of government spending on public works to take up the slack in the economy. "If

94 *New Republic,* 17 (16 Nov. 1918), p. 61.

95 "The Conservation of the New Federal Standards," *Survey,* 41 (7 Dec. 1918), pp. 291–3. This was an address delivered in New York to the "Conference on Demobilization and the Responsibilities of Organized Social Agencies" arranged by the *Survey* in late November 1918.

96 "Between War and Peace," *Survey* 41 (16 Nov. 1918), pp. 179–85 at p. 182. This lengthy article was prepared in cooperation with members of the *Survey* staff. *Survey,* 41 (7 Dec. 1918), p. 287.) See also Social Democratic League of America, *A Program of Social Reconstruction* (Girard, Kans., 1918), pp. 9, 12; Weyl, *End of the War,* pp. 307–8; *New Republic,* 17 (21, 14 Dec. 1918), pp. 206–7, 183; *Independent,* 96 (30 Nov. 1918), p. 278; White to Will H. Hays, 17 Sept. 1918, to Charles F. Scott, 9 Nov. 1918, and to Theodore Roosevelt, 18 Nov. 1918, White Papers; Rowell to Will H. Hays, 18 July 1918, Rowell papers; Russell, *After the Whirlwind,* pp. 230–7, 287; "The Readjustment of Labor and Capital . . . IV, Needed Reforms in Education, etc.," McClure Newspaper Syndicate, 13 Apr. 1919, Russell papers; Hapgood, "A Programme of Reconstruction," p. 72.

97 AP to John F. McNamee, 8 Aug. 1918, Amos Pinchot Papers, box 35.

98 *New Republic,* 17 (16 Nov. 1918), p. 60; Devine, "Between War and Peace," p. 183; Russell, *After the Whirlwind,* pp. 289–90; White to Elmer Peterson, 17 May 1918, White Papers; Social Democratic League, *A Program of Social Reconstruction,* pp. 9–10; *Survey,* 41 (30 Nov. 1918), pp. 256–7.

99 Howe, "A Constructive Program for the Rehabilitation of the Returning Soldiers," *Annals,* 80 (Nov. 1918), pp. 150–2; *The Land and the Soldier;* White to Franklin K. Lane, 1 July 1918, to Theodore Roosevelt, 18 Nov. 1918, White Papers; Rowell to Will H. Hays, 18 July 1918, Rowell Papers; Russell, *After the Whirlwind,* p. 294; *New Republic,* 16 (21 Sept. 1918), pp. 218–

we can spend twenty-four billion on current expenses in one year of war, we can spend say six billion as a capital investment to get started after the war," Hapgood argued.[100] "The large lesson of the war," Devine maintained, "is that for vital ends and recognized common advantage everybody must and can pay taxes and if necessary lend something as well."[101] A third element was the hope that the idealism of the war would be carried over to peace in the form, as Adler put it, of a "feeling that this had been a war of liberation and that the effects of it must be the liberation of the disadvantaged people of the world."[102] "The mass of mankind has been quickened," the *Public* observed, "and there is no person to whom the words liberty and opportunity have not come with a new meaning. . . . This soul awakening . . . is the fruit of the war."[103]

The circumstances might be unusual, but the prescriptions were familiar. The program adopted by the Conference on Demobilization organized by the *Survey* "read like an updating of the social justice planks of the old Progressive party."[104] In his obituary tribute to Theodore Roosevelt, Kellogg remarked that the issues raised by his 1912 campaign "will again be uppermost in the reconstruction period," while those other former Bull Moosers, White and Rowell, maintained that what was needed now was a program along the same lines but more radical.[105] Among the continuities with the pre-war era, of course, were differences of view among progressives, of which the most significant remained that between antimonopolists and collectivists. Amos Pinchot, under the guidance of George Record, was already showing the heightened sensitivity to the importance of this division that was to lead him in 1920 to abandon the reform organization to which he had devoted most of his energies for the previous eighteen months.[106] For the most part, however, doctrinal dif-

20; *Public*, 21 (12 Oct. 1918), p. 1279; Social Democratic League, *Program of Social Reconstruction*, p. 15.

[100] "A Programme of Reconstruction," p. 71.

[101] "Between War and Peace," p. 183. See also *Public*, 21 (12 Oct. 1918), p. 1279; *New Republic*, 17 (16 Nov., 14 Dec. 1918), pp. 60, 182–3; Howe, "A Constructive Program," p. 151; *Survey*, 41 (22 Feb. 1919), p. 730; Russell, *After the Whirlwind*, p. 285.

[102] "A New Purpose," p. 289.

[103] *Public*, 21 (28 Dec. 1918), p. 1538.

[104] Chambers, *Kellogg*, p. 70.

[105] *Survey*, 41 (18 Jan. 1919), p. 529; White to Theodore Roosevelt, 25 Mar. 1918, White Papers; Rowell to W. H. Hays, 18 July 1918, to W. D. Lewis, 29 Jan. 1919, and to Harold L. Ickes, 20 Dec. 1919, Rowell Papers.

[106] See AP to William B. Colver, 28 Aug. 1918, Amos Pinchot Papers, box 36. The reform organization in question was the Committee of 48. On this and Amos Pinchot's relationship, see Pinchot's *History*, ed. Hooker, pp. 72–5; and Noggle, *Into the Twenties*, pp. 184–6. For Pinchot's resignation, see AP to J. A. H. Hopkins, 26 Nov. 1920, Amos Pinchot Papers, box 40.

ferences remained subordinate to a sense of common purpose.[107] At the programmatic level, there was still a considerable degree of overlap, with the Social Democratic League calling for a tax on land values, and the *Public,* albeit on antimonopolist grounds, for the "socialization" not only of the railroads and the mines but also of "the Steel Trust."[108] Beyond this, there was general agreement on basic principles. None would have dissented from the *New Republic*'s declaration that "the whole issue hinges on social control. . . . We shall require a subordination of class and sectional interests in the interests of the nation."[109] In other words, the common good remained the paramount value.[110]

The postwar period demonstrated clearly that for most progressives the principle had two, somewhat contrary, implications. The first was the necessity for that move toward a more equal distribution of wealth and power which they had long demanded. "The democracy" Americans had fought for, Russell insisted, "can never be made to square with conditions under which only a small percentage of the population has ever a chance to know life in the true meaning of the word, one element being engaged in a bitter, blinding struggle for daily bread and another in a sordid effort to outwit other men and take from them a disproportionate share of the fruits of the earth."[111] "The workers must be given a larger share in the control of industry and a larger proportion of the product of industry," concluded the *Independent.*[112] "We are not wedded to means: only to ends," the *New Republic* declared. "The uncertainty that has attended labor incomes must be lifted, that is the fundamental requirement."[113]

That the workers themselves would contribute toward the realization of this objective was anticipated, and indeed to an extent relied upon.[114] Nevertheless, the second implication of the supremacy of the common good was that their interests, too, had to be set in a wider context. The Bolshevik revolution had sharpened the edge of the Marxist challenge to bourgeois reformers, but the idea that class struggle was a necessary, or

[107] On this point, see Shapiro, "Twilight of Reform," pp. 362–3.
[108] Social Democratic League, *A Program of Social Reconstruction,* p. 14; *Public,* 22 (15 Nov. 1919), pp. 1061–2.
[109] *New Republic,* 17 (16 Nov. 1918), pp. 60–1.
[110] See Chapter 3, "Progressive Values."
[111] *After the Whirlwind,* pp. 307–8.
[112] *Independent,* 98 (7 June 1919), p. 352.
[113] "The Meaning of Reconstruction," *New Republic,* 17 (14 Dec. 1918), p. 183. See also Weyl, *End of the War,* pp. 306–8; Hapgood, *The Advancing Hour,* p. 162; White, "What the War Did for Brewer," *Yale Review,* n.s., 8 (Jan. 1919), pp. 243–51.
[114] For example, Croly, "The Obstacle to Peace," p. 406; Rowell to Hiram Johnson, 15 May 1919, Rowell Papers; White, *Martial Adventures of Henry and Me,* pp. 316–26.

even desirable, means of progress was rejected as firmly as ever by almost all of these publicists. Even those most sympathetic to the Soviet regime were no exceptions in this respect.[115] At a low moment in Paris, Steffens had become convinced that "the stupid class war is inevitable all over Europe," but six months later he was declaring himself "a pacifist against the class war. It is too fierce, too expensive, too atrocious . . . the diagnosis is fake, and evolution is POSSIBLE."[116] Weyl, who devoted more thought to the question than most, expressed both moral and strategic reservations about the doctrine of class war. "We must not believe that wage-earners are noble merely because the attainment of many of the ends they strive for run parallel to the line of social development," he reminded himself. "There are limits of generosity of American wage-earners to European or Japanese workers, of white to black."[117] Moreover, "an industrial and social democracy . . . cannot be attained in our country by a mere struggle between the wage-earning proletariat and all who possess capital, since the latter constitute the majority of the people and the overwhelmingly preponderant group."[118]

These basic attitudes were evident in the responses of progressive publicists to the strikes that were such a prominent feature of 1919. On the one hand, there was general sympathy for the workers and their claims, which were often seen as attempts to maintain wartime gains and fulfill wartime promises. The attention bestowed on labor during the war had given rise to "a feeling of importance, a sense of power," Creel observed. "Labor is no longer *submissive,* people are no longer content to suffer injustices, and the glaring inequalities of American life will no longer be tolerated by the victims of these inequalities."[119] Reporting the steel strike, Baker stressed that the immigrant workers of Gary had been taught "that this was a war for democracy and that when it was over

---

[115] Ironically, the only real exception to this generalization remained Walling, who was of course extremely hostile to bolshevism. For his postwar views, see *Sovietism: The ABC of Russian Bolshevism – according to the Bolshevists* (New York, 1920).

[116] Steffens to Allen H. Suggett, 13 Apr. 1919, 14 Sept. 1919, *Letters,* 1, pp. 466, 486.

[117] Weyl Diary, 13 June 1919.

[118] *End of the War,* pp. 307–8. For Weyl's engagement over the years with the challenge of Marxism, see Charles B. Forcey, "Walter Weyl and the Class War" in *American Radicals: Some Problems and Personalities,* ed. Harvey Goldberg (New York and London, 1957), pp. 265–76.

[119] "Politics and Presidents," *Leslie's Weekly,* 129 (19 July 1919), pp. 96, 118. See also Russell, "The Readjustment of Labor and Capital," McClure Newspaper Syndicate, 30 Mar., 6 Apr. 1919, Russell Papers; White to Charles F. Scott, 27 Oct. 1919, White Papers; Amos Pinchot, "What's Back of Bolshevism?" *Lackawanna (N.Y.) Daily Journal,* 30 June, 1 July 1920, Amos Pinchot Papers, subject file 57.

everything would be different and better."[120] On the other hand, apart from Walling none of these writers was prepared simply to give organized labor unqualified support. In particular, there was little enthusiasm for the calling of strikes. The *New Republic* pointed out that "the strike is not a powerful weapon for the unskilled workers outside the A.F. of L., and by basing their whole campaign on it the wage-earners will accomplish their end, if at all, with a maximum of loss, bitterness of feeling and social friction."[121] Some, like the *Public* and Amos Pinchot, stressed the inefficacy of strikes, particularly in the absence of public support,[122] but there was more emphasis on the damage they caused. "Both sides try to prove atrocities," Baker remarked, as he developed a comparison between strikes and wars, "and always the noncombatant (the public) is the chief sufferer."[123] It was frequently observed that the whole community had a common interest in increased production. While not defending "the present unfair distribution of wealth," the *Independent* declared that "labor and capital in fighting each other have in large part lost what they were fighting for."[124] Even Howe, one of those most sympathetic to labor in these years, acknowledged that, in sabotaging production, "labor is not striking against the employer alone. . . . Labor is striking against society. For society wants wealth. It wants food, coal, lumber, machinery, clothes, shoes and commodities of all kinds."[125] Lippmann predicted that strikes in industries producing "immediate necessities" would not continue to be tolerated forever.[126] "Mr. Gompers and his friends notwithstanding, there is a Public to be protected," Spargo insisted. "Some means of adjusting labor disputes and lessening the number of strikes and the injury arising from them must be found."[127]

The contrary tendencies in progressive thought — sympathy for labor's objectives, dislike of its methods — permitted considerable variation in

---

[120] *The New Industrial Unrest: Reasons and Remedies* (New York, 1920), pp. 51–2. See also pp. 53–5, 67, 121–2, 133–4, 151–2. David Brody has emphasized the effect of the war in raising steelworkers' aspirations. See *Labor in Crisis: The Steel Strike of 1919* (Philadelphia, 1965), pp. 72–4, 114, 155–7.

[121] *New Republic*, 18 (26 Apr. 1919), p. 399.

[122] *Public*, 22 (22 Nov. 1919), p. 1085; AP to Edward Nockles, 21 May 1920, Amos Pinchot Papers, box 40.

[123] *The New Industrial Unrest*, pp. 47, 147–8.

[124] *Independent*, 97 (8 Mar. 1919), p. 320.

[125] *Revolution and Democracy* (New York, 1921), pp. 4–5.

[126] "Can the Strike be Abandoned?" *New Republic*, 21 (21 Jan. 1920), p. 226.

[127] "The Public in Industrial Warfare," *Independent*, 103 (14 Aug. 1920), p. 226.

attitudes to particular disputes and specific issues. This was vividly illustrated in the fall of 1919 when there was a printers' strike in New York.
While the *New Republic* and the *Public,* refusing to use nonunion labor,
ceased publication for a time, the *Independent,* condemning the strike as a
breach of faith by the union, produced several issues through the process
of "callitypy," a form of reproduced typewriting that it hailed as the
successor to printing.[128] Similarly, there was a clear division of opinion
over proposals to restrict the right to strike. Compulsory arbitration in
some form or other was advocated by the *Independent,* Spargo, and White,
but firmly opposed by the *Survey,* Russell, and Walling.[129] Indeed, Russell, explicitly reversing his pre-war endorsement of the New Zealand
compulsory arbitration law, maintained that any limitation of the right to
strike would be tantamount to slavery.[130] Baker expressed skepticism
about the efficacy of making strikes illegal, comparing such proposals
with Prohibition: "In this moment we have a pathetic faith in laws passed
– a long-developing American defect."[131] The *New Republic* adopted a
similarly pragmatic position when Attorney General Palmer attempted to
forestall a miners' strike by securing an injunction under the terms of the
Lever Act: "Until the industry has been fundamentally democratized,
[and] until adequate and scientific machinery for investigation and mediation has been established, . . . it will be the part of wisdom to refrain
from coercive measures against the miners."[132]

In thus identifying the only real solutions to the problem of industrial
unrest, the *New Republic* was expressing views shared by progressives of all
schools of thought. In the first place, even those who opposed any restriction of the right to strike favored some form of inquiry or mediation

---

[128] *New Republic,* 20 (8 Oct. 1919), p. 275; *Public,* 22 (15 Nov. 1919), p. 1059; *Independent,* 100 (1,
29 Nov. 1919), pp. 33, 115. The *Survey* maintained an irregular service to its subscribers by
printing some issues in a union shop in New Jersey. See *Survey,* 43 (25 Oct. 1919), p. 43. For the
issues of the strike, see ibid. (13 Dec. 1919), pp. 231–3.

[129] *Independent,* 100 (8 Nov. 1919), p. 61; Spargo, "The Right to Strike," paper produced for the
president's industrial conference, Oct. 1919, Spargo Papers, box 1; Spargo to Stokes, 6 Oct.
1919, Stokes Papers, box 31A; White to Henry Allen, 4 Jan. 1920, to S. Pemberton Hutchin-
son, 15 Jan. 1920, White Papers; *Survey,* 44 (3 Apr. 1920), pp. 8, 48; Social Democratic
League, "An Appeal to Progressives to Unite on a Non-Partisan Basis and Program," 13 Sept.
1920, Walling Papers.

[130] "Compulsory Arbitration the Next Battle Prize: Why It Failed in New Zealand," *Reconstruction,* 2
(Apr. 1920), pp. 150–3.

[131] Notebook 26, 10 Nov. 1919, pp. 54–5, R. S. Baker Papers.

[132] *New Republic,* 21 (10 Dec. 1919), pp. 43–4. The *Public's* position on the coal injunction was
similar, although Amos Pinchot's opposition to the administration's action was characteristically
less qualified. See the *Public,* 22 (29 Nov. 1919), pp. 1106–7; telegram to John L. Lewis, 6 Nov.
1919, Amos Pinchot Papers, box 39.

procedure that would elicit the facts of the situation and enable public opinion to make an informed judgement. [133] It was recognized that there existed much public hostility to organized labor, but this "prejudice" was attributed to "misrepresentation." [134] Nonetheless, as Lippmann observed, the conviction persisted "that there is a Public Group, that it is the guardian of the Public Thing, that somehow it manages to represent the disinterested thought of the community. . . . The idea of a Public is simply a short way of expressing the great faith that a group of men and women will always disentangle themselves from their prejudices and will be sufficiently powerful to summon the partisans before the bar of reason; and that evidence, not mere jaw, will then decide." [135] It was this faith that animated Baker as he undertook his investigation of the industrial situation: "If the American people can *see* and *know* and *understand* these things they will decide aright concerning them." But "how can a democracy succeed unless there are those who will honestly inform it?" [136]

Beyond the desirability of some more effective representation of the public interest in labor disputes, progressives agreed in seeing the prevalence of unrest as evidence of the need for more fundamental reform in industrial relations. In defending his opposition to compulsory arbitration, John Fitch of the *Survey* declared himself "interested in removing the cause of strikes, and if that can be done strikes will take care of themselves, just as typhoid fever will if you look after the water supply. . . . What we want is a self-reliant, independent, free people, capable of working out their own destinies." [137] Or, as Hapgood put it, "the stability of business and society today is threatened by the proletariat. The only remedy is to abolish the proletariat." [138] The favored means of achieving this goal remained "industrial democracy," though as the issues of the day obliged these publicists to give somewhat fuller indications of what they understood by the phrase, significant differences emerged. To the

---

133 In addition to the *New Republic*, 21 (10 Dec. 1919), pp. 43–4, see Russell, *After the Whirlwind*, pp. 284–5; *Survey*, 41 (16 Nov. 1918), pp. 183–4, and 42 (9 May 1919), pp. 193–5; *Public*, 22 (29 Nov. 1919), p. 1108; Baker, *The New Industrial Unrest*, pp. 203–4; Post to W. J. Bryan, 18 Feb. 1921, Post Papers.

134 Russell, "Collective Bargaining in the President's First Industrial Conference," *Annals*, 90 (July 1920), p. 69. See also *New Republic*, 20 (20 Aug. 1919), pp. 69–71; Baker, *The New Industrial Unrest*, p. 11; Croly, "The Eclipse of Progressivism," *New Republic*, 24 (27 Oct. 1920), p. 212.

135 "Unrest," *New Republic*, 21 (12 Nov. 1919), p. 320.

136 *The New Industrial Unrest*, pp. 11–12; Notebook 26, 8 Nov. 1919, pp. 49–50, R. S. Baker Papers.

137 *Survey*, 44 (29 May 1920), p. 303.

138 *The Advancing Hour*, pp. 208–9.

Independent, it meant simply "that wage earners must have the right to join unions, and that collective bargaining must be between employers and unions organized by the men themselves."[139] To many, however, the term implied participation by workers in management, though there remained both uncertainty and disagreement about the form that this should take. Hapgood became an advocate of cooperatives.[140] Baker, like the *Survey* and Spargo, was greatly impressed by the Shops Council system in the clothing industry that had developed following Sidney Hillman's initial agreement with Hart, Schaffner, and Marx in Chicago in 1911.[141] The Whitley Councils established in England seemed for a time a promising model to some,[142] but greater interest was shown in the more radical ideas of the Guild Socialists.[143]

In the United States, however, the most specific proposal of this kind in 1919 was the Plumb Plan for the railroads, under which the railways were to be bought by the nation and then operated by a board on which the government, the managers, and the employees would be equally represented – net profits being split equally between the government and labor.[144] This scheme, which was sponsored by the Railroad Brotherhoods, met a friendly reception in the liberal weeklies, though both the *New Republic* and the *Public* insisted that wage rates ought to be determined by the government representatives on the board since "no man can be judge in his own cause."[145] The Plumb Plan appealed to a wide spectrum of progressive opinion. Not only was it forthrightly endorsed by Russell, Walling, and Spargo of the Social Democratic League, but it also attracted the active support of Howe, Lippmann, and (for a time) Amos Pinchot.[146] Howe, indeed, became the director of the organization found-

[139] *Independent,* 98 (21 June 1919), p. 437. This editorial was signed by Giddings.

[140] *The Advancing Hour,* chap. 7.

[141] *The New Industrial Unrest,* chaps. 15–16; *Survey,* 41 (1 Feb. 1919), p. 640; Spargo, *The Jew and American Ideals* (New York, 1921), pp. 132–3.

[142] *New Republic,* 17 (30 Nov. 1918), p. 124. Later, the practical operations of the Whitley Councils were seen as rather disappointing. See *Survey,* 44 (5 June 1920), pp. 336–8.

[143] *New Republic,* 14 (2 Mar. 1918), pp. 151–2; *Survey,* 41 (1 Feb. 1919), pp. 643–4; Spargo to Harry W. Laidler, 11 Nov. 1919, Stokes Papers, box 31A; Howe, *Revolution and Democracy,* pp. 199–200, 230.

[144] The title of the book in which the railroad lawyer, Glenn E. Plumb, made the case for his scheme was *Industrial Democracy: A Plan for Its Achievement* (New York, 1923). See Milton Derber, *The American Idea of Industrial Democracy,* pp. 148–51.

[145] *New Republic,* 20 (20 Aug. 1919), pp. 71–2, 74–7, and (27 Aug. 1919), p. 106; *Public,* 22 (16, 30 Aug. 1919), pp. 869, 926; *Survey,* 41 (8 Mar. 1919), p. 825.

[146] Walling and Russell, "Open Letter to the American Federation of Labor from the Social Democratic League of America," 30 Sept. 1919, Stokes Papers; Spargo, *The Psychology of Bolshevism* (New York, 1919), pp. 56–7; WL to Howe, 9, 14 Sept. 1919, and Howe to WL, 14 Sept.

ed to promote the scheme, though when he invited White to join the Advisory Council of the Plumb Plan League he met a rebuff. "I am as anxious as you to take the control of industry out of the hands of the bankers," White replied, "but I feel that the community should be primarily interested in the transfer of power rather than anyone else, even the workers."[147] Yet, while deploring "the nationalization of any industry for the benefit, not of the consumer, but of labor," White was committed to "the policy of bringing labor up to the middle class."[148] To this end, he, like other progressive publicists, advocated measures to secure regular employment, shorter hours, better conditions, and a higher standard of living for the wage-earning part of the population.[149]

Yet if class warfare was rejected as a means of progress, the question remained how else goals such as these were to be achieved. Reflecting on the Marxist challenge during the Paris Conference, Croly saw only one answer: "It comes back to the amount of idealism which the democratic peoples bring to the new task. They depend for their deliverance from choice between unredeemed capitalism and revolutionary socialism upon the ability of the 'ideologists' to plan and to effect a redeeming transformation in a real world. And the richest source of the needed ideology is the gospel of Jesus Christ."[150] A few months earlier, White had expressed an essentially similar sentiment more simply and more optimistically. "Whatever progress has been made during the ages has been made by the slow and inexorable rise in our human relations of the spirit of mutual help among men," he asserted. "That spirit has come to men through their desire to ameliorate the hard lives of their fellows, and essentially it is the practical application in human institutions of the golden rule."[151]

For some months after the Armistice, a number who had been among the most enthusiastic supporters of America's war effort continued to maintain that it had given impetus to such moral advance. "I think the

1919, Lippmann Papers, box 14, folder 570; AP to Howe, 22 Sept., 21 Oct. 1919, Amos Pinchot Papers, box 39. Later, Pinchot decided that the Plumb Plan was "unsound." See AP to James H. Maurer, 4 Feb. 1920, Amos Pinchot Papers, box 41.

[147] White to Howe, 2 Oct. 1919, White Papers.

[148] White to General Leonard Wood, 7 Aug. 1919, White papers.

[149] White to Paul U. Kellogg, 2 Dec. 1919, White Papers. See also, for example, Hapgood, *The Advancing Hour*, chap. 9; Russell, "The Readjustment of Labor and Capital," McClure Newspaper Syndicate, 23 Mar.–18 May 1919, Russell Papers; Lippmann, "Can the Strike be Abandoned?" pp. 226–7; Spargo, *Psychology of Bolshevism*, pp. 141–50; Amos Pinchot, "What's Back of Bolshevism?" *Lackawanna (N.Y.) Daily Journal*, 1 July 1920, Amos Pinchot Papers, subject file 57.

[150] "Obstacle to Peace," pp. 406–7. See also Baker, *The New Industrial Unrest*, p. 231.

[151] "What the War Did for Brewer," p. 250.

spiritual in man is ascending above the material," Russell declared in April 1919, as he observed that "in the new view of life that the war has forced upon us, the only basis of reward that society can recognize is use."[152] Others remained persuaded that idealism would be reinforced by a more enlightened variety of self-interest following the war's effect in hastening the rise of professional managers possessed of what Hapgood called "the powerful engineering mind" and more interested in production than profits.[153] "Business is as much out of sympathy with mere money making as labor itself," claimed Devine in the *Survey* as he expressed the belief "that radical social changes may be made without raising any controversial issues whatever." "Programs of reform and progress are apt to be divisive and controversial," he admitted in March 1919. But "unless we have been living in a fool's paradise these two years, we have now changed all that."[154]

The "red scare" and the rejection of progressivism

Devine's confidence, so ironical in retrospect, must have seemed a little behind the times even when his article was published. Some weeks earlier, a writer in the *Public* had concluded that, indeed, "we have many of us been living in a fool's paradise."[155] The occasion was Wilson's message to Congress in December 1918 in which, though recommending public works and endorsing the Lane plan, he had called for the speedy winding up of the wartime agencies and the liberation of "our spirited businessmen and self-reliant labourers" from "any leading strings."[156] The liberal weeklies made no attempt to disguise their disappointment. "Those who hoped that the President's address would promise vigorous leadership for the period of reconstruction must now be thoroughly disillusioned," the *New Republic* observed.[157] As the apparatus of wartime collectivsm was dismantled, the *Independent* condemned the "precipitate abandonment of all those principles of organized cooperation between the Government and individuals which were so loudly acclaimed when we were organizing for

---

[152] "The Readjustment of Labor and Capital . . . III, The Present High Wage Scales," McClure Newspaper Syndicate, 6 Apr. 1919, Russell Papers. See also *After the Whirlwind*, pp. 276–8.

[153] Hapgood, *The Advancing Hour*, pp. 224–6. See also Baker, *The New Industrial Unrest*, pp. 209–18.

[154] "A Nation Wide Drive for Social Reconstruction," *Survey*, 41 (1 Mar. 1919), p. 784.

[155] John Merriman Gaus, "A Challenge to Liberals," *Public*, 21 (21 Dec. 1918), pp. 1522–4.

[156] Albert Shaw, ed., *The Messages and Papers of Woodrow Wilson* (New York, 1924), 1, pp. 564–7.

[157] *New Republic*, 17 (7 Dec. 1918), pp. 146–7.

war" and the rush "back into the merry old ways and irresponsibilities of *laissez faire.*"[158]

The attitudes of Wilson and the Congress did, however, reflect the political climate. Not only was there little substantial support for the progressive visions of reconstruction, but the wave of antiradical hysteria that swept the country in 1919 threatened to engulf even the most moderate critics of the capitalist system.[159] Early in the year, Kellogg warned that "a spell of Tory-minded terrorism" was threatening to put all liberals "under the ban."[160] By the summer, those returning from the peace conference were shocked by the state of American opinion. "You can hardly conceive the bewilderment of mind over here," Lippmann reported to Bernard Berenson. "It is exploited in the interests of the blackest reaction our generation has known. . . . My crowd is distinctly unpopular – parlor-'bolsheviki' etc."[161] "In these days what shall a liberal do?" Baker asked himself. "If he try to see honestly what is happening he is promptly tagged . . . as a pro-German, or a bolshevist, or an agitator."[162] Those of these publicists who were in some way within the political arena were likely to find themselves targets of direct attacks. Howe was forced to resign as Commissioner of Immigration after a House of Representatives Committee investigation into his reluctance to deport aliens accused of anarchism had taken on "the characteristics of a witchhunt."[163] Hapgood, who had been nominated by Wilson as minister to Denmark in February 1919, resigned in November when it was clear that the Senate would not confirm his appointment because he was considered too sympathetic to the Soviet government in Russia.[164] The following year, Post was threatened with impeachment for his actions as assistant secretary of labor in canceling warrants for the deportation of aliens arrested in the Palmer raids.[165] In such an atmosphere, it was not perhaps surprising that there were calls for Steffens (safely in Europe) to be jailed, but it is still somewhat startling to find that epitome of respectability, Hamilton Holt, having to defend himself from charges of guilt by associa-

[158] *Independent,* 97 (22 Feb. 1919), pp. 243–5.
[159] See Robert K. Murray, *Red Scare: A Study of National Hysteria, 1919–1920* (New York, 1964).
[160] *Survey,* 41 (1 Feb. 1919), pp. 648–9.
[161] WL to B. Berenson, 16 July 1919, Lippmann Papers, box 3, folder 138.
[162] Notebook 25, July 1919, p. 111, R. S. Baker Papers.
[163] Neil Thorburn, "A Progressive and the First World War: Frederic C. Howe," *Mid-America,* 51 (April 1969), pp. 117–18. See also Murray, *Red Scare,* pp. 205–6; Howe, *Confessions,* pp. 273–7.
[164] Marcaccio, *The Hapgoods,* pp. 135–8.
[165] Murray, *Red Scare,* pp. 247–9.

tion.[166] "At this moment," Lippmann concluded in November 1919, "the man who in domestic policy stands about where Theodore Roosevelt stood in 1912 and in foreign affairs where Woodrow Wilson stood when he first landed in Paris, and in his doctrine of toleration where John Milton stood two and a half centuries ago, is certain, absolutely certain to be called pacifist, pro-German and Bolshevist."[167]

As the epithets listed by Lippmann indicated, the "red scare" had to be seen as a legacy of the war. "When in 1917 I first read the generalization about history that in a war the belligerents are likely to exchange national characteristics, I was faintly interested," Hapgood wrote in January 1920. "Just now my interest is grave. . . . The United States in five years, mainly in three years, has passed into a despotic spirit comparable only to what Russia and Prussia were before 1914."[168] Deploring the "carrying over into a period of peace" of "the appetite for suppression and persecution, the intolerance of opposition and the glorification of blind and unruly popular feeling which was stimulated by the war," the *New Republic* maintained that "the government unleashed the passion for persecution by beginning to prosecute and jail Socialists for declaring that America entered the war in the interest of capitalist domination."[169] Even some of those, like White, who had been most bellicose during the war, were now prepared to admit that the government had been "too stiff in their regulations of press and of speech."[170] The campaign for amnesty for those imprisoned under the Espionage Act, notably Eugene Debs, attracted strong support from progressive journals and publicists.[171] Even those most friendly to Wilson found the administration's intransigence on this issue indefensible, as Spargo warned the president in August 1919.[172] Spargo's memorandum received a gracious reply but when, a year later, no action had been taken, he publicly denounced "the brutal and czaristic

[166] Kaplan, *Lincoln Steffens*, p. 266; Stein, "Lincoln Steffens," pp. 252–3; Holt to A. E. Stevenson, 12 May, 9 June 1920, and Stevenson to Holt, 3 June 1920, Holt Papers, box 2, folder 4.
[167] "Unrest," p. 317.
[168] "The Storm Cellar," *New Republic*, 21 (28 Jan. 1920), pp. 255–7. See also *The Advancing Hour*, pp. 2–12, 255–6.
[169] *New Republic*, 17 (7 Dec. 1918), pp. 149–51.
[170] To Senator Arthur Capper, 29 July 1919, White Papers.
[171] *Public*, 22 (26 July 1919), p. 787; *New Republic*, 20 (27 Aug. 1919), pp. 107–8; Amos Pinchot, "Protecting the Old Order," 12 Mar. 1919, Amos Pinchot Papers, subject file 55; Russell et al., telegram to Woodrow Wilson, 18 Mar. 1919, Stokes Papers, box 31A; Lippmann to Newton D. Baker, 1 Apr., 23 July 1920, N. D. Baker Papers, box 12; Steffens to Allen H. Suggett, 18 Nov. 1920, *Steffens Letters*, 2, pp. 556–7; Hapgood, *The Changing Years*, p. 289.
[172] Spargo to Woodrow Wilson, 25 Aug. 1919, Spargo Papers, box 1.

spirit which those in authority have manifested since the cessation of hostilities."[173]

Spargo found it difficult to persuade his colleagues in the Social Democratic League to join him in urging an amnesty for all those convicted during the war for the "mere expression of opinion"; some wanted to go no further than making a special case for Debs on the grounds of his "advanced age" and "his high moral character."[174] This hesitation reflected not only the persistence of wartime emotions but also the related preoccupation of this group of pro-war Socialists with the fight against bolshevism. Indeed, Spargo himself contributed as energetically as any to this cause, delivering many lectures and publishing no fewer than four books on various aspects of the subject in 1919 and 1920.[175] However, while not outdone by anyone in his hostility to the Soviet regime, which he accused of betraying democracy, socialism, and civilization itself, Spargo maintained that attempts to destroy revolutionary communism, whether in Russia or elsewhere, by the use of force and repression were bound to be counterproductive.[176] In contrast, Walling positively fanned the flames of the red scare. Not only did he contribute material to the National Security League, one of the leading disseminators of antiradical propaganda,[177] but he laid great emphasis on the threat posed by Bolshevik sympathizers in the United States. Far from being "comparatively harmless" as was generally thought, "parlor Bolshevism," he insisted, constituted "a serious, persistent and world-wide attack on the foundations of democratic civilization – more insidious, more flexible and more dangerous than Bolshevism itself."[178] His obsession with the enemy within led him to claim in a private letter that "every revolutionary movement in Europe from the mild and revolutionary Socialism of Henderson to Bolshevism has been largely sustained for the last two years by

---

173 Wilson to Spargo, 29 Aug. 1919, Wilson Papers, ser. 2, box 192; "Democracy Must Not Be Vindictive," *Independent*, 103 (11 Sept. 1920), pp. 303–4.

174 Spargo to Henry L. Slobodin, 15 Mar. 1919; to Stokes, 24 Mar. 1919; Russell et al., telegram to Woodrow Wilson, 18 Mar. 1919, Stokes Papers, box 31A. Also Friedberg, "Marxism in the United States," pp. 271–3.

175 *Bolshevism: The Enemy of Political and Industrial Democracy* (New York and London, 1919); *Psychology of Bolshevism; Russia as an American Problem* (New York and London, 1920); *The Greatest Failure in All History: A Critical Examination of the Actual Workings of Bolshevism in Russia* (New York and London, 1920); Spargo to Henry L. Slobodin, 15 Mar. 1919, Stokes Papers, box 31A.

176 *Psychology of Bolshevism*, pp. 95–108, 136–40; *New Republic*, 20 (20 Aug. 1919), pp. 89–90.

177 R. M. McElroy to Stokes, 2 Jan. 1919, Stokes Papers, box 44. On the National Security League's role, see Murray, *Red Scare*, pp. 84–6.

178 *Sovietism*, p. 130.

the Wilson appointees" and to complain in public about the editorial policy of such journals as the *Annals of the American Academy of Political and Social Science,* which gave "the strange 'evidence' of the pro-Bolshevists as much space as their most scrupulous and competent critics, thus causing the uninformed to remain in doubt as to their position."[179] When in January 1920, Walling supported the move to expel the five Socialist members from the New York Assembly on the grounds that the party was an antiparliamentary conspiracy, he precipitated Spargo's resignation from the Social Democratic League.[180]

Apart from Walling, the most susceptible of these publicists to the antiradical hysteria was Giddings, who at the end of the war transferred to the Bolsheviks the anathema he had earlier pronounced on hereditary rulers.[181] While the deportation of alien radicals following the Palmer raids was deplored by the *New Republic* and the *Survey,* the *Independent* not only welcomed it but warned that there were "still assiduously at work hundreds, perhaps thousands, of times 300 equally extreme radicals who have not even yet been apprehended, and who are doing their best to overthrow our established government by force."[182] However, the actions of the New York Legislature in 1920, not only in expelling the Socialists but also in passing the Lusk bills requiring the certification of teachers' loyalty and the licensing of schools, were too much even for Giddings, though the terms in which he attacked the Lusk bills were double-edged. "This sort of thing is not Americanism," he declared. "It is Leninism: it is pure and unalloyed Bolshevism, which means that it is neither more nor less than newfangled jargon for tyranny."[183]

In thus contesting the claim of the superpatriots to the national tradition, Giddings was employing an argument common among these pub-

[179] To Willoughby Walling, 19 May 1919, Walling Papers; *Sovietism,* p. 146.

[180] Spargo to Walling, 20 Jan. 1920; Spargo to Editor, *New York Tribune,* 20 Jan. 1920, Stokes Papers.

[181] "The Bolsheviki Must Go," *Independent,* 97 (18 Jan. 1919), pp. 97–9. See also *Independent,* 96 (16, 23 Nov. 1918), pp. 196–7, 240–2.

[182] *Independent,* 101 (3 Jan. 1920), p. 18. See also ibid. (17 Jan. 1920), p. 99; *New Republic,* 21 (24 Dec. 1919, 14 Jan. 1920), pp. 96–8, 186; *Survey,* 43 (10, 17 Jan. 1920), pp. 391–2, 419.

The *Public* had by this time ceased publication. However, following the bomb incidents of May 1919, an editorial had approved of the deportation of alien radicals advocating "the doctrine of sabotage." *Public,* 22 (24 May 1919), pp. 536–7.

[183] *Independent,* 102 (10 Apr. 1920), pp. 53–5. See also ibid., 102 (17 Apr. 1920), p. 88; *New Republic,* 21 (4 Feb. 1920), pp. 279–80, and 22 (14, 28 Apr. 1920), pp. 200–2, 259; *Survey,* 43 (31 Jan. 1920), pp. 487–90, 503, and 44 (1, 29 May 1920), pp. 186, 298.

On the Lusk bills, see Julian F. Jaffe, *Crusade against Radicalism: New York During the Red Scare* (Port Washington, N.Y., 1972), pp. 134–6.

licists, the great majority of whom were more unequivocal critics of the red scare. Thus White declined an invitation from the National Security League to write an article on "One Hundred Per Cent Americanism" by declaring: "My idea of one hundred per cent Americanism is an American who has intelligent faith enough in his country and his ideals to allow any other American however stupid and however crooked and however malicious to say what he pleases. . . . I fear that the standard of Americanism of your League doesn't come up to that."[184] "Just now the real conservators of the sound American tradition are the very radicals and the aliens whom the real law-breakers are trying to outlaw," observed Devine.[185] To Baker, the lesson was that "the American elements in our population are fully as much in need of training in Americanism as most of the foreigners: for Americanism is not a language, or a flag, or even a constitution, but a certain free and generous point of view."[186] Howe maintained that the repression had "made Americanization impossible. For even the alien is discerning enough to realize that freedom is an empty thing if it is stripped of those liberties and civil rights which distinguish America from the Old World."[187]

Such sentiments would not have sat easily with any real sympathy with bolshevism, but in truth there was little of that to be found among these progressives. A contrary impression could be given by the strength of antipathy to the anti-Bolshevik campaign, which most saw as reactionary in both its purposes and its methods. These objections certainly encompassed any military intervention in the Russian civil war, which in addition violated the principle of self-determination. "The Russian people too have a right to choose their own ways of life and obedience," Lippmann stressed.[188] The popular appeal of this principle encouraged radical anti-imperialists to "play up" the issue in 1918–19, as Steffens observed at the time.[189] At a rally in New York City (at which Amos Pinchot also spoke),

---

184 White to Charles B. Orth, 1 Nov. 1920, White Papers.
185 "To Presidential Candidates," *Survey*, 44 (17 Apr. 1920), p. 106. See also "To Governor Smith," ibid. (29 May 1920), p. 298.
186 *The New Industrial Unrest*, p. 108.
187 "Lynch Law and the Immigrant Alien," *Nation*, 110 (14 Feb. 1920), pp. 194–5. See also Creel, "The High Cost of Hate," *Leslie's Weekly*, 129 (5 July 1919), p. 22; *Survey*, 42 (3 May 1919), pp. 196–8.
188 *The Political Scene*, pp. 78–9. See also Devine, "Between War and Peace," pp. 180–1; *New Republic*, 17 (4 Jan. 1919), pp. 267–70; AP to Hiram W. Johnson, 9 Dec. 1918, Amos Pinchot Papers, box 36.
189 Steffens to Laura Suggett, 24 Dec. 1918, *Steffens Letters*, 1, p. 451. For some confirmation of this view, see AP to Philip Francis, 20 Dec. 1918, Amos Pinchot Papers, box 37.

Howe declared that the "organization to overthrow the revolutionary movement in Russia is as portentous to the world as was the coalition against the French revolution."[190] The continued presence of American forces in Russia attracted increasing criticism. One month after the Armistice, Hapgood, as president of the League of Free Nations Association, cabled House in Paris that the troops "absolutely must" be withdrawn "because the reasons for their being there, whatever those reasons may have been previous to the victory [over Germany], are now wholly shallow and unacceptable."[191] In March 1919, the *Independent,* which had supported intervention in 1918 as an aspect of the war against Germany, concluded that it had "strengthened the Bolsheviki instead of weakening them."[192] The *New Republic* repeatedly called for the ending of intervention, and by September the *Public* was describing the continued presence of "American troops in a foreign country with which we are not at war" as "the blot on the escutcheon of the Administration."[193]

Notwithstanding this almost unanimous opposition to military intervention, there were significant differences of opinion among these publicists over policy toward Russia. At one extreme, Spargo, Walling, and to a lesser extent the *Independent,* favored positive attempts to weaken the Bolsheviks through the use of economic assistance, and even through the provision of supplies to the White forces.[194] Naturally they firmly opposed recognition of the Soviet government; indeed, Spargo seems to have been the effective author of the "Colby Note" of August 10, 1920, in which the policy of nonrecognition was proclaimed by the U.S. government.[195] On the other hand, Amos Pinchot demanded the recognition of the Soviet government as well as the lifting of the blockade and the fostering of normal commercial relations.[196] During 1919, most pro-

---

[190] "Justice to Russia," *Bulletin of the People's Council of America,* June 1919, Amos Pinchot Papers, box 39.

[191] Hapgood to House, 18 Dec. 1918, E. M. House Papers. See also Hapgood to House, 25 Dec. 1918; to Frank L. Polk, 26 Dec. 1918, ibid.

[192] *Independent,* 97 (1 Mar. 1919), pp. 279–80. Cf. ibid. 95 (20 July, 14 Sept. 1918), pp. 77, 342.

[193] *New Republic,* 17 (4 Jan. 1919), pp. 267–70, and 19 (9, 16 July 1919), pp. 299–300, 343–4; *Public,* 22 (13 Sept. 1919), p. 973. See also *Emporia Gazette,* 17 Sept. 1919; Russell, *After the Whirlwind,* p. 262.

[194] Spargo, *Russia as an American Problem;* Walling, *Sovietism; Independent,* 97 (1 Mar., 6 Sept. 1919), pp. 279–80, 318.

[195] Ronald Radosh, "John Spargo and Wilson's Russian Policy, 1920," *Journal of American History,* 52 (Dec. 1965), pp. 548–65.

[196] "The Economic Blockade – an Enormous Crime," *Bulletin of the People's Council of America,* June 1919; AP to Santeri Nuorteva, 9 Feb. 1920, and to Bainbridge Colby, 1 March 1920, Amos Pinchot Papers, boxes 39, 41.

gressive commentary took an intermediate position, often recommending economic assistance as a means of weakening the Bolsheviks. [197] Hapgood, who developed a particular interest in the question, urged that aid should be directed to the cooperative associations on the grounds that these were still independent of Bolshevik control. [198] In October, he summed up his case against existing policy in a letter to the State Department from his post in Copenhagen: "Our blockade and our support of Denikin and Kolchak are creating Bolshevism in western and central Europe, driving an increasing number of progressive publicists from President Wilson in America, and making it possible for the Bolshevists to keep their despotic power in Russia, whereas normal conditions (peace and free foreign business) would have ended them long ago." [199]

Hapgood's argument was doubtless tailored to his audience but there is no reason to question the sincerity of his hostility to bolshevism. It is true that by 1920 he had come to advocate recognition of the Soviet government, but this was simply on the basis that "it is usually well to recognize facts." [200] Baker, who took a similar view, emphasized that "we ought to recognize the Soviet government of Russia, not because we believe in the doctrines of Bolshevism – which we do *not* – but because it is the de facto government." [201] It is not, of course, surprising that Leninism did not greatly appeal to reformers for whom democracy was such a central value. As Weyl, who tried to adopt a more understanding approach, noted: "The great charge is that it is undemocratic. From President Wilson down, down to John Spargo this is the charge." [202] To some, notably the pro-war Socialists, the Bolsheviks remained guilty of betraying the Russian revolution. "These victims of a strange delusion came in and spoiled the greatest democratic promise the world had so far lighted," Russell asserted. [203] Apostles of gradualism, however, saw the re-emergence of autocracy in Russia as proof that revolution was an illusory method of

---

[197] See, for example, *New Republic*, 17 (4 Jan. 1919), pp. 267–70, and 18 (15 Feb., 29 Mar., 19, 26 Apr. 1919), pp. 70–2, 261–3, 364–5, 400–2; *Survey*, 41 (1 Feb. 1919), p. 632.

[198] Hapgood to House, 19 Mar. 1919, House Papers; Hapgood to Woodrow Wilson, 26 May, 30 June 1919, Woodrow Wilson Papers; Hapgood, *The Advancing Hour*, pp. 93–4.

[199] Hapgood to Frank Polk, 9 Oct. 1919, House Papers. For further extensive criticism of U.S. policy, see White, "Litmus Paper of the Acid Test," *Survey*, 44 (5 June 1920), pp. 343–6.

[200] *The Advancing Hour*, p. xiii. See also "More Brains, Good Lord," *New Republic*, 24 (1 Sept. 1920), pp. 17–19.

[201] Notebook 30, 14 Aug. [1920], p. 46, R. S. Baker Papers.

[202] Diary, 14 Aug. 1919.

[203] "The Danger of Bolshevism in the United States," McClure's Newspaper Syndicate, 27 Apr. 1919, Russell Papers. See also Spargo, *Bolshevism*, pp. 209, 274–5.

advance. "Progress is a *stream*," Baker insisted.[204] Even those most friendly to the Soviet regime did not try to disguise its authoritarian character. "The present Russian government is the most autocratic government I have ever seen," Steffens wrote in his report on the Bullitt mission. Although, like Weyl, he argued that the Soviet Union was committed to an "economic democracy" more fundamental than "political democracy," Steffens was not entirely enchanted.[205] "There must be liberalism," he declared. "The Socialists haven't it at all, and they will need it most of all, as Russia shows."[206] "Unhappily Russia too . . . is sabotaging freedom," Howe observed, as he hoped this might be "merely a transition stage."[207]

Although there were no unqualified defenders of the Soviet government among this group, there were obviously vast differences in the degree of antipathy felt for bolshevism and the extent to which it was seen as a serious threat within the United States. However, there was one response they all shared – like the domestic labor unrest associated with it by the conservative propagandists of the red scare, bolshevism showed the need for the sort of reforms these progressives had long advocated. Thus Spargo, while declaring that "just as the world of civilized mankind recognized Prussian militarism as its deadly enemy, to be overcome at all costs, so too, Bolshevism must be overcome," maintained that "the remedy for Bolshevism is a sane and far-reaching program of constructive social democracy."[208] Amos Pinchot, on the other hand, doubted "that bolshevism (even if it were all that it is imagined to be) is the 'greatest evil'," but emphasized that such appeal as it had in America derived from the "absurdly unjust distribution of the country's wealth."[209] "It is the unrest, the unhealthy conditions, that cause the Bolshevism; not the Bolshevism that causes the unrest," Baker explained.[210] "The Red is an economic problem, an engineering job," White stressed. "I should not fight Bolshevism with guns, but with steady employment."[211] Indeed, it was

---

[204] Notebook 30, p. 57, R. S. Baker Papers.

[205] Winter and Shapiro, eds., *The World of Lincoln Steffens*, pp. 55–66; Weyl Diary, 14, 15 Aug. 1919.

[206] Steffens to Jack Hollister, 21 Feb. 1920, *Steffens Letters*, 2, p. 536. See also Steffens to Laura Suggett, 29 Mar. 1920, ibid., 539–40.

[207] *Revolution and Democracy*, pp. xviii–xix. See also pp. 194–5.

[208] *Bolshevism*, pp. 322–23. See also *Psychology of Bolshevism*, pp. 141–50. For similar views, see Russell, "Needed Reforms in Education, etc.," "The Danger of Bolshevism in the United States," McClure's Newspaper Syndicate, 13, 27 Apr. 1919, Russell Papers; statement by the Social Democratic League of America on Bolshevism, 5 Jan. 1920, Walling Papers.

[209] "What's Back of Bolshevism?" Amos Pinchot Papers, subject file 57.

[210] *The New Industrial Unrest*, p. 56.

[211] "Leaven of the Pharisees," *Saturday Evening Post*, 192 (29 May 1920), p. 21; WAW to Paul U. Kellogg, 2 Dec. 1919, White Papers.

generally argued that the repression of radicalism was counterproductive. "Bolshevism is the perverted child of popular distress," the *New Republic* observed. "It thrives on suppression just as Christianity throve under persecution." The only effective way to fight it was "honestly to try to accomplish by democratic methods and without violence the revolutionary improvement in the condition of the poor and the dispossessed that Bolshevism is attempting to accomplish by violence."[212] "American democracy must be made so broad and so impartial that no man will have an excuse for starting a class movement," insisted the *Public*.[213] It followed that those who resisted such change were the de facto allies of the Bolsheviks. "The persistence of the reactionary spirit of ingrained arrogant Bourbonism" was, Creel argued, "as much responsible for the present revolutionary tendency as the philosophy of Lenin and Trotzky."[214] "With the standpatters," Hapgood concluded, "rests the choice between painless evolution and evolution by shock."[215]

Numerous and variously couched as such appeals were, they clearly did not accord with the prevailing sentiment of postwar America. Indeed, it became evident that many people did not wish to hear them. The public's taste for critical studies of social problems and calls for reform, perceptibly declining before American involvement in the war, had not been revived by the subsequent excitements.[216] Thus Baker found that his articles and book on *The New Industrial Unrest* aroused little interest. He contrasted the public response to the muckraking days when "I had had a feeling . . . that I was speaking to men who had a real appetite for the truth, and that they intended to act immediately and vigorously to change existing injustices and wipe out official corruption."[217] For writers who had identified themselves with the cause of reform, this change in the mood of the reading public could have very direct implications. Steffens's reputation for radicalism had for some time prevented his publishing anything other than fiction in the middle-class magazines. His impressions of the peace conference had been conveyed in letters to his family; the only reports of his from Paris that appeared in print were much altered

---

212 *New Republic*, 17 (7 Dec. 1918), pp. 149–51. For similar arguments, see ibid., 20 (1 Oct., 26 Nov. 1919), pp. 245–6, 360–2; Lippmann, "Unrest," pp. 315–22.
   Steffens endorsed the analysis but not, overtly, the preference. See Steffens to Marie Howe, 28 Dec. 1919, *Steffens Letters*, 1, p. 519.
213 *Public*, 22 (29 Nov. 1919), p. 1106. See also ibid. (14 June, 19 July 1919), pp. 622, 759.
214 Address to St. Louis Advertising Club, 28 Apr. 1919, Creel Papers.
215 *The Advancing Hour*, pp. 30–1.
216 See Chapter 4, "The Domestic Scene: The Decline of Progressivism."
217 *American Chronicle*, pp. 467–8.

and under someone else's name. "My friends in the business in New York write me that the magazines will have nothing that is not either trivial or propaganda against the things I stand for," he explained.[218] In this climate, the reform journals, too, found life difficult. The *New Republic* lost circulation in 1919–20, as did the *Survey,* whose financial problems were aggravated by its pro-labor approach to industrial relations.[219] The *Public* had to cease publication in December 1919 when its deficit had reached proportions its patron, Mrs. Fels, no longer considered tolerable.[220] The *Independent,* having lost money steadily in the postwar period, was taken over in September 1921 by the conservative *Weekly Review.* Thereafter, before assuming the presidency of Rollins College, Florida, in 1925, Holt was reduced to rather embarrassingly touting for business as a lecturer.[221] For those without a private income, a career as a reform publicist was now hard to sustain.

As the size of their audience diminished, these writers also found their more direct forms of involvement in political life reduced or marginalized. As we have seen, Howe and Hapgood were forced to resign their official positions during the red scare.[222] Creel had been unceremoniously ejected from office in June 1919 when Congress abolished the Committee on Public Information,[223] while Baker's official assignment had, of course, ended with the peace conference. The more informal contacts with the Wilson administration, which had been so numerous and extensive, also declined.[224] Some progressives distanced themselves by their increasingly critical attitude following the Versailles treaty, Wilson's lack of leadership over reconstruction, and then Attorney-General Palmer's actions during the red scare. But in the postwar political climate, the administration seemed less interested even in those who remained loyal. No response was made to a suggestion from Hapgood, as the election of 1920 approached, that an organization be formed along the lines of the Woodrow Wilson Independent League of 1916 "to reach those liberal and radical

---

[218] *Steffens Letters,* I, pp. 434, 440–3, 452.

[219] Forcey, *Crossroads of Liberalism,* p. 292; Chambers, *Kellogg,* p. 81.

[220] *Public,* 22 (29 Nov. 1919), p. 1103; Post, "Living a Long Life Over Again," (renumbered), p. 262, Post Papers.

[221] Kuehl, *Holt,* pp. 37–9, 158–75. For a disenchanted view of Holt's indefatigable self-promotion, see Ernest M. Hopkins, president of Dartmouth College, to N. D. Baker, 3 Nov. 1921, N. D. Baker Papers.

[222] See the discussion earlier in this section.

[223] *Rebel at Large,* pp. 222–4.

[224] Some particular relationships survived, of course, notably those between Lippmann and Newton Baker and between Hapgood and House.

leaders who are showing impatience."[225] Those in the Republican Party
fared at least as badly. White's emphatic pleas to national leaders that the
party adopt a progressive stance were disregarded, and his political influence was evidently "at a low ebb."[226] In California, Rowell also found
himself in the wilderness after his support of the League of Nations had
caused a breach between himself and Hiram Johnson.[227] By writing
editorials "suggesting that the Progressive platform of 1912 be made the
model, brought up to date, of course, for the Republican platform of
1920," Rowell wrote to Harold Ickes, "I am kicking myself pretty effectively out of politics and am luxuriating in the privilege of saying whatever I please, especially the things that lose votes."[228] Such active political involvement as there was now tended to be on the radical fringes,
where Howe devoted his energies to the Plumb Plan League and Amos
Pinchot was one of the leading members of the Committee of 48, an organization consisting mostly of former Bull Moosers, which by December 1919
had become committed to the launching of a new third party.[229]

However, the national convention organized by the Committee of 48 in
July 1920 resulted in the emergence of a Farmer–Labor Party that
Pinchot found unacceptably class-oriented and socialistic.[230] This outcome was characteristic of these men's experiences in the election year of
1920, which were variously but consistently discouraging. "In this abominable election," Croly complained in October, "every attempt . . . to
give effective political expression to the aspirations of a progressive to
make his vote count on behalf of human liberation" becomes "pale with
unreality."[231] Earlier in the year, Herbert Hoover had seemed an attractive presidential possibility to Croly, as he had to many, including Lippmann, Baker, Rowell, White, and even the devout Democrat, Creel.[232]
But Hoover had disappointed progressives even before he shocked them

[225] "If you approve, I feel confident Ray Stannard Baker would be willing to collect such a club,"
Hapgood wrote. Hapgood to Woodrow Wilson, 25 Sept. 1919, House Papers.
[226] WAW to Will H. Hays, 17 Sept. 1918, 6 Aug. 1919; to Leonard Wood, 29 July, 7 Aug., 12
Nov. 1919; to Ogden L. Mills, 2 Mar. 1920, White Papers. Also McKee, *White*, p. 156.
[227] Rowell to Meyer Lissner, 9 Feb. 1920, Rowell Papers.
[228] Rowell to Harold L. Ickes, 20 Dec. 1919, Rowell Papers.
[229] See Pinchot's *History*, ed. Hooker, pp. 72–3.
[230] Ibid., pp. 73–5; J. A. H. Hopkins, "Facts about the Chicago Convention," Amos Pinchot
Papers, subject file 11.
[231] "The Eclipse of Progressivism," *New Republic*, 24 (27 Oct. 1920), pp. 215–16.
[232] Forcey, *Crossroads of Liberalism*, p. 299; Lippmann to Felix Frankfurter, 7 Apr. 1920, Lippmann
Papers, box 10, folder 421; Baker, *American Chronicle*, pp. 476–8; Rowell to Roy V. Bailey, 27
Dec. 1919, Rowell Papers; *Emporia Gazette*, 6 Jan. 1920; White, "Leaven of the Pharisees," p.
21; Creel, "Politics and Presidents," pp. 96, 118.

by endorsing Harding.[233] "He somehow lacked the necessary vision," Baker reported to Brand Whitlock. "And finally, he actually added his strength to the most reactionary group of them all."[234] "When Mr. Hoover rallied to a candidate such as Harding," Croly observed, "middle of the road liberalism skidded . . . until it reached the declivity of the far right."[235] While Harding's nomination was deplored by all,[236] his Democratic rival, James M. Cox, aroused little enthusiasm, though he did secure the support of those to whom the League of Nations seemed the crucial issue. This group included the Republican Holt, and the Socialist Spargo, as well as Creel, Hapgood, and, eventually, Baker.[237] The tone and character of the whole campaign depressed many. "Two provincial, ignorant politicans entirely surrounded by special interests, operating in a political vacuum," Lippmann reported to his friends in England. "I can remember no time when the level of political discussion was so low."[238] "Nothing could exceed the weak turgidity of Harding's utterances," Baker noted. "The public is apathetic, giving itself over to senseless pleasure."[239] Hapgood anatomized the prevailing mood as "mental fatigue, impatience to ideas, desire to be rid of everything except 'business'."[240] In these circumstances, the Harding landslide was not surprising, but it confirmed for Spargo that "we have definitely entered upon a period of reaction such as this nation has rarely experienced."[241] "I fear that it is more than the sunset of an Administration," White wrote. "I feel that it is the twilight of an era."[242]

233 Lippmann to Frankfurter, 7 Apr. 1920, Lippmann Papers, box 10, folder 421.
234 Baker to Brand Whitlock, 11 Aug. 1920, *American Chronicle*, pp. 478–9. Steffens had earlier come to a similar view. "Hoover sees things pretty much as Allen's other engineering friends see them – as trees walking," he reported after talking to him in Paris. Steffens to Laura Suggett, 8 Apr. 1919, *Steffens Letters*, 1, pp. 464–5.
235 "The Eclipse of Progressivism," p. 210.
236 "Of all the men who aspired to the presidency, Harding was the only impossible one," Rowell later wrote. Rowell to Hiram Johnson, 7 Apr. 1921, Chester Rowell Papers.
237 Holt, "The Successful League of Nations," *Independent*, 104 (23 Oct. 1920), pp. 123–4; Spargo, *Independent*, 103 (24–31 July 1920), pp. 110–12; ibid., 104 (20 Nov. 1920), pp. 264–5; Hapgood, *Independent*, 103 (7, 21, Aug., 4 Sept. 1920), pp. 143–4, 208–9, 271–3; ibid., 104 (30 Oct. 1920), pp. 155–6; Creel, Scrapbook, September 1920, Creel Papers; Baker, Notebook 30, 14 Aug. [1920], pp. 44–5, and Notebook 31, 4 Nov. [1920], p. 113, R. S. Baker papers; *American Chronicle*, pp. 478–9.
238 WL to S. K. Ratcliffe, 10 Aug. 1920; to Graham Wallas, 31 Aug. [1920], Lippmann Papers, box 28, folder 1023; box 33, folder 1246.
239 Notebook 29, 5 Aug. 1920, p. 40, R. S. Baker Papers.
240 "Why Vote for Cox," *Independent*, 104 (30 Oct. 1920), p. 155.
241 "A Socialist View of the Landslide," *Independent*, 104 (20 Nov. 1920), p. 264.
242 White to Rep. Phillip Campbell, 14 Dec. 1920, White Papers.

Responses to reaction

There is no doubt that the emphatic rejection of progressivism at home, following the failure of hopes for a new world order, cast a deep pall of gloom. "What a God damned world this is!" White wrote to Baker in December 1920. "I trust you will realize I am not swearing," he assured his puritanically inclined friend, "merely trying to express in the mildest terms what I think of the conditions that exist. . . . If anybody had told me ten years ago that our country would be what it is today, and that the world would be what it is today, I should have questioned his reason."[243] In his diary, Baker had already made the same contrast, sadly reviewed the course of events, and drawn a lesson. "We had things pretty well and smugly settled in our own minds when this war broke out," he recalled. "How I advocated this: cried out for that! Then the War came: and the bitter Peace Conference: and the bitterer return to America and the disillusioning discussions at Washington − and the veil fell from my eyes." "Our prophecies were false, our remedies vain," he concluded.[244]

In their sharing of a sense of defeat and of alienation from the postwar world, but also in the rather different character of their responses − defiant or self-reproachful − White and Baker were typical of these publicists. The extent and nature of postwar "disillusionment" among progressive intellectuals has been variously assessed by historians; as several have recognized, this reflects the diversity of the phenomenon itself, for individuals interpreted and responded to their experience in different ways.[245] Indeed, after 1919–20 these writers can no longer be regarded as a group. The sense of common purpose they had shared before 1914 had been eroded, as we have seen, by the conflicts arising out of the war and the Russian revolution. In the 1920s for many it became little more than a memory, as they went their various ways. Nevertheless, certain patterns can be discerned in their political thinking in the postwar period, and these reflect responses to challenges presented to some of their pre-war

---

[243] White to R. S. Baker, 28 Dec. 1920, White Papers.

[244] Notebook 25, July 1919, pp. 138–9; Notebook 29, [July 1920], p. 24, R. S. Baker Papers.

[245] See, for example, May, *The End of American Innocence*, pp. 393–8; Lasch, *The New Radicalism in America*, pp. 251–6; Arthur S. Link, "What Happened to the Progressive Movement in the 1920s?" *American Historical Review*, 64 (July 1959), p. 844; Otis L. Graham Jr., *The Great Campaigns: Reform and War in America, 1900–1928* (Englewood Cliffs, N.J., 1971), pp. 114–20; Stuart I. Rochester, *American Liberal Disillusionment in the Wake of World War I* (University Park, Pa., 1977), chaps. 8–9; Kennedy, *Over Here*, pp. 292–5.

assumptions by the subsequent course of events. These challenges had highlighted the tensions implicit in the set of beliefs that had constituted the core of the progressive consensus.

One of the more notable effects of the wartime and postwar experience had been to induce greater concern with the question of individual freedom. In the pre-war period, as we saw, this issue had attracted little attention from progressives by comparison with those of economic inequality and democratic control. Indeed, the language of individual rights had been more often invoked by conservatives defending the economic status quo. However, the attacks on freedom of speech and other civil liberties after, as well as during, the war awakened them to the continuing merits of a tradition that they had been prone to regard chiefly as an outmoded rationalization of laissez-faire. Thus, whereas Croly had once emphasized the limitations and unfortunate consequences of "the great formative English political idea – the idea of liberty,"[246] it was now invoked in a much more respectful spirit. "Is there among us in America none of that pride that makes famous Englishmen dissent from the enraged majority no matter how hot the issue?" Hapgood asked at the height of the red scare, as he called on his countrymen to "give battle for those conceptions of freedom handed down to us in the noble English tradition and carried along by the great names in our own history."[247] "Probably you would think it a joke to be compared with John Milton or Daniel De Foe or Sidney Smith," Devine wrote in a public letter to Al Smith, who, as governor of New York, had vetoed the Lusk bills. "But the fact is that all of these men owe their high place as prose writers partly to the accident that in their time also there were . . . just such chances as you had to defend freedom and to denounce bigotry."[248]

This heightened consciousness of their allegiance to the Whig, and classical liberal, tradition gave a certain appropriateness to the increasing tendency for these men to call themselves liberals rather than progressives. In fact, this change of usage seems to have resulted less from a self-conscious redefinition of their political philosophy than from the broader international perspective produced by the war and the consequent sense of identification with liberals abroad, and, also, as Lippmann suggested, the

---

[246] See *Promise of American Life*, pp. 230–9, and Chapter 4, "War and Reform."

[247] "The Storm Cellar," *New Republic*, 21 (28 Jan. 1920), p. 257. See also Hapgood, "Oases of Freedom," *Nation*, 112 (9 Feb. 1921), pp. 211–13.

[248] "To Governor Smith," *Survey*, 44 (29 May 1920), p. 298.

appropriation by the Bull Moose party of the designation progressive.[249] Nevertheless, it was disturbing to many that the threats to rights previously taken for granted had come from forces whose authority progressives had generally sought to enhance – namely, government and public opinion. Regarding the former, it is true that one school of progressive thought – the New Freedom or antimonopoly strain – had always been hostile to any form of concentrated power, and also that some indications of antipathy to bureaucracy had been more widely apparent in progressive writings. Nevertheless, before the war, as we have seen, progressives of all types had joined in stressing the need for some enlargement of the sphere of government action, and had also generally emphasized the claims of the community as a whole, and of the state as the community's agent, against those of the individual.[250] The experiences of the war and postwar years prompted not only many more frequent and intense expressions of antibureaucratic sentiment[251] but also a few more drastic reassessments of the nature of the state.

The war itself, of course, had raised obvious questions about the desirability of enhancing either the power of states or the degree of allegiance they commanded from their citizens. The work of the German sociologist, Franz Oppenheimer, which traced the origins of the state to the political organization of medieval tribes, had enjoyed currency among anti-war progressives since the early years of the war.[252] Oppenheimer's thesis was adopted by Randolph Bourne in his essay, "The State," on which he was working at the time of his death from influenza in November 1918. "A modern country represents a long historical and social process of disaggregation of the herd," he wrote, but this process was reversed by war. "War is the health of the State. Only when the State is at war does the modern society function with that unity of sentiment, simple uncritical

[249] See Richard Crockatt, "American Liberalism and the Atlantic World, 1916–17," *Journal of American Studies,* 11 (Apr. 1977), pp. 123–43. According to Lippmann, "the word, liberalism, was introduced into the jargon of American politics by that group who were Progressives in 1912 and Wilson Democrats from 1916 to 1918. They wished to distinguish their own general aspirations in politics from those of the chronic partisans and the social revolutionists." *New Republic,* 21 (31 Dec. 1919), p. 150. Presumably, Lippmann meant that the latter two groups had appropriated, respectively, the terms "progressive" and "radical."

[250] See Chapter 3.

[251] For example, *New Republic,* 17 (30 Nov. 1918), pp. 113–14; *Survey,* 41 (7 Dec. 1918), pp. 301–3; Russell, *After the Whirlwind,* pp. 68–70; Spargo, *Psychology of Bolshevism,* pp. 59–60, 142; Hapgood, "The Sabotage of Capitalism," *Independent,* 102 (22 May 1920), p. 249.

[252] Franz Oppenheimer, *The State: Its History and Development Viewed Sociologically* (Indianapolis, Ind., 1914); Max Eastman to Amos Pinchot, 16 Nov. 1915, Amos Pinchot Papers, box 22.

patriotic devotion, co-operation of services, which have always been the ideal of the State lover." "The State," Bourne concluded, "represents all the autocratic, arbitrary, coercive, belligerent forces within a social group, it is a sort of complexus of everything most distasteful to the modern free creative spirit, the feeling for life, liberty and the pursuit of happiness."[253]

Such views might seem closer to Herbert Spencer's than to the socialism Bourne had professed before the war. It is true that, like Oppenheimer, Bourne emphasized that a hierarchy of classes was an essential feature of the state,[254] but, by relating this to the institutionalization of privilege rather than the social relations of capitalism, he remained within that broad stream of American political thought that included both Jefferson and Henry George.[255] Progressives whose thinking had always been much influenced by this tradition were naturally receptive to Oppenheimer's ideas. Thus Amos Pinchot cited Oppenheimer's authority for the proposition that "all states' main motivation has always been to provide political means for acquiring and protecting wealth," and Howe incorporated his historical theories into his account of the state in *Revolution and Democracy* (1921), in which he described the institution as "little more" than "an agency of an economic class" and "an agency of suppression."[256] In this work, Howe maintained that "freedom involves the enactment of but a few laws" – essentially, the Single Tax, the "socialization" of transportation, a cooperative, localized banking system, and some form of industrial democracy, possibly Guild Socialism.[257] There were, of course, clear elements of continuity between this program and the proposals Howe had made in previous writings, but he himself insisted that his attitude to the state had been profoundly altered by his experiences. Thus in 1919 he explained to White that having seen at close quarters "the deadening effect of public office on the minds of men" had been "one of the things which turned me from Government Ownership to the Plumb Plan."[258] And in *The Confessions of a Reformer* (1925) Howe was to stress

---

253 "The State," in Bourne, *War and the Intellectuals*, ed. Resek, pp. 65–104. Quotations on pp. 76, 84–5.
254 Ibid., p. 93.
255 Despite his limiting remarks on what "Jeffersonian Democracy" had "meant in practice." Ibid., p. 99.
256 AP to W. B. Colver, 28 Aug. 1918, Amos Pinchot Papers, box 36; Howe, *Revolution and Democracy*, pp. 98–118.
257 *Revolution and Democracy*, pp. 198–200, 230.
258 Howe to White, 29 Sept. 1919, White Papers.

that his fights on behalf of helpless aliens with Washington bureaucrats had had lasting effects upon his political thinking. "The war had changed an abiding faith in the state into questionings of it," he wrote. "It seemed to want to hurt people; it showed no concern for innocence; it aggrandized itself and protected its power by unscrupulous means."[259]

If the agrarian and Single Tax elements in Howe's thought had always possessed a potentially anti-statist aspect, the same could hardly be said of Croly's pre-war views. Yet the doubts that the war had induced in him, too, were confirmed and broadened by the postwar experience. "The state, as now organized, is essentially the embodiment of power rather than justice," he declared in December 1919. Its "commands . . . are intended in nine cases out of ten to secure to the property-owner not only the undisturbed but usually the exclusive and irresponsible enjoyment of his property." Yet it attracted an excessive devotion. "Men glorify the state, cling to it and worship it as a God because their vision of religious truth has ceased to possess authority and integrity."[260] As a more mundane antidote to the international dangers of the nationalist emotion he had once seen as a beneficent force, Croly continued to be attracted by pluralism. "The authorization by conscious collective consent of semi-independent but cooperative classes within a nation," he argued, "erects the surest safeguard against the kind of headstrong mob rule in which war so often originates and whose flare-up in this country during the recent war was so largely responsible for the disappointing end of its crusade in Europe."[261]

As Croly indicated, the state was not the only institution in which it now seemed that progressives had placed excessive trust. Public opinion had to bear a large share of the responsibility not only for the treatment of political dissenters but also for the failure of progressive hopes both abroad and at home. The two issues – the state and public opinion – were, of course, intimately related. On the one hand, as we have seen, much of the case against the national state rested on the attitudes that it induced, by one means or another, in its citizenry. On the other hand, the conviction remained that the state was potentially a force for good – even Howe continued to maintain that "it should be an agency of cooperation and help," while Croly's objections had been to "the state *as now orga-*

---

[259] *Confessions*, pp. 317, 279–82. See also pp. 255–6.
[260] "Disordered Christianity," *New Republic*, 21 (31 Dec. 1919), pp. 136–9.
[261] "Liberalism versus the War," *New Republic*, 25 (8 Dec. 1920), pp. 35–8.

nized."[262] But the most obvious obstacle to efforts to change the character of the state, as to other desirable changes, was the electorate's evident lack of enthusiasm for progressive programs.

One could, of course, seek to make a distinction between the outcomes of the electoral process and true public opinion. This involved emphasizing, as progressives had long done, the undemocratic features of the political system. Thus, Howe argued that the nature of the Constitution and the obstructive role of the courts accounted for the public's loss of interest in reform. "As a result of these many limitations," he explained, "democratic movements have to survive a series of elections to achieve their ends. . . . The average man is moved by the desire for results. Yet when success is subject to innumerable obstacles, when the end desired is distant and highly problematical, when the fruits of effort are subject to veto by officials unresponsive to the public will, initiative and effort are discouraged."[263] Generally, however, the Constitution, and even the judiciary, were criticized less often than they had been before the war, now that their potential role in protecting individual rights was more highly valued.[264] By contrast, the political parties, another long-standing target, attracted much hostile comment in these years. In "the State," Bourne described "the party system" as "the means of removing political grievance from the greater part of the populace, and of giving to the ruling classes the hidden but genuine permanence of control which the Constitution had tried openly to give them."[265] This was an extreme view, but many argued that the parties contrived both to engender a damaging divisiveness and to obfuscate the crucial issues. That the struggle between Democrats and Republicans was essentially one for place and patronage in no whit abated its bitterness, Creel pointed out. The "theory of politics as a vast employment agency has its logical development in the perfection of slander and abuse as legitimate campaign weapons."[266] To Croly, the election of 1920 represented the triumph of the professional party politicians "and their combination of realistic machine methods with unlimited patriotic pretense."[267] Baker, who had earlier deplored

262 *Revolution and Democracy*, pp. 98–9; "Disordered Christianity," p. 137. My italics.
263 *Revolution and Democracy*, pp. 102–10 at 109–10.
264 See, for example, Weyl Diary, 28 July 1918; *New Republic*, 20 (26 Nov. 1919), pp. 360–2; AP, telegram to John L. Lewis, 6 Nov. 1919, Amos Pinchot Papers, box 39; Hapgood, "Oases of Freedom," pp. 211–13; and, even, Howe, *Revolution and Democracy*, p. 87.
265 *War and the Intellectuals*, p. 104.
266 *The War, the World and Wilson*, p. 64. See also Hapgood, *The Advancing Hour*, pp. 70–1.
267 "The Eclipse of Progressivism," p. 211.

the division of Americans "into two great crude amorphous, political lumps called parties," attributed Harding's victory to "the forces of reaction, negation, opposition, partisanship."[268] As evidence of the debilitating effect of traditional party allegiance on the movement for progressive reform, some of these publicists needed to look no further than their own relationships. "It is indeed a bit funny that we are not together. We who hold eighty per cent of our political opinions in common," White, the Republican, wrote to Creel, the Democrat. "I hope the day comes when there will be a thorough-going radical party with a thorough-going radical program."[269] This desire for a political realignment along ideological lines was frequently expressed. What was needed, Hapgood declared, was "one party that fairly represents the liberal minds of the country, now divided up, being a minority among the Republicans, the Democrats, the Socialists, with a number who have remained independent because of the absence of a liberal party."[270]

Yet despite the claim that the existing parties were unrepresentative, Hapgood was here admitting that liberal sentiment was limited to a minority. In view of their pre-war optimism, this state of affairs demanded explanation, as many progressives recognized. Perhaps the most comforting recourse was to attribute the public mood to the unfortunate, but presumably temporary, influence of events. War, White remarked, "is a stimulant that leaves an awful bust head. America was thirty years getting over the bust head of the Civil War. Heaven knows how long we may have to wallow in reactionary conservatism after this one."[271] "A relaxation after the long and terrible tension of these five years was inevitable," Russell concluded almost complacently. "Any one familiar with history could easily have predicted in 1917 and 1918 that the end of the war would see in America a season of unexampled cynicism and pessimism."[272] More ominously, Lippmann commented in November 1920 that "unless one is prepared to regard the election as the final twitch of the war mind (that is the way I regard it), there would be cause for profound discouragement with universal suffrage."[273]

---

[268] Notebook 29, p. 73; Notebook 31, Nov. 4, [1920], p. 109, R. S. Baker Papers.

[269] White to Creel, 13 Nov. 1918; also White to Croly, 16 Nov. 1918, White Papers.

[270] Hapgood, *The Advancing Hour,* pp. 85–6. See also Rowell to J. A. H. Hopkins, 14 June 1919, Rowell papers; Howe, *Revolution and Democracy,* p. 126.

[271] White to Rodney Elward, 13 Mar. 1920, White Papers.

[272] Lectures, "The Idealism of America" [1919?], "The Assault on Democracy" [1921], Russell Papers.

[273] WL to Graham Wallas, 4 Nov. 1920, Lippmann Papers, box 33, folder 1246.

The nature of the presumed connection between war and reaction was variously interpreted. Sometimes the war spirit was evoked nostalgically. "For two years while we were in the throes of a problematic struggle it looked as if the American people were largely under the influence of an altruistic and beneficent purpose," the *Public* observed. "As the weeks go by the unsocial vices of avarice and cruelty become more open and insistent, showing that our fine display of other-regarding feeling in war time was mostly an excursion of emotion rather than a just expression of settled character."[274] "The moment the war ceased," Baker recalled, "the bottom fell out of idealism! The great moment had passed, there had been no miracle, we were back at the old controversies, selfish interests were again rampant."[275] But on another occasion, Baker lamented that "everyone has learned the lesson our patriots tried to instill during the war: that men should look to their own interests first."[276] The ambivalence of the war experience for progressives was captured by Lippmann in a single sentence: "I sometimes think that the terrific morale we developed during the war exhausted the public spirit of this country for a generation and that nobody will be enthusiastic about anything until the generation grows up that has forgotten how violent we were and how unreasonable."[277] Some saw a direct connection between the postwar reaction and the temper of the country during the war. "Privilege reached the height of its power at the end of the European war," Howe claimed. "The press and agencies of public opinion organized for war propaganda, became an agency for the support of the status qu."[278] This line of argument was particularly favored by those who opposed intervention, for there was a natural tendency to find an explanation that justified one's pre-existing views. Thus Russell and Walling laid the blame not only for the red scare but for the whole postwar reaction upon the Bolsheviks and their sympathizers. "One year of his [Lenin's] agitation," according to a Social Democratic League statement, "has threatened to destroy not only all the democratic advance won in the five years of the war, but a large part of the gains of the last fifteen years of progress."[279]

The impression made by events depended, of course, upon the way they

274 *Public*, 22 (2 Aug. 1919), p. 817.
275 *The New Industrial Unrest*, pp. 9–10.
276 Notebook 26, Oct. 1, [1919], p. 9, R. S. Baker Papers.
277 WL to S. K. Ratcliffe, 10 Aug. 1920, Lippmann Papers, box 28, folder 1023.
278 *Revolution and Democracy*, p. 75.
279 Statement on bolshevism by the Social Democratic League of America, 5 Jan. 1920, Walling Papers. See also Russell, lecture, "The Assault on Democracy," Russell Papers.

were reported and presented. These journalists and writers were not likely to underestimate the influence upon public opinion of the media of communications. Their belief in the value of their own role was premised upon the importance of bringing information into the public arena and upon the educative potential of journalism. Even in 1919 Russell reaffirmed his faith that "to right any wrong in the United States is, after all, a simple process. You have only to exhibit it where all the people can see it plainly."[280] As he was about to embark on his investigation into the steel strike, following the great success of his articles on "What Wilson Did at Paris," Baker assured himself that "the greatest service in the world today is to try to present the *facts* regarding the present discontent." "The trouble is," he noted, "that most editors and writers do not believe in . . . real democracy."[281] The concern that, in practice, the power of the press did not serve the cause of truth and justice but distorted events in the interest of antidemocratic forces was not new.[282] It was, however, greatly increased by the wartime and postwar experience.

As we have seen, the belligerent and nationalistic tone of much of the American press during the war had distressed many of these progressives.[283] Amos Pinchot had no doubt that it reflected sinister interests. "To some extent at least," he wrote to Congress, "the statement that this is a government by newspapers is warranted. And, that this newspaper government does not represent the public's will is quite inevitable, since most of our important journals are owned by wealthy men whose aims are not, generally speaking, parallel with the people's."[284] Pinchot's sense of the importance of this issue only grew in the next few years. "There should be an organization to stop the influence of the large newspapers," he wrote to a correspondent in December 1918.[285] By 1921 he had reached the conclusion that "our main difficulty . . . does not lie in our political machinery or in its failure to register the public will. The public will is registered well enough whenever public will exists. But the serious fact in the situation is that public will or opinion is formed largely by the press, by our educational system, the stage and the screen. All these factors are controlled by the privileged class, which in all ages and places

[280] *The Story of the Nonpartisan League; A Chapter in American Evolution* (New York, 1920).
[281] Notebook 26, 8, 4 Nov. 1919, pp. 49–50, 34, R. S. Baker Papers.
[282] See Chapter 3, p. 50.
[283] See Chapter 6, "The War at Home: Civil Liberties and Public Opinion."
[284] Open letter to the Conference Committee of the Senate and the House of Representatives, 18 Sept. 1917; see also AP to Edwin S. Potter, 31 Oct. 1917, Amos Pinchot Papers, boxes 34, 33.
[285] AP to J. Bates Gay, 19 Dec. 1918, Amos Pinchot Papers, box 37.

has, with an unerring instinct of self-preservation, been opposed to free discussion of important issues."[286]

As an open opponent of intervention, Pinchot had had particular cause to be sensitive to the performance of the American press during the war. So, too, had Creel, as chairman of the Committee on Public Information and himself a target of attack in Republican newspapers. His postwar verdict was as severe as anyone's. "The average newspaper," he wrote, "made for confusion rather than clarity; its appeals were to the emotions, not to the mind; it muddled thought instead of molding it; it cluttered public discussion with rumors, false report and hysteria." Observing that "the newspaper has lost its interpretative, informative and educational qualities," he, too, argued that "the causes go back of the workers to the owners; back to the belief and insistence of these owners that the newspaper is a strictly commercial proposition operated entirely for private profit, and without the slightest recognition of the great truth that the press *is* vested with a high public use, and *is,* in fact, a public utility." In 1919, Creel stressed that "reform *must* come" to the press, but by 1924, he was noticeably more pessimistic. "The very *existence* of a forceful, effective public opinion is much to be doubted," he maintained. "It is these joined causes – the indecencies of partisanship, the noise and unintelligibility of a large portion of the press, the lack of trustworthy information, the dreary routine of mud-slinging that passes for political discussion – that have killed public opinion, or rather deafened it, confused it, bored it, disgusted it."[287]

It was Creel's old antagonist, Lippmann, who was to explore most thoroughly the significance of what in 1920 he called "the crisis in journalism."[288] It would be wrong to see Lippmann's famous study, *Public Opinion* (which appeared in 1922),[289] simply as a product of his experiences during and after the war. His manuscript diary shows that as early as 1915 he had been planning a work on the implications for orthodox democratic theory of the way in which public opinion was formed in the real world.[290] Nevertheless, there is no doubt that his concern with the problem was intensified not only by his personal experi-

[286] "A Letter to the Editors," *Freeman*, 20 Apr. 1921, p. 137. See also AP to Upton Sinclair, 15 Apr. 1919, Amos Pinchot Papers, box 38.

[287] "The American Newspaper: What It Is and What It Isn't," *Everybody's*, 40 (April 1919), pp. 40–4, 92; "The 'Lash' of Public Opinion," *Colliers*, 74 (22 Nov. 1924), pp. 8–9, 46.

[288] *Liberty and the News* (New York, 1920), p. 4.

[289] *Public Opinion* (New York, 1922).

[290] Diary, especially pp. 31–39, 20 May 1915, Lippmann Papers.

ences in government service, to which so much implicit reference is made in *Public Opinion,* but also by the disappointment of the hopes he and his fellow progressives had shared. This is evident from the writings in 1919 in which he first began to analyze "the pseudo-environment of reports, rumors, and guesses" in which ordinary people had to make most of their political judgments.[291] Not only did he emphasize the unfortunate consequences at the peace conference of that "lack of information which kept public opinion from affecting the negotiations at the time when intervention would have counted most," but among the necessary qualifications for a journalist he included "a steady sense that the chief purpose of 'news' is to enable mankind to live successfully toward the future."[292] He appealed to "organized labor and militant liberalism" to establish "a great independent journalism, setting standards for commercial journalism, like those which the splendid English co-operative societies are setting for commercial businesses." "An enormous amount of money is dribbled away in one fashion or another on little papers, mass-meetings and what not," he observed. "If only some considerable portion of it could be set aside to establish a central international news-agency, we should make progress."[293]

A few years later, Lippmann was explicitly to reject the view that the purification of news would be a sufficient solution to the problem of public opinion in a modern democracy.[294] Similarly, while several of these publicists in the postwar years referred to the reactionary influence of the press,[295] there was a growing recognition that it could not bear the full responsibility for the electorate's deficiencies. "The American people prefer to confine the business of thinking to their own personal affairs." Creel observed in 1920. "When they turn to politics, it is for amusement, for excitement, for indignation, but never for intellectual activity."[296] White implicitly admitted that progressives had expected too much from the democratization of the political process. "A reform does exactly what it is primarily expected to do; that is all," he concluded. "Establish the primary

---

[291] "The Basic Problem of Democracy, 1, What Modern Liberty Means," *Atlantic Monthly,* 88 (Nov. 1919), pp. 616–27 at 624.
[292] "The Basic Problem of Democracy," p. 627; "Liberty and the News," *Atlantic Monthly,* 88 (Dec. 1919), pp. 779–87 at 783.
[293] "Liberty and the News," pp. 786–7.
[294] *Public Opinion,* chap. 24. See also *The Phantom Public* (New York, 1925).
[295] For example, Howe, *Revolution and Democracy,* pp. 77, 81–4; Hapgood, *The Advancing Hour,* pp. 260–2; Russell, "The Assault on Democracy," 1921, Russell Papers.
[296] *The War, the World and Wilson,* p. 34.

and you give the people potential power; but you don't endow them incidentally with sense and independence and leadership."[297] "Weren't you a bit naive yourself at first?" Howe's wife challenged Steffens in 1925. "When did you discover that people wanted to be let alone – wanted a comfortable acceptance of things as they are? . . . Everybody hates moving day and hates moving, even though they move into a larger apartment. And they hate the moving man."[298]

This correspondence had been prompted by the publication of Howe's autobiography, *The Confessions of a Reformer*. In this, Howe had concluded that, although his experiences during and after the war had compelled him into much "unlearning" of previously held assumptions, he had "made one reconciling discovery: my dreams – the things I wanted – were still alive under the ruins of most of what I had thought." "I wanted . . . a world of equal opportunity," he recalled. "I wanted, too, an orderly world – a world that had the distinction that aristocracy gave; all of the personal distinction of individualism, and all of the wealth that human ingenuity could create, dispensed as its creators desired. . . . I still wanted all this. But I had been wrong about the way to get it."[299] In this reaffirmation of his social ideals, Howe spoke for the great majority of these progressive publicists, particularly in the first few years after the war. Yet without some plausible strategy for realizing their ideals, they would be unable to meet the challenge Steffens posed earlier the same year as he considered his own "life of unlearning." "The liberal notions you and I used to agree upon," Steffens wrote to Brand Whitlock, "seem to me now to have been cultivated human wishes and purposes, having no parallels in nature and no foundation in science."[300]

Howe's own answer to the question of how "to get" his "dreams" was through "working with labor." "The one thing I had clung to all these years was a belief in my class convinced by facts," he wrote. "I now began to see that men were not concerned over the truth. It did not interest them when economic interests were at stake. . . . The new truth that a free world would only come through labor was forced on me." It was in this spirit that he had become director of the Plumb Plan League. Howe was not the only one to reach the conclusion that "the place for the liberal

[297] "Why I Am a Progressive," *Saturday Evening Post*, 193 (23 Apr. 1921), p. 4.
[298] Marie Howe to Steffens, 25 Nov. [1925], Steffens Papers, reel 2.
[299] *Confessions*, pp. 317–25 at 324.
[300] Steffens to Brand Whitlock, 28 Jan. 1925, Steffens Papers, reel 5. This passage was omitted from the version of the letter published in *Steffens Letters*, 2, pp. 683–5.

was in labor's ranks."[301] It grew naturally, of course, out of their enthusiasm for the British Labour Party,[302] which, despite its limited electoral success, continued to seem an attractive model in the postwar years, not least because of its prominent middle-class component.[303] In 1919–20, the *Public,* the *New Republic,* and the *Survey* had expressed hopes that an American equivalent might emerge from the movement toward independent political action within some of the state Federations of Labor.[304] Neither in its character nor in its strength did the Farmer–Labor Party constitute the true fulfilment of such hopes, but it was nonetheless endorsed by Croly on the grounds that "the future political power of liberalism depends upon its ability to secure the voting support of those who live by labor" and that "it is . . . the liberals rather than labor who should initiate such a partnership."[305] In his 1919 essay on "tired radicals," Weyl observed that "radicals by environment" generally possessed more staying power than "radicals by temperament."[306] Following the election of 1920, both Spargo and Hapgood expressed the view that the AFL should repudiate Gompers's approach and form "a genuine labor party."[307] On the other hand, Walling, who took the policy of "working with labor" to characteristic extremes, thoroughly endorsed Gompers's attitude to politics along with the rest of the labor leader's judgments. An open letter in 1919, which stressed that "the Social Democratic League of America merely addresses itself to labor and accepts labor as the court of final appeal," thoroughly justified Walling's later claim to Selig Perlman that he was "perfectly willing . . . to take his orders from organized labor rather than to play the Messiah to labor."[308]

Neither politically nor industrially, however, was American labor to prove a source of great strength to any cause in the 1920s. The frustration of political impotence was undoubtedly the background to what John Diggins has called the "flirtation with Fascism" of some American pro-

---

[301] *Confessions,* pp. 322, 324–5, 329–32.

[302] See Chapter 6, "Friends and Foes of a Democratic Peace."

[303] See, for example, *New Republic,* 19 (24 May 1919), pp. 102–4; *Survey,* 44 (11 Apr., 19 June 1920), pp. 110–11, 416–17; Hapgood, "The Sabotage of Capitalism," *Independent,* 102 (22 May 1920), p. 251; Spargo, *Psychology of Bolshevism,* pp. 16–17.

[304] *Public,* 22 (25 Jan. 1919), pp. 78–9; *New Republic,* 18 (26 Apr. 1919), pp. 397–400; *Survey,* 44 (22 May 1920), p. 267.

[305] "The Eclipse of Progressivism," *New Republic,* 24 (27 Oct. 1920), pp. 210–16 at p. 213.

[306] *Tired Radicals and Other Papers* (New York, 1921), pp. 9–10.

[307] Spargo, "A Socialist View of the Landslide," p. 264; Hapgood, "Oases of Freedom," pp. 212–13.

[308] "Open Letter to the American Federation of Labor from the Social Democratic League of America," 30 Sept. 1919, Stokes Papers; Walling, ed., *Walling,* p. 90.

gressives in the middle years of the decade.[309] Of these publicists, the only two affected in this way were Croly and Steffens. Croly seems to have thought that fascism was inspiring the sort of spiritual regeneration that by this time he saw as the only hope of real progress. He warned liberals against "outlawing a political experiment which aroused in a whole nation an increased moral energy and dignified its activities by subordinating them to a deeply felt common purpose."[310] Steffens made it even plainer that it was the ability to achieve results that attracted him to Mussolini as it had to Lenin. "Can there be any real reform except by a dictatorship?" he asked.[311] He was not concerned, he told the *Survey*'s readers in 1927 about "Fascist aims": "The method of doing whatever is to be done in any country is what I would like to see considered and discussed. . . . No real progress is being made by the old, approved ways of liberalism, political democracy, and representative parliaments. The only changes that have been made are in Russia, surely, and possibly, in Italy, where the same method has been applied; a new-old method quite different from ours in the pre-war period when we American reformers were so utterly defeated."[312]

A year earlier, Steffens's fellow muckraker, Baker, had drawn a strikingly different lesson from their shared experience. "We 'pre-war radicals' were just like all the other politicians," he wrote. "We were more interested in bossing people than in knowing them; we wanted to boss our neighbours into our own little plans for goodness, or efficiency, or justice. We did not understand that growth does not come from without or above, but from within and deep down."[313] Baker published these views in his contribution to a symposium in the *Survey* provoked by Howe's *The Confessions of a Reformer,* but he had reached these conclusions several years earlier. In the eighteen months following his return from Paris in the summer of 1919, he had, as mentioned earlier, filled pages of his notebooks with what he called "the Confessions of a Bruised Idealist."[314] The

[309] John P. Diggins, "Flirtation with Fascism: American Pragmatic Liberals and Mussolini's Italy," *American Historical Review,* 71 (Jan. 1966), pp. 487–506.

[310] John P. Diggins, *Mussolini and Fascism: The View from America* (Princeton, N.J., 1972), pp. 230–1.

[311] "Trotzky, Mussolini, La Follette," TS. [1925], Steffens Papers, reel 10.

[312] "Stop, Look, Listen!" *Survey,* 57 (1 Mar. 1927), pp. 735–7, 754–5 at 754–5.

[313] "Where Are the Pre-War Radicals?" *Survey,* 55 (1 Feb. 1926), pp. 556–66.

[314] Notebook 25, July 1919, pp. 143–53, R. S. Baker Papers. See also Notebook 25, pp. 125–34; Notebook 26, pp. 7–11, 16–17, 143–9; Notebook 27, pp. 6–11, 21–3, 134–5; Notebook 28, pp. 45, 46–7; Notebook 29, pp. 19–27, 31–2, 40, 50, 53–4, 86–7, 144; Notebook 30, pp. 6, 12–16, 21, 37–9, 57, 117–21, 143–4, 192–4; Notebook 31, p. 103, ibid.

burden of these repetitious and insistent jottings was that, without a fundamental change in people's attitudes, "the whole political method" was "hopeless."[315] Hence "the only true seat of reform" was "the soul of man."[316] From here it was but a short step to the discounting of all forms of institutional reform. "Economic adjustments, social improvements, will of themselves never satisfy the man who does not possess his own soul," he wrote in 1920. "How hopeless all this re-arrangement of external machinery."[317] As to how the necessary change of spirit was to be brought about, Baker was sometimes a little coy: "We must arise and return to our father."[318] Yet, for all his own difficulty in accepting the tenets of orthodox Christianity, Baker was sure that "the great majority of people are now, and always have been, and always will be, religious in one way or another. And the surest way to reach them to-day is to give them a new idea of God: and a new faith."[319]

Neither in his disenchantment with politics nor in his revived interest in religion was Baker alone among these publicists. As we have seen, Croly had for some time been stressing that the achievement of liberal political goals depended upon the revitalization of Christian faith.[320] "The love and reverence for human life born of the imitation of Christ constitute the substance of a truth which in so far as it is acknowledged really has some chance of setting mankind free," he declared in December 1919.[321] The following year, he published a chapter from a projected book (which was never to appear) on "the Breach in Civilization" that had been caused by the unnecessary and disastrous divorce of science and religion. He was to remain preoccupied with this issue through the 1920s.[322] At a totally different level of intensity, Spargo, having come to the conclusion by 1921 that "there can be no socialization of society until we have changed the consciousness and motives of the individuals comprising society," also came to view his local church with more respect.[323]

---

315 Notebook 25, July 1919, p. 151, ibid.
316 Notebook 26, Oct. 1 [1919], pp. 10–11, ibid.
317 Notebook 29, pp. 20, 50, ibid.
318 Notebook 29, p. 54, ibid.
319 Notebook 27, April 1920, p. 22. ibid. On Baker's own religious beliefs, see Notebook 25, July 1919, pp. 125–34.
320 See "Versailles and After," and "Reconstruction and the Persistence of Progressivism."
321 "Disordered Christianity," *New Republic*, 21 (31 Dec. 1919), p. 139.
322 "Regeneration," *New Republic*, 23 (9 June 1920), pp. 40–7. See also ibid., 22 (3 Mar. 1920), p. 35; Forcey, *Crossroads of Liberalism*, p. 305. According to Forcey, Croly withdrew the book from publication because it was too "journalistic."
323 "The Reconstruction of the Social Order," 1 Dec. 1921, quoted in Friedberg, "Marxism in the

The majority of these publicists, however, abandoned neither their commitment to the processes of democratic politics nor their belief in the sort of reform they had advocated for so long. Of none was this more true than Kellogg, who not only continued to see the British Labour Party as a model but also retained his conviction that the way to promote progress was by publicizing "the true facts."[324] For those who kept some variant of this faith through the dispiriting decade of the 1920s, America's wartime experience retained its ambivalence. On the one hand, it continued to be seen, together with the unprecedented prosperity, as one of the chief explanations for the prevailing conservatism. "The war set us back about ten years," Kellogg stated flatly in 1927.[325] On the other hand, a rather selective recollection of events could be a source of comfort, even inspiration. White recalled "the spirit of idealism that prevailed during the war," while Baker insisted that "nothing can ever rob us of that great moment" when "we forgot ourselves; we were greater than ourselves."[326] When, after the collapse of prosperity, reformers were presented with a greater opportunity than they had ever enjoyed during the Progressive Era to put their ideas into practice, their response would be significantly affected by an idealized memory of the collectivist organization and social spirit of World War I.[327]

United States," p. 303; Spargo, "Reminiscences," p. 352. See also Spargo to Stokes, 12 July 1921, Stokes Papers.

[324] Chambers *Kellogg,* pp. 105, 99.

[325] Ibid., pp. 77–8. See also AP TS., 22 Oct. 1925, Amos Pinchot Papers, subject file 80; Hapgood, "The Future of Radicalism," *Jewish Daily Forward,* 20 May 1926.

[326] White to Ralph M. Sheldon, 15 June 1920, White Papers; Baker, *The New Industrial Unrest,* pp. 151–2, cf. 133–4.

[327] See William E. Leuchtenburg, "The New Deal and the Analogue of War," in *Change and Continuity in Twentieth-Century America,* eds. John Braeman, Robert H. Bremner, and Everett Walters (Ohio State, 1964), pp. 81–143, especially pp. 84–94.

CHAPTER 8

Conclusion

For most of its best-known publicists, progressivism always remained a set of largely unfulfilled aspirations. The precise character of these aspirations varied from individual to individual, although, as we have seen, they all sought a more equal and more cooperative – in their eyes, a more genuinely democratic – society. In the years before the war, they were also in broad agreement on the general direction change must take if this goal was to be achieved. For all their professed optimism, there were signs as early as 1914 that they were becoming frustrated by the difficulty of bringing about the sort of reform measures they thought necessary. By 1920, they were generally in a state of despair about the possibility of doing so in the foreseeable future.

Although the names of many of these writers and journalists often figure prominently in historical accounts of it, they constituted, of course, only one element in the progressive movement. Nevertheless, their experience does throw an interesting light upon the broader phenomenon. The general thrust of much of the revisionist historiography in the 1960s and 1970s has been to suggest that the real character of the political and economic reforms that were instituted in the early twentieth century revealed the democratic pretensions of progressive reformers to be misleading, if not dishonest. Those who have more recently sought to reconcile the traditional view of this period with the findings of the "organizational" school of historians have emphasized the distinction between the intentions of reformers and the character of the eventual outcome.[1] This is a proper distinction, and one that seems to illuminate the history of some regulatory measures in particular.[2] However, the fact that these publicists were so largely dissatisfied with the state of affairs in 1914 (let alone 1920) suggests that, in large part, progressivism (as they understood it)

---

[1] McCormick, "The Discovery that Business Corrupts Politics," pp. 273–4; William L. O'Neill, *The Progressive Years: America Comes of Age* (New York, 1975), pp. x, 157–8.
[2] See, for example, Stanley P. Caine, *The Myth of a Progressive Reform: Railroad Regulation in Wisconsin, 1903–1910* (Madison, Wisc., 1970).

was a movement that simply failed to accomplish its objectives. In other words, the chief distortion in the traditional picture may have been not the portrayal of the values of "the progressives" but the assumption that they dominated "the Progressive era."

Such a conclusion would help to explain why historians have found what Daniel T. Rodgers has called "the search for that great overarching thing called 'progressivism' "[3] so unrewarding. For this search is based upon the implicit premise that whatever gave a comparatively short period of American history its distinctive character must provide a key to understanding the most significant developments of the time. Yet the legislation of the early twentieth century, to say nothing of the changes in other aspects of American life, surely owed less to the rather diffuse climate of opinion that marked these years than to the variety of more specific impulses and interests that historians have now identified.[4] The thrust of several of these forces was, of course, in directions significantly different from those favored by the publicists we have been considering.[5]

The diverse, and sometimes contradictory, nature of these forces meant that the notion of a broad-based progressive movement was always largely illusory. The unstable and shifting character of the electoral support received by progressive political leaders confirms this.[6] This illusion was no doubt a product of the reforming mood that prevailed in the years around 1910. Yet this ethos, like that associated with the 1960s, may well have been a more superficial and transitory phenomenon than it seemed to many at the time.

From this perspective, the "decline" of progressivism would seem to have been inevitable, even had the First World War never occurred. Indeed, as we have seen, it is clear that the political appeal of progressive rhetoric was already much reduced by the time of the 1914 elections, earlier than it is plausible to attribute much influence to a conflict still somewhat remote to most Americans. No doubt, the emotions later aroused by the debate over intervention and then by American participation in the war affected the political climate. Indeed, these experiences seem to have led directly to the virulently antiradical mood of the imme-

---

[3] "In Search of Progressivism," *Reviews in American History*, 10 (December 1982), p. 127.
[4] See Chapter 1.
[5] For a fuller development of this argument, see J. A. Thompson, *Progressivism* (British Association for American Studies Pamphlet, 1979).
[6] For a summary of the evidence on this, see John D. Buenker in Buenker et al., *Progressivism*, pp. 57–9.

diate postwar period – but this, too, was to prove short-lived. Yet the passing of the red scare did not restore the public's taste for the language of progressive reform, or revive the illusions that this had created.

If the war was not primarily responsible for the decline of progressivism, the decline of progressivism does seem to have played a significant part in shaping the responses to the war of several of the publicists with whom we have been concerned. The difficulty they were already experiencing in developing public support for their point of view may even have made them more willing to turn their attention to the European conflict. It surely strengthened the tendency to seek in the apparent requirements of successful warfare additional justification for the case against laissez-faire. Through this connection, and in other less direct ways, the weakening of progressivism seems to have increased the readiness with which many accepted, and others welcomed, American participation in the war. The reliance upon the exceptional experience of belligerency, or the unique opportunity of postwar reconstruction, to produce the kind of transformation in American social and economic organization that they sought surely reflected their diminishing confidence in the prospects for achieving their goals through the normal processes of democratic politics in peacetime.

In other ways, too, the attitudes of these publicists to the issues raised by the war seem to have reflected their progressive outlook. As we have seen, they were predisposed toward an anti-imperialist perspective on international affairs and to the belief that the overriding purpose of American foreign policy should be to secure a peaceful world. However, these general inclinations were not precise enough to foreclose debate on specific questions of policy nor were they by any means the only considerations that weighed with them. Indeed, their views on foreign policy questions were shaped by a wide variety of concerns, which included both emotional involvement with the fate of other countries, and preoccupation with the perceived domestic implications of particular courses of action. In this, they were perhaps typical of their countrymen generally, who seem to have shared an assumption that vital American interests were sufficiently secure to permit the United States a choice between a wide range of viable options in the field of foreign policy.

On domestic reform also, the positions these progressives occupied had some not uncommon features. This was particularly true in respect of the more fundamental issues by which they were confronted in these years. Reform-minded intellectuals at many times and in many places have wrestled with the problems of reconciling the liberal values of individuality and freedom with the social goals of equality and community. They have also become familiar with the difficulty of securing popular support for programs and policies that seem to them essentially democratic in character. If among this particular generation of American reformers these recurring dilemmas eventually produced an exceptional amount of discouragement, disillusionment, and reassessment, that can be seen as a form of testimony to their earlier confidence. This confidence had been based upon their perception of the way the world was moving in the prewar period. That perception, which has contributed not a little to the subsequent image of the Progressive Era, surely owed something to the unusually important role that they, as publicists, had seemed to play in the politics of the early twentieth century. The recognition that this role had been at best transitory added a very personal dimension to the more cosmically depressing experiences of the war and postwar years.

Index

Aaron, Daniel, 34n
Abrams, Richard M., 33n
Addams, Jane, 15, 123, 177, 178n; as
  associate editor of the *Survey,* 27; and
  opposition to intervention, 162
Adler, Felix, 248, 250
Allen, H. C., 75n
Allen, Henry J., 182, 232
Allen, Howard W., 117n
American Alliance for Labor and Democracy, 181–2
American Committee on War Finance,
  183, 184, 215–16
American Federation of Labor (AFL), 79,
  181, 208–9, 213, 253, 283
American League to Limit Armaments,
  128, 131, 135
American Magazine, 15, 31, 89
American mission, idea of, 120–7, 149,
  245–6
American participation in World War I:
  as ambivalent experience for progressives, 212, 230–1, 286; debate
  over, 150–9; division over, 159–68,
  214–15; engenders intolerance, 177–
  80, 184; and progressive advance at
  home, 154–6, 212–20, 249–50,
  257–8; Russell first to advocate,
  132
American Red Cross: Kellogg and, 181;
  White and Henry J. Allen and, 182
American Review of Reviews, 92n
American Union Against Militarism
  (AUAM), 128, 136, 150, 161, 169,
  178, 184, 186, 221
anti-imperialism, 165; as basis of progressive approach to foreign policy,
  148–9; and opposition to preparedness, 136–8; as predisposition of most
  progressives, 120, 130

Association for an Equitable Federal Income Tax, 30, 140–1
Austria-Hungary, 102, 200–1, 202

Baker, Newton D., 178, 182, 184, 214,
  215, 221, 227, 239
Baker, Ray Stannard, 10n, 11, 15, 27,
  28, 30, 31, 34, 38, 39, 40, 42, 58,
  61, 63, 65, 73, 74, 78, 79, 83–4,
  107, 108, 109, 126, 128, 131, 141,
  144, 165, 189, 200, 210, 219, 223,
  227, 233, 234, 235, 239, 256, 259,
  269–70; on America's role in the
  world, 121–2, 123, 245; background
  and personality, 12–13; and Bolshevism, 237–8, 265, 266; on British
  Labour Party, 206–8; decline of progressivism and, 113–16, 267; and democracy, 49–50, 54–5, 65, 206,
  255, 276–7; disillusionment of, 242,
  247, 271, 284; his view of role, 30,
  255, 279; and intervention, 160, 162,
  168, 174–5; and league of nations,
  134, 240, 270; notebooks of, 13, 88–
  9, 237–8, 271, 284–5; and pacifism,
  131, 133, 135, 168; and peace conference, 236–8, 240, 245, 268; and
  peace terms, 194, 202, 204–5; and
  postwar strikes, 252–3, 254; and progress, 76, 88–9, 91, 266; and religion, 44–5, 285; reports from
  Europe (1918), 181, 193, 204–5,
  206–7, 211; on socialism, 35; and
  war in Europe, 86, 88–9, 91, 101–2;
  and wartime experience, 180, 182–3,
  184, 213, 216, 229, 230, 232, 278,
  286; and Wilson, 143, 148–9, 169–
  70, 171–2, 235, 237–8, 243
Bannister, Robert C., 35n, 38n, 60n,
  62n, 78n, 79n

291

148, 197, 207, 222, 225, 230, 231,
234, 248, 262; on America's role in
world, 119–20, 122–3, 126, 136,
145; on Bolsheviks, 191, 262, 264;
and British Labour Party, 208, 231,
248; character and history of, 20–1,
268; condemns German government,
152, 153, 184, 189; on labor, 214,
251, 253, 254, 256; on peace settlement, 145, 157–8, 241; praises
Wilson, 143, 202; skeptical on national self-determination, 125, 198–9;
and wartime collectivism, 108, 213,
219–20, 232, 258–9
"industrial democracy," 80, 255–7
Industrial Workers of the World (IWW),
73, 79, 222–3, 227, 228
Inquiry, the, 186, 200, 205, 236; memorandum of, and the Fourteen Points,
202
Intercollegiate Socialist Society, 34, 36
Irwin, Will, 11n
Israel, Jerry, 3n
Italy: entry into war, 98, 99; reverses in
1917, 187

Jaffe, Julian F., 262n
James, William, 23, 141
Jeffreys-Jones, Rhodri, 77n
Johnson, Donald, 221n
Johnson, Hiram, 17, 269
Johnson, Paul Barton, 248n
Johnson, Tom L., 18, 36, 37, 49
Johnson, Walter, 31n, 43n, 74n, 115n,
182n
Joseph Fels Fund, 25, 170

Kaplan, Justin, 10n, 37n, 119n, 182n,
260n
Kelley, Robert, 39n
Kellogg, Paul U.: and antimilitarism,
128, 129; background and personality,
26–7; and British Labour Party, 207,
209, 286; during war, 177, 181, 221;
as editor of the *Survey*, 10, 28, 32,
33, 73, 79, 90, 97, 107, 136, 140,
169, 259, 286; founds LFNA, 197,
246; and opposition to intervention,
151, 152, 157, 161, 162, 165; and
peace, 147, 185, 241
Kennan, George F., 191n, 192n

Kennedy, David M., 5n, 212n, 214n,
216n, 224n, 227n, 271n
Kenynes, John Maynard, 243
Kernek, Sterling J., 200n
Kidd, Benjamin, 55n
Kolko, Gabriel, 4n
Kreuter, Kent and Gretchen, 179n,
210n
Kuehl, Warren F., 20n, 22n, 35n, 64n,
124n, 135n, 195n, 240n, 268n

labor disputes: Colorado (1914), 70, 73,
79–80; Lawrence (1912), 79, 115–16;
in 1919, 253–6; progressive attitudes
to, 77–80, 251–6
La Follette, Robert M., 18, 36, 150,
151, 168
Lamont, Hammond, 109n
Lane, Franklin K., and plan for returning soldiers, 249, 258
Larson, Simeon, 182n
Lasch, Christopher, 34n, 130n, 172,
190n, 191, 271n
Lawrence strike (1912), *see* labor disputes, Lawrence (1912)
League of Free Nations Association
(LFNA), 264; "Statement of Principles," 197–8, 246
League of Nations: debate over U.S. participation in, 241–2, 246, 270; and
democratic peace, 194; and need for
flexibility and inclusiveness, 146–8,
157, 197–8, 235, 241; support for,
124, 134–5, 239–41; view of Allies
as nucleus of, 196–7
League to Enforce Peace, 124, 134–5,
142, 146, 147, 151, 196, 197, 236
Leib, Franklin A., 117n
Lenin, V. I., 15, 190, 232, 243, 284
Leuchtenburg, William E., 117–18,
286n
Lever Act (1917), 212, 215, 254
Link, Arthur S., 1n, 100n, 123n, 141n,
143n, 148n, 150n, 152n, 169, 271n
Lippmann, Walter, 7, 23, 25, 27, 28,
29, 30, 31, 48, 54, 57, 60, 66, 78,
82, 85, 86, 90, 107, 114, 134, 143,
146, 160, 169, 172, 189, 212, 219,
220, 222, 263, 269, 270, 278; background and personality, 24–5; on democracy and public opinion, 51, 99–

5 1/95